Spinoza, Liberalism, and the
Question of Jewish Identity

STEVEN B. SMITH

Spinoza, Liberalism, and the Question of Jewish Identity

Yale University Press
New Haven and London

Printed in the United States of America by BookCrafters, Inc., Chelsea, Michigan.

Library of Congress Cataloging-in-Publication Data
Smith, Steven B., 1951–
Spinoza, liberalism, and the question of Jewish identity / Steven B. Smith.
p.   cm.
Includes bibliographical references and index.
ISBN 0-300-06680-5 (cloth : alk. paper)
1. Spinoza, Benedictus de, 1632–1677.   Tractatus theologico-politicus.
2. Jews — Identity.   3. Judaism and philosophy.   4. Liberalism.   5. Philosophy and religion.   6. Free thought.   I. Title.
B3985.Z7S55   1997
199'.492 — dc20   96-34870

A catalogue record for this book is available from the British Library.

The paper in this book meets the guidelines for permanence and durability of the Committee on Production Guidelines for Book Longevity of the Council on Library Resources.

10 9 8 7 6 5 4 3 2 1

For Joshua

"All things excellent are as difficult as they are rare." — Spinoza

Contents

Acknowledgments

This book began as an attempt to inquire into the relation between Judaism and liberalism in modern political theory. Spinoza was to occupy one chapter, but one chapter turned into two, then two into three, and so on. The story is a familiar one. What is not so familiar is the place occupied by Spinoza and especially his *Theologico-Political Treatise* in the larger story that I want to tell—a story partly about the attempted secularization of religion during the Enlightenment and the subsequent creation of a modern Jewish identity. Writing a book on such a topic poses unusual opportunities and risks. I have been sustained throughout this venture by the image of Isaac Bashevis Singer's fictional character Dr. Nahum Fischelson, the Spinoza of Market Street, and have been constantly mindful of Dr. Fischelson's final, mournful plea.

Several nonfictional persons have given time, understanding, and friendship in helping me see this work to completion. Among them I would like to mention my colleagues Bruce Ackerman, Shelly Burtt, Ian Shapiro, Stephen Skowronek, Rogers Smith, and Norma Thompson. The diligence, probing queries, and many useful suggestions made by Peter Berkowitz, Edwin Curley, Barbara Koziak, and Nathan Tarcov have made this a better book than it would otherwise have been, and for this I am grateful. I alone accept responsibility for the uses to which their suggestions have been put.

Parts of this work have been presented publicly over the years. An early version of the argument as a whole was presented at a seminar at Princeton University, where it benefited from the friendly but skeptical questioning of George Kateb and Harry Frankfurt. Later versions were presented at the Hebrew University in Jerusalem and the University of Tel Aviv during the spring of 1994. I would like to thank Shlomo Avineri, Yaron Ezrahi, Jeffrey Macy, and Yossi Shain for their generosity and for encouraging me to pursue a subject that remains of vital importance for the future of the state of Israel. Different parts of the manuscript have been presented to the fellows of Ezra Stiles College and the Whitney Humanities Center at Yale University. With special pleasure I note that this book was written and completed during my tenure as a fellow of the Whitney Humanities Center, and I would like to thank its last two directors, David Bromwich and David Marshall, for their support. Finally, I want to acknowledge a group of extremely talented graduate students, "the friends of Spinoza," who devoted one evening a week for an entire semester to reading and discussing Spinoza with me and who caused me to reconsider several key points of my argument when the manuscript was nearing completion.

In an age when people speak unceasingly about the decline of the family, it has been my good fortune to be sustained by a loving and generous one. My wife, Susan, has listened patiently and offered her opinions at virtually every twist and turn of the book's progress. My father and I discussed this book, and I deeply regret that he did not live to see it into print; I think he would have liked it. The one to whom the work is dedicated represents my hopes for the future.

Introduction

The term "Jewish Question" is probably best known among students of political philosophy as the title of a short essay by the young Karl Marx. In *Zur Judenfrage,* Marx put forward his views on such themes as the distinction between "political" and "human" emancipation and between civil society and the state; only at the end of the essay does he address the announced topic, the civic emancipation of the Jews. Expressing many of the dominant stereotypes of his era, Marx denied that bourgeois society should withhold civil liberties from the Jews, because the Jews more than any other group embodied the commercial essence of that society. Even though Marx evinces no compelling knowledge of Judaism in the essay, he succeeded in joining issue with a topic that was widely discussed not only among German intellectuals but among European intellectuals generally, who were living in the wake of the French Revolution. The Jewish Question concerned the place to be occupied by the Jews in those modern states, notably France, Germany, England, and the United States, where the influence of the Enlightenment had been most palpably felt. What is not so well known, however, is that the Jewish Question was prepared, even created, by a far more original Jewish heretic and radical: Baruch de Spinoza.

My decision to write a book devoted to Spinoza's *Theologico-Political Treatise* derives from a combination of personal and academic reasons. Spinoza has not been given his due as one of the founders of modern political philosophy. In spite of the enormous attention given in recent years to the political thought of the Renaissance, Reformation, and early modernity, scarcely any of this considerable body of literature has been devoted to Spinoza. Those who have turned to him have done so for illumination on questions pertaining to his metaphysical and speculative philosophy. His views on such matters as the unity of Substance, the mind-body problem, and the nature of causality have been extensively and elaborately studied. Only rarely is Spinoza regarded, as he will be here, as someone who thought long and deeply about the fundamental problems of political life.

For reasons that will become clear in the first chapter of this book, the core of Spinoza's philosophy might be called the theologico-political problem. Spinoza was by no means the first or the only thinker to elevate this problem to the virtual center of his philosophy. It suffices, for instance, to consider his two great contemporaries Thomas Hobbes and John Locke, both of whom made the relation between church and state, theology and politics, the core of their thinking. What distinguishes Spinoza from the other major figures of the early Enlightenment is, in my opinion, not only that he was a greater and more learned biblical philologist and interpreter but also that he was the first thinker of European standing to make the question of Jews and Judaism central to his theologico-political inquiries. I do not believe that it is a falsehood or an exaggeration to say that the Jewish Question was the main theme of Spinoza's reflections from very early on. My aim is to show that Spinoza made the Jewish Question an essential ingredient of modern political thought.

The study of Spinoza's relation to Jewish thought and philosophy has been a staple of modern scholarship since Manuel Jöel's pioneering work in the nineteenth century (*Spinozas Theologisch-Politischer Traktat auf seine Quellen geprüft* [1870]) and Harry Wolfson's in the twentieth (*The Philosophy of Spinoza* [1934]). Both of these interpreters addressed Spinoza's dependence on such diverse medieval influences as Maimonides, Hasdai Crescas, and Leone Ebreo. Although there is much to learn, and much I have learned, from these early critical studies, Spinoza is often reduced therein to little more than the sum of his sources. His genuine novelty gets lost in the mass of borrowings from earlier writers whose texts he quoted or paraphrased and whose terms he adapted for his own purposes.

Spinoza was not a friend and admirer of his predecessors but an often fierce and uncompromising critic. Indeed, he found himself excommunicated from the Jewish community of Amsterdam. But it would be equally misleading to view him as radically detached from the needs and concerns of this community. If Spinoza chose to live alone, his work as a whole represents an ongoing dialogue with the Torah, the prophets, the rabbis, and the philosophers, chief among them Maimonides. Spinoza was not a devout Jew (far from it), and it is not my purpose to attempt to exonerate him. Spinoza put Jewish concerns and problems at the forefront of his thought in order to exercise a profound transformation of them. Not conversion but secularization was the final aim of the *Treatise*. It was an attempt to turn Judaism from an authoritative body of revealed law into what today would be called a modern secular identity.

The *Treatise* represents the first and most profound expression of the Jewish-liberal symbiosis that has survived to the present. Spinoza did as much as anyone to create the historical affinity between Judaism and liberalism, that is, the assimilation of Judaism to the norms and principles of the modern liberal state. But if liberalism has been the precondition for Jewish emancipation, so, too, have liberal government and institutions derived, in Spinoza's view, from Jewish sources. For Spinoza, Judaism served perhaps as a basis for liberalism not because it was a religion of reason, as Moses Mendelssohn believed, but because it was a body of law. The priority of law in Jewish ethics made it ideally suited to serve liberal ends, even while liberal ends required that it be divested of its transcendent and revealed status. The chief advantage of law is that, besides being enunciated in public statutes, it deals almost entirely with externals and outward behavior, leaving unaffected the freedom of mind and the individual's disposition toward virtue. Spinoza was not interested in Judaism per se, but in how Jews could live with dignity, on a footing of legal equality, with their non-Jewish neighbors. Only a liberal democracy based on the rule of law could avoid the evils of religious persecution and provide a common framework under which Jews and Christians might share a common citizenship.

For Spinoza, this kind of liberalism entailed more than a state that was neutral or tolerant of religious differences; it also entailed a new kind of theology, or what I call the theology of the liberated individual. His proposal for a new, rational theology whose cardinal precept was the teaching of toleration was intended to form the basis of the new liberal identity. The new theology would be freed from the old and "primitive" ceremonial law, purged of religion's transcendent and other-worldly longings, and redirected toward the liberal and secular ends of toleration and freedom of belief. Spinoza presented this trade as a small, even welcome, price to pay for the benefits of citizenship and legal equality; but others have felt a combination of fear and doubt at the thought of the betrayal of an ancient tradition. When the tradition in question is one like Judaism that claims a divine or revealed origin, this concern is all the more intense.

Spinoza's solution to the theologico-political problem forces us today to reconsider what is sometimes called the Enlightenment project. Central to this project is the call to liberation or emancipation. The *Treatise* promises liberation from an ancient tradition that has been the cause of Jewish passivity and weakness. It offers a new, rational theology that provides for civic equality in place of the old Mosaic law with its notions of special providence and divine promises. It proffers a new promised land, as it were, based on freedom: freedom of religion, freedom of commerce, freedom of inquiry. But the question is, At what cost? Is Spinoza's promised land a new Jerusalem or a fool's paradise? Is the the liberated individual of the *Treatise* a real person of flesh and blood or an abstraction based on the decomposition of tradition and communal life? Does the liberal state offer Jews genuine toleration and equality before the law, or is it but a first step toward eventual absorption into the mainstream of modern secular culture?

Long before Marx or Freud, Spinoza symbolized the emancipated or secular Jew. But the benefits of emancipation—religious toleration, civil rights, citizenship—have brought problems that Spinoza did not fully anticipate. Among these are the psychological consequences of self-denial that have attended the impulse to assimilation. Emancipation meant liberation for the individual, not for the Jew. The individual, once liberated, was often alone and adrift in a society that remained predominantly Christian in its values and modes of organization. Further, the abatement of the power of Christianity did not necessarily mean a decrease in anti-Semitism, to say nothing of more subtle forms of discrimination. Lacking the traditional resources of communal life, the emancipated Jew was torn between the extremes of self-hatred and the revolutionary desire to "force the end," that is, to put an end to Jewish suffering by putting an end to Judaism.

The Jewish Question has haunted modernity ever since its inception. It remains the most vivid form of the question of the Other, or human diversity, with which liberal society has labored to come to terms. At the onset of modernity Jews and Judaism were regarded as the quintessential Other, the cultural alien whose assimilation was evidence that society was becoming more rational and more tolerant as a result of the expenditure of conscious moral energy. The cultural differences of the Jews were even exaggerated to demonstrate the universality of human nature. In Spinoza's time the problem of the Other was understood through largely theological categories and concepts. Seeing it mainly in terms of secular categories like race, ethnicity, and gender does not alter the fundamental problem. In this respect the Jewish Question remains a question coeval with humanity as such.

This study is an attempt to reverse a common conception of Spinoza as a rationalist metaphysician just viewing himself and the world *sub specie aeternitatis*. Without denying Spinoza's important contributions to modern philosophy, I want to establish his stature as a political theorist first and foremost. This entails reading the *Treatise* as a text with a unity and integrity of its own, neither as a stage in Spinoza's "development" nor as an example of the application of a priori philosophical principles to the changing and contingent nature of political reality. Spinoza did not develop his understanding of politics from a set of metaphysical premises independently derived; instead, he developed it from a study of biblical narrative and history, to say nothing of the European situation in the seventeenth century. He was deeply attuned to the realities of political power and in the idiom of his time sought to reach an understanding of the human condition as it really was, not as it was imagined or wished for. Spinoza was passionately political, and he made the theologico-political predicament the wellspring of his thought. The Spinoza that emerges in this book has a much deeper awareness of history, both sacred and secular, than is often thought to be the case; he has greater respect for the power of the prophetic imagination and more acceptance of the fragility of human rationality.

The organization of this book follows, but does not duplicate, Spinoza's order of presentation in the *Treatise*. In Chapter 1 I expound upon and develop the themes of the Jewish Question and the theologico-political problem only briefly touched on in this preface. In Chapter 2 I examine Spinoza's account of the psychology of religious belief in intellectual and political context. In Chapter 3 I analyze his critique of the authority of Scripture. The principle of *Interpretatio naturae* is used to view Scripture as a historical text adapted to the prejudices and needs of its time. In Chapter 4 I reconstruct the *Treatise*'s account of prophetic history from Moses to Spinoza himself. Spinoza ranks the historical religions on a progressive scale from Judaism to Christianity, culminating in the *fides universalis*, his own rational theology. In Chapter 5 I explore Spinoza's account of democracy as the *optima Respublica*, or "best regime." I bring out the relation between, on the one hand, the account of natural right and the social contract, which provides the groundwork for Spinoza's political theory proper, and, on the other, the account of the divine law, which circumscribes the highest form of individual perfection.

In Chapter 6 I reconstruct the secular history in the *Treatise* beginning with the ancient Hebrew theocracy and culminating in the modern commercial republic of Amsterdam. In Chapter 7 I explore the subsequent appropriation of certain important Spinozist themes in the German Enlightenment. The conception of the role of Jews and Judaism in the *Treatise*, I argue, exercised a profound and determinative influence on the writings of Mendelssohn, Lessing, Kant, and Hegel. It was Spinoza's reception in Germany at the end of the eighteenth century and the beginning of the nineteenth that helped prepare the reception for the German-Jewish synthesis that persisted well into the twentieth century and whose last great representative was Hermann Cohen. I hope to follow this study with a companion volume on those archetypal "non-Jewish Jews" Heine, Marx, and Freud and proceed to a reconsideration of the benefits of emancipation and secularization presented in the works of Franz Rosenzweig, Gershom Scholem, and Leo Strauss.

Throughout this book I use words like "democratic," "republican," and "liberal" to describe Spinoza's politics. The first two terms are Spinoza's own. He was the first modern thinker of note to describe himself as a democrat, by which he meant that sovereignty resides in the people in their collective capacity. He also speaks of republican government, which in context has both antimonarchical and anticlerical overtones. A republican form of government, contrasted to a monarchy, is one in which all religious organizations are put under the authority of the civil sovereign. Spinoza harbored none of the nostalgia for the ancient or bygone republics thought characteristic of Renaissance humanism. He was skeptical of the language of civic virtue, maintained a healthy respect for the primacy of self-interest in human actions, preferred the urban patriciate and its values to the rural squirearchy, and viewed history not as the story of corruption and moral decay but as the story of human progress and humankind's triumph over superstition, fear, and ignorance.

Spinoza did not use the term "liberal" to describe his system of politics: the word meant no such thing in the seventeenth century. My use of the term to describe Spinoza's politics might be thought of, then, as deceptively anachronistic. But if to be a liberal means to have a lively sense of the autonomy and dignity of the individual, to defend the values of freedom of speech and opinion, to prefer a diverse and tolerant commercial society, and to entertain a belief in the benefits derived from the progress of the arts and sciences, then Spinoza can be described as a liberal. He helped found the proud tradition of political thought that can boast such later luminaries as Locke, Montesquieu, the authors of *The Federalist Papers*, Kant, Tocqueville, and John Stuart Mill.

Still, it is not my purpose simply to assimilate Spinoza into the mainstream of liberal thought. His work, like that of all weighty thinkers, is sui generis. He defies easy classification. Although he lived at the onset of modernity, he stood with one foot in the premodern world. If he has been a hero to Enlightenment liberals, he has also found favor among romantic anti-liberals. If he has been decried as an atheist, has also been heralded as a "God-intoxicated man" and called the "divine Spinoza." If he was a favorite of the German idealists, he has also been embraced by Marxian materialists. And if he was an advocate of a religiously tolerant liberal state as one solution to the Jewish Question, he was also a founder, perhaps *the* founder, of political Zionism. One of the great pleasures of reading Spinoza is coming to the realization that there is virtually no current of modern thought that he has not touched and vitally transformed.

Note on the Text

Throughout this study I refer to the *Theologico-Political Treatise* simply as the *Treatise*. The most widely used edition of the *Treatise* was translated over a century ago by R. H. M. Elwes. This translation, part of *The Chief Works of Spinoza,* is badly out of date and in need of revision. A partial translation of some of the more political chapters appeared in A. G. Wernham's edition of the *Political Works.* A new translation of the *Treatise* by Samuel Shirley came out in 1991, and another by Edwin Curley is under way — it will appear in his edition of the *Collected Works.* I am very grateful to Professor Curley for allowing me to quote throughout from a typescript of his translation of the *Treatise,* which, we can only hope, will be forthcoming sooner rather than later. I have made occasional minor changes in Curley's translation where I have deemed appropriate.

In the notes I cite the standard Latin edition of the *Treatise,* edited by Carl Gebhardt, which appears in volume 3 of the *Spinoza Opera.* I also refer to the Elwes translation of the *Treatise* for the convenience of readers who have no other ready access to Spinoza's text.

I

The Return of the Theologico-Political Problem

The religious issue that was hotly debated at the onset of modernity has once again acquired urgency. The rise of religious fundamentalism in the United States and other quarters of the globe has created problems that would not have seemed possible even a generation ago. Until very recently, the religious issue seemed to belong to a dark, atavistic past from which we had only slowly emerged. Secularization theorists confidently averred that religious conflicts, along with their attendant tribal and ethnic animosities, would wither away with the advance of modernity. Social and economic development would bring the conditions for stable democratic government, and with democracy, society would be liberated from the dominance of religious symbols and institutions.[1]

Political theorists have fared little better in providing the intellectual resources necessary for coming to terms with the religious issue.[2] Contemporary liberals have everywhere affirmed the dominance of a certain type of enlightened, secular individual — rational, self-interested, risk averse — which is precisely what the return of religious problems has called into question. Liberals have found themselves taking refuge behind the concept of a "wall of separation" between church and state while refusing to see why the legitimacy of that wall was being assailed by those on the other side of the divide. The return of the religious question, then, has not only caught liberals unawares but has found them without even an adequate language to address it. For this reason alone, it is incumbent upon us to reconsider the roots of the dilemma.

With the return of the "theologico-political problem," the optimism that once attended our faith in modernity has been significantly shaken. Its return has eclipsed the moral certainties that upheld an earlier faith in the triumphal march of progress, secularization, and enlightenment. As the name implies, the theologico-political problem has two dimensions: Should religion rule politics, or should politics rule religion? To some degree, the entire history of Western political thought and practice can be seen as a series of attempted answers to these questions. Indeed, the much vaunted separation of church and state is one, but only one, solution to the problem. The vulnerability and inherent contestability of all such solutions is very apparent today, perhaps even more evident than at any time in the recent past. The return of this problem provides striking evidence for what the French political theorist Claude Lefort has called the permanence of the theologico-political.[3]

The return or reemergence of the theologico-political problem would scarcely have surprised the founders of liberal democracy, who were all immersed in theological studies and treated them as inseparable from politics. Hobbes, Spinoza, Locke, Leibniz, and Kant, to name just the most famous, helped establish the genre of political writing called secular theology.[4] This genre was secular in that it was the product of men outside the established clergy. Furthermore, the fundamental questions of the genre concerned the world *ad seculum* rather than individual salvation and divine truth. From the outset, the secular theologians took aim at biblical orthodoxy, or what Hobbes tellingly called the kingdom of darkness, considering it equivalent to the rule of superstition and priestcraft.[5] Their biblical commentaries and interpretations were attempts to supplant Scripture, the traditional authoritative guide and teacher of humanity, with some kind of new, rational theology. These thinkers intended more than biblical scholarship and research: they intended wholesale cultural and political transformation — nothing short of the replacement of the God of Scripture by unassisted human reason, the establishment of human reason as our "only Star and compass," in Locke's luminous phrase.[6]

The Enlightenment of the seventeenth and eighteenth centuries provides us with the grounds for the liberal answer to the theologico-political problem. The answer characteristically worked out by the most advanced thinkers of this period was some form of separation of religion and politics. This separation was related to, but not altogether identical with, the later liberal distinction between the private and the public realms or, in the language of John Stuart Mill, the spheres of "self-regarding" and "other-regarding" actions.

Henceforth politics would concern itself only with what Locke called civil goods, such as the protection of life, liberty, health, and material possessions.[7] Religion would be confined to the precincts of personal disposition and inclination. Deprived of the trappings of public office and the coercive power of the state, religion would be privatized, left to the conscience or inner light of the individual believer. To be sure, none of the leading exponents of the Enlightenment believed even for a moment that political life could dispense with religion altogether. A commonwealth of atheists was thought to be an impossibility, even if Pierre Bayle had tried to imagine it.[8] A link of some sort had to be found to join the inner and the outer, the private and the public, civil society and the state. Increasingly, the idea of culture, especially in those lands touched by the Protestant Reformation, was made to do the work of bridging the gap between a wholly secular public space and the realm of values, to which religion was often consigned.

The separation of religion and politics came in many different shades and acquired several rationales. One strategy — we could call it the pluralist strategy — was to encourage the proliferation of religious sects within a broad framework of mutual toleration. The classics of this genre were works like Milton's *Areopagitica,* Locke's *Letter on Toleration,* and Voltaire's *Philosophical Letters.* On this view, the differences between individuals and groups on religious and metaphysical questions were deep, not to say intractable. The optimal way of eliminating religious-based coercion was not through the imposition of a common faith but through the creation of a competitive market in religious sects.[9] For reasons that Madison would develop at length in the *Federalist* No. 10, the defenders of religious pluralism argued that a multiplicity of sects would lead to moral restraint and the disavowal of violence as an acceptable means of achieving conversion.

Another strategy taken by several leading Enlightenment thinkers — let us call it the rationalist strategy — was to develop, even invent, new, rational forms of religion that would gradually replace the older Scriptural theology. By a rational religion was meant not historical, institutional, or popular religion but what all revealed religions were thought to have in common, that is, a belief in divine providence, order, and wisdom and a short list of fundamental moral commandments. On this view, the Enlightenment was a kind of second Reformation intended to purify still further the areas of morality and religion. Examples of works in this genre are Locke's *On the Reasonableness of Christianity,* Toland's *Christianity Not Mysterious,* and Kant's *Religion Within the Limits of Reason Alone.* Sometimes these works were thinly veiled efforts to demonstrate the original rationality of Scripture that had become encrusted with centuries' worth of commentary and interpretation. The task of Enlightenment on this account was not merely to control or contain religious diversity but to purify and refine religious morality, to give it a more cosmopolitan and universalist perspective. Perhaps the high-water mark of this rationalist strategy was Thomas Jefferson's expression of a hope that after him all future generations of Americans would be Unitarians.[10]

The pluralist and rationalist approaches to the religious question could be equally described as the soft and hard versions of the Enlightenment.[11] Both versions equally defend the separation of politics and religious faith, but each carries different implications for the conduct of public and private life. The soft version of the Enlightenment grew out of the experience of the murderous wars of religion, and adherents saw the achievement of civil peace and the avoidance of conflict as the only legitimate ends of political life. Toleration of religious differences was the most efficacious means of achieving these goals. But even here the Enlightenment's endorsement of toleration fell far short of an embrace of diversity. Toleration was extended for the most part to the dissenting Protestant sects. Catholics and atheists found themselves, at least initially, outside the circle of what was deemed tolerable. The point was to validate not every way of life and set of moral beliefs but only enough of them to avoid the dangers of civil war.[12]

The hard version of the Enlightenment aspired not merely to the toleration of religious differences but to the transformation of those differences into a form of rational religion that conformed to the requirements of universal human morality. As such, it opposed all particularistic moralities embedded in distinctive religious cultures and forms of life. Orthodox Judaism and other traditional religious practices clearly fell outside the orbit of this version of the Enlightenment. Rational religion thus exhibited a preference for certain Protestant forms of inwardness and emphasized communities of faith over law. The hard version of the Enlightenment was thus responsible for creating its own forms of secular intolerance. Religions that promoted moral self-direction and individual autonomy were deemed superior to those based on adherence to tradition and a body of sacred texts. Reason tolerates only the religion of reason, a point at odds not only with true toleration but also with an appreciation of moral and religious diversity. From the use of reason to undermine faith in popular religion it was but a short step to the critique of even rational religion as incompatible with the demands of courage, probity, and intellectual resoluteness.[13]

The new liberal solution to this age-old problem promised great benefits. In the first place, it promised an end to the destructive wars and crusades that had so ravaged Europe and its colonial peripheries. Not only did the separation of religion and politics promise an era of peace, but Enlightenment skepticism

also brought the idea that because certainty in religion is not available, toleration is the only reasonable alternative. By extending the mantle of toleration to
all (or nearly all), society could enjoy the benefits of peace and avoid the worst
forms of sectarian zealotry and religiously inspired cruelty. Second, by making
religion a matter of private belief or conscience, the separation of the spheres
would tend to abolish the hierarchical and authoritarian features of established churches and religious institutions. What was already the case for many
other features of civil life would apply to religion as well; that is, churches
would become voluntary associations of believers. And finally, by redefining
the scope of religious authority, the privatization of religion would deprive
power-hungry clerics of their influence over political life. The result would be a
toleration for religious minorities and other dissenters.

The Enlightenment's solution to the religious question has, to be sure, gar-
nered considerable success. The politics of toleration took shape slowly and
unevenly in places like Holland and England, but nowhere more clearly than
in the newly founded American republic.[14] It is a peculiarity of the original
American constitution that its only explicit reference to religion seems intended to severely circumscribe its scope. In Article 6 it is noted that there
should be no "religious test" as a requirement for public office. Beyond this the
First Amendment scrupulously prohibits Congress from passing any law "re-
specting an establishment of religion and prohibiting the free exercise there-
of." In these few words the Constitution intimates the belief that the best
guarantee for the freedom of religion is to deny any public recognition to it.
We are faced with the ongoing paradox that a nation consisting overwhelmingly of Christians should steadfastly deny its status as a Christian nation.[15]

The success of the Enlightenment's solution to the theologico-political problem has not, however, been complete. The wall of separation between church
and state has been battered by recurrent waves of religious "enthusiasm,"
from the Great Awakening to the Christian Coalition.[16] The insistence on
strict separation flies in the face of a society that was and remains persistently
and obdurately religious. The type of tolerant religiosity favored by Washington, Madison, and Jefferson, though embraced by elites, has not always found
favor with subsequent generations of Americans.[17] The framers' rationalistic
creed seemed to lack the primordial sense of awe, power, and mystery that
Hobbes called the natural seed of religion.[18] Nor, more recently, has the Enlightenment project necessarily fared well in controlling religious zealotry and
cruelty, to wit, the resurgence of militant Christianity, Judaism, and Islam.

Furthermore, some believe that the secularization of public life has been permitted to go too far. A growing number of academics and ordinary citizens
think that the politics of contemporary liberal regimes are openly hostile to

religious devotion. Official political and legal institutions now actively promote a "culture of disbelief," which seeks positively to discourage public
expressions of religious devoutness and sentiment.[19] According to Stephen
Carter, it is well to remember that religious communities remain important
intermediary associations standing between the individual and an intrusive
bureaucratic state.[20] It is wrong, he argues, to paint all religious believers with
the same broad brush. If some have fostered a climate of right-wing intolerance, it is equally true that such cherished liberal causes as abolitionism and
the civil rights movement would have been unthinkable without the zeal of
religion.[21] Furthermore, if diversity is a value appreciated by liberals, then
today the energy coming from religion helps to keep this value alive in a society
that is becoming monochromatically secular and skeptical in orientation.[22]

Secularization has meant not merely the privatization of religious belief but
its peripheralization. The result has been to deprive even liberal societies of the
moral authority and legitimating symbolism that they need to sustain themselves. What we are faced with today is, in the language of Jürgen Habermas,
nothing short of a legitimation crisis. The privatizing of religious faith that
was a staple in the works of the founders of liberal democracy is now said to be
responsible for pushing religion to the very margins of society, leaving the
"public square" dangerously "naked" and vulnerable to ominous forms of
indoctrination and control.[23]

To judge the Enlightenment project a failure on the basis of some recent developments would be unjustifiable and prematurely harsh. Still, a more balanced assessment of its strengths and weaknesses is long overdue. One reason
for the failure to address the religious question head on is the assumption that
the framers of the Enlightenment triumphed, and the defenders of religion
lost. Their very success in winning the positive judgment of posterity has produced a remarkable blindness to the permanence of the theologico-political.
To put the problem in perhaps its most paradoxical light: liberal theory has become the victim of its own success. The resurgence of the theologico-political
would scarcely have surprised the leading avatars of the Enlightenment, but
the very success of their arguments has prevented us, their descendants, from
grasping the full extent of the problem.

Only by returning to the early modern expressions of the theologico-
political problem can we hope to shed some light on our current dilemmas and
controversies. Precisely because the founders of modernity did not live in a
world shaped by the separation of church and state and an ethic of toleration,
they give us a window on how we have come to arrive at our own self-
understanding. The contributors to this debate were not shaped by the forces
of modernity; they moved within a universe governed by the language, sym-

bolism, and imagery of an older scriptural tradition. Indeed, it is a partial testimony to the success of their critiques of this tradition that no political theorist writing today has anything close to the mastery of scriptural texts and knowledge of ancient languages exhibited by these earlier secular theologians. To understand the return of the theologico-political problem, we must return to those who most profoundly shaped our understanding of it.

Spinoza and the Enlightenment

Who was Spinoza? A few biographical facts can help with the answer.[24] Spinoza was born in Amsterdam in 1632, a descendent of Portuguese Marranos. The Marranos were Iberian Jews who had fled the Catholic Inquisition during the fifteenth and sixteenth centuries for the relative safety and toleration of Holland, where after the Dutch revolt from Spain, the requirement of religious uniformity was abolished. Virtually nothing is known of Spinoza's early years. He attended a Jewish yeshiva, where he learned Hebrew and studied the Torah and Talmud. Early on, his intellectual gifts were noted. He spoke Spanish, Portuguese, and Dutch and later learned Latin, the language in which he wrote his scholarly works, from a former Jesuit priest named Van Den Enden.

There were for all intents and purposes no outward signs of Spinoza's later nonconformity. We do not know what ideas were fermenting in the mind of the young Spinoza. For reasons that are still a matter of dispute, in 1656, when he was twenty-four, the elders of the synagogue pronounced on him a *herem*, or edict of excommunication, making him "banned, cut off, cursed, and anathematized," no longer one of the people of Israel. Indeed, not only was Spinoza put to the ban, but the text of the *herem* concludes with the ominous warning that anyone who seeks to contact him, either orally or in print, do him any favor, or "read anything composed or written by him" will suffer the same fate.[25] Reading this angry denunciation from a distance of more than three hundred years, it is almost impossible not to ask how a people, many of whom had barely escaped the Inquisition themselves, could perpetuate the same spirit of persecution with one of their own members? Why would a people who had for centuries been victims of persecution and intolerance continue the same practice?

These are today almost inevitable questions, but they are not necessarily the same questions that Spinoza's contemporaries would have raised. In spite of the harsh, even fiery, language of the *herem*, such excommunications were not at all uncommon, and the terms for readmission were fairly mild. In imposing these edicts, Jews were maybe doing nothing other than adapting themselves to the customs and practices of the Gentile lands where they lived, often precariously. The world of the seventeenth century, even the relatively enlightened, cosmopolitan world of Amsterdam, was still a world determined by a corporate medieval structure. A person was defined by his or her theologico-political identity. Holland may have permitted a fairly wide degree of toleration among sects, but what went on within sects was an entirely different matter. The later Lockean idea of a church or synagogue as a voluntary association had no basis in reality. The idea of the autonomous individual standing outside or above tradition had yet to win recognition.

The reasons for Spinoza's excommunication are vague. The text of the *herem* refers to certain "horrible heresies," "awful deeds," and "evil opinions" without specifying what these were. Several different hypotheses have been advanced. According to Jean M. Lucas, an eighteenth-century biographer, Spinoza was excommunicated for his "contempt for the Law" and "want of respect for the Law of Moses."[26] Johannes Colerus, another early biographer, traces the excommunication to Spinoza's early study of natural philosophy, which led him to question the authority of the rabbis, whose "ridiculous doctrine and principles. . . are only built upon the authority of the rabbis themselves . . . and without the least appearance of reason."[27] More recently, scholarly research has pointed to the possible influence of such notable Marrano freethinkers as Uriel de Costa, Isaac Orobio de Castro, and Juan de Prado, whom Spinoza knew during these years.[28] It has even been suggested that Spinoza was excommunicated not for theological reasons but because he was a social and political radical whose beliefs threatened the commercial elite who ruled the Jewish community of Amsterdam.[29]

For all of his differences with the authorities, however, Spinoza was not an apostate. He refused to convert to Christianity but lived alone and aloof from all sects and attachments. According to biographical tradition, instead of seeking readmission to the synagogue, he wrote an apologia in Spanish on his decision to leave, which served as a draft copy for the *Theologico-Political Treatise*.[30] His very loneliness made him a kind of philosophical, even literary, hero to many.[31] In his years of exile he was befriended by members of some of the more liberal Protestant sects, like the Collegiants and Mennonites, who saw him as a potential ally. These sects tended toward republicanism in politics and latitudinarianism in theology. It was also during these years that Spinoza came to identify with Jan de Witt, leader of the republican faction in Dutch politics and opponent of the monarchy represented by the House of Orange and supported by the Calvinist clergy. The brutal murder of de Witt and his brother by an angry mob in 1672 led to Spinoza's withdrawal from political involvement; Spinoza commented that the behavior of the crowd represented the *ultima barbarorum*, "the height of barbarism."[32]

In addition to these associations, Spinoza had contact with the leading philosophers and scientists of his day. Leibniz and Huygens both sought out his views, as did Henry Oldenburg, the secretary of the Royal Academy in London and confidant of Sir Isaac Newton. Even though Spinoza was not a Christian, he was offered a professorship at the University of Heidelberg, which he turned down on the grounds that it would compromise his freedom of mind.[33] Around the same time Spinoza was approached by an emissary of the Prince de Condé with the prospect of a pension from Louis XIV if Spinoza would dedicate one of his books to him. Spinoza declined the offer "with all the civility he was capable of," saying, "I am a good republican and I always aimed at the glory and welfare of the state."[34] He earned a living as a lens grinder until his death in 1677 at the age of forty-four.

Spinoza exercised an unusual combination of boldness and reticence in his writing. As an excommunicant, living alone and unprotected, he knew at first hand the sting of religious persecution and the dangers of speaking one's mind openly. His signet ring bore the Latin inscription *caute*, or "caution." He took pains to conceal his opinions even from those most intimate with him. With the exception of an early commentary on Descartes's *Principles of Philosophy*, followed by his own *Metaphysical Thoughts*, no other work published by Spinoza during his lifetime bore his name on its cover. His major work of political philosophy, the *Theologico-Political Treatise*, was published anonymously in 1670 carrying the name of a fictitious Hamburg publishing house.[35] The work for which he is best known, the *Ethics*, was published posthumously for reasons of prudence and safety. A shorter work, the *Political Treatise*, promised a more detailed defense of democracy than the defense set out in the *Theologico-Political Treatise*, but he did not live to finish writing it.

For reasons that we will examine more fully in the next chapter, Spinoza often presented his views in an "Aesopian" rhetoric intended to conceal his most radical opinions. There is by now a large and fairly comprehensive literature dealing with the detection and interpretation of multilevel writing in philosophy, religion, and the history of political thought.[36] Evidence for this type of writing may take the form of systematic ambiguity, paradox, and even outright contradiction. Multilevel writing may be motivated by a fear of persecution but also by a sense of intellectual elitism. It may be intended to preserve the truth from the uninitiated but also to win converts to philosophy. As we shall see, the audience for the *Treatise* was not philosophers as such but those "left"-leaning members of dissenting sects ("Chrétiens sans église," in Leszek Kolakowski's memorable phrase) who may have been susceptible to Spinoza's arguments.[37] Spinoza himself referred to this group as the *libera multitudo*, the "free people," the party of liberty, those most likely to aid the cause of republican government and religious toleration.

The *Treatise* was intended not as a work of timeless philosophy but as a political tract, a *Tendenzschrift,* written to advance the fortunes of a cause.[38] Spinoza therefore adapted the language and outlook of the party most likely to favor that cause. Aware of the principle that "Scripture speaks the language of man" (*Scriptura humane loquitur*), Spinoza accommodated his language to those around him. Security and personal safety were always a consideration, but Spinoza adopted his broadly "dialectical" technique of appealing to biblical authority, which he knew would be widely accepted among his readers, to draw out lessons and arguments that could then be used against theological orthodoxy. Biblical hermeneutics was for Spinoza the activity of finding a common ground with his audience in order later to undercut the very ground that had been fictitiously established.[39] The following passage from chapter 5 of the *Treatise* typifies Spinoza's manner of expression:

> If someone wishes to teach some doctrine to a whole nation, not to mention the whole human race, and wishes it to be understood in every respect by everyone, he is bound to confirm his teaching solely by experience and for the most part to accommodate his arguments and the definitions of the things to be taught to the power of understanding of the common people, who form the greatest part of the human race. He should not connect his arguments or give definitions according to how they serve to connect his arguments. Otherwise he will write only for the learned, i.e., he will be intelligible to only a very few men compared with the rest.[40]

Despite his protestations of caution and reticence, no one reading the *Treatise* could fail to see it as anything other than a bold, even audacious, work. Spinoza gives uncompromising expression to the Enlightenment's critique of Scripture in its most radical form. Taking up the themes of prophecy, miracles, and providence, he submits each in turn to withering criticism. Yet the book was more than a challenge to scriptural authority. The critique of religion was inseparable from a program for political reform. In the *Treatise* Spinoza champions the freedom of thought and opinion and the toleration of religious heterodoxy, argues for the subordination of the clergy to the secular powers, and defends the independent use of reason as an inalienable human right. But so boldly did Spinoza express himself that his writings were almost universally proscribed. From the time the book first appeared it became embroiled in a controversy from which it has never fully recovered. "Few books occasioned as many refutations, anathemas, insults, and maledictions," Gilles Deleuze has written. "The words 'Spinozism' and 'Spinozist' became insults and threats."[41]

Among the foremost critics of Spinoza were not only defenders of the various religious orthodoxies but also proponents of the Enlightenment, for whom Spinoza's chief error lay in expressing his claims recklessly. Thus Hobbes, a man not ordinarily known for caution, remarked to Aubrey that the *Treatise* had "cut through him a bar's length" for "he durst not write so boldly."[42] The judicious Locke, under attack from the Bishop of Worcester, found it necessary to remark, "I am not so well read in Hobbes and Spinoza," adding a word about "those justly decried names."[43] Similarly, the French Huguenot Pierre Bayle, in his article on Spinoza in the *Historical and Critical Dictionary,* could describe the *Treatise* as "a pernicious and detestable book in which [Spinoza] slips in all the seeds of atheism."[44] According to Bayle, Spinoza's doctrine of the unity of Substance commits him to the view that God alone is responsible for all the cruelty, suffering, and inhumanity that takes place in the world. This is the "monstrous hypothesis" that surpasses "all the extravagances" of the pagan poets, none of whom dared to approach the idea that God is the agent of "all the crimes that are committed and all the infirmities of the world."[45]

It could be argued that Bayle's article is based on certain fundamental misunderstandings of Spinoza.[46] This did not, however, prevent it from becoming the authoritative interpretation for at least the next century. The French *Encyclopédie* treats Spinoza extensively under the entry on atheism, where the author confines himself to a virtual paraphrase of Bayle's synopsis.[47] One might have thought that Spinoza's iconoclasm would have appealed to the skeptical spirit of Hume. Nothing could be further from the case. In *A Treatise of Human Nature* Hume repeats Bayle almost verbatim. Spinoza's "hideous hypothesis" regarding the unity of Substance is said to form the "fundamental principle of the atheism" that has made his name "universally infamous."[48] Montesquieu, in his "Defense of the Spirit of the Laws," felt compelled to denounce Spinoza's fatalism and atheism.[49] And Rousseau, in the *Discourse on the Sciences and the Arts,* could praise Bacon, Newton, and Descartes as the "preceptors of the human race" but still condemn the invention of typography for enabling "the dangerous dreams" of Hobbes and Spinoza to last forever.[50] This war of words continued through the eighteenth century, culminating in the debate between Mendelssohn and Jacobi over the alleged Spinozism of Lessing.[51]

Only toward the end of this period did the appraisal of Spinoza begin to change. The demonization that began almost immediately after the publication of the *Treatise* gave way, initially in Germany, to the virtual sanctification of his name. Although Spinoza had been attacked earlier as an atheist and materialist, the romantics now heralded him as a mystic and pantheist, a "God-intoxicated man," to use the phrase of Novalis. Spinoza came to be seen as the founder of a new kind of piety and a new kind of church opposed to both the Enlightenment and orthodoxy. This was the religion of culture and the church of the cultured individual. What played a particular role in Spinoza's rehabilitation was the belief that a good person could not be the carrier of bad ideas, and Spinoza, it was alleged, had lived a life of exemplary piety, self-denial, and devotion to truth. He came to be seen as more than an ordinary philosopher — as a kind of philosophic saint, like Socrates.[52]

This massive reconsideration of the life and work of Spinoza was initiated by Goethe's consternation at reading Bayle's article on Spinoza. In his autobiography, *Dichtung und Wahrheit,* he recalls "the feeling of calm and clarity" that passed over him after paging through the works of that "remarkable man." This confidence in Spinoza, Goethe opined, was based on the "peaceful effect" that his writings induced, which was only confirmed "when I heard my beloved mystics being accused of Spinozism."[53] Although Goethe's Spinoza was still something of a philosophical pagan, the belated process of Christianization was part of his makeover. In the *Biographia Literaria* Coleridge, one of the first to introduce Spinoza in England, could describe him as one of the great mystics who had prevented him "from being imprisoned within the outlines of any single dogmatic system."[54] Later in the same work Coleridge cites a passage from the *Ethics* (V, P 42) as evidence that Spinoza's teachings were "thoroughly *Pauline*" and "compleatly accordant with the doctrines of the established Church."[55] The same current of Christian apologetics flowed through the nineteenth century. In an influential article entitled "Spinoza and the Bible" Matthew Arnold enthused about Spinoza's "life of unbroken diligence, kindliness, and purity" and compared the purity of his "beatific vision" to that of Saint Augustine and Fra Angelico.[56] "His life," he quotes Heine as saying, "was a copy of the life of his divine kinsman, Jesus Christ."[57]

This beatification of Spinoza has contributed more than anything else to our inability to come to terms with his thought. In fact, there has been a tendency among contemporary students of Spinoza to perpetuate the obfuscation, no doubt unwittingly, in their depiction of him as representing "the metaphysical mind and temperament at its purest and most intense," "the perfect example of the pure philosopher."[58] This image of the philosopher untouched by experience, untroubled by human contingency, looking down on human affairs, as it were, *sub specie aeternitatis,* driven only by the imperatives of "pure philosophical thinking," contributes to the myth of Spinoza as an ascetic saint, devoted to constructing "a single metaphysical system."[59] The idea that Spinoza was a political figure deeply concerned with the theologico-political issues of his time who wrote as an excommunicated Jew with a passionate volatility has hardly ever been allowed to intrude.[60]

My aim here is to restore a more human and a more political dimension to

Spinoza's accomplishments. The *Treatise* is perhaps the least read work of political theory by a philosopher of the first rank, no doubt because it is overshadowed by the *Ethics*. But to see Spinoza as a "pure" philosopher first and a political theorist only derivatively or to view the *Treatise* as only a propadeutic to the *Ethics*, a stage in Spinoza's "progress," is to court serious misunderstanding.[61] The *Treatise* was written prior to the *Ethics*, its concerns being foremost in Spinoza's mind during the years leading up to and after his excommunication. Furthermore, we are only now beginning to see the *Ethics* as a more political work than it has been traditionally depicted. Once again Deleuze proves to be supremely helpful: "The *Ethics* is a book written twice simultaneously: once in the continuous stream of definitions, propositions, demonstrations, and corollaries, which develop the great speculative themes with all the rigors of the mind; another time in the broken chain of scholia, a discontinuous volcanic line, a second version underneath the first, expressing all the angers of the heart and setting forth the practical theses of denunciation and liberation."[62]

The Spinoza to appear in this book, then, is neither the pure metaphysical-system builder, nor a Christian mystic, nor a putative *Naturphilosoph*. Rather, he was a crucial figure in the Enlightenment's formulation of the theologico-political problem. This is not to say that Spinoza was especially representative of the Enlightenment. In crucial respects he was not. But because he often said bluntly what others said more timidly he can serve as a litmus of the Enlightenment's view of the religious question. His outspokenness is also what allows us to see Enlightenment aspirations in all their folly and grandeur. Before turning to the substance of the *Treatise*, however, another set of issues central to this study must be addressed.

The *Treatise* and the "Jewish Question"

Spinoza's treatment of the theologico-political problem is important because it tells us something about the nature and limits of liberalism. But Spinoza is also the first writer to consider seriously the place of the Jews within modern liberal society. To use a somewhat anachronistic turn of phrase, Spinoza was the first exponent of what in the nineteenth century was called the Jewish Question.[63] By the Jewish Question is meant the terms by which Jews, after centuries of separation and ghettoization, would be granted the rights of membership in, or admission to, the polity. The expression may today have a sinister ring. Why, after all, should Jews and Judaism be a question? Although the Jewish Question was often debated by people with a fervent, even profound, hostility to Judaism, it remains inseparable from the Enlightenment.

The debate over the Jewish Question concerned the conditions under which Jews would be admitted to the rights of citizenship. As Pierre Birnbaum and Ira Katznelson have recently argued, no single model or unitary path toward emancipation was followed by all Jews everywhere.[64] Emancipation took a variety of forms depending on national context and circumstance. In France emancipation was essentially a creation of the Revolution, which established a unitary republican state with a cohesive national identity. In Germany, where there was no national state until 1871, emancipation proceeded along largely cultural rather than legal-political lines, whereas in the United States the liberal structure of the Constitution made it possible for widely different particularist cultures to coexist without undergoing any formal process of conversion or self-renunciation.

The idea of Jewish emancipation was not an initiative of the Jews themselves. Rather, it was was an afterthought to the historical transformations of the major European polities beginning as early as the sixteenth century. The emergence of the centralized territorial state as the single locus of sovereign power is without doubt the most important fact in the history of early modern Europe. The rise and development of the state was intended to put an end to the divisive conflict of authority and allegiance that had dominated the medieval world and expressed itself in the famous doctrine of "the king's two bodies."[65] Legal and philosophical fictions like the state of nature, the social contract, and the sovereign were invented to represent the view that only a central unitary state could create order, prevent chaos, and maintain the individual in a condition of peace and security. Further, the vast increase in state power was presented not as a usurpation but as the emancipation of the individual from such traditional sources of authority as the church, school, guild, and patriarchal family. The so-called absolutist monarchies and enlightened despotisms were aimed at creating a new "neutral" power capable of imposing its own solution on the theologico-political problem.[66]

Jewish emancipation, then, was something of an afterthought among these larger dynamics of state building and the concentration of political power. Jews, who had traditionally lived in semiautonomous communities and administered their own body of corporate law, were merely one such partial association that the modern state was trying to absorb. The state may have claimed to be the sole instrument of legitimacy, but it also promised to treat the Jews with the same legal equality guaranteed to other citizens. In place of the old "state within a state" would come a new complex of individual rights, freedoms, and equalities—above all, the right to participate in the operations of society.[67] The assimilationist logic of the modern state was given powerful expression in a famous exchange that took place on the floor of the French

National Assembly in 1789. In response to the demand of the Parisian Jews to be treated according to the same civil code as all other French citizens, the Comte de Clermont-Tonnerre proclaimed: "Everything must be denied the Jews as a nation and everything granted to the Jews as individuals. . . . They must no longer form either a political body, or an order in the State; they must be citizens individually."[68] Emancipation was to be formally granted, but on condition of the complete submersion of Jewish particularism.

Although there may have been no single model of emancipation, what characterized the process of integration everywhere was the gradual shedding of an ancient identity. The paradoxical result of emancipation was the creation of secular forms of anti-Semitism. Many of the enlighteners and emancipators believed that Judaism would wither away once Jews had the opportunity to mingle with and become part of the larger society. The European democratic movements sought to emancipate Jews from enforced legal and social ghettoization, but they continued to regard Judaism as inimical to the Enlightenment values of liberation and emancipation. Judaism was castigated not, as in the ancien régime, for its refusal to recognize the truth of Christianity but for its obdurate insistence on and loyalty to a traditional way of life. Moreover, emancipation generally took the form of integration into societies that remained largely Gentile in their cultural values and forms of social life. Not conversion but acceptance of these values was imposed as the price for an admission ticket to the benefits of civil privileges. While individual Jews may have been granted civil rights, Judaism as a set of institutions and a way of life was barely tolerated. A common saying of the German Jewish community throughout the nineteenth century was that Jews had been emancipated, but Judaism had not.[69]

There is, as the economists say, no such thing as a free lunch. Emancipation has its price. A bargain of sorts was struck: in exchange for the granting of equal rights and protection under the law, Jews agreed to renounce their "particularity," that is, their claims to exclusivity and loyalty to a particular tradition. Obviously, in countries like fifteenth-century Spain or tsarist Russia where Jews lived apart as a "foreign" nation within the host country, such an exchange was never a consideration. Only in those nations undergoing liberalization or modernization did extending civil and political rights to Jews become a question. Nowhere was the Jewish Question debated more intensely than in Germany. German Jews, more than Jews of any other nation, sought to replace their ancient identity with fidelity to the Enlightenment's project of emancipation through *Bildung,* or self-formation.[70]

Emancipation did not necessarily require the destruction of traditional Jewish identity, but it did entail an often profound transformation of it. The paradoxes of emancipation often expressed themselves in new, sometimes comic, sometimes pathetic roles for Jews, who took on identities ranging from pariah to parvenu.[71] With the loss of faith in the God of one's fathers, there emerged that distinctively modern phenomenon known as the secular or "god-less Jew" (*gotlosser Jude*), or what Yosef Yerushalmi has recently dubbed the Psychological Jew. Yerushalmi's description of this type is worth quoting at some length:

> The Psychological Jew was born before Freud. If, for all secular Jews, Judaism has become "Jewishness" of one kind or another, the Jewishness of the Psychological Jew seems, at least to the outsider, devoid of all but the most vestigial content; it has become almost pure subjectivity. Content is replaced by character. Alienated from classical Jewish texts, Psychological Jews tend to insist on inalienable Jewish traits. Intellectuality and independence of mind, the highest ethical and moral standards, concern for social justice, tenacity in the face of persecution — these are among the qualities they will claim, if called upon, as quintessentially Jewish. . . . Floating in their undefined yet real Jewishness, they will doubly resent and fiercely resist any attempt on the part of the surrounding society to define them against their own wishes. The worst moments are those in which, as a result of anti-Semitism, they are forced to realize that vital aspects of their lives are still determined by ancestral choices they may no longer understand and which, in any case, they feel they have transcended or repudiated.[72]

"It is therefore no accident," Yerushalmi has added, that long before Freud or even Marx "the first great culture-hero of modern secular Jews was Spinoza."[73]

Spinoza is the prototype of the emancipated Jew. Emancipation meant liberation from tradition and authority. More than that, emancipation meant universality and, therefore, renunciation of Jewish particularity. The emancipated Jew did not substitute one identity for another but embodied the free or autonomous individual, what Franz Rosenzweig has called the abstract man-in-general.[74] To prove one's credentials as a truly emancipated individual, one must be prepared to submit one's own tradition to a critical analysis. Spinoza ridicules the idea of a divine election of the Jewish people and regards their survival over centuries of Diaspora as simply "nothing to wonder at."[75] Thus, throughout the *Treatise* Spinoza consistently demeans the Hebrew Bible in comparison to the Christian revelation. Judaism is depicted as narrow and particularistic, scarcely a religion at all, while Christianity is praised as universalistic and ethical. Further, Moses is disparaged as a cynical and calculating politician in comparison to "Christ," who is portrayed as a teacher and philosopher in intellectual communion with God. Spinoza, who claims to write *sine ira et studio,* may well have known that these comparisons were unjust and ideologically loaded. Why, then, did he engage in what must surely be considered a powerful and emotionally charged polemic against his own people?[76]

The answer to this question illustrates the dilemmas of emancipation in a particularly vivid form. The *Treatise* presents itself as one of the great works of autoemancipation. The aim of the work as a whole is the liberation of the individual from bondage to superstition and ecclesiastical authority. Spinoza's ideal is the free or autonomous individual who uses reason to achieve mastery over the passions. The *Treatise* culminates in an exhilarating vision of republican government where citizens live in peace and toleration and everyone is free "to think what he likes and say what he thinks."[77] Though presenting himself at the same time as a man who rises above all bias and prejudice, Spinoza does not cease from carrying out a scathing attack on Judaism. Indeed, this attack is made all the more troublesome in that it is carried out by a learned Jew steeped in biblical and talmudic studies who uses religious sources as weapons against Judaism itself. Why does he do this? Why does Spinoza consistently debase Judaism before a predominantly Gentile audience? Why does he play deliberately and self-consciously to anti-Jewish prejudice?

Three hypotheses have been offered in response to the question. One widely held view is that Spinoza's defamation of Judaism was the result of Jewish self-hatred. Spinoza was the archetype of the self-hating Jew. In an influential essay Hermann Cohen attributed Spinoza's critique of Judaism to his "unconcealed hatred" of his own people.[78] Cohen ascribed the premises of the *Treatise* to a desire to take "revenge" on the rabbis of Amsterdam for excommunicating him. According to Cohen, Spinoza's naturalism blinded him to the ethical idealism of the prophets and the universalism of their teaching. Spinoza's chief sin was his depiction of Judaism as a purely carnal political legislation void of moral content. Accordingly, he was denounced as a "renegade" and an "apostate."[79] He derogated Judaism, trafficking in anti-Jewish stereotypes that were to become the source of later hostility toward Jews. Spinoza thus stands condemned of a "humanly incomprehensible betrayal."[80]

The view that Spinoza is a defiler of Judaism was reiterated recently by the French philosopher and talmudist Emmanuel Levinas. In an essay entitled "The Spinoza Case" Levinas questions the wisdom of Ben Gurion's attempt to have the ban against Spinoza lifted.[81] Indeed, he remarks that the case of Spinoza still constitutes an "essential question" for the Jewish people. Within the history of ideas, Levinas asserts, Spinoza exerted an influence that was both "decisive and anti-Jewish."[82] Repeating Cohen's verdict, Levinas maintains that Spinoza remains "guilty of betrayal" for his subordination of the Hebrew Bible to the Christian Scripture and calling them simply stages in the development of reason. To Levinas, lifting the ban on Spinoza appears both unnecessary and unjust — unnecessary because Spinoza's rationalism has already emerged triumphant and unjust because removing the ban would merely sanction his slanders against Judaism.

A second and less hostile explanation of Spinoza's strategy is offered by Leo Strauss, who in an early essay denies that Spinoza's philosophy can be understood as motivated simply by a desire for revenge.[83] Cohen's emphasis on Spinoza's excommunication as a motive for writing the *Treatise* is at best a "conjecture," given that Spinoza seems to have been working along the same lines well in advance of his expulsion from the synagogue. According to Strauss, Spinoza was motivated above all by a desire to liberate philosophy from ecclesiastical supervision, a move that could have been accomplished without any untoward hostility toward Judaism. Instead, Spinoza's critique of the Old Testament was aimed at the spiritual and political domination of Dutch Calvinists, who saw themselves as the heirs of the ancient Hebrew theocracy. Spinoza's *Treatise* was directed less at seeking revenge on the Jewish community than at liberating the sect-ridden Netherlands of the seventeenth century from ecclesiastical control.[84]

Forty years later Strauss embellishes upon his position without fundamentally altering it.[85] He argues that Spinoza, to achieve his objective, the liberation of philosophy from theology, had to appeal to the prejudices of his predominantly Gentile audience. Spinoza's strategy of demeaning Judaism before his non-Jewish readers was part of an elaborate rhetorical ruse to gain a hearing; it did not derive from any animus against Judaism as such. Strauss goes so far as to suggest that Spinoza even felt a sympathy for his people that he had to conceal if he were to gain a popular audience for his cause. Spinoza may have hated Judaism, according to Strauss, but he did not hate the Jewish people.[86] This is not to say that Strauss was Spinoza's defender. "Our case against Spinoza," he writes, "is in some respects even stronger than Cohen thought."[87] Spinoza's strategy of appealing to anti-Jewish prejudice, while dictated by considerations of prudence, was nevertheless Machiavellian in the literal sense; that is, he used base or ignominious means to achieve a lofty goal. Spinoza's betrayal of Judaism may have been humanly comprehensible, but he was still playing "a most dangerous game," even an "amazingly unscrupulous" one.[88]

A third explanation for Spinoza's critique looks to his Marrano background. Yirmiyahu Yovel, in a two-volume study of Spinoza, has depicted the philosopher as having internalized a pattern of thought and behavior typical of *converso* mentality.[89] The *conversos* were Jews of Iberian descent who had converted to Catholicism during the fourteenth and fifteenth centuries but who remained secret practitioners of their ancient faith. These *conversos* may have paid lip service to official Catholic doctrine, but they remained subterranean judaizers, even to the point of confusing or mixing up their Judaism with the symbolism and imagery of the Catholic church. Over time this dual existence became internalized to such a degree that their successors, like Spinoza, who never stepped foot in Catholic Spain, wore the mask of the *converso* almost as second nature.[90]

According to Yovel, the Marrano model fits Spinoza like a glove. Among the features ascribed to Marranism are, first, a skepticism about revealed religion and traditional routes to salvation. Marranos were often those who had lost one faith but were incapable of ever fully accepting another.[91] Second, the Marrano experience was typified by a propensity for multilevel language and the elaborate use of other literary disguises. Brought up with a fear of inquisitorial methods, the true Marranos dissembled their views out of a cautious fear of persecution.[92] Third, the propensity for esotericism was coupled with a philosophical elitism. For Spinoza this meant that redemption was attainable through neither the Christian sacraments nor the law of Moses but through the use of reason. Reason understood as *scientia intuitiva* acquired an almost mystical status leading to a state of *beatitudo,* or the intellectual love of God. The practice of rationality was the preserve of a tiny minority, with the majority of humankind condemned to live a life of superstition under the sway of *imaginatio.*[93]

Each of these explanations sheds some light on the dilemmas of emancipation, but none is, in my opinion, satisfactory. The argument from Jewish self-hatred is perhaps the least adequate. To explain Spinoza's critique of Judaism as motivated by a desire for revenge is both simplistic and reductionist. More important, it cannot explain those parts of the *Treatise* where Spinoza expresses a genuine sense of Jewish pride and self-respect. The *Treatise* is, to my knowledge, the first modern work to advocate the restitution of Jewish sovereignty and a Jewish state.[94] Cohen and Levinas both miss the extent to which Spinoza's critique of Judaism is also indirectly a critique of Christianity. Being unable to attack Christianity directly, he does so through the back door. For reasons that I will develop at length, Spinoza moves Judaism to center stage largely in order to facilitate the establishment of a state that is indifferent to — that is, tolerant of — the differences between Christians and Jews.

Strauss's view has the advantage of focusing on Spinoza's famed passion for secretiveness and self-concealment. Spinoza often put forward shocking and novel opinions while professing moderation and conformity with prevailing orthodoxies. Even his apparently boldest statements, when sufficiently unpacked, conceal layers of meaning that turn out to be bolder still. But Strauss's claim that the ultimate purpose of the *Treatise* is the liberation of philosophy from religion, though surely correct, downplays the political character of the work. Spinoza wrote not only to liberate philosophy from religion but also to liberate politics from religion and to subordinate the clergy to the authority of the secular state. To be sure, Strauss is closer to the truth than Cohen when he pronounces Spinoza's apparent betrayal of Judaism humanly comprehensible, but he attributes the intelligibility of Spinoza's motives to a strategy of achieving the liberation of philosophy from Scripture rather than achieving the control of the clergy by the state.[95]

Finally, Yovel's explanation of Spinoza's treatment of Judaism as the result of the Marrano experience, though biographically illuminating, is philosophically unpersuasive. In the first place, Spinoza's use of strategies of deceit and duplicity was a common literary trope used by many non-*converso* authors during the Renaissance. To describe this rhetorical device as specifically Marrano is to bend the term out of all proportion. Second, notwithstanding the depiction of Spinoza as the "Marrano of reason," Marranism remains deeply embedded in the outlook of the medieval Jewish experience. Spinoza's *Treatise* ultimately has less in common with the classics of *converso* literature than with the language and outlook of enlightened Europe. Whereas Marranism represented a strategy of survival for Jews living in hostile lands, Spinoza's arguments for freedom of conscience and toleration of religious difference became the basis for Moses Mendelssohn's appeals for Jewish emancipation and civil equality a century later.[96]

I argue that Spinoza's treatment of the Jewish Question is inseparable from his liberal political theory. His denigration of Judaism cannot be seen simply as the result of self-hatred, or the desire to emancipate philosophy, or his Marrano background. Each of these explanations is essentially outside or external to his politics. Spinoza's critique of religion is the direct consequence of his political aspiration: the creation of a new kind of liberal polity with a new kind of liberal citizen. This effort to establish a new liberated individual who inhabits a modern secular state could not but represent a profound break with historical Jewish experience. His attack on the ceremonial law as an instrument of worldly well-being, his denigration of Moses and the prophets as men of fervid imagination but enfeebled intellect, his depiction of the Scriptures of Israel as *antiqui vulgi praejudicia* were all intended to divest Jews of their traditional identities and their attachments to an ancient tradition. His efforts to undermine and replace the older theologico-political identity is, I suggest, a key premise of the modern liberal state.

Spinoza adopted the strategy that he did, not out of an anti-Jewish animus, much less self-hatred, but for the supremely political reason that Christians excelled Jews in power and influence. The hope for a liberal and tolerant society was more likely to be expedited by appealing to Christians, rather than Jews, and to those potential philosophers among the Gentiles. Such a tactic could be described as Machiavellian; more accurately we could say that it is constitutive of Spinoza's liberalism. The centerpiece of this liberalism was the attempt to replace the historical religions based on Scripture with a new kind of civil theology based on reason. The Bible would have to be shown to contain nothing offensive to society, and its teachings would have to be reinterpreted to support the requirements of civil life. When all is said and done, the doctrinal core of this religion is reducible to a handful or so of basic dogmas, specifically the injunction to practice toleration and avoid persecuting others. With a civil theology, professions of faith are by and large a private matter, and in any case, individuals will understand their faith according to their own capacities. The *fides universalis,* the "universal faith," is the theology of the rational or liberated individual, the person for whom the *Treatise* was manifestly intended.

The *Theologico-Political Treatise,* I believe, presents the most powerful and profound statement of the Jewish Question. The Faustian bargain presented by Spinoza is the exchange of an ancient Jewish identity for a modern secular one. It is an exchange that many have found irresistible. Indeed, not for nothing does Spinoza belong to that distinguished line of thinkers that the Marxist historian Isaac Deutscher has called non-Jewish Jews.[97] Like Yerushalmi's Psychological Jew, Deutscher's non-Jewish Jew is one who lives on the margins of Judaism and for whom the traditions of orthodoxy have become "too narrow, too archaic, and too constricting."[98] The archetypal non-Jewish Jews were all those who rebelled against their own Judaism and, in doing so, revealed something about "the quintessence of Jewish life and the Jewish intellect." What Deutscher finds quintessentially Jewish in such a diverse lot as Spinoza, Heine, Marx, Rosa Luxemburg, and Freud is that

> they were *a priori* exceptional in that as Jews they dwelt on the borderlines of various civilizations, religions, and national cultures. They were born and brought up on the borderlines of various epochs. Their minds matured where the most diverse cultural influences crossed and fertilized each other. They lived on the margins or in the nooks and crannies of their respective nations. Each of them was in society and yet not in it, of it and yet not of it. It was this that enabled them to rise in thought above their societies, above their nations, above their times and generations, and to strike out mentally into wide new horizons and far into the future.[99]

Deutscher uses the term "non-Jewish Jew" to identify the Jewish heretic who seeks to transcend the boundaries of Judaism in order to adopt a universal "human" perspective. "Spinoza's ethics," Deutscher has demurred, "were no longer Jewish ethics but the ethics of man at large."[100] But are the ethics of "man at large" real or chimerical? Is the exchange of a particular and historical identity for a universal human identity a real exchange or something like an offer to buy the Brooklyn Bridge? Must not any set of ethics be the ethics of someone? Liberal ethics or Marxian ethics are not the ethics of man-in-general but the ethics of liberals and Marxists. The Jewish Question thus remains the most tangible expression of the problem of any person or group faced with the offer of emancipation. The value of Spinoza is his ability to help us understand the costs and benefits of this offer.

Spinoza's Democratic Liberalism

Spinoza's reputation as a Jewish heretic is perhaps better known than his political theory. The *Ethics* remains widely read as a classic of early modern philosophy along with the works of Descartes and Leibniz. The *Treatise,* at least chapter 7, is well known among students of the history of religion for its pioneering critique of Scripture and Spinoza's anticipation of the "higher criticism" of the nineteenth century. But only rarely has Spinoza been read by political theorists. Even when the *Treatise* has been read, Spinoza has been seen merely as applying the principles of a dogmatic metaphysics to the changing and variable nature of political reality. Spinoza is accused of lacking a serious understanding of history and of operating with a static conception of the political regime as nothing more than a "closed mechanical system."[101] This neglect of Spinoza is both surprising and unfortunate: surprising because of the enormous interest evinced in recent years in the historical origins of modern political thought and unfortunate because Spinoza is the first modern political theorist to endorse democracy as the best regime (*optima Respublica*).[102]

It is easy to disregard the *Treatise* as a political text. Spinoza's political theory is buried three-quarters of the way through it and comes to light only after a long and painstaking discussion of biblical philology and criticism. His defense of democracy is undergirded by a ruthlessly naturalistic psychology that is even more immoralistic than Hobbes's. And he entertains certain elitist and aristocratic views of human perfection. The distinction between the few who live according to *ratio* and the many who live according to *appetitus* seems to undercut his democratic commitments.

Perhaps the greatest benefit to be obtained from a recovery of the *Treatise* is that it would compel us to reconsider many of our standard genealogies of liberalism. Ever since Tocqueville, it has been common to think of liberal democratic ideology as a direct continuation of Christian and especially Calvinist theology.[103] Liberal doctrines of individualism, the rights of man, moral equality, along with a suspicion of hierarchy, can all be traced back to the wellsprings of dissenting Protestantism. Spinoza provides us with an alternative route to liberalism by way of Judaism. For Spinoza, Judaism, not Christianity, is the paradigm for liberalism—so much so that the *Treatise* could almost have been called a defense of liberalism *aus den Quellen des Judentums*. Spinoza reaches liberal democratic conclusions by grappling with the issues of Jewish law, political identity, and history. He locates the essence of Judaism in its orthopractic character. Judaism is for him not a theology or set of credal beliefs but a body of authoritative law. Insofar as the liberal state is limited to the control of external behavior and is tolerant with respect to beliefs and opinions, it shows a marked affinity with Judaism.[104] In the *Treatise*, rather than mechanically applying metaphysical principles to the subject matter of politics, Spinoza shows a richly developed sense of history, making elaborate use of biblical narrative and entering into dialogue with both rabbinic and medieval philosophical sources.[105]

These considerations notwithstanding, the *Treatise* gave an important impulse to later developments in democratic thought. Spinoza derives the legitimacy of democracy from premises at least in part borrowed from his most notorious contemporary, Hobbes. Like Hobbes, Spinoza begins with a perfectly realistic, not to say hard-boiled, picture of human nature in which every living being has a natural right to preserve itself by whatever means are at its disposal. Like Hobbes, Spinoza invokes the metaphor of a social contract as a means by which individuals agree with one another to reduce the state of war to a condition of peace. Yet Spinoza departs from Hobbes in two interesting, indeed crucial respects. Unlike Hobbes, who displays a marked preference for monarchy, Spinoza finds that only a democratic sovereign can ensure protection against the dangers of arbitrary rule stemming from the investiture of power in the hands of one person. Because the natural right of every being is said to be identical with its power, he draws the conclusion that the majority in any community have by definition the preponderance of right on their side. And unlike Hobbes, who maintained that the avoidance of war is the greatest political good, Spinoza endorses democracy for its enhancement of human freedom. Democracy is desirable because it fosters the conditions of reason and the expression of individual faculties. To a degree developed later by Rousseau and Kant, not peace and security but freedom becomes the true end of political life.[106]

The kind of democracy advocated by Spinoza is what today would be called a liberal democracy. A central feature of this democracy is its incorporation of the widest possible freedom of thought and opinion. The *Treatise* provides several, not necessarily consistent justifications for toleration. Toleration is said to follow from the doctrine of natural right strictly understood. If the right of nature means the liberty to do whatever our power permits, then by nature the sovereign's power must be limited to the control of external behavior. Because no one's mind can possibly lie wholly at the disposition of another, the sovereign must leave the contents of the mind entirely to individual discretion.

In the *Treatise* Spinoza also argues that historically and politically attempts to control the content of thought have invariably backfired. Rather than producing consensus and harmony, policies of intolerance and persecution have bred conflict and opposition. The effort to criminalize opinion has led even honorable men to don the mantle of revolution. Note that unlike later defenders of toleration, Spinoza does not say that the effort to control thought violates some sacred or privileged sphere of individual privacy. Persecution is wrong not because it is immoral but because it is inherently self-defeating.

Most important, Spinoza defends freedom of speech because it fosters a certain kind of human being with distinctive traits of character and mind. This new type of human being so much admired by Spinoza, as well as by Machiavelli, Hobbes, and Montaigne, was just beginning to make an appearance on the European scene. The kind of human being envisaged by Spinoza is one for whom "nothing is considered to be dearer or sweeter than freedom."[107] A person is liberated who, as far as possible, does not depend on mere authority, who wishes to think for himself, who seeks to understand and hence master the passions, who acts rather than being acted upon, who thinks and acts not out of envy and fear but out of love and friendship. Above all, this person thinks of nothing so much as life itself and the means necessary to its enhancement. Although Spinoza's idea of the liberated individual has certain ancient precedents, it remains a modern creation to a considerable degree. It is based much more radically on the ideas of independence, self-mastery, and, above all, courage (*fortitudo*) than earlier conceptions were.[108]

The *Treatise* is one of the first works in which it is argued that the fruits of toleration are beneficial not merely for the individual but also for society as a whole. Spinoza draws an explicit connection between freedom of speech and the progress of the liberal arts. Like Descartes, Spinoza saw the tremendous potential locked inside the emergent sciences of nature, especially medicine, to increase the ease and comfort of life.[109] But Spinoza also recognized that intellectual and scientific progress does not take place in a vacuum. He links the progress of the arts and sciences to issues of trade and commerce. Intellectual and religious freedom are possible only in an environment that encourages commercial liberty. Spinoza's democracy is, then, necessarily a commercial republic with economic, political, and religious freedom.

Spinoza's preference for the modern commercial republic is based on an emphatic rejection of both the older classical republic and biblical theocracy. For the ancients, the polity was a small polis-like body characterized by a high degree of moral and religious homogeneity. Spinoza's defense of commercial and intellectual freedom indicates a preference for large, cosmopolitan, open societies marked by a diversity of opinions and ways of life. Furthermore, the ancient polities, whether Greek or Hebrew, had a severity and moral austerity demanding from members a self-sacrificing devotion to the laws. Conversely, Spinoza's commercial republic is characterized less by virtue than by freedom in its various dimensions. Freedom, says Spinoza, brings not only the progress of the arts and sciences but also the refinement and improvement of behavior. The *Treatise* concludes with ringing praise for the commercial republic of Amsterdam, where the effects of liberty are on display for all to see.[110]

For these and other reasons to be adduced, the *Treatise* ought to be considered a classic of modern liberal democratic theory. Liberal democracy is inseparable from the Enlightenment's solution to the religious question. This solution is based on the model of the free or liberated individual. This individual is free not only in the philosophical sense that comes with the exercise of one's rational powers but in the ordinary sense that comes with liberation from ecclesiastical tutelage and supervision. The tenets of Spinoza's civil religion, like the rational theologies expounded by the other framers of liberal democracy, were intended to frustrate the power of ecclesiastics, who have a professional stake in multiplying the obscurities of religion. The aim of the *Treatise* was to divest religion of its transcendent and otherworldly trappings and redirect it toward more sociable, peaceful, and civil ends.

The point of this discussion is not to establish Spinoza as a member in good standing in the pantheon of liberal saints but to allow us to reconsider the role of the critique of religion in the original formulation of liberal doctrine. The *Treatise* represents the most radical form of the Enlightenment's critique of religion, and the critique of Judaism in the *Treatise* forms the essence of that critique. With Spinoza begins that line of distinctly modern thought which holds that Jews can be free not only when they have been granted freedom of religion but also when they have been emancipated from Judaism. To many during the Enlightenment, Judaism was the archetype of a clerical religion, and as such, it seemed inimical to the values of freedom and autonomy. This view made it possible for them to extend a hand to individual Jews while at the same time carrying on a cultural war against Judaism.

The *Treatise* was the first book to treat the persistence of a distinctive Jewish identity as emblematic of the obstacles to the creation of a state in which the individual, not the group, was the fundamental political unit. To be sure, Spinoza attacks Judaism as an opening gambit to get at Christianity. His real target, however, was Christian sectarianism and intolerance, not Jewish particularity and exclusivity. This distinction between targets corresponds to what might be called the esoteric and the exoteric dimensions of the *Treatise*. That Spinoza's derogation of Moses and the prophets is in the service of a state that is ostensibly tolerant of the differences between Jews and Gentiles is clear. What this state was to effect, however, was nothing short of a transformation of Judaism. Jews were to be welcomed into the new liberal polity so long as they ceased to be distinctively or recognizably Jewish. Toleration was to extend to individuals as a first step toward their assimilation into modern secular-Christian culture. It is this transformation that Spinoza was the first to propose. It has remained the unspoken premise of liberalism ever since.[111]

2

Spinoza's Audience and Manner of Writing

The great theme of the *Treatise* is the freedom to philosophize.[1] The lengthy subtitle declares that not only is freedom of thought compatible with the necessity of civil peace but the attempt to censor and control thought is the cause of public discord. It reads: *Containing Several Discussions in Which It Is Shown That Freedom of Philosophizing Not Only Can Be Granted Without Harm to Piety and the Peace of the State, but Also Cannot Be Abolished Unless Piety and the Peace of the State Are Also Destroyed.*[2] Indeed, the subtitle bears a quotation from the Christian Scripture suggesting that persecution is both a cause of conflict and a form of impiety.[3] Freedom of mind is apparently mandated by piety and true religion, then, as well as reason.

The means to accomplish the end of intellectual freedom is the now familiar strategy of separating philosophy and religion. This separation is in turn supported by two arguments that are integral to the structure of the *Treatise*. The first is Spinoza's claim that philosophy and theology represent two different kinds of knowledge with two different objectives.[4] Philosophy or reason aims at truth, the truth about nature, the truth about causes, the truth about mind and its powers. Theology, by contrast, aims not at truth but at acts of piety and obedience, which Spinoza interprets to mean justice and charity.[5] It follows from this distinction that those who fail to observe and uphold the radical incommensurability of philosophy and religion must either corrupt reason by forcing it to comply with the teachings of Scripture or corrupt religion by making it conform to the demands of speculative truth. The conclusion to which this line of reasoning points is that "Scripture leaves reason absolutely free, and that it has nothing in common with philosophy," for "each rests on its own foundation."[6]

The separation of philosophy and theology is at the root of Spinoza's liberal politics, according to which actions, not words and opinions, are the only valid objects of civil legislation.[7] Having declared that philosophy concerns the search for knowledge of causes, whereas theology concerns obedience and strength of character, Spinoza now declares that religion, not philosophy, belongs under the control of the secular political authority. Rather than arguing for a strict separation of church and state, Spinoza seeks an alliance with the political sovereign to control religion. The argument running through the *Treatise* is that not philosophy but religion is the source of public discord and that society has nothing to fear from allowing complete liberty of mind to its citizens. The unprecedented argument of the *Treatise* is that this freedom is beneficial not only to philosophers and "intellectuals," for whom ideas offered in free exchange are, so to speak, their stock-in-trade, but for society as a whole. The "free republic" (*libera respublica*) of Amsterdam provides a test case for what Spinoza thinks will become a model for all civilized nations.

Before developing these themes, Spinoza must engage in a protracted critique of the obstacles to their realization. The chief obstacle to the separation of philosophy and theology is the power of clerical or ecclesiastical authority, which has become an arbiter of opinion. It was precisely Spinoza's challenge to the authority of the clerics that led to his expulsion from his own religious community and later caused even those in the latitudinarian circles with whom he associated to shun his work.

The attack on and opposition to Spinoza's work from even these relatively tolerant and enlightened circles, I suggest, was not utterly groundless or grounded in beliefs left over from an age of superstition. Spinoza's challenge to clerical authority was one front of a two-front war. Spinoza attacked the power of the divines in order to undermine the source from which their power derived, namely, Scripture itself. Spinoza typically appeals to the literal meaning of Holy Writ in order to attack certain corrupt and dangerous ecclesiastical practices, while elsewhere appealing to reason to undermine the very words of Scripture. Unless we keep this twofold strategy in mind, we run the risk of missing altogether the radical nature of Spinoza's enlightenment project.

The Critique of Religion and the Problem of Imaginatio

According to no less an authority than Kant, the Enlightenment is "the age of criticism."[8] To be sure, the Enlightenment was a vast movement of thought forged by a variety of thinkers working on different problems in different national and religious contexts. The French Enlightenment was different from the Scottish, and the German *Aufklärung* different from the Italian risorgimento.[9] For all their differences, however, the names of Bacon, Descartes, and Newton arise again and again as the initiators of a new age in philosophy, science, politics, and theology.[10]

Despite the very real differences separating these thinkers on a host of issues, what is characteristic of the Enlightenment is a conception of public criticism and even ridicule of many accepted doctrines and opinions. The true object of the Enlightenment's polemical assault was the pervasive power of religion, or "the kingdom of darkness," in Hobbes's colorful phrase. Spinoza did not invent the category of superstition, but more than perhaps anyone else he helped define the Enlightenment as an almost unrelenting war on "superstition" (*superstitio*) and "prejudice" (*praejudicia*) in all of its varieties — as a war on the pervasive power of prejudice, as what Hans-Georg Gadamer has called the Enlightenment's prejudice against prejudice.[11] He could just as easily have used as an epigraph for his *Treatise* Kant's motto for the Enlightenment: *Sapere aude*, "Dare to know."[12] Prejudice meant for Spinoza more than an error of reasoning or a fallacy of logic; it meant a comprehensive body of false beliefs. His specific contribution to the Enlightenment's debate over prejudice was to connect the power of these beliefs to the sway of the passions, especially the imagination.

The *Treatise* begins, in fact, with a reference to the causes of superstition and its hold over the human mind:

> If men could manage all their affairs by a certain plan, or if fortune were always favorable to them, they would never be in the grip of superstition. But since they are often reduced to such straits that they can bring no plan into operation, and since they generally vacillate wretchedly between hope and fear, from an immoderate desire for the uncertain goods of fortune, for the most part their hearts are ready to believe anything at all. While they are in doubt, a slight impulse drives them this way or that; and this happens all the more easily when, torn by hope and fear, they are at a loss to know what to do; at other times they are too trusting, boastful and overconfident.[13]

The causes of superstition, then, are the twin powers of "hope and fear," which hold the mind in a state of perpetual oscillation, although superstition is caused, maintained, and preserved principally by fear (*superstitio oritur, conservatur, et fovetur, metus est*).[14] Like Hobbes before him, Spinoza treats fear as the overriding passion of our emotional life.[15] He treats fear not as the dread of any particular object but as a general terror of the unknown. It is because we are ignorant of the natural causes of our particular fortunes and misfortunes that we find ourselves uniquely prone to error and credulity. Thus in times of good fortune people are convinced that their success is attributable to their own wise choice and judgment, but when their luck changes they seek desperately for any remedy that seems near at hand. Out of such confusion and mental anguish religion is born. Spinoza hopes that knowledge of causes will liberate us from the twin vices of arrogance and servility, both of which flow directly from the power of the passions.[16]

But for Spinoza superstition is more than a general condition of psychological uneasiness or dread. It is related to an historically specific phenomenon, the birth of God or the gods. It is the belief in an intending deity who acts for purposes as do we — a belief that is for Spinoza not just any prejudice but the prejudice underlying all prejudices.[17] This belief in an intending deity arises from a pervasive dread and fear of the unknown. The task of the *Treatise* as a whole is, then, to liberate its readers from the terrors of superstition and prepare the way for the transition from a life dominated by the passions to one directed by reason. Although Spinoza is correctly known as one of the greatest rationalists in the history of thought, his confidence in reason did not blind him to the power of the passions and the emotions in human life. Reason is weak in comparison with the twin pressures of hope and fear. It is precisely because we do not understand the causes of our emotions that we find ourselves dominated by them.

The purpose of the *Treatise* is the therapeutic one of liberating reason from superstition or, what comes to the same thing, the power of the imagination (*imaginatio*).[18] Just as Hobbes had maintained that the imagination is "nothing but decaying sense," so for Spinoza it is simply the condition of the body.[19] The imagination is not a source of reliable knowledge about the external world but a record of the mental and physiological dispositions of the body. Thus Hobbes regards the imagination, or "fancy," as the source of our ability to make comparisons and construct metaphors, whereas Spinoza sees it as the cause of myth, fantasy, and religion.[20] By locating the source of religious belief firmly in the faculty of the imagination, Spinoza implies that it is basically a psychological phenomenon, or, in the language of Nietzsche, a "sign language of the affects."[21]

Because reason is fragile Spinoza believes the majority of humankind is condemned to live in perpetual servitude to their passions and emotions. These terms have for him none of the implications of later nineteenth-century romanticism but signify a life governed by "delusions of the mind" and other "impulses of frenzy."[22] The imagination, far from being a source of intellectual creativity, is a prime cause of error and confusion. It is ultimately fear of the unknown brought about by ignorance of natural causes that has led human beings to abdicate the free use of their reason. It is as though God had ceded authority to the inspiration and promptings of "fools, madmen, and birds."[23]

Spinoza converts his argument about the weakness of reason into a far-ranging political critique. Because knowledge of causes is difficult to attain, we find ourselves led by those who would capitalize on popular credulity as a means of gaining power. As with Hobbes, Spinoza traces the prestige of religion to the weakness and gullibility of human beings who cede their right of self-legislation to power-hungry priests and kings.[24] It is not true religion that Spinoza claims to oppose here but priestcraft. As a consequence of human gullibility, faith has become "nothing now but credulity and prejudices," and true religion a tissue of "absurd mysteries."[25] Most dangerous of all, the church in alliance with the state uses its power to control not only the actions but the minds of subjects. In attempting to criminalize opinions, the guardians of theological orthodoxy become the unwitting purveyors of conflict and civil war: "For it is completely contrary to the common freedom to fill the free judgment of each man with prejudices, or to restrain it in any way. As for the rebellions which are aroused under the pretext of religion, they surely arise only because laws are instituted regarding speculative matters, opinions are regarded as wicked and condemned as crimes, and their defenders and followers are sacrificed, not to the public well-being, but only to the hate and barbarism of their opponents."[26]

The attempt to liberate the mind from fear and superstition is hardly novel to Spinoza. The fear theory of religion has origins going as far back as Epicurus, who joins Democritus and a few other Greek atomists as the only ancient thinkers who win Spinoza's praise.[27] In a letter to a correspondent Spinoza remarks that "the authority of Plato, Aristotle, and Socrates does not carry much weight" with him, adding that they are the inventors of "occult qualities, intentional species, substantial forms, and a thousand other trifles."[28] What makes Spinoza's critique of religion unusual is not even his rehabilitation of Epicureanism, which was already well under way in his time, but the attempt to wed the materialistic or atomistic theory of the Epicureans with a political program aimed at popular enlightenment and a democratic republican form of government. This point calls for a word of explanation.

The Epicurean critique of religion found its greatest expression in Lucretius's prose poem *De rerum natura,* a work devoted to the exploration and extirpation of religious fear. This poem makes the classic statement that the antidote to fear of death and terror of divine punishment is the knowledge of natural causes. Lucretius refers to an unnamed Greek (Epicurus) who was "the first to raise the shining light out of tremendous dark" by demonstrating the power of mind over nature.[29] Long before Bacon promised to harness the forces of nature for "the relief of man's estate" or Descartes claimed that the correct scientific method could render us "the masters and possessors of nature," Lucretius promised to banish the terrors of death by liberating the mind from religious dread. Lucretius may not boast of the utilitarian benefits following from his critique of religion, but he does suggest that his critique will achieve the therapeutic end of fostering freedom from fear and hence genuine peace of mind (*ataraxia*).[30]

The purpose of the scientific account of the soul in the third and best known book of *De rerum natura* was to demonstrate the irrationality of the fear of death. Only when we come to understand that the soul, like the body, comes into being and passes away, will death cease to be terrifying and will human beings stop debasing themselves by seeking comfort in religion. All of our attempts to avoid the torments of hell in the afterlife merely contribute to making our life hell on earth.[31] The problem with which Lucretius struggles in the poem is why the majority of people refuse to listen, are indeed hostile, to the very Epicurean philosophy that claims to liberate them from their fears. By the end of the poem Lucretius can only speculate that it is the strangeness of his ideas that has prevented their adoption.[32] Rather than being a source of tranquillity and peace of mind, Lucretius's teaching seems to have been a cause of increased anxiety. The very austerity of *De rerum natura* has prevented its popularity.

Spinoza's bold project was to combine something like the naturalistic theory of the origins of religion with a program of radical political transformation. Unlike the Epicurean critique of religion, the Spinozist critique was passionately political. Its aim was not just to liberate the mind from fear and superstition but to liberate the body from a combination of ecclesiastical and monarchical authority. Thus Spinoza's critique of religion was tied to his defense of a democratic republican state. It is precisely the problematic relation between his defense of democracy and his critique of religion that is our special concern.

To be sure, Spinoza was not the first to contemplate such a bold combination of religious criticism with political activism. Hobbes, in his *Leviathan,* sets out a similar program of reform. Even the most superficial comparison of *Leviathan* with the *Treatise* shows Spinoza's profound indebtedness to his slightly older English contemporary. The idea of the social contract and natural rights are both found in Hobbes, to say nothing of Hobbes's own use of the fear theory of religion to advance his arguments about secular control over the clergy.[33] He pioneered a critique of such topics as prophecy, miracles, and the authorship of Scripture that Spinoza would later submit to a more thoroughgoing analysis. Hobbes's use of Scripture seemed to many of his contemporaries a pious front to conceal a fundamentally materialistic and atheistic teaching.[34] But even Hobbes, as his biographer John Aubrey confirms, did not press his controversial points as far as Spinoza does. Upon reading the *Treatise* Hobbes could do no more than declare that "he durst not write so boldly," for the work had "cut through him a bar's length."[35]

To take but one example: in *Leviathan* Hobbes speaks of miracles as anything that compel wonder or "causeth admiration."[36] It is sufficient to designate an event as miraculous if it seems strange, unlike anything we have seen or experienced before, and if its causes seem so remote that "we cannot imagine it to have been done by natural means."[37] Thus Hobbes describes the first rainbow as a miracle because a rainbow had never been seen before, although rainbows have ceased to be miraculous because they appear frequently and their causes are well understood. The inference is that as our knowledge of natural causes increases, miracles cease to exist, and what are still called miracles are deceptions.[38] Whereas Hobbes describes miracles as unusual natural events, Spinoza describes the very concept of miracles as contradictory, for nothing can happen contrary to the laws of nature.[39] Among the "ancients" (*antiqui*) a miracle was no more than an event for which they had no explanation.[40] Thus miracles were popularly understood to be occurrences contrary to the ordinary course of nature, especially if such events brought with them "profit or advantage."[41] Spinoza reverses this popular belief by arguing that miracles, such as they are, are governed entirely by the laws of natural causality. The miraculous is not that which defies the order of nature but what conforms to it. Spinoza, by assimilating God's will to his intellect, is enabled to argue that nature is nothing other than the "fixed and immutable eternal order" which operates according to its own eternal laws.[42] To believe that God would act to contravene this order is not merely an "absurdity" but an impiety.[43]

We will return in Chapter 5 to the relationship between Spinoza and Hobbes. For now it is enough to note that Spinoza went beyond Hobbes in his advocacy of liberation of the individual not only from superstition but also from "monarchic rule" (*regiminis Monarchici*). For Spinoza, superstition implied the creation of an ecclesiastical elite who would capitalize on popular credulity as a means of gaining power and, beyond that, the emergence of monarchic rulers who use their power "to keep men deceived and to cloak in the specious name of Religion the fear by which they must be checked."[44] The church in alliance with the state uses its power to keep its subjects in a perpetual condition of ignorance and superstition. Such a system has been brought to perfection in Turkey, says Spinoza, where open discussion is regarded as a mark of impiety.[45]

Unlike Hobbes, who was known throughout the seventeenth century not as the founder of liberalism but as the great defender of monarchical absolutism, Spinoza posited that superstition is always the helpmate of monarchy; this is a central thesis of the *Treatise*. Monarchy and free thought were as much opposed to one another as superstition and freedom of mind were opposed to one another. Spinoza's defense of the free republic, the *libera respublica,* is that it is the only regime compatible with human freedom. Hobbes's attempt to combine monarchical politics with greater economic and intellectual freedom was a half solution that could not succeed. Only in a republic "where everyone is granted complete freedom of judging" can one have the freedom to worship God in one's own fashion.[46] This freedom of worship is conducive to public peace, and it is also the precondition for the exercise of genuine piety. The extraordinary implication of Spinoza's argument is that monarchy is the enemy of not just public order but also true religiosity.

Spinoza's preference for the democratic republic, "where nothing is considered to be dearer and sweeter than freedom," is based to some degree on classical sources. Indeed, it was the "Greek and Latin writers" who Hobbes thought to be among the great causes of war and sedition for making regicide seem a noble and heroic deed.[47] Spinoza turns not to the classical political philosophers but to the ancient historians Curtius and Tacitus for his evidence.[48] But the free republic to which Spinoza alludes is by no means the same as the republic of antiquity. To state the most obvious differences, Spinoza maintains that toleration of religious differences and freedom of thought are the hallmarks of the modern republic, but no one could plausibly maintain this of the ancient republic based on a stern conception of civic virtue and the subordination of self-interest to the commonweal. Furthermore, the model for Spinoza was Amsterdam, a commercial or trading republic. He was averse to the classical restrictions on trade and the acquisitive arts.[49]

Spinoza's republican sympathies had a precedent in modern times. Not Hobbes but Machiavelli was Spinoza's true political teacher and guide.[50] From Machiavelli, Spinoza took over a certain kind of realism whose adherents claimed to study human beings as they are rather than as they ought to be. Recalling the fifteenth chapter of *The Prince*, where Machiavelli speaks to "the effectual truth of things" (*verità effetuàle della cosa*), Spinoza begins the *Political Treatise* (unfinished at the time of his death) by chastening philosophers for their failure to say anything useful.[51] Their failure in this regard is related directly to their prior failure to understand the nature of the passions. Instead of viewing the passions as natural phenomena, they insist on regarding them as moral vices to which we should attach judgments of praise or blame. His statement that we should view the passions with the same sangfroid as we study any natural phenomenon, like heat or cold or thunder, brings to mind his famous boast in the *Ethics* to study the emotions "geometrically" (*in more geometrico*).[52] Rather than treating the passions as species of vice or instances of weakness of will, Spinoza asserts that "I shall consider human actions and appetites just as if it were a question of lines, planes, and bodies."[53]

Spinoza's claim to provide a scientific account of the passions in the *Ethics* often diverts attention from his moral, rhetorical, and pedagogical purposes, which are buried in the various prefaces, appendices, and scholia of the text.[54] The language of geometry was as much a matter of rhetoric and metaphor as of demonstration. Spinoza's official doctrine is that every animate body contains a *conatus,* that is, an inner mechanism or life force that seeks to sustain, preserve, and enhance its power and well-being.[55] We will return to this issue later in the context of Spinoza's political theory proper. In spite of the pretensions of scientific metaphysics to provide an understanding of the passions as nothing more than "modes" of Substance, Spinoza, as much as any previous moralist, is at pains to encourage some emotional dispositions at the expense of others. He wants to turn negative and what he regards as life-destroying passions like anger, jealousy, and hatred into positive and life-enhancing passions like love, joy, and courage, or self-mastery.[56]

Spinoza puts the problem of the control of the passions at the forefront in the *Political Treatise*:

> Philosophers regard the passions that torment us as vices into which we fall through our own fault; and so their habit is to deride, deplore, and revile them, or else, if they want to seem more pious than the rest, to denounce them in God's name. Such conduct they take to be godlike, and they think they have reached the acme of wisdom when they have learnt to sing the praises of a human nature nowhere to be found, and to rail at the sort which actually exists. In fact, they conceive men, not as they are, but as they would like them to be. The result is that they have generally written satire instead of ethics, and have never conceived a political system which can be applied in practice; but have produced either obvious fantasies, or schemes that could only have been put into effect in Utopia, or the poets' golden age, where, of course, there was no need for them at all. Thus while theory is supposed to be at variance with practice in all the sciences which admit of application, this is held to be particularly true in the case of politics, and no men are regarded as less fit to govern a state than theorists or philosophers.[57]

It is because they have misunderstood the nature of the passions that the theorists or philosophers are deemed utterly incompetent to handle public affairs. But his evident contempt for the "philosophers" (*philosophi*) and "theorists" (*theoretici*) notwithstanding, Spinoza is equally reluctant to cede political matters to the "statesmen" (*politici*). If the philosophers are too unworldly, the politicians are too cynical and manipulative to be entrusted with public affairs. Although statesmen have generally written more usefully about politics than have the philosophers, they study the passions primarily to anticipate them and make them serve their own interests. If the philosophers have spoken uselessly but also harmlessly, the politicians "have a greater reputation for cunning than for wisdom."[58]

Because neither the theorists nor the politicians can be trusted to do a creditable job of ruling, Spinoza turns to the multitude (*multitudo*) as the only solid basis of a free society. From Machiavelli, whom he praises as the great advocate of republican rule, he learned that the people are more reliable than the prince.[59] Neither Machiavelli nor Spinoza had any great confidence in the intelligence or moral capacity of the multitude. Machiavelli prefers the people because "the nature of the masses is no more reprehensible than the nature of princes."[60] Also, the effects of power unregulated by law are less dangerous in a people than in a prince. A "licentious and turbulent populace" (*un populo licenzioso e tumultuario*) can be brought under the constraint of law more easily than can a prince, for whom there is no remedy except the sword. Finally, the brutalities of the people are invariably directed against those suspected of conspiring against the common good, whereas the cruelties of the prince are directed against those suspected of conspiring against his own interests.[61]

The passage from the *Political Treatise* in praise of Machiavelli deserves citation in full:

> The means which a prince whose sole motive is lust for despotic power must employ to strengthen and preserve his state have been described at great length by that shrewd observer Machiavelli; but there seems to be some uncertainty about the purpose of his account. If he had some good purpose, as we must believe of so wise a man, it was probably to show the folly of attempting — as many do — to remove a tyrant when the causes which make a prince a tyrant cannot be removed, but become rooted more firmly as the prince is given more reason to be afraid, which happens when a people has made an example of its prince, and boasts of its regicide as though it were a glorious deed. Perhaps he also wished to show how chary a free people should be of entrusting its welfare entirely to one man, who, if he is not a vain fool who thinks that he can please everybody, must go in daily fear of plots; and thus is forced in self-defense to plot against his subjects rather than to further their interests. This interpretation of that wise statesman seems to me particularly attractive in view of the well-known fact that he was an advocate of freedom, and also gave some very sound advice for preserving it.[62]

Spinoza's remarks are extraordinary — especially his belief that Machiavelli was a republican. On the basis of this passage, Spinoza goes on to assert that

Machiavelli wrote *The Prince* primarily to warn the people against the dangers of monarchic rule. He extols the capacity of the free multitude for self-government and enjoins them to be extremely cautious about entrusting their affairs to a prince. It is Machiavelli's reputation as a "shrewd observer" (*acutissimus*), "the most prudent" (*prudentissimo*) man, a "wise man" (*viro sapiente*), that recommends him as a giver of "very sound advice" (*saluberrima consilia*).

The free multitude in the passage from the *Political Treatise* stands in marked contrast to the fear-ridden and superstitious multitude of the *Theologico-Political Treatise*. Fear of the multitude coupled with a belief in the possibility of democratic rule and popular enlightenment is a paradox that cuts through the middle of both *Treatises*.[63] We could even say that Spinoza's attitude toward the multitude vacillates between hope and fear. Spinoza never entertained the belief that one could educate the people and bring them to reason. Like all things excellent, reason remains as difficult to acquire as it is rare.[64] Nevertheless, it might be possible to reform political institutions so they control the dangers arising from the passions of ordinary people and thereby bring peace and security to all.[65]

To control for the effects of the passions is possible only if one knows how to control for the causes. Among the multitude, the chief danger to be averted is the evil of intolerance and persecution arising from fear and superstition. To better understand how this danger arose in the past and how it might be avoided in the future, Spinoza set himself a historical task in the *Treatise*. The question that he asks us to consider there is, How did Christianity, which began as a religion of love and charity, evolve into a religion of persecution?[66] How did theological dogma and ecclesiastical hierarchy come to replace Christian professions of love and kindness? Earlier religious reformers who sought to divest Christianity of vestiges of paganism and ecclesiastical corruption also asked this question about the contradiction between Christian teaching of love and the practice of persecution.

Spinoza, as I have already implied, provides a double answer to this complex historical problem. In the *Treatise* he turns from the church, the synagogue, and other institutions of ecclesiastical control and appeals directly to the teachings of Scripture in its most primitive and uncorrupted form. The same procedure was adopted by the Protestant reformers who appealed to the principle of *sola scriptura* as a guide to determining the authentic meaning of biblical texts. Yet at the same time that he appeals to Scripture as a means of condemning persecution, he appeals to reason and freedom of thought as a means of undercutting the authority of the Bible. It is not so much the corruption of religion that haunts the pages of the *Treatise* as the love of freedom.

Spinoza's method throughout is to appeal to Scripture in opposing superstition and then to appeal to reason in opposing Scripture.

Is There an Esoteric Teaching in the Treatise?

An important, if not decisive, fact about Spinoza's *Treatise* is that it was written by a Jew living in a Protestant country during an age of persecution. From the beginning Spinoza sought to conceal his identity as the author of the work. The *Treatise* was published anonymously, although its author was soon discovered. What is more, the subtitle carries a quotation from the Christian Scripture giving further credence to the view that he sought to conceal his identity from the public. As an excommunicated Jew living on the margins of Dutch society, Spinoza wrote with an eye to the religious orthodoxies of his time. It was no doubt his opposition to these orthodoxies that earned him his expulsion from the Marrano community of Amsterdam as well as his reputation for atheism.[67]

Spinoza's passion for secrecy is by now one of the better known secrets of his work. That he feared persecution at the hands of religious authorities and even possible assassination are attested to by the facts of his biography.[68] An author who held strong heterodox opinions could not expect to express himself openly without incurring serious repercussions. Indeed, the use of veiled or Aesopian language was a literary strategy used by a number of important seventeenth- and eighteenth-century authors, as several recent interpretive studies have made clear.[69] But just how far or deep Spinoza's secrecy ran and what it means for the assessment of his ideas remains a subject of lively debate.[70]

In this most literal sense, an author may resort to literary strategies of irony, indirection or even outright deception as a means of self-protection. If, like Spinoza, the author lives in an age of even relative intolerance, such strategies may prove necessary so as not to jeopardize his other interests. To attribute a rhetoric of caution and discretion to Spinoza's manner of writing is by no means the same as alleging intellectual dishonesty or duplicity.[71] Spinoza's choice of rhetoric is not a moral judgment but a political one. He did not live in a world where the freedom to express one's opinions openly and candidly was a cherished human right enforced with constitutional guarantees. His decision to write as he did is more a matter of political prudence than a violation of the norms of honesty and integrity. His statement in the *Ethics* that the free man will never act in *dolo malo,* "in bad faith," should not be taken to mean that the free man will never employ discretionary or deliberately ambiguous speech.[72] Far from demonstrating inconsistency, Spinoza's method is of a piece with his general philosophical outlook. If the primacy of self-preservation is the fundamental drive of all living species, as is asserted in both the *Treatise* and the *Ethics,* then Spinoza's strategy of intentional deception is mandated by the very principles of natural right.

Yet in the case of Spinoza it would be at best a half truth to say that his manner of writing was dictated by the fear of persecution. He adopted this practice from Maimonides, who remained his *Gesprächspartner* throughout much of the *Treatise.*[73] But for Maimonides and for his Arab predecessor and teacher Alfarabi, the need for secrecy was only in part dictated by a concern for safety and physical survival. Multilevel writing was for both a means of conveying certain religious ideas in an idiom that readers could comprehend and, more precisely, a means of shielding those readers from some of the more disturbing implications of the truth. Maimonides and Alfarabi lived in societies where obedience to religious law—whether laid out in the Torah or the Quran—was mandatory. To avoid unsettling the beliefs of those around them, for political as well as theological reasons, they addressed different kinds of readers with different needs and abilities in different ways. One point of adopting various ways of writing was pedagogical, to encourage the development of potential philosophers among the audience without necessarily tipping their hand to the nonphilosophers. Again, this is not a matter of questioning the authors' intellectual integrity or commitment to the truth but an assessment of the theologico-political climate in which they lived.[74]

Spinoza's world was far different from that of Maimonides and Alfarabi. He spoke with a bluntness that would have seemed reckless beyond imagining to his medieval predecessors. One of his strategies was to take terms or concepts embedded in the philosophical and exegetical literatures and begin subtly to revise and ultimately undermine their meaning. In this way he could claim to remain faithful to tradition while at the same time signaling his departures from it. It was this dual strategy of presenting a conventional or orthodox exoteric teaching to one audience and a more radical heterodox esoteric teaching to another that earned Spinoza a reputation for duplicity. Pierre Bayle, for one, likened his works to the theology of a certain Chinese sect that divided its doctrines between a pious exterior, "which is the one that is publicly preached and taught to the people," and an atheistic interior, "which is carefully hidden from the common people and made known only to the initiates."[75]

Spinoza's passion for concealment was not merely defensive but grew out of his deepest convictions concerning the relation between philosophy and society. Spinoza's writings teem with allusions to the distinction between the few who live according to reason and the many who are governed by passion and imagination. This distinction he took to be a permanent aspect of human nature — not that he despaired altogether of achieving some degree of popular enlightenment, but such enlightenment as he expected was more likely to come about indirectly from above than directly from below. The hope in the *Treatise* was not for a world where all men would be philosophers but for the far more modest achievement of a liberal society that would provide philosophers and heterodox thinkers freedom from persecution. Even there he believed distrust or suspicion of philosophy to be a permanent human phenomenon.[76]

Spinoza's reputation for caution (*caute*) has been explained in a number of ways.[77] From an early date he was linked with Descartes, whose epigone he was considered to be. As such, he was thoroughly embroiled in the atheism controversies of the 1660s and 1670s. The publication of his *Renati des Cartes principia philosophiae*, a work from which he took pains to distance himself, contributed to his embroilment.[78] On numerous occasions he intentionally accommodates his prose to public opinion. In a letter to Oldenburg he mentions dictating parts of a commentary on Descartes's *Principles of Philosophy* to a young man "to whom I did not want to teach my own opinions openly."[79] He demonstrates the same reticence regarding the published version of his commentary on Descartes, which contained an explicit warning to the reader that the author did not acknowledge all the opinions contained in the work, adding, "I had written many things in it which were the very opposite of what I held [to be true]."[80]

This caution in matters of self-expression was acknowledged by Spinoza's friend and student Lodewijk Meyer, who appended a preface to Spinoza's commentary. Meyer goes out of his way to distinguish the opinions of Spinoza and Descartes, suggesting that in many controversial issues Spinoza's views remain unstated.

> Our Author has only set out the opinions of Descartes and their demonstrations, insofar as these are found in his writings, or are such as ought to be deduced validly from the foundations he laid. For since he had promised to teach his pupil Descartes' philosophy, he considered himself obliged not to depart a hair's breadth from Descartes' opinion, nor to dictate to him anything that either would not correspond to his doctrines or would be contrary to them. *So let no one think that he is teaching here either his own opinions, or only those which he approves of.* Though he judges that some of the doctrines are true, and admits that he has added some of his own, nevertheless there are many that he rejects as false, and concerning which he holds a quite different opinion.[81]

Spinoza's method of cautious dissimulation was motivated, then, by more than the negative and somewhat crude desire to avoid persecution.[82] He was also motivated by his desire to attain a positive political or pedagogical goal.

In the same letter to Oldenburg cited above, he mentions his hope that in publishing his work "it will induce some who hold high positions in my country to want to see other things I have written, which I acknowledge as my own, so that they would see to it that I can publish without any danger of inconvenience."[83] But this desire to publish securely in the future is still coupled with a strong measure of reticence. If his works do not find a receptive audience among the ruling classes, he concedes that "I shall be silent rather than force my opinions on men against the will of my country and make them hostile to me."[84] His aim was to gain the ear of those in "high positions" in order to promote political and theological innovations.

Far from displaying a "habitual attitude of timid caution," Spinoza expresses a combination of caution and boldness that varied by degrees both with his understanding of his situation and with the different audiences that he sought to address.[85] He speaks in different voices to different people depending on the circumstances. Thus in the *Ethics,* a work addressed principally to other philosophers, he adopts the severe language of mathematics and geometric demonstration. The imposing architecture of the *Ethics* is no doubt intended to intimidate and scare off all but the most committed readers. Even here the rebarbative presentation was intended precisely to conceal the non-geometrical portions of the work full of rhetorical rebukes and ridicule.[86]

The *Treatise* was not a work written for philosophers but for those in "high positions," so it does not employ the language of geometry but the language of Scripture and history. There is evidence to believe that Spinoza regarded the *Treatise* as an "exoteric" or public work and wrote it with at least three different audiences in mind. The first was the *multitudo,* those under the sway of theological orthodoxy.[87] The concept has a quasi-technical meaning in Spinoza's vocabulary, suggesting not merely the "vulgar" (*vulgus*) or the "ignorant" (*ignari*) but all those who live under the power of *imaginatio.* Membership in the multitude, then, is correlated with a system of teleological beliefs that stem from an ignorance of natural causes. The chief of these beliefs is the conception of free human will associated with the representation of God as a master, creator, or legislator of the universe. This combination of teleological and anthropomorphic beliefs keeps the *multitudo* in a condition of *fluctatio animi,* a fluctuation between hope and fear.

Second, he wrote for members of the free multitude alluded to in the *Political Treatise.* The free multitude is not the same group as the passion-ridden and superstitious multitude. Rather, they were people seeking to lessen the hold of orthodoxy, readers who might be enlisted in the struggle for a democratic-republican state. One might expect to find members of this group in the commercial and patrician classes among those with moderate to liberal religious convictions. Such readers were not altogether free of superstition, and it was with them in mind that Spinoza composed the seven dogmas of the "universal faith" (*fides universalis*) set out in chapter 14 of the *Treatise*.

This group needs to be distinguished from a third, not often taken to form a distinct class within society, namely, the "prudent" or "philosophical" readers. The interests of this group are not primarily in political or commercial liberty but in the freedom of mind, the freedom to philosophize. The group may consist, not of philosophers in the strict sense, but of those "left"-leaning members of the Marrano and Mennonite communities who represented a new kind of political party, a party of liberty. This is the group that Spinoza hoped to nurture, holding out the possibility of freedom of religion, perhaps even freedom from religion.

These three potential audiences are adverted to with tolerable clarity in his correspondence with Henry Oldenburg in 1665, five years before the publication of the *Treatise*. In a letter to Spinoza, Oldenburg, who had obviously been informed of Spinoza's work on the *Treatise,* asked to be filled in on its details: "I see that you are not so much philosophizing as, if I may say so, theologizing; for you are writing down your thoughts about angels, prophecy, and miracles. But perhaps you are doing this in a philosophical manner. However that may be, I am sure that the work is worthy of you, and especially desired by me. Since these very difficult times hinder freedom of intercourse, I ask you at least not to mind telling me in your next letter your plan and object in this work of yours."[88] In his reply Spinoza acceded to Oldenburg's request and set out his reasons as follows:

> I am now writing a Treatise about my interpretation of Scripture. This I am driven to do by the following reasons: 1. The Prejudice of the Theologians; for I know that these are among the chief obstacles which prevent men from directing their minds to philosophy; and to remove them from the minds of the more prudent [*prudentiorum*]. 2. The opinion which the common people have of me, who do not cease to accuse me falsely of atheism; I am also obliged to avert this accusation as far as it is possible to do so. 3. The freedom of philosophizing, and of saying what we think; this I desire to vindicate in every way, for here it is always suppressed through the excessive authority and impudence of the preachers.[89]

This statement provides an unusually frank expression of Spinoza's purpose. The second aim is in one sense the most revealing. It is directed at the "common people" (*vulgus*) and their leaders who continue to think of Spinoza as an atheist. It is to avert the accusation of atheism that he moderates his attack on religion. The third aim is directed to the needs of the free multitude who desire freedom of speech and the freedom of living without the direct supervision of the clerics. The *Treatise* was intended in large part as an exercise in the political education of this group, who seem to be the potential or actual democrats among Spinoza's audience. It is, however, the first aim that is the most radical, directed to the "more prudent" readers who desire freedom of thought and opinion and who also wish to turn their minds to philosophy, that is, liberation from religion.

The question of Spinoza's audience is raised explicitly in the preface to the *Treatise,* where once again he returns to the distinction between the "philosophical reader" (*Philosophe lector*) to whom the book is addressed and the "multitude" (*multitudo*) who are under the power of fear and superstition and "carried away by an impulse to praise or blame."[90] The philosophical reader here is the same as the prudent reader referred to in the letter to Oldenburg. But after so identifying his audience, Spinoza immediately goes on to qualify his statement. The *Treatise* is addressed not to philosophers in the strict sense but to friends of philosophy. For the true philosopher, "the main points" of the work are "more than adequately known." We can assume that Spinoza did not write the *Treatise* to bore his readers with what they already know. The prudent readers described here are most likely to be would be or potential philosophers, recruits drawn from the ranks of the nonphilosophers.

Just as the audience for the *Treatise* are not philosophers in the strict sense, neither are they from the ranks of the "vulgar" (*vulgus*). This term encompasses not so much the common people as the clerics and pastors who lead and influence public opinion. In seventeenth-century Holland the clergy that Spinoza had in mind were the Calvinist branch of the Dutch Reformed church, whose principles were confirmed by the Synod of Dort (1618–19). It was above all the Calvinist clergy who exercised an implacable system of government and thought control, arrogating to themselves the power to direct education, suppress blasphemy, and excommunicate those suspected of heresy. Indeed, readers will misunderstand large portions of the *Treatise* unless they see its appeal to the *respublica Hebraeorum* as a comprehensive rejection of the Calvinist claim to subordinate civil authority to the power of the pastorate. It is precisely this learned multitude who Spinoza claims have perpetuated the accusation that he is an atheist and for whom the *Treatise* will prove useless or worse than useless.

Spinoza's prudent or philosophical reader, then, is neither a Jew nor a Christian but a new kind of person who might be called the liberated individual. This type of individual, delineated in the pages of Machiavelli, Hobbes, and Montaigne, was just beginning to make an appearance on the European scene. Such a person is liberated as far as possible from dependence on tradition and authority, is master of his passions and tolerant of others, and puts the highest premium on self-respect. Although this idea of the free individual had certain classical antecedents in the philosophy of Plato and the Stoics, it was based much more than before on the idea of personal autonomy. Where did such a reader come from? Where was such a one to be found?

The Intended Audience for the Treatise

The audience for the *Treatise,* then, was neither the philosophers nor the theologically orthodox, but those would-be philosophers who, for reasons to be demonstrated, were most likely to be found among the dissenting Protestant sects. The evidence for this last proposition is considerable. Spinoza did not intend the *Treatise* to be a theoretical study written *sub ira et studio.* The work was nothing short of a political tract written to advance the fortunes of a cause.

This cause was the republican faction in Dutch politics led by Jan de Witt, the "grand pensionary of Holland," against the monarchist faction led by the House of Orange.[91] Spinoza was closely identified with the de Witt faction until the murder of de Witt and his brother by an angry mob in 1672. For Spinoza, like the Dutch Arminians and Mennonites with whom he associated, republicanism meant primarily a state where "everyone is granted complete freedom of judging" and where each may worship God "according to his understanding."[92] The murder of the de Witts, an event that Spinoza called "the ultimate barbarism" (*ultima barbarorum*), merely indicated an extreme of theologically inspired cruelty.[93] Legend has it that Spinoza and de Witt were close personal associates, but more recent evidence suggests that they may not even have known one another. Spinoza's admiration for de Witt is well documented, although it is not known to what extent this admiration was reciprocated. In particular, de Witt's conception of toleration applied only to the Reformed church, excluding Catholics, Jews, and some lesser sects.[94]

The de Witt faction adopted the strategy of the subordination of the clergy in civil matters and a policy of toleration or latitudinarianism among competing religious sects. Among those associated with de Witt's "party of liberty" were Pieter de la Court, who argued in his influential *The Interest of Holland* (1662) that trade and commerce did more to contribute to the national interest than did the courts of monarchs with their wars of ambition.[95] The argument for *doux commerce,* as Montesquieu was later to call it, was directed not only against the Orangist conduct of foreign policy but also the Calvinist insistence on sumptuary laws and the independence of the pastors. Throughout the seventeenth and eighteenth centuries the Dutch model acted as a kind of European miracle at which foreign observers could but wonder.[96]

Consider the case of Sir William Petty, founder of the modern science of political economy.[97] In his *Political Arithmetick* (1690) he focused on such mundane factors as shipbuilding and control of the herring trade as the secret to Dutch commercial success but paid particular attention to the relation between religious and commercial liberty.[98] Liberty of conscience, Petty declared, was the first principle of the Dutch policy. The desire to avoid the impositions of the clergy had led to the break with Spain and was the key to Dutch success. Eschewing the desire to impose uniformity, the Dutch adopted toleration, because "to force men to say they believe what they do not, is vain, absurd, and without honour to God." The Dutch understand that they are not an "infallible Church" and therefore allow all sects to seek salvation as they see fit, "how erroneous soever their opinions be."[99]

Petty even suggests an inverse relation between attempts to impose orthodoxy and the persistence of dissent. Where attempts to impose orthodoxy have been most pronounced, there heterodoxy has flourished. He goes so far as to suggest that diversity is endemic to human nature and suggests that if by some miracle the heterodox portion of a given population were removed, it would only be a matter of time until a new heterodoxy reappeared, "it being natural for men to differ in opinion in matters above sense and reason."[100] More to the point, Petty attributes the economic success of nations to the heterodox part, for example, the Banians in India, the Jews and Christians in Turkey, and the Jews and nonpapists in the Italian city-states. In contrast to the Weberian thesis of a peculiar affinity between Protestantism and capitalism, Petty asserts that "trade is not fixt to any species of religion as such" but is always carried out most vigorously by the heterodox elements of the community, whatever religion they may be.[101]

The other great observer and analyst of the Dutch experiment was the English diplomat and statesman Sir William Temple.[102] Temple observed that the remarkable feature of Dutch prosperity was the ironic coupling of a large population and penurious natural resources. The industry of the Dutch people grew out of the effort, ingenuity, and parsimony forced on them by the paucity of their resources. Indeed, the success of the Dutch economy was nowhere better illustrated than in a contrast with the Irish economy, where a small population and an abundance of natural resources conspired to maintain the population in indigence and poverty.[103] Whereas the Malthusian doctrine posits that population inevitably outstrips the means of subsistence, Temple maintains, at least in the Dutch case, that a large population is the greatest natural resource.

Like other observers, Temple notes the relation between Dutch prosperity, its form of government, and religious toleration. He says that the great strength of the Dutch state, its stability over time, derives in large part not from the imposition of uniformity but from the presence of diversity. The very presence of "so great a concourse of people of several nations, different religions, and customs" has led to a common bent for industry.[104] The result is that Holland has become a haven for refugees from all over Europe, where "industrious people" come to "enjoy safety under laws from [in]justice and oppression."[105]

Similarly, Temple praises Dutch religious policy as perhaps making the greatest contribution to liberty and to an unprecedented toleration of religious heterodoxy. Temple attributes this to the Treaty of Utrecht in 1579, which allowed each province freedom to establish its own religion, but also to the fact that in Holland the clergy never became one of the official estates of the realm: "The great care of this state has ever been to favour no particular or curious inquisition into the faith or religious principles of any peaceable man, who came to live under the protection of their laws, and to suffer no violence or oppression upon any man's conscience, whose opinions broke not out into expressions or actions of ill consequence to the state. A free form of government, either making way for more freedom in religion, or else, having newly contended so far themselves for liberty in this point, they thought it the more unreasonable for them to oppress others."[106]

Freedom of religion, more than any other type of freedom, has ensured not just peace and stability but a new spirit of cosmopolitanism and "humanity." In a passage that could have come directly from Locke's *Letter on Toleration* or Spinoza's *Treatise*, Temple writes:

> But in this commonwealth, no man having any reason to complain of his oppression in conscience, and no man having hopes, by advancing his religion, to form a party, or break in upon the State, the differences in opinion make none in affections, and little in conversation, where it serves but for entertainment and variety. They argue without interest or anger; they differ without enmity or scorn; and they agree without confederacy. Men live together like citizens of the world, associated by the common ties of humanity, and by the bonds of peace, under the impartial protection of indifferent laws, with equal encouragement of all art and industry, and equal freedom of speculation and inquiry; all men enjoying their imaginary excellencies and acquisitions of knowledge, with as much safety as their more real possessions and improvements of fortune.[107]

Temple concludes his discussion of the benefits of toleration by noting that "religion may possibly do more good in other places," but in Holland "it does less hurt."[108]

In addition to the policy of religious toleration, the de Witt faction opened its doors to those currents of Cartesianism in philosophy that lent themselves to the adoption of quantitative methods for handling fiscal matters. De Witt had been himself educated by Cartesians and was the author of a commentary on Descartes's *Geometry* that appeared under the title *The Elements of Curved Lines* (*Elementa curvarum linearum*).[109] In particular, de Witt drew fire for extending political protection to those theologians, chiefly Arminians, who accepted the tenets of the new philosophy. The resolution of September 30, 1656, which formally condemned the teachings of Cartesianism, attempted to reach an accommodation between the clergy and the philosophers that extended the freedom to philosophize by establishing that each group stick to its own domain. In the years following this edict — which, incidentally, was promulgated in the year of Spinoza's ostracism — Spinoza's association with the de Witt circle began.

The attack on Cartesianism began, according to Descartes himself, with the publication of Voetius's disputations on atheism in 1639.[110] Throughout the seventeenth century Cartesianism remained in many circles synonymous with atheism. Despite Descartes's official affirmation of the innateness of the idea of God, his philosophy of systematic doubt was widely held responsible for contributing to an atheistic climate of opinion.[111] The term "atheism" is difficult to specify precisely and applies to a range of phenomena, some relatively precise and others wildly polemical. For the most part, however, the controversy over Cartesianism was carried out by different wings of the Dutch Reformed church, so it had much the character of an intramural debate.[112]

The seventeenth-century debate over Descartes's alleged atheism concerned not so much the letter of his beliefs as their implications, both logical and practical. Thus critics of the new philosophy were compelled to distinguish between speculative and practical (or indirect) atheism.[113] The speculative atheist was widely held to be a logical impossibility; the systematic denial of the existence of God was inconceivable. The practical atheist, however, was one who acknowledged the existence of God but who denied any means of access to God's will. For all practical purposes, it was as if God did not exist. Descartes's assertion, then, that reason alone is adequate for understanding the cosmos was thought to have dangerous atheistic implications, for it seemed to deny such things as particular providence and to boast reason's proud independence of religion. Skepticism was the natural ally of atheism.

The debate over Cartesianism was carried out with greatest intensity in Holland.[114] The anti-Cartesian party, headed by Voetius, was based in Utrecht, the center of Calvinist orthodoxy. The pro-Cartesian party, led by Johannes Cocceius, was centered in Leiden. The issue between the two camps turned on the extent to which Cartesian rationalism either undermined or reinforced

Christian doctrine. The Voetians feared that Cartesian theology was more than an attempt to reform philosophy, that it was an attempt to introduce nothing short of a new divinity. For the Cocceians, the greater danger to religion was not rationalism but uncertainty, doubt, and irresolution. Only by extending the method of Cartesian skepticism to divine matters, they reasoned, could religion and philosophy be harmonized. These two factions formed the immediate theological backdrop to Spinoza's discussion of skepticism and dogmatism in the *Treatise*.[115]

The audience to whom Spinoza appealed were those liberal theologians among the de Witt camp associated with the variety of dissenting Protestants abounding in Holland whom Leszek Kolakowski has called "Chrétiens sans église."[116] This paradoxical formulation is intended to underscore a rejection of the strict Calvinist insistence on the church as a necessary precondition for the achievement of salvation. Rejection of the sanctifying agency of the church carried with it a repudiation of several other specific Calvinist tenets. Among these were a denial of the dogma of predestination, which had the function of dividing humanity into the saved and the damned; a distinction between the historical Jesus, teacher of a purely human morality, and Christ, the mystical son of God; and an affirmation of religious toleration and a rejection of clerical authority and hierarchy. It was among these Reformed sects known as Remonstrants and described by their Calvinist rivals as libertines that one found the beginnings of something like a democratic opposition to the monarchic principles of the House of Orange in alliance with with the Calvinist clergy.

Spinoza's association with these Protestant dissenters went back to the period after his expulsion from the Jewish community, when he left Amsterdam to settle in the suburb of Rijnburg. Here Spinoza met and was befriended by members of the Collegiant-Mennonites who later became part of the Spinoza circle.[117] These thinkers, as Kolakowski has noted, turned toleration from a doctrine of convenience into an authentic principle of Christianity.[118] Toleration was not claimed as the exclusive privilege of one minority sect or dissenting group. Rather, the Collegiants put their emphasis on the absolute equality of all believers and made the freedom to "prophecy" into a universal doctrine of toleration. It was through association with this group that Spinoza met Jarig Jelles, who later wrote the preface to Spinoza's *Opera posthuma,* and Pieter Balling, who translated Spinoza's early study of Descartes into Dutch.[119]

At first the Collegiants were pleased to welcome an excommunicated Jew into their midst. But the extent to which Spinoza's views were consistent with Collegiant-Mennonite theology remains problematic. Did he share the Collegiant views on such things as the "inner light" and the personal nature of religious experience? Or did he find it merely convenient to associate with the "colleges," or "societies" (associations of free Christians independent of any formal church), as a means of propagating a more radical, secular teaching? What we do know is that from virtually the moment the *Treatise* was published its author was excoriated as an atheist, a radical Cartesian, and a Hobbesian who attacked the authenticity of Scripture and the possibility of miracles. Even those ostensibly closest to him suspected Spinoza of failing to come clean on a range of vexing topics. His correspondence with Oldenburg shows how even those most sympathetic to Spinoza were deeply perplexed and troubled by his work.[120]

In a series of letters between Spinoza and Oldenburg the latter expresses the view that the *Treatise* was a dangerous work and its author was not being altogether candid with his readers. In his letter of June 8, 1675, Oldenburg remarks that his initial reaction to the book was quite negative but that "after having examined and weighed the matter more closely" he has come to revise that opinion.[121] Nevertheless, he appends the following words of caution: "Certain things in it seemed to me, at the time, to tend to harm religion, when I measured it by the standard furnished by the crowd of theologians, and the accepted formulae of the creeds (which seem to be too much inspired by partisanship). But, on reconsidering the whole matter more closely, many considerations occur to me which go to persuade me that you are so far from intending any harm to true religion and sound philosophy that, on the contrary, you labor to commend and establish the true object of the Christian religion, and the divine sublimity and excellence of a fruitful philosophy."[122] Oldenburg then asks Spinoza if he would share any of his current work, adding, "I sacredly promise you that I will not divulge a syllable to anyone, *if you enjoin silence*."[123]

We do not know Spinoza's reply to Oldenburg's request, if any, but from the next letter we learn that Spinoza had announced his plan to publish the *Ethics* in five books. Oldenburg replies that it would be less than a friend's duty if he failed to warn Spinoza "not to include anything which may appear to undermine the practice of religious virtue."[124] Such a warning would have been absolutely unnecessary had Spinoza not already acquired the reputation for impiety or even atheism.

Spinoza maintains in his reply that his reputation for atheism is completely unfounded, the product of "certain theologians" who have it in for him, as well as of the "stupid Cartesians" (*stolidi praeterea Cartesiani*) who distorted his views in their attempts to sponsor them.[125] Spinoza then thanks his correspondent for his "friendly warning" and inquires, perhaps disingenuously, which ideas he was referring to that seem to militate against religion and piety.

"I beg you," he writes, "to point out to me the passages in the *Tractatus Theologico-Politicus* which have caused uneasiness to learned men, for I want to illustrate that treatise with notes, and to remove if possible the prejudices conceived against it."[126]

Oldenburg in his reply of November 15, 1675, approves of Spinoza's desire to "soften" (*mollire*) those passages in the *Treatise* "which have given pain to its readers."[127] Among the "ambiguities" in the work Oldenburg notes Spinoza's famous doctrine of *deus sive natura,* which "a great many people think you have confused." In addition he mentions Spinoza's skepticism regarding miracles and therewith the possibility of divine revelation. And finally he complains that "you conceal your opinion concerning Jesus Christ, the Redeemer of the world," and requests a "clear explanation" of Spinoza's beliefs on these subjects.[128]Later we will examine Spinoza's views on these and other important subjects. To say the least, Oldenburg is correct to point out that the *Treatise* fails to reveal its author's opinions on a host of problems, or does so only in an obscure, indirect, and contradictory manner.

Spinoza's work was not so respectfully received by all its early readers. Shortly after the work was published the Cambridge Platonist Henry Moore proclaimed that Spinoza was a "perfect Cartesian" and "no less than an infidel and an atheist."[129] The same opinion was true for the Dutch Remonstrant theologian Philippus van Limbroch, who wrote to a Cambridge associate, Oliver Doiley, that he could not remember ever reading "so pestilential a book"; he added that the *Treatise* was evidence for "what monsters our Holland brings forth."[130] A similar sense of outrage was expressed by Willem van Blijenbergh, a correspondent of Spinoza's, who remarked that the *Treatise* "is a work full of curious but abominable discoveries" that "every man of sense, ought to abhor" for its effort "to overthrow the Christian religion and baffle all our hopes which are grounded upon it."[131]

It was widely recognized that Spinoza was an esoteric writer whose concealment of his views made him all the more dangerous. Limbroch was one of the first to note Spinoza's deceptions and concealments, stating that "he deliberately writes obscurely in order not to show all too plainly the godlessness of his opinions."[132] Elsewhere the same critic observes that this "subtle author" intended "to instill his noxious opinions by ambiguity in incautious minds" in order that he might "conceal his venom in the mutilated and incomplete expression of his opinions, that thus he may decoy the careless readers to his point of view before they plainly see whither he tendeth."[133] Although many of Spinoza's early readers, as Rosalie Colie has deftly shown, correctly identified the subversive character of his beliefs, few were able to penetrate the depths of Spinoza's concealments.[134]

Spinoza's Provisional Morality

It is clear by now that the potential philosophers, the "prudent readers" to whom Spinoza appealed, were neither simply the Dutch republican camp of de Witt, who kept an excommunicated Jew at arm's length, or even the Collegiant-Remonstrants, who could not countenance Spinoza's attack on the biblical account of creation and the divinity of Christ. To some degree, the party of Spinoza was a construction of the author's own making ("le veritable 'parti de la liberté' *est a constuire*," as Etienne Balibar has noted).[135] The audience for the work was neither Christian nor Jewish but the autonomous individual. By appealing to independent human reason, Spinoza sought to achieve two ends. He hoped to break the historical bonds of authority and belief that held together the competing religious sects of seventeenth-century Europe. At the same time, he hoped to persuade citizens to submit their private judgment to a new kind of secular political authority. With an enlightened rational mind, citizens would perceive the reasonable grounds of submission to authority.

The issue of submission to authority is raised by Spinoza at the very outset of the *Treatise*:

> I begin with the natural right of each person, which extends as far as that person's desire and power extend. By the right of nature no one is bound to live according to the understanding of another person, but each one is the defender of his own freedom. Moreover, I show that no one really gives up this right unless he transfers his power of defending himself to someone else, and that he to whom everyone has transferred his right to live according to his own understanding, together with his power to defend himself, must retain this natural right absolutely. From this I show that those who hold supreme authority have the right to do whatever they can do, that they alone are the defenders of right and freedom, and that all others must do everything according to their decree alone.[136]

At the very end of the preface Spinoza personalizes this theoretical statement by expressing his willingness to submit himself and his book to "the examination and judgment" of the civil authority. He expresses his readiness to retract anything that the authorities deem to be "in conflict with the laws of the country, or harmful to the general welfare."[137] And the preface concludes with the author's recognition of his own fallibility and desire to remain "entirely consistent with the laws of my country, with piety and with morals."[138]

These passages raise a number of difficulties. How can we reconcile Spinoza's bold challenge to liberate human reason from ecclesiastical authority with his apparently mouselike expression of submission of his own reason to the political rulers, which comes in virtually the same breath? How can we accept both his radical endorsement of the absolute sovereignty of individuals to think and read what they like and his seemingly conservative social philosophy that teaches submission of judgment to the institutions of the state with its presumptive right of censorship? Spinoza's answer to this question follows up on his twofold strategy outlined earlier.[139]

Spinoza's profession of willingness to submit to the judgment of the secular arm of government is a way of defying the clergy's presumptive right of education and censorship. The strategy is intended to establish himself and the *Treatise* on the side of secular power while at the same time assuring the representatives of the government that they had nothing to fear from philosophy. There is, Spinoza would have us believe, a harmony of interests between a strictly secular government and the interests of philosophy. However, Spinoza's stated wish that his writing be "entirely consistent" (*omnino responderet*) with the laws of his country is by no means his final word on the subject. It is entirely consistent with his passion for secrecy and concealment. His hope that his writings would conform to the prevailing morality is of a piece with his claim in the *Treatise* and elsewhere that he always accommodated himself to the opinions and practices of those around him. In fact, this statement of external conformism and this profession of loyalty merely underscore the heterodox views and independence of judgment contained in the body of the text.

Spinoza's strategy of outward conformity combined with a program for achieving intellectual and political independence was in crucial respects modeled after Descartes's code of "provisional morality" outlined in the *Discourse on Method*.[140] To the well-known procedure of radical doubt announced at the beginning of the *Discourse* Descartes attached certain restrictions seemingly aimed at mitigating the political consequences of his method. In particular he cautioned against bringing the new method to bear on questions of theology and morality precisely to rope them off from the corrosive effects of skepticism. Thus his first rule of conduct was always "to obey the laws and customs of [one's] country," including constant adherence to the established religion. In all matters of practical action Descartes enjoins following "the most moderate in nature and the farthest removed from excess," both because the moderate is best suited for practice and "all excess has a tendency to be bad." The consequence of this rule is that in matters of morality it is "most expedient" to harmonize one's opinions with those of one's neighbors and to follow not one's own opinions but those of people "on whose judgment reliance could be placed."[141]

Students of Descartes often forget that his *morale provisoire* is exactly what it claims to be, namely, provisional, not definitive. A policy of outward conformity helps to mask the attitude of ironic detachment or skeptical distance that Descartes places between himself and his received moral opinions. Thus in the *Discourse* he says that because of "the corrupt state of our manners there are few people who desire to say all that they believe" and that his morality was written under the force of social pressure and does not necessarily represent his true convictions.[142]

The tension between professions of conformity and submission to authority, on the one hand, and repeated challenges to all authority, on the other, exists in Spinoza's political philosophy as well as Descartes's. Indeed, Spinoza can be called a Cartesian in politics to the extent that he follows this double strategy. If imitation is the sincerest form of flattery, then he is a flatterer: he copies Descartes's provisional code of conduct to a tee. At the outset of his *Treatise on the Emendation of the Intellect* Spinoza remarks that he is "compelled" to enunciate certain rules of conduct as "provisionally good." The first of these rules is simply "to speak in a manner intelligible to the multitude, and to comply with every general custom that does not hinder the attainment of our purpose."[143] And in a statement dripping with Machiavellianism, Spinoza adds that this method of "accommodation" will not only procure a "friendly audience" for his purpose but the goodwill of the multitude, from which "no small advantage" can be expected. This reference in the *Emendation* to the accommodation to the multitude is essentially the same as the statement in the *Treatise* that what he says is "in agreement" with morality and the law. Both texts combine stunning bluntness with a remarkable air of secrecy and reticence in expressing the author's true or definitive opinions.

The contrast between Spinoza's proud declaration of independence for human reason and his abject willingness to submit his judgment to the oversight of the political authorities is just one of the most obvious contradictions running through the *Treatise*. Consider the following. At times Spinoza defends, at other times undermines, the idea that revelation or prophecy is possible. He develops a hermeneutic that would deny any cognitive status to Scripture, declaring an absolute separation of reason and theology; yet elsewhere he proclaims that Scripture announces a profound moral truth that can be corroborated by reason and that amounts to the injunction to practice charity and love one's neighbor. How, then, to understand these very evident contradictions that cut through the heart of the *Treatise*?

It seems reasonable to conclude that the contradictions of the *Treatise* are best understood as part of Spinoza's strategy of accommodation to the opinions of the multitude. The multitude in question is not the *vulgus*, who are prone to fear and superstition and who are for Spinoza the object of fear and loathing. Spinoza's views are adapted to the free multitude, the *libera multitudo,* consisting of a coalition of Dutch republicans of the de Witt party and a variety of nonconfessional Reformed sects of the Collegiant-Mennonite type. To the more political readers of his text, Spinoza sought to make a show of his loyalty and even subservience to political authority, whereas to his more theological readers he gave assurances of piety and his defense of true religion against ecclesiastical hierarchy and paganism. Among these groups, many of them still under the sway of certain theological dogmas and prejudices, Spinoza sought both to discover and to create an audience for the *Treatise*.

Spinoza's strategy of accommodation can be understood to employ two principles. First, when two statements contradict one another, it is safe to assume that the more extreme or heterodox view is Spinoza's actual opinion. Second, when an argument from theology or Scripture is put alongside an argument from reason or philosophy, we can infer that the secular argument is Spinoza's actual opinion and the theological argument merely adapted to prevailing prejudice.[144] Only by consistently following this strategy could the *Treatise* create an audience capable of guaranteeing the success of what Spinoza called his purpose.

3

The Critique of Scripture

At the outset of the *Treatise* is a series of questions that Spinoza asks the reader to consider: Why is the human mind so beset by fear, doubt, and uncertainty? Why does religion, which asks for acts of loving-kindness, so often result in its opposite, cruelty, persecution, and intolerance? If "nothing is considered to be dearer and sweeter than freedom," why is freedom so difficult to attain and, once won, so hard to hold? The answers to these questions all derive from a basic phenomenon that Spinoza bent all his efforts to expose: the power of revealed religion.

All errors and superstitions are species of one fundamental prejudice. The prejudice on which all other prejudices rest is the authority that people have accorded to a single book, the Bible or Scripture. Spinoza uses "Bible" and "Scripture" (in the singular) to refer to both the Old and the New Testaments.[1] Yet even the most superficial reading of the *Treatise* shows that the vast majority of its materials derive from the Jewish rather than the Christian Scripture. This may be partly explained by the contingent fact that as a Jew, Spinoza simply knew the Jewish sources better and did not wish to poach in areas not his own.[2] It has also been suggested, not unreasonably, that Spinoza's professed intention to liberate his readers from prejudice is in reality an attempt to liberate them from Judaism. His biblical criticism is criticism of the Jewish Bible only.[3] An even more plausible suggestion is that Spinoza's biblical criticism performs the double-pronged strategy referred to earlier. Spinoza attacks the Hebrew Scripture as a means of gaining the confidence of his Gentile readers. He then uses this confidence to undermine their confidence in their own beliefs.

Spinoza attacks the view that the Bible is not merely a book but The Book, the divinely inspired declaration of the will of God in all the most important matters. Spinoza lived and wrote at a time when the authority of Scripture remained absolute even though the meaning attributed to it was becoming increasingly problematic. It is the authority of Scripture or, more precisely, the conflict between the rival interpreters of Scripture, that stands as the most formidable obstacle to freedom and toleration. Even if it could be demonstrated—and Spinoza believes it cannot—that Scripture is a divine or revealed work, it is necessary to remember that the interpreters of Scripture are merely human and hence fallible. Rather than subordinating Scripture to reason ("dogmatism") or reason to Scripture ("skepticism"), Spinoza undertakes to return authority to the individual as the sole arbiter and guide of biblical meaning. This is the revolutionary new teaching of Spinoza.

Spinoza and His Predecessors

Spinoza's answer to the pervasive power of Scripture over human life is unexpected at first. Not philosophy but historical philology is the antidote to the authority of Scripture and the key to humanity's liberation from spiritual and ecclesiastical tutelage. The *Treatise* stands at the beginning of what would later become known as the "higher criticism" of the Bible.[4] This higher criticism aims at nothing less than the historical understanding and reconstruction of the Bible. Spinoza's biblical criticism is, then, historical criticism; its goal is the historicization or secularization of the biblical text. It is a testimony to Spinoza's power of mind that three centuries after the publication of the *Treatise* modern philologists continue to work out the implications of his historical insights.[5]

Long before Julius Wellhausen in the nineteenth century popularized the idea that the biblical text was composed by different authors living in different periods, Spinoza led the charge against the ascription of divine authorship to the Torah. According to the traditional view on which Spinoza had been brought up, the Torah, or "Five Books of Moses," had been dictated directly by God to Moses, who gave it in turn to Joshua; it passed from him to the elders, from them to the prophets, then to the men of the Great Assembly, and finally to the rabbis, all in a long chain of unbroken tradition. For the traditional exegete, every word, indeed, every letter down to and including its particular shape and size, was pregnant with divine meaning.[6] In contrast to this exegetical method is the historico-genetic method of Spinoza, who takes an almost perverse delight in applying it to bring out the incoherencies, contradictions, and anachronisms in the text.[7] In particular, he makes much of the fact that Moses could not be the sole author of the Pentateuch because his death is recorded there (Deut. 31:14–22). Once you remove Mosaic authorship from the Torah, it becomes a collection of ancient fairy tales, and a not very impressive one at that.

To be sure, both secular and theological scholars had noted this before Spinoza. Hobbes took up this issue in *Leviathan,* maintaining that "it is not argument enough that [the books of the Pentateuch] were written by Moses because they are called the Five Books of Moses."[8] For evidence Hobbes points to Deuteronomy 34:6, where it is recorded that the whereabouts of the tomb of Moses is unknown, a statement that could not have been made if Moses were then still alive.[9] Similar, but even more radical, charges were leveled against the claims of Mosaic authorship by Isaac La Peyrère, a contemporary of both Hobbes and Spinoza, whose *Prae-Adamitae* (Men Before Adam) was published in 1655.[10] In *Prae-Adamitae* he argued many heretical ideas, chiefly that even before Adam the world was populated by human beings living in a condition of nature. Using a wide range of anthropological evidence, La Peyrère maintained that the Bible offered the history of the Jews, not the history of the entire human race. Specifically, on the basis of an internal examination of the text, he speculated that Scripture as handed down is not the word of God but a record made by many hands, "a heap of Copie confusedly taken."[11]

The extent of La Peyrère's influence on Spinoza is largely a matter for conjecture. We know that he visited Amsterdam between the winter of 1654 and the spring of 1655, shortly before Spinoza's excommunication. Spinoza makes no explicit reference to La Peyrère in any of his works, but this may be because of the sensitive nature of the materials and La Peyrère's reputation for heresy. However, a copy of *Prae-Adamitae* was found in Spinoza's library at the time of his death.[12] Some even suspected that La Peyrère had established a sect in Amsterdam consisting of "preadamites," "atheists," and "theologico-politicians," the last being an unequivocal reference to Spinoza.[13] Rather than adducing the authority of the notorious La Peyrère to make his case, Spinoza refers to the considerably more reputable Abraham Ibn Ezra, "a man who possessed an independent mind" (*liberioris ingenii vir*) and had "no slight learning" (*non mediocris eruditionis*).[14] Spinoza writes as if he and the twelfth-century Spanish exegete agree that the forty lines of Deuteronomy dealing with Moses' death demonstrate that Moses did not write the passage in question and that the Pentateuch as a whole is a human compilation.[15] But although Ibn Ezra maintained this embarrassing insight behind a veil of secrecy, Spinoza pursued the implications with a ruthless, almost fanatical consistency: if Scripture has human authorship, it belongs to the species of ancient literature and is a work to be read and studied the same way Homer's *Iliad* or Virgil's *Aeneid* is.

The idea that the *Treatise* offers something like the foundations of historical criticism will seem peculiar to readers who have been taught to approach Spinoza principally as the author of the *Ethics*.[16] For the Spinoza of the *Ethics*, not history but mathematical physics served as the paradigm for all knowledge. Returning to the Parmenidean injunction that "to be" means "to be always," Spinoza was led to doubt the veracity of any knowledge based on time, contingency, or empirical fact. Historical knowledge belonged to the medium of the imagination, which, we have seen, produces just error and confusion. Only what derives from the immutable structure of reason can be called true in the highest sense of the term.[17]

In the *Treatise* history plays a much different role than in the *Ethics*.[18] History fulfills a didactic or pedagogic purpose: to liberate the reader from the power of passions and prejudice. When applied to the study of Scripture, historical understanding shows that the teachings of the prophets were neither absolutely true nor absolutely false but attuned or "accommodated" to the understanding and language of the peoples to whom they were addressed. Spinoza was far from trying to overturn religious language and imagery as such. Rather than denying the imagination any value, he believed that however vague, incomplete, or inadequate the language of Scripture may be, it is still functionally related to the social and psychological needs of the age of which it treats. By regarding biblical prophecy not as divine inspiration but as the product of the times, Spinoza's scriptural hermeneutics serves an essentially emancipatory function; it is a seventeenth-century precursor of nineteenth-century *Ideologiekritik*. His professed aim was the liberation of readers from the authority of those who traced their authority back to Scripture. Spinoza's biblical hermeneutics could have been the foundation of Marx's later statement that "the critique of religion is the premise of every critique."[19]

The premises of Spinoza's biblical hermeneutics will be considered in detail below. These premises form the basis of Spinoza's liberal politics and his effort to free philosophy from the authority of Scripture. He also realizes that the separation of philosophy from theology is a conclusion that he must reach in the *Treatise*, not a dogma with which to begin. To reach that conclusion,

Spinoza elaborates a new, correct method for reading Scripture. The premises of this method can be reduced to three:

1. the principle of *interpretatio naturae,* or the view that the Bible can be understood by the same method used to understand the world of nature
2. the separation of meaning from truth
3. the self-sufficiency of reason as a new basis of authority

Interpretatio naturae *as the Principle of Spinoza's Biblical Hermeneutics*

Spinoza is keenly aware that the *Treatise* stands or falls on the viability of the method that he proposes therein for the interpretation of Scripture. The leading principle of this hermeneutic method is stated boldly in chapter 7:

> The method of interpreting Scripture does not differ from the method of interpreting nature [*dico methodum interpretandi Scripturam haud differre a methodo interpretandi naturam*], but agrees with it completely. For just as the method of interpreting nature consists above all in putting together a history of nature, from which, as from certain data, we infer the definitions of natural things, so also to interpret Scripture it is necessary to prepare a straightforward history of Scripture [*sic etiam ad Scripturam interpretandam necesse est ejus sinceram historiam adornare*] and to infer the mind of the authors of Scripture from it, by legitimate reasonings, as from certain data and principles. For if someone has admitted as principles or data for interpreting Scripture and discussing the things contained in it only those drawn from Scripture itself and its history, he will always proceed without any danger of error, and will be able to discuss the things which surpass our grasp as safely as those we know by the natural light.[20]

Spinoza's proposal for reading Scripture is apt to strike the modern reader as bizarre. In particular, he brooks one of the major conventions of contemporary hermeneutics, that is, the distinction between the sciences of nature and the study of culture. We are inclined to believe that the methods used for the study of natural phenomena are different in kind from those used to study intentional human activities. The methods of the natural sciences are, strictly speaking, explanatory, whereas those of the human or social sciences are interpretive. Interpretation applies only to those beings or artifacts that exhibit or express conscious human intelligence, which animals and inanimate objects do not. The implication, as Vico and others have maintained ever since, is that natural phenomena — like the tendency of bodies to fall — are not fully intelligible. They merely happen, and for no necessary reason. Intentional human activities, however, happen for reasons, reasons that we can understand because the subject and object of the inquiry share a common mind.[21]

In contrast to this dual structure of understanding, Spinoza everywhere maintains that there is a single form of explanation. Both the "book of nature" and the "book of books" are susceptible to the same laws and thus the same kind of explanation. There is no reason to think that human objects and artifacts, including divinely ascribed texts, are an exception to the rules governing the production and reproduction of other events and occurrences. It is part of Spinoza's scientific metaphysics that political and human life are nothing more than "modes" of Substance, to be studied and analyzed no differently from any other class of phenomena. This metaphysics provides the foundation for a new scientific politics in which human behavior is conceived as exhibiting the same regularities as the movements of any other nonhuman bodies.

The principle of *interpretatio naturae* entails at least two implications. First, it implies that we should attempt to explain the content of Scripture by means of strictly natural causes. Just as a scientist explains natural phenomena by means of causes that are endogenous to the system of nature without recourse to miracles or other supernatural events, so must the biblical exegete examine Scripture in its own terms and using the same assumptions without drawing on extraneous standards of truth or rationality. Reading the text *sola Scriptura* is the hermeneutic equivalent of Galileo's discoveries about the motion of falling bodies.[22]

The idea that the Bible can be understood naturalistically, that is, in terms of the laws of physical causation, is part of Spinoza's plan to desacralize or humanize the text. Partly, this means naturalizing the various myths, miracles, and other happenings recorded in Scripture. Thus in chapter 2 of the *Treatise* Spinoza "explains" the miracle recorded in Joshua (10:12–14), where the sun is reported to have stood still. From this report Spinoza draws the inference that "nothing in Scripture is clearer than that Joshua, and perhaps also the author who wrote his history, thought that the sun moves around the earth, but that the earth is at rest, and that the sun stood still for some time."[23] Rather than trying to force science to conform to Scripture or to explain away the evidence, it is best to think that Scripture and science are marked by different purposes. Here, it is unnecessary to believe that because Joshua was a brave soldier, he was also "skilled in astronomy."[24]

No longer is the Bible, then, the key to the understanding of nature; rather, nature is the key to understanding the Bible. By nature, Spinoza means a vast and interlocking network of efficient causes; to explain means ultimately to know the causes whereby things are determined. The principle of strict causal explanation entails the rejection of divine purposes. These are rejected as no more than an "anthropomorphic" projection of human desires and appetites onto the structure of the universe. Indeed, so great are the advantages to be gained from explanation by efficient causes alone that Spinoza promises that if his method is followed rigorously, it will produce results that are certain and "without any danger of error."

Second, Spinoza's method of reading implies not merely that Scripture is a natural phenomenon controlled by natural laws but that it is a purely historical document whose meanings need to be uncovered or unearthed in the manner of an archaeologist studying the remains of an ancient civilization. To be sure, Spinoza was not the first person to propose a historical investigation into the meaning of Scripture. A century and a half before Spinoza, Renaissance humanists like Lorenzo Valla and Erasmus sought to purge Christianity of its historical accretions by returning to the letter of the Gospels.[25] But for Spinoza these humanistic efforts to recover a pristine form of Christianity could not but fail because ultimately they were trying to reconcile biblical teachings with philosophy. Spinoza's immediate predecessor, Hugo Grotius, was the greatest disciple of this school of Erasmian humanism.

Spinoza's principle of *interpretatio naturae* had its source more immediately in a new attitude toward history growing out of the Baconian-Cartesian philosophies of science. Neither Bacon nor Descartes was a historian in the strict sense (although Bacon wrote a *History of the Reign of King Henry VII*), but they brought together the intellectual methods from which the principles of Spinoza's historiography arose. It was these principles that, in Ernst Cassirer's view, led Spinoza to become "the originator of the idea of the historicity of the Bible" and enabled him to be "the first to develop it with sober precision and clarity."[26]

Spinoza's indebtedness to Bacon has only occasionally been recognized.[27] In the *Advancement of Learning* Bacon took over from Aristotle and the Renaissance humanists a division of all knowledge into the three categories of philosophy, poetry, and history.[28] These three branches of knowledge were said to "emanate" from three distinct human "faculties." Reason is to philosophy what imagination is to poetry and what memory is to history.

> History is properly concerned with individuals, which are circumscribed by place and time [*Historia proprie individuorum est, quae circumscribuntur loco et tempore*]. For though Natural History may seem to deal with species, yet this is only because of the general resemblance which in most cases natural objects of the same species bear to one another; so that when you know one, you know all. And if individuals are found, which are either unique in their

species, like the sun and moon; or notable deviations from their species, like monsters; the description of these has as fit a place in Natural History as that of remarkable men has in Civil History. All this relates to the Memory [*Haec autem ad memoriam spectant*].[29]

What Bacon calls "memory" he later calls "sense," or knowledge derived through experience. Indeed, the study of Scripture or revelation, far from constituting an independent branch of inquiry, a divine science, is incorporated into what can be known through ordinary empirical means. "The information derived from revelation and the information derived from the sense," Bacon writes, "differ no doubt both in the matter and in the manner of conveyance; but the human mind is the same, and its repositories and cells the same. It is only like different liquids poured through different funnels into one and the same vessel."[30]

Spinoza was deeply indebted to the Baconian method of induction, which he claimed to be reluctant to criticize. "It is not my custom," he wrote with explicit reference to Bacon, "to expose the errors of others."[31] Nevertheless, by suggesting that memory is the controlling faculty of history, Bacon provided no critical means for sorting out and analyzing the data provided by the senses. Bacon, Spinoza believed, was correct to distinguish the merely relative truths of history from the truth provided by philosophy. It is a mistake to look to history as a repository of truths or as the revelation of a rational plan. Just as we must de-anthropomorphize nature by denying it final purposes, so must we confront the facts of history in all their stark "otherness" or their manifest unintelligibility rather than artificially assuming that history is the manifestation of providence. In the case of Bacon, however, there is no way of proceeding from induction, the collection of data, to the principles of order or the reasons why. In the end, Spinoza's judgment of Bacon is that "he simply narrates" (*sed tantum narrat*).[32]

The empirical or inductive spirit of Baconianism had to be combined with the more skeptical and critical temperament of Descartes. From Descartes, Spinoza inherited a radical distrust of everything that could not justify and defend itself at the bar of reason. In the *Discourse on Method* and other writings Descartes was prepared to dispense with all knowledge that did not appear to him as "indubitably true" and "incapable of being doubted." Such an austere conception of knowledge coupled with Descartes's skepticism regarding the evidence of the senses would not seem to be a promising starting point for the study of history.

In part I of the *Discourse* Descartes undertakes a survey of the various branches of learning, including history — considered as a species of "eloquence" (rhetoric) — law, medicine, and languages. The study of languages, Descartes admits, is useful for reading the works of "ancient literature," which might "charm" the mind by recalling the "memorable deeds" of ancient heroes.[33] He even suggests that to learn "the histories and fables" of the ancients is a useful part of education. Furthermore, the study of history is is a hedge against parochialism and insularity: "For to converse with those of other centuries is almost the same thing as to travel. It is good to know something of the customs of different peoples in order to judge more sanely of our own, and not to think that everything of a fashion not ours is absurd and contrary to reason, as do those who have seen nothing."[34]

The problem is that to spend one's energy studying the charms of other times and places makes one a stranger to one's own. The danger with this kind of intellectual tourism is that "when one is too curious about things which were practiced in past centuries, one is usually very ignorant about those which are practiced in our own time."[35] The study of history, in other words, fosters romantic escapism, which leads the student to exaggerate and misrepresent the deeds of the past in order to render them more worthy of study in the present. Descartes critiques history for preferring the past to the present, whereas he wants the reader to develop a preference for the present and even the future.

Far from representing an obstacle to historical inquiry, Descartes's skepticism about the value of historical knowledge proved a challenge and an inspiration.[36] From Descartes, Spinoza drew the lesson that the testimony of written sources could not be accepted at face value without submitting them to critical scrutiny. Taking Descartes's point that previous historical narratives had grossly exaggerated the splendors of the ancients, Spinoza set out to use the methods of history to debunk the authority of the past. The term "ancient" had for him the double meaning of not just old and venerable but also primitive and uncouth. Spinoza turned to history in the spirit of Descartes. He turned to the ancient "histories and fables" of the Bible, not for evidence of a golden age or for examples of timeless truths, but for a propadeutic to our liberation from false ideas and bondage to superstition. History is intended to fulfill an emancipatory function.

Spinoza's use of nature as a model for interpreting Scripture is the basis for his later statement that "all knowledge of Scripture must be sought only from Scripture itself" (*Scripturae cognitio ab ipsa sola peti debet*).[37] Spinoza's principle of reading Scripture according to Scripture is emblematic of his attempt to secularize or naturalize the text:

> But to establish clearly that this way is not only certain, but also the only way, and that it agrees with the method of interpreting nature, we must note that

Scripture very often treats things which cannot be deduced from principles known to the natural light. For historical narratives and revelations make up the greatest part of it. . . . Moreover, the revelations were also accommodated to the opinions of the prophets . . . and they really surpass man's power of understanding. So the knowledge of all these things, i.e., of almost everything in Scripture, must be sought only from Scripture itself, just as the knowledge of nature must be sought from nature itself.[38]

Interpretatio naturae, or understanding Scripture by using Scripture, consists of three parts. First, Spinoza recommends that the biblical interpreter cultivate a thorough knowledge of "the nature and properties" of the Hebrew language.[39] Second, the exegete must perform a kind of content analysis on each book of the Bible, noting down all the passages "which are ambiguous or obscure or which seem inconsistent with one another."[40] Finally, the investigator must relate the context and environment of each book to "the life, the character and concerns of the author of each book," as well as to the reception of the various books by subsequent redactors. This historical assessment includes what today would be called the study of canon formation to show how these many diverse works came to be "accepted among the sacred books" and "unified into one body."[41]

Spinoza did not regard his development of this hermeneutic procedure as universally applicable to all texts. Unlike contemporary interpretivists, he is *not* saying that the world is a text and that everything requires interpretation. We need rules of interpretation only for what confronts us as mysterious and unintelligible. It is because Scripture is unintelligible that we need a method to help us understand it. The Bible is a book containing "incredible or incomprehensible things" (*res incredibiles aut imperceptibiles*) written in "very obscure terms" (*obscuris scriptum*).[42] Spinoza even compares its narrative content to that of other fantastic stories in Ovid and the tales of Orlando Furioso.[43] Like the apparently haphazard workings of nature, such stories are inexplicable without understanding their "history."

Interpretatio naturae is appropriate, then, only for objects that are problematic or make no sense. What is intelligible, by contrast, needs no interpretation. Thus Spinoza distinguishes between historical works like the Bible, the true meaning of which, he admits, is in many places "incomprehensible," from essentially "intelligible" books like Euclid's *Elements.*[44] Although everyone can understand the truth of Euclid's propositions "even before they are proved," for "hieroglyphic" works like the Bible, which seem to surpass the bounds of sense, a method must be used that can render intelligible the narrator's meaning (*mentem auctoris*).[45] The difference is that Euclid begins with definitions and first principles; the Bible does not. Neither nature nor Scripture begins with definitions, hence both require interpretation.

The difference, then, between Euclid and the Bible is not that they require two different kinds of interpretation. It is, rather, that intelligible works require no interpretation; they are for all practical purposes self-interpreting.[46] For example, one does not need to be a profound scholar of Greek to learn geometry, or to study the circumstances of Euclid's life and times to understand the properties of a triangle. Spinoza distinguishes in the sharpest possible manner between hieroglyphic texts that require interpretation from self-interpreting works that require only an ability to follow a chain of reasoning from premises to conclusion: "Euclid, who wrote only about things which were quite simple and most intelligible [*simplices et maxime intelligibiles*], is easily explained by anyone in any language. For to grasp his intention and to be certain of his true meaning, it is not necessary to have a complete knowledge of the language in which he wrote, but only a quite common and almost childish knowledge. Nor is it necessary to know the life, concerns and customs of the author, nor in what language, to whom and when he wrote, nor the fate of his book, nor its various readings, nor how nor by whose deliberation it was accepted."[47]

What Spinoza says here of Euclid is indeed true of all authors who write of things "by their nature comprehensible" (*natura perceptibilibus*), including, by implication, the author of the *Ethics*. Spinoza's *Ethics* is a work written *in more geometrico* and as such can do without the stories, narratives, and histories provided in Scripture. The audacious but unstated claim of the *Treatise* is to use the method of *interpretatio naturae* in order ultimately to dispense with it. The pedagogical aim of the *Treatise*, we have seen, is to use Scripture against the clerics and then to use reason against Scripture. Spinoza hopes to prepare his audience to substitute his *Ethics* for Scripture or to turn the *Ethics* into a new Scripture or new dispensation.

Spinoza and the Skeptics

The principle of *interpretatio naturae* is a necessary but insufficient condition for the emergence of Spinoza's critical project. It is not enough that the content of Scripture be viewed naturalistically, as governed by the same kinds of causes that determine the motions of other objects. Rather, it is necessary to distinguish the "meaning" (*mens*) of Scripture from its truth: "For we are concerned only with the meaning of the utterances, not with their truth. Indeed, we must take great care, so long as we are looking for the meaning of

Scripture, not to be preoccupied with our own reasoning, insofar as it is founded on the principles of natural knowledge (not to mention now our prejudices). But lest we confuse the true meaning with the truth of things, that meaning must be found out solely from the usage of language, or from reasoning which recognizes no other foundation than Scripture."[48]

This distinction between meaning and truth, so apparently innocent and yet so vital, can be fully understood only when seen in the light of the argument of the *Treatise* as a whole. In the *Treatise* Spinoza defends the radical separation of reason (philosophy) from theology. By further separating meaning from truth and then defining truth as a function of reason, the unstated premise of Spinoza's biblical hermeneutic is that Scripture cannot speak the truth. This does not prevent Scripture from issuing moral commands that remain useful for life in society, such as the injunction to practice love and charity. But we should be careful not to confuse moral claims, however salutary, from epistemic truths. These latter belong to philosophy or reason alone. Judgments of truth pertain exclusively to the discovery of causes, whereas morality pertains to action and behavior.[49]

The confusion or "accommodation" of the meaning and truth of Scripture is what has vitiated all previous efforts at understanding. Accommodationism has given rise to two equally dangerous fallacies that the separation of meaning and truth can prevent. These fallacies are identified in the fifteenth chapter of the *Treatise* as skepticism and dogmatism, respectively.[50] Both isms are instances of a generic or "astronomical" problem, that is, the failure to take seriously the distinction between the meaning of the text and its truth value.[51] We shall consider these two alleged fallacies in turn.

The skeptics to whom the *Treatise* refers are those who, disbelieving in their own rationality, argue that "reason must be accommodated to Scripture."[52] The skeptics here are not those, like Spinoza, who would be skeptical of Scripture, but those who are skeptical about reason. The result of this skepticism is that they are forced "to admit as divine teachings the prejudices of the common people of long ago" (*antiqui vulgi praejudicia*).[53] Chief among these skeptical exegetes is the orthodox rabbi Jehuda Alpakhar. Alpakhar was a central participant in the Maimonidean Controversy in Spain in the 1230s. In a letter to David Kimchi he attacked Maimonides' allegorical reading of Scripture and in general sought to discredit the intrusions of philosophy into Judaism.[54]

For Spinoza, Alpakhar's skepticism ironically committed him to a biblical literalism in which the truth of Scripture in all matters must be affirmed because of the insufficiency of reason. Literalists, whether traditional rabbinic exegetes or contemporary Protestant theologians, take the surface or literal meaning of Scripture as true, no matter how contradictory or inconsistent statements may be. To some degree, as we shall see, Spinoza has no quarrel with the claim that the literal meaning of Scripture expresses the intentions of its authors; where he attacks the skeptics is in their belief that the literal meaning of the text is also true.

Spinoza takes a malicious glee in exposing evident discrepancies in the biblical texts and asking disingenuously how a rational being, even Rabbi Alpakhar himself, could possibly believe the texts to be true without falling into absurdity. The discrepancies fall into three sorts: anachronism, contradiction, and anthropomorphism.

The examples of biblical anachronism refer mainly to the circumstances of the composition of the text that Spinoza maintains cannot be attributed to Moses. In addition to the last twelve verses of Deuteronomy, where the death and funeral of Moses are recorded, Spinoza points to the verse "and Moses wrote the law" (Deut. 31:9).[55] The repeated references to Moses in the third person are sufficient for him to doubt Mosaic authorship.[56] Spinoza notes, too, that other statements, like "There arose not a prophet since in Israel like unto Moses," could not have been written in the time of Moses but were probably written considerably later.[57]

There are further instances of biblical anachronism. Spinoza makes much of the statement after the passage recording Abram's journey through Canaan to Shechem: "the Canaanites were in the land" (Gen. 12:6). The passage implies that at the time of composition the Canaanites were no longer in the land, although the land was still occupied by the Canaanites at the time of Moses' death.[58] Furthermore, Mount Moriah is called the mount of God, although it did not acquire this name until it was selected by God as the site of the Temple (Gen. 11:14).[59] Spinoza also notes a parenthetical expression regarding Og: "For only Og, the king of Bashan, was left of the remnant of the Rephaim; behold, his bedstead was a bedstead of iron; is it not in Rabbah of the Amonites?" (Deut. 3:11). By implication, the passage was written long after the time of Og, who was a direct contemporary of Moses. Spinoza speculates that the mode of speaking is appropriate to a time considerably later, perhaps when the bedstead and other "relics" were discovered by David, who conquered the city of Rabbah (2 Sam. 12:30).[60]

Besides anachronism there is the problem of contradictory predication, or the attribution of contradictory attributes to God. Spinoza's proof texts here are Samuel's denial and Jeremiah's affirmation that God repents of his decisions (1 Sam. 15:29; Jer. 18:8–10).[61] For reasons to be examined in the next chapter, Spinoza attributes these contradictions to the different psychological states and dispositions of the prophets and speakers whose judgments they express.

Finally, there is the more serious problem of biblical anthropomorphism, the attribution of human features or characteristics to God. At various points God is called jealous and compared to a fire (Ex. 34:14: Deut. 4:24, 6:15).[62] Elsewhere he is depicted as coming down to Mount Sinai, as moving about, and speaking (Deut. 19:20).[63] Throughout the Bible, there are innumerable references to the eyes of God, the mouth of God, the face of God, and so on. Yet there are also powerful injunctions against all such depictions of God in corporeal form as tantamount to idolatry. The absolute unity of God is affirmed as incumbent upon all Jews to accept ("Hear, O Israel: The Lord our God is one Lord"), as is the denial of his resemblance to any visible thing in heaven or on earth ("Since you saw no form on the day that the Lord spoke to you . . . beware lest you act corruptly by making a graven image for yourselves, in the form of any figure" — Deut. 6:4, 4:15–16). The belief that God is multiple or corporeal is further said to be a grave offense against the Jewish people, which may result in expulsion.[64]

Spinoza's point is that a work with so many factual errors and inconsistencies cannot all be true, at least at the level of detail. Here he seeks to drive a wedge between reason and biblical literalism. If the skeptic who adheres to literalism can be made to admit that Scripture is sometimes allegorical, why should this interpretation not extend to other details and perhaps even to the work as a whole? Failure to recognize this possibility must lead the skeptic cum literalist to accept as authoritative everything contained in Scripture, which Spinoza believes he has shown cannot be done.

The problem with skepticism, then, is that it preserves the dignity and sanctity of the biblical text, but at the expense of reason:

> Again, I ask who can accept something in his mind in spite of the protests of reason? Surely I cannot marvel enough that people should want to make reason, the divine light, [God's] greatest gift, subordinate to dead letters, which could have been distorted by the wicked conduct of men. . . . They think it pious to trust nothing to reason and to their own judgment, but impious to doubt the reliability of those who handed down the Sacred Books to us. This is mere folly, not piety. What are they worried about? What are they afraid of? Can religion and faith not be defended unless men deliberately know nothing about anything, and say farewell to reason completely? Surely if they believe this, they are more fearful for Scripture than trusting in it.[65]

For any careful reader of the *Treatise* it should be evident from the biting and polemical tone of this passage that Spinoza is concerned with more than the obscure Jehuda Alpakhar. It is conceivable that Alpakhar was a stand-in for Spinoza's contemporary critic Isaac Orobio de Castro.[66] But the unnamed target of Spinoza's critique was, I want to suggest, the Protestant fideists of the seventeenth century who held that faith alone provides the road to truth and that reason or philosophy counts for little or nothing. It is important to recall here that skepticism reappeared in modern European thought as an ally not of reason but of religion. Not until much later were skeptical arguments used against religion.[67]

The appearance of skeptical fideism was a common Renaissance trope with Pico della Mirandola and Lorenzo Valla, but it was given a greater sense of urgency with the rise of Luther's Protestant hermeneutics.[68] It was this skeptical critique of reason that a century after Spinoza would still inform the work of Kant. The *Critique of Pure Reason* was nothing short of an attempt to give philosophical expression to this theological tendency: Kant found "it necessary to deny knowledge, in order to make room for faith."[69] For Luther and the tradition of Protestant hermeneutics that he helped to establish, the doctrine of justification through faith was intended precisely to circumscribe the role of reason in securing human salvation. The official Lutheran position was that Scripture is the word of God and as such directly intelligible without dependence on the mediating institutions of either the church or man's corrupted reason.[70]

At first glance this denial of the need for rational justification in theology seems in accord with Spinoza's insistence on the radical separation of reason and theology. But nothing could be further from Luther's Protestant hermeneutics than Spinoza's insistence that Scripture is a "hieroglyphic" text fundamentally in need of critical exegesis and reconstruction. For Luther, the understanding of Scripture is something lived or experienced, the result of opening oneself to the transformative power of the text. Understanding is not so much the fruit of reason as it is a product of the hermeneutical situation in which Scripture is encountered.[71] For Luther, however, reason and the chief among reasoners, Aquinas, were principally responsible for the corruption of Scripture and for the substitution of Aristotle for Saint Paul. Reason was no longer understood as the crown of creation, as in Thomas's magisterial synthesis, but as the "devil's whore," "the fountain and headspring of all mischiefs."[72] Aquinas in particular bore primary responsibility for introducing this "dead heathen" into the universities, where his influence "has conquered, obstructed, and almost succeeded in suppressing the books of the living God."[73] For Luther, the profound and unfathomable mystery of such things as the Christian doctrine of the Trinity underscored the insufficiency of reason.

This kind of Protestant hermeneutic is, I suggest, the actual, though unstated, target of Spinoza's attack on the harmless Jehuda Alpakhar. The connection between skepticism and Protestantism is made explicit, however, in a letter to the Calvinist grain merchant and amateur philosopher Willem van Blijenbergh written some years before the publication of the *Treatise*. Here Spinoza writes with considerable frankness, shedding his "characteristic caution" and even allowing himself to "drop his mask" before a correspondent who he senses might be hostile and perhaps even hateful.[74] The overt theme of the correspondence is the problem of evil, which becomes very quickly a question of how God can be the cause of an evil will such as Adam's desire to eat the forbidden fruit. Spinoza makes some unusually candid remarks about the relation between reason and Scripture.

In a letter, dated January 28, 1665, Spinoza begins by expressing doubt that their differences over the question of evil could ever be resolved through an exchange of letters. The causes of their disagreement go to their very different understandings of the power of reason to grasp the truth. "For I see that no demonstration, however solid it may be, has weight with you unless it agrees with that explanation which you, or theologians known to you, attribute to sacred Scripture."[75] If Spinoza's correspondent believes "that God speaks more clearly and effectively through sacred Scripture than through the light of the natural intellect," there is nothing that Spinoza can do to prevent him from "bending your intellect to the opinions you attribute to sacred Scripture." In a moment of supreme irony Spinoza replies "without circumlocution" (*sine ambagibus*) that he does not understand Scripture even though admitting to have spent "several years on it"; he repeats himself almost verbatim in the *Treatise*.[76] Instead of bending his reason to conform to a work that he "confesses" not to understand, Spinoza asserts a buoyant, even dogmatic, confidence in the power of the natural intellect. So confident is he in the power of unaided reason that he claims to entertain no suspicion that he might be dangerously deceived or that his reasoning might contradict Scripture (which he does not understand anyway). Furthermore, even if the fruits of the natural intellect could be proven false, Spinoza avers that this would still make him happy on the grounds that it would allow him to climb "a step higher" toward the recognition of truth ("the greatest satisfaction and peace of mind").[77]

Always mindful to avoid the appearance of atheism, Spinoza says later in the same letter that his opinions are not intended to cast doubt on the authority of Scripture. "I believe I ascribe as much, *if not more,* authority to it, and that I take care, far more cautiously than others do, not to attribute to it certain childish and absurd opinions."[78] Among these "childish and absurd opinions" is the belief that everything contained in Scripture is literally true, as asserted in both Protestant and Jewish skeptical hermeneutics. Though denying that he understands Scripture, he now claims to know that many of its teachings are wrapped in parabolic or enigmatic language addressed or accommodated to the needs of its audience. For this reason he doubts the "explanations" of "ordinary theologians," who always take Scripture "according to the letter and external meaning." Indeed, "except for the Socinians," there has never been a theologian "so dense" as to deny the essentially parabolic and hence nonliteralist meaning of Scripture.[79]

Maimonides and the Dogmatists

If the error of skepticism is that it forces reason to accord with Scripture, the problem with dogmatism is precisely the opposite, that of forcing Scripture to agree with reason. As a result, the dogmatists "ascribe fictitiously to the prophets many things they did not think of even in their dreams" and which would be easier for a layman to think up than for a scholar to discover in Scripture.[80] To save the truth or rationality of Scripture, it must be bent out of all proportion, and intentions at odds with the literal meaning of the text must be attributed to its author. The method of the dogmatists, then, is to uncover hidden, symbolic, or esoteric truths in Scripture hidden below the surface meaning.

The chief "dogmatist" identified in the *Treatise* is Maimonides, "the first person among the Pharisees who frankly maintained that Scripture should be accommodated to reason."[81] Maimonides practices a form of reading that came to be known as allegorization or, in the talmudic tradition, *derash*. *Derash* means "to seek" in the sense of inquiring from an oracle or a prophet. When applied to Scripture, it means to seek divine knowledge that had been secretly encoded in the text and that had to be gleaned from such things as the style, order, and even spelling of particular words.[82] The method of *derash*, the tendency to search for the allegorical or symbolic meanings of words, is, for Spinoza, as great a danger as the skeptic's adherence to the literal meaning of the text. The great confidence in the power of reason that he had expressed when addressing the skeptic is now turned against reason when addressing the dogmatist.[83] Whereas the skeptic saves Scripture but at the expense of his own reason, the dogmatist saves reason but at the expense of Scripture. Scripture must be tortured to reveal its esoteric truths no matter how evident the surface meaning may be. In fact, no matter how clear or evident the meaning, the dogmatist "will not be able to be certain of the true meaning of Scripture . . . so long as he can doubt the truth of the matter or so long as it is not established for him."[84]

Spinoza's critique of dogmatism centers on Maimonides' theory of interpretation. Maimonidean *derash* proceeds from exactly the opposite premises as does Spinozistic *peshat,* or the method of historical contextualization. For

Maimonides the Torah is a divine work containing the sum total of human knowledge, both moral and metaphysical, but for Spinoza it is a human work that needs to be interpreted within its historical, linguistic, and even psychological context. Scripture is not the word of God but a historical work and, as such, "very much accommodated to the prejudices of [its] age" (*maxime accommodatae sunt uniuscujusque aevi praejudiciis*).[85]

Maimonidean interpretation proceeds from the assumption that Scripture is a secret or esoteric work and that its teachings may be pronounced, so to speak, only among consenting adults in private.[86] In the introduction to *The Guide of the Perplexed* Maimonides announces his purpose: "to explain the meaning of certain terms occurring in the books of prophecy." He later modifies this to read: "the explanation of very obscure parables occurring in the books of the prophets."[87] Shortly thereafter Maimonides identifies these parables with the "Account of the Beginning" in the book of Genesis and the "Account of the Chariot" in Ezekiel 1 and 10. These he takes to refer to the sciences of physics and metaphysics, respectively.[88]

The problem, so far as the *Guide* is concerned, is that its author labors under a rabbinic injunction that the speculative doctrines contained in the Torah be taught only in a secret or esoteric manner. The precise wording of this injunction is: "The Account of the Chariot ought not to be taught even to one man, except if he be wise and able to understand by himself, in which cases only the chapter headings may be transmitted to him."[89] Not only does Maimonides profess strict adherence to this injunction, but he goes beyond it, stating that even the chapters are not arranged in any coherent order in the *Guide* but are "scattered and entangled with other subjects" so that "the truths [are] glimpsed and then again concealed."[90] The purpose of the *Guide* is, then, to reveal these truths, but in a way that does not fully reveal them. The truth is to be expressed in an enigmatic or parabolic manner so as to maintain, so far as possible, the "Secrets of the Torah" from outright exposure.

Why does Maimonides choose such a deliberately obscure, not to say perverse, mode of presentation in the *Guide*? Because the Torah itself is a secret or esoteric book. The esoteric character of the Torah is revealed through its use of stories and parables to convey its teachings. Just as there are intentional contradictions in the Bible, so are there in the *Guide*, and they must be read in the same way. Thus Maimonides prescribes for readers of his work that they "connect its chapters one with another" and, further, "grasp each word that occurs in it in the course of the speech, even if that word does not belong to the intention of the chapter."[91] In spite of the arbitrary appearance of its composition, Maimonides assures us that "the dictation of [the *Guide*] has not been chosen at haphazard" and that "nothing has been mentioned out of its place."[92] He even warns the reader not to comment on so much as "a single word" of the book or to explain to another anything that has not been interpreted by some previous authority.

Maimonides suggests that even he lacks full command of the meaning of Scripture. Interpretation is not a matter of all or nothing but of more or less. It remains at best like an occasional flash of light in greater or lesser periods of darkness:

> You should not think that these secrets are fully and completely known to anyone among us. They are not. But sometimes truth flashes out to us so that we think that it is day, and then matter and habit in their various forms conceal it so that we find ourselves again in an obscure night over whom lightning flashes time and time again. Among us there is one for whom the lightning flashes time and time again, so that he is always, as it were, in unceasing light. . . . There are others between whose lightning flashes there are greater or shorter intervals. Thereafter comes he who does not attain a degree in which darkness is illumined by any lightning flash.[93]

The *Guide* is a parabolic work because the Torah is a parabolic work containing many anomalies and contradictions. To take but the most obvious example: The Torah frequently speaks of God as a lawgiver and judge endowed with specific moral and psychological attributes. God is presented variously as angry, just, merciful, and compassionate. At the same time, however, that Scripture uses openly anthropomorphic terms, it also refers to God's unity, omniscience, and incorporeality. How can a being possessed of unity also be said to have distinct parts and capacities? How can a being who is incorporeal be embodied in human shape? Maimonides sets out to account for these anomalies.

He does so by means of a commentary on a biblical parable. According to Solomon, "A word fitly spoken is like apples of gold in settings of silver" (Prov. 25:11).[94] Maimonides interprets this to mean that every biblical parable will have two meanings, an internal and an external one. The external or public meaning will be like the silver filigree that frames a golden apple. He adds that a parable is well constructed if, when viewed "from a distance" or with "imperfect attention," it appears as though the apples were made of silver or as though the external meaning is identical to the internal one. A parable is well designed, then, if it succeeds in hiding its real meaning. But Maimonides goes one step further in suggesting that the external and internal meanings are addressed to radically different audiences. The external meaning is intended for the multitude and conveys necessary truths that pertain to "the welfare of human societies." The internal meaning is intended for the few and refers to

but to stick as closely as possible to what the language meant for those who used it.[100]

Against what Spinoza takes to be Maimonides' hyperrationalism he sets a proof text: the discussion of the biblical doctrine of the creation versus the Aristotelian conception of the eternity of the world in the *Guide*, II, 25. The relevant passage is worth quoting:

> Know that our shunning the affirmation of the eternity of the world is not due to a text figuring in the Torah according to which the world has been produced in time. For the texts indicating that the world has been produced in time are not more numerous than those indicating that the deity is a body. Nor are the gates of figurative interpretation shut in our faces or impossible of access to us regarding the subject of the creation of the world in time. For we could interpret them as figurative, as we have done when denying His corporeality. Perhaps this would even be much easier to do: we should be very well able to give a figurative interpretation of those texts and to affirm as true the eternity of the world, just as we have given a figurative interpretation of those other texts and have denied that He, may He be exalted, is a body.[101]

In this difficult passage, Maimonides opens up the possibility that the biblical doctrine of the creation of the world may itself be an allegory or fable. After all, he admits, if the depiction of the deity as a body has been shown to be parabolic, why might this not also apply to the biblical view of God's creations in Genesis? He candidly admits that "the texts indicating that the world has been produced in time are not more numerous than those indicating that the deity is a body," so nothing could be easier than to provide a figurative interpretation of those texts in order to make them conform to Aristotle's doctrine of the eternity of the cosmos.

But Maimonides adduces two reasons for adhering to the biblical view of creation rather than relying on his usual method of allegorical interpretation:

> Two causes are responsible for our not doing this or believing it. One of them is as follows. That the Deity is not a body has been demonstrated; from this it follows necessarily that everything that in its external meaning disagrees with this demonstration must be interpreted figuratively, for it is known that such texts are of necessity fit for figurative interpretation. However, the eternity of the world has not been demonstrated. Consequently in this case the texts ought not to be rejected and figuratively interpreted in order to make prevail an opinion whose contrary can be made to prevail by means of various sorts of arguments.[102]

It is not merely an assertion but a "demonstration" of Scripture that the deity is not embodied. All biblical texts to the contrary must therefore be interpreted allegorically to support rational belief. However, the eternity of the world, Maimonides believes, has never been conclusively established but remains at best a working hypothesis that we are free to either accept or reject.[103] Because the eternity of the world has not been conclusively established, it follows that creation in time is at least a logical possibility. More important, the Aristotelian theory of eternity appears to deny God's will and volition and to affirm necessity. The belief in creation in time is thus more compatible with a number of other moral beliefs about the nature of God, man, and the world and supports the biblical view regarding the promises of divine justice. Because the belief in divine necessity has not been conclusively demonstrated, it is more reasonable, so Maimonides believes, to accept the biblical view that the world was created in time.[104]

Spinoza objects to the apparently arbitrary and capricious manner of Maimonidean *derash*. Beginning from the premise that truth and the meaning of Scripture cannot be at odds and therefore that no statement in the Bible can be against reason, Maimonides has to decide which passages in Scripture accord with truth as they stand and which have to be interpreted allegorically to make them so accord. Thus in the passage alluded to above, Maimonides asserts that both the philosopher and the prophets agree regarding the noncorporeality of God. But, Spinoza counters, had Maimonides been convinced by sufficient reason that the world is eternal rather than created in time, he would not have hesitated to turn the biblical texts inside out to make them conform to that belief.[105]

In criticizing Maimonides, Spinoza takes up the more orthodox position of Alpakhar, who saw the *Guide* as an attempt to force the Torah to conform to the dictates of Aristotelian logic. The clear implication is that if Aristotle's notion of the world's eternity had been philosophically demonstrable, Maimonides would have had no difficulty in accommodating the biblical text to that teaching. In this case, Spinoza asserts that Maimonides would have chosen, without compunction, "to twist Scripture and to explain it in such a way that it would finally teach the very same thing" as the pagan philosophers.[106] What seemed untenable was the Maimonidean attempt to make philosophy, a pagan interloper, the monitor of the law of Moses. It is one thing to welcome the biblical promise that Japeth dwell in the tents of his brother Shem (Gen. 9:27). It is another to give philosophy and things Greek (which, according to tradition, derive from the line of Japeth) authority over where to pitch the tent. If one were to follow Spinoza's reasoning, Maimonides, not he, would appear to be the heretic.

There is a fundamentally political problem at the core of this dispute. Spinoza accuses Maimonides of using his method of interpretation to set up a new kind of priestly or rabbinical authority to adjudicate conflicts over scriptural interpretation. Ultimately, he accuses Maimonides of harboring ambitions to set himself up as philosopher-king. Consider the following:

> If [Maimonides'] opinion were true, I would concede without qualification that we need some other light beyond the natural to interpret Scripture. For hardly any of the things which are found in these texts can be deduced from principles known by the natural light . . . and so the power of the natural light cannot establish anything for us about their truth, and hence, it also cannot establish anything for us about the true meaning and intention of Scripture. For this we would necessarily need another light.
>
> Again, if this opinion were true, it would follow that the multitude, who for the most part have no knowledge of demonstrations, or cannot give their time to them, will be able to admit nothing about Scripture except on the unaided authority and testimonies of those who philosophize. So they will have to suppose that the philosophers cannot err concerning the interpretation of Scripture. This would obviously introduce a new authority into the Church, and a new kind of minister or Priest, which the multitude would mock rather than venerate.[107]

Underlying Maimonides' hermeneutic, then, is a "Platonizing" political doctrine aimed at establishing a new scholarly caste of philosopher-kings.[108] It is clearly this tendency that is referred to later on in the *Treatise* where, without mentioning Maimonides by name, Spinoza polemicizes against certain philosophizing authors: "If you ask what mysteries they see hidden in Scripture, you will find nothing at all but the inventions of Aristotle or Plato or someone else like that."[109] These interpreters have found nothing in Scripture that was not already "a commonplace among the Pagan philosophers," to whom they have made their own speculations conform.[110] A typical case in point is Maimonides' interpretation of the Garden of Eden story in the *Guide,* I, 2, where Adam is depicted as a philosopher who stayed in perpetual communion with the *intelligibilia* until his sin forced him to abandon speculation and concern himself with the merely human problems of good and evil.[111]

We are now in a position to see that the intention of Spinoza's scriptural hermeneutics is not simply the scholarly reconstruction of biblical meanings but the substitution of one type of authority for another. The aim of the *Treatise* as a whole is nothing less than the replacement of the prophet-priest of the past with the historian-philologist of the present as the authoritative interpreter of Scripture. Spinoza seems aware of the objection that his own form of *peshat* may end up substituting a new secular clerisy for the older priests and rabbis. "Our method requires knowledge of the Hebrew language for which the multitude also cannot give time," Spinoza admits, "but it does not follow that the multitude must trust in the testimony of interpreters."[112]

Rather than attempting to establish himself and followers of his method as a new secular priesthood, Spinoza denies having any such ambitions. "All the things necessary for salvation can easily be perceived in any language, even though the reasons for them are not known, because they are so ordinary and familiar [*communia et usitata*]" and not dependent on the testimony of learned commentators.[113] That Spinoza's actual, as opposed to professed, aim is to create a new clerisy capable of eliciting the multitude's free consent remains the overriding, though never fully stated, theme of the *Treatise*.

The Authority of Reason in the Interpretation of Scripture

Spinoza's insistence in the *Treatise* on the separation of truth and meaning leads him to the conclusion that reason (or truth) should not be subordinated to the claims of Scripture, nor should Scripture be subordinated to the demands of reason. But the separation of meaning and truth by no means entails an abandonment of reason as such. In fact, nothing short of a new conception of reason is necessary to defend the interpretation of Scripture that the *Treatise* sets forth. Thus after dispensing with what he regards as the two major rivals to the correct interpretation of Scripture, Spinoza proceeds to demonstrate the superiority or essential correctness of his own method of reading.

According to the *Treatise,* truth is not a property of Scripture but pertains exclusively to the method of interpreting Scripture. Rather than harmonizing truth with the Bible or the Bible with truth, truth becomes a property of the process of interpretation alone. Spinoza expresses confidence that the *Treatise* contains "the true method of interpreting Scripture" (*veram methodum Scripturam interpretandi*), requiring nothing beyond "the natural light itself."[114] At the end of the seventh chapter, we are told that "the standard of interpretation must be nothing but the natural light which is common to all [*lumen naturale omnibus commune*]."[115] Because reason is "accommodated to the natural and common intelligence and capacity of men" (*naturale et communi hominum ingenio et capacitati accommodata*), it follows that the right of interpretation belongs to everyone individually.[116]

Spinoza's insistence that "the natural light" of reason is the supreme property of every individual denies interpretive authority to a priestly-philosophic elite and gives the individual's natural reason primacy over Scripture. But this method is applicable only to those works whose subject matter consists principally of narratives and events that "surpass our grasp" and what "we know by the natural light" (*limine naturali cognoscimus*).[117] The *Treatise* thus proposes a method that will reduce the unintelligible, the things that "surpass" our understanding, to the intelligible; put another way, it proposes to use principles of intelligibility derivable from "the natural light" of reason alone. The purpose of interpretation in the light of natural reason, then, is not to discover whether what Moses and the prophets said was true but simply to find out what they believed. "We must not in any way infer our answer from the fact that [Moses'] opinion agrees with reason or is contrary to it," Spinoza writes, but only from the reasonableness or the reverse of the method.[118] What, then, ensures the reasonableness of the method?

Spinoza warns the reader that once we are in possession of Scripture and the necessary historical and philological skills to understand it, we must prepare for the task of investigating the beliefs of the prophets. In doing so, we must keep one rule in mind:

> In examining natural things we strive, before all else, to investigate the things which are most universal and common to the whole of nature [*res maxime universalis et toti naturae communes*] — viz., motion and rest, and their laws and rules, which nature always observes and through which it continuously acts — and from these we proceed gradually to other less universal things. In just the same way, the first thing to be sought from the history of Scripture is what is most universal, what is the basis and foundation of the whole of Scripture [*Scripturae basis et fundamentum*], and finally, what all the Prophets commend in it as an eternal teaching, most useful for all mortals."[119]

We can see from this passage that for Spinoza the meaning of Scripture is located in those teachings that appear most universal in two senses of the term. First, what are most universal are those teachings that are applicable to all human beings whatever their circumstances and, second, those repeatedly or consistently asserted teachings that provide "the basis and foundation of the whole of Scripture." Taken together these two meanings constitute the principle of sufficient reason.

Spinoza writes *as if* reason provides a clear-cut procedure for distinguishing which passages in Scripture evince a universal intent and thus serve as a basis for all other biblical teachings and which are obscure and contradictory. This question is hardly minor, as Maimonides' allegorizing method had shown. For Spinoza, however, it is not the obscure, out-of-the-way, or problematic passages of Scripture that contain its meaning but those that are everywhere, consistently repeated. Thus he expresses his "unceasing astonishment" as those "Kabbalistic triflers" whose "insanity" leads them to believe that every jot and tittle of Scripture, even the markings of the particular letters, contain divine secrets.[120] The task of Spinoza's interpretation of Scripture is to distinguish those passages that are clearly, universally significant and accessible to reason from those that have arisen from no "defect in the powers of the natural light but only from the slackness (not to say wicked conduct) of the men who neglected the history of Scripture while they could still put it together."[121]

Once we have discovered what the Bible universally teaches, we can descend to the secondary or derivative teachings, which are explicable only in terms of the particular circumstances and contexts in which they occurred. These secondary teachings are compared to "streams" that flow from a common source but that can only be understood historically, that is, in terms of "what occasion, and at what time, and for whom they were written" (*qua occasione, quo tempore, vel cui scripta fuerint*).[122] Spinoza provides an application of this method to one of the central doctrines of the New Testament:

> When Christ says "blessed are those who mourn, for they shall receive comfort" (Matthew, 5:4), we do not know from this text what kind of mourner he means. But because he teaches later that we should be anxious about nothing except the kingdom of God and his justice, which he commends as the greatest good (see Matthew, 6:33), from this it follows that by mourners he understands only those who mourn for the kingdom of God and the justice which men have neglected. For only this can be mourned by those who love nothing but the divine kingdom or fairness, and who completely scorn what fortune may bring. So also, when he says "to a man who strikes you on the right cheek, turn to him the other also," etc. (Matthew, 5:39).[123]

Spinoza's use of "et cetera" (*et quae deinde sequuntur*) indicates that the injunction to turn the other cheek is not to be understood as universally valid but as valid only for those who find themselves in circumstances similar to the speaker's. Thus Spinoza goes on to say that Christ uttered this injunction not as a lawgiver (*Legislator*) like Moses but as a private person. Furthermore, these words were delivered to those living in corrupt times when the conditions of justice were utterly neglected. A similar doctrine can be found in Lamentations just before the first destruction of Jerusalem (Lam. 3:25–30).[124]

The universal teachings of Scripture are those that are continually asserted without contradiction or inconsistency. For reasons to be examined more fully in the next chapter, the speculative teachings of Scripture are contradictory to one another.[125] Consequently, the universal doctrines consist almost entirely of the moral precepts of Scripture. Among the precepts commended by all the prophets as "eternal and most useful for all mortals" (*aeterna et omnibus mortalibus utilissima*) we find the belief that God is one, that he is omnipotent, that he alone should be worshiped, and that he loves those who worship him and who love their neighbor as themselves.[126] These tenets "and similar things" are everywhere repeated in Scripture so frequently that "there has never been anyone who disputed [their] meaning."[127]

Like the student of physics, the biblical exegete will want to proceed from the diverse evidence provided by Scripture to "certain data and principles."[128] The fewer and more general these principles the better, until one arrives at a single comprehensive principle from which all the biblical teachings follow. For Spinoza, this one simple principle is stated in a variety of ways. Sometimes he speaks of "the teachings of true piety" (*Verae enim pietatis*), which are expressed "in the most familiar words," words that are "very ordinary" and "no less simple and easy to understand."[129] Later he refers to "simplicity and sincerity of heart" as the single, overriding biblical command.[130] Elsewhere, however, Spinoza refers to "the universal foundation" of both Testaments as "the teaching of loving-kindness," which is commended everywhere "in the strongest terms."[131] And he cites Paul (Rom. 13:8) to the effect that obedience to God consists solely in the love of one's neighbor.[132] Other questions are of no matter so far as Scripture is concerned and should be left entirely apart from theology.

The *Treatise*'s clearest and most definitive expression of the universal teaching in Scripture is this: "For from Scripture itself we have perceived its general tendency without any difficulty or ambiguity: to love God above all else, and to love your neighbor as yourself. But this cannot be an interpolation, nor can it be something written by a hasty or erring pen. For if Scripture ever taught anything other than this, it would also have had to teach everything else differently, since this is the foundation of the whole religion. If it were taken away, the whole structure would collapse in a moment. And so such a Scripture would not be that same book we are speaking about here, but an entirely different one."[133]

The one powerful, overriding command of both the Hebrew and Christian Scriptures is, then, love of neighbor, which Spinoza interprets to mean no persecution, no intolerance on the basis of religion. This is a teaching of the highest political importance. It suggests that not only does the Bible forbid persecution but those who practice intolerance stand condemned of heresy. It suggests that intolerance not only is bad as policy but is at odds with the "universal foundation" of religion. Toleration carries the weight of reason behind it ("the supreme right of thinking freely, even concerning religion, is in the hands of each person") and the weight of Scripture.[134] Reason and religion converge on the same moral end.

But does this conclusion not present a problem for Spinoza's method of reading? The teaching of toleration or freedom of mind is the great conclusion of the *Treatise*. That Scripture and the *Treatise* reach the same conclusion seems to contradict Spinoza's initial assertion that reason and theology stand on totally different footings.[135] The separation of truth and meaning in the *Treatise* seems to be contradicted by Spinoza's assertion that "Scripture hands things down and *teaches* them as each person can most easily perceive them."[136] Further, his statement that the conclusions of the *Treatise* are "more confirmed" by the fact that the prophets "*taught* no moral doctrine which does not agree most fully with reason" strikes at the core of his injunction to read Scripture as a "hieroglyphic" work without concern for its truth value.[137] Does not Spinoza here appear to be doing exactly what he accused Maimonides of, namely, accommodating Scripture to his own reason or harmonizing reason and theology? Is he not producing the same kind of rational theology that he elsewhere implies is a contradiction in terms?

Spinoza's answer to this evident contradiction is to maintain that the separation of reason and theology applies only to reason in its scientific or theoretical guise. It need not apply to questions of morality and conduct. There is for Spinoza, following Aristotle and anticipating Kant, a distinctively practical use of reason that is capable of generating moral norms and that is autonomous or semiautonomous from the theoretical or speculative use of reason. The practical use of reason, that is, of the "natural light," does not produce a priori truths like those found in Euclidean geometry. But it can produce moral truths like the prescription for toleration or nonpersecution, which is true not in any speculative sense but in the human and political sense of "most useful for all mortals." Thus although the speculative propositions of Scripture may be no more than primitive or ancient "prejudices," its moral injunctions are more than the relics of an early civilization: they constitute the very core of morality. The command to practice charity and love one's neighbor is as true today as in the time of Moses.

This apparently happy reconciliation of Scripture and moral truth cannot be Spinoza's last word on the subject. In the *Treatise* he maintains that not only are reason and theology two different modes of knowledge, but they operate on two different objects. Theology enjoins obedience to God's law, interpreted to mean no persecution or tolerance of heterodoxy. Philosophy aims at the truth regarding the necessary causes of things.[138] There seems to be no way that Spinoza can consistently harmonize these radically separate spheres of operation.

The most plausible way to account for this contradiction is to note that for the vast majority of humankind a rational ethics is inconceivable. Charity and love of neighbor require a belief in revelation in order to lend them "moral certainty" (*Morali certitudine*).[139] Spinoza understands that certainty in the saving power of Scripture cannot be demonstrated by reason alone. The only basis for the authority of Scripture remains the testimony of the prophets and the apostles.[140] The prophets demonstrated their authority not by their reason and judgment but by their ability to convince people of their authority, that is, by their powers of persuasion. Yet Spinoza also maintains that the authority of the prophets is a prejudice and one that Spinoza hoped to replace with the power and sufficiency of the individual's own rational capacities. Although for many readers "the utility and necessity" (*utilitatem et necessitatem*) of Scripture remains "very great," and Scripture has been "a very great source of comfort to mortals," the goal of the *Treatise* is to replace Scripture with a new moral and political doctrine attuned less to moral comfort than to liberty.[141]

We must conclude that Spinoza's attempt to derive a rational ethics from the very words of Scripture is spurious or at best a strategy "accommodated" to the understanding of his contemporaries. In spite of his effort to vindicate the moral teachings of Scripture, the more radical thrust of the *Treatise* is to show that these teachings are based purely on the imaginative power of uneducated men. Such teachings may continue to be of service for the moral and political education of the multitude, but for the more "prudent" readers Spinoza's aim was to replace Scripture as a basis for authority with individual critical reason

"the truth as it is" or "demonstrated truth giving satisfaction to a single virtuous man."[95]

If we use Maimonides' midrash on this parable as providing the key to his
understanding of Scripture as a whole, we reach the following conclusion. The
Torah is a book for everybody. But precisely because it is a book for everybody,
it will have to address readers with very different talents and intellectual abilities. It will have to speak in different languages to readers with different
capacities. It follows, then, that the figurative or representational language of
the Bible need not be taken as its true teaching. The various biblical an-
thropomorphisms are like the silver settings around the golden apple in Solomon's parable. The external or exoteric meaning is intended for the needs
and psychology of the multitude of readers who have no time, interest, or
aptitude for philosophical speculation and study. The surface meaning of
Scripture serves the socially useful purpose of instilling correct beliefs and
attitudes regarding those things prescribed by the law of Moses.[96]

Spinoza is in fundamental agreement with Maimonides so far as the surface
meaning of Scripture is concerned. He disagrees that there is anything below
or underneath the surface. Thus in the *Treatise* he avers that it is correct to say
that "each passage of Scripture admits various meanings, indeed, contrary
meanings" (*imo contrarios sensus admittere*).[97] It is incorrect, however, to
believe that these "contrary meanings" should be made to yield some rational
interpretation or truth. Thus it is false to proceed from the fact of contradictory meanings to the principle that if the literal meaning clashes with one's
own reason, then the passage must be interpreted in some allegorical sense in
order to bring it into alignment with the truth. The fallacy, then, of Maimonides' "dogmatic" hermeneutics is its claim to bring the Bible into accord with
reason or to make Scripture talk sense.[98]

The principle of Spinoza's *peshat* is that the meaning of a passage derives
solely from the way words and language are used by its author. Whereas
Maimonides approaches biblical language in the manner of a philosopher
seeking layers of meaning, Spinoza does so in the manner of a philologist
asking what an author or text could have meant given the range of linguistic
resources conventionally accessible at the time. Sounding more than a bit like
a contemporary linguistic philosopher, he asserts that "it could never be useful
to anyone to change the meaning of some word" (*nam nemini unquam ex usu
esse potuit, alicujus verbi significationem mutare*) and adds that although it
may be possible for someone to alter or corrupt a speech from some "very rare
book," no one could ever change the meaning of a language to which people
have become accustomed "in speaking and in writing."[99] When reading a
biblical passage, we must be careful "not to be preoccupied with our own
reasoning, insofar as it is founded on the principles of natural knowledge,"

4

From Sacred to Secular History

According to no less an authority than Hegel, Spinoza marks a "testing point" in modern philosophy. Of modern philosophy "it may truly be said: You are either a Spinozist or not a philosopher at all."[1] Spinoza occupies for Hegel an almost unique position in the history of philosophy. What he says of Spinoza he says of virtually no other thinker. "Thought must begin by placing itself at the standpoint of Spinozism; to be a follower of Spinoza is the essential commencement of all philosophy."[2]

The uniqueness of Spinoza's philosophy consists of his demand that philosophy take its point of departure from the one absolute Substance that contains both mind and body. "When one begins to philosophize, the soul must commence by bathing in this ether of the One Substance, in which all that one has held as true has disappeared; this negation of all that is particular, to which every philosopher must have come, is the liberation of the mind and its absolute foundation."[3] What constitutes the "grandeur" of Spinoza's thought is, then, his claim "to renounce all that is determinate and particular, and restrict himself to the One, giving heed to this alone."[4]

Yet it is precisely the "grandeur" of Spinoza's demand that philosophy consider everything under the aspect of eternity that conceals, according to Hegel, its greatest weakness. Spinoza lacked an adequate conception of time or temporality. In his haste to proceed *sub specie aeternitatis,* Spinoza forgot that all thought, including his own, is written *sub specie durationis,* which cannot but affect the content of what is thought. Spinoza's philosophy, we are told, is fixated on the absolute Substance, which alone is actual or real. The human and political world is said to be merely a "mode" or articulation of this Substance and, as such, is strictly subordinate to the eternal or divine order. For this reason, Hegel avers, Spinoza's philosophy might best be called an Acosmism, for in it the "particular" lacks any intrinsic meaning, and intelligibility is ascribed to God, who alone is substantial.[5]

What is "philosophically inadequate" in Spinoza is said to derive from a failure of the historical sense: "For Spinoza . . . there exists only absolute universal substance as the non-particularized, the truly real—all that is particular and individual, my subjectivity and spirituality, has . . . no absolute existence. . . . As all differences and determinations of things and consciousness simply go back into the one substance, one may say that in the system of Spinoza all things are merely cast down into this abyss of annihilation. But from this abyss nothing comes out. . . . This is what we find philosophically inadequate with Spinoza."[6] A fact that has gone virtually unrecognized is that Hegel traces Spinoza's lack of a historical sense back to his Jewish roots. The "profound unity" of Spinoza's philosophy, "the identity of the finite and the infinite in God," is said to be "an echo from Eastern lands."[7] The chief difference between Spinoza's standpoint and Hegel's is that "through the agency of Christianity concrete individuality is in the modern world present throughout in spirit."[8] Spinoza's "Oriental" philosophy of identity failed not only to admit particularity but also to recognize the triune nature of the absolute.[9]

I cite these passages because they (or others like them) are often used to indict, sometimes to commend, Spinoza as an "unhistorical" thinker.[10] To be sure, this view is not false. But the commonplace that Spinoza lacks a theory of history also misidentifies the ways a thinker's ideas may be properly called historical. In the preceding chapter we saw how Spinoza's reading of Scripture helped to initiate a profound revolution in biblical criticism and hermeneutics according to which Holy Writ must be understood not as the revealed word of God but as a historical document that can be properly understood only in context.[11] Spinoza's contextual reconstruction of biblical meanings is itself a modification of the medieval hermeneutic of accommodation. This principle of accommodation turned on the Latin phrase *Scriptura humane loquitur,* or roughly "Scripture speaks the language of man."[12] Spinoza took the phrase to mean that not only does Scripture speak or accommodate itself to human language but it is uniquely adapted to the cultural and political circumstances of its time. Scripture speaks the language of man and is a thoroughly human book.

Spinoza went even further than traditional biblical exegetes by transforming the principle of accommodation into a full-blown theory of the relation between political institutions and time. In the *Treatise* he reworked biblical narrative, transforming it from a sacred history (*historia sacra*) to a secular history (*historia profana*). Spinoza was not the first person to think about the relation between the eternal order of ideas and the temporal order of human passions, actions, and institutions. Medieval philosophers and exegetes like Maimonides had accommodated their views on human and historical time to the account of creation in the book of Genesis. According to this account, the analysis of human political institutions remains suspended between two eternities. Between God's creation of the world, which marks the beginning of time, and his redemption of humanity (or some portion of it), which marks the messianic age yet to come, the world of earthly polities remains, so to speak, suspended in midair. Spinoza turned the apocalyptic and messianic motifs of scriptural theology into a radically secular theory of political time, substituting an idea of progress for the older rhetoric of accommodation.

Secularization is inseparable from the general dynamics of modernity.[13] In spite of the wealth of connotations that the word has acquired over time, as a term of both abuse and proud defiance, the modern world is thought to be a secularization of biblical themes in virtually all of its dimensions. Modern economic life has been called a secularization of the Puritan idea of the "calling," with its ethic of worldly asceticism and outward activity.[14] Modern democracy with its doctrine of equal human rights is called a secularization of the Christian idea of the dignity and equality of each individual in the eyes of God. And even modern revolutionary movements, like communism, with their expectation of political redemption, are characterized as secularizations of apocalyptic messianism and the biblical conception of paradise.[15] Indeed, as a twentieth-century observer has put it, "all significant political concepts are secularized theological concepts."[16]

At the beginning of the modern era, the concept of secularization had a relatively precise meaning. "Secularization" is the English equivalent of the Latin *saeculum*, which means something like "age," "world," or "generation." In medieval Europe secularization meant the legal or canonical act whereby a person left the cloister or monastery to return to the *saeculum*, thus becoming a secular person. From the Carolingian age onward, the term acquired a political meaning designating the appropriation of church lands and other religious holdings by the state or worldly powers, as in England under the reign of Henry VIII. The secularization of monasteries and ecclesiastical properties meant their passage or transfer from the sphere of religious meanings and functions to the world of "everyday life."[17]

Secularization was simultaneously hastened by developments within Protestant theology. Protestantism has been described as "an immense shrinkage in the scope of the sacred in reality, as compared to its Catholic adversary."[18] This "shrinkage" concerns a reduction of the sacramental apparatus of religion and the general "desacralization" of the world, a quantitative reduction in the size and scope of the sacred in reality. This process entailed a separation of political and intellectual sectors of society—and even the separation of aspects of theology itself—from the protective band of religious institutions and symbols. The result of this secularization was the creation of a reality polarized between a radically transcendent divinity shorn of all anthropomorphic attributes and an utterly worldly humanity void of all sacred qualities.[19] The state and society were progressively cut off from God's grace, and religion became subject to "internalization" or privatization. Under these changed circumstances, religion came to occupy a special "private" sphere of its own increasingly cut off from its traditional societal and public functions.

Secularization first presented itself not as a break with religion but as a return to original elements of the Bible. The secularization of the world, hastened by the Protestant Reformation, was seen as the completion or perfection of an original biblical teaching. Modern thought, especially the philosophy of history, was the bearer of the highest realization of the Christian spirit.[20] Hegel, writing in the first generation after the French Revolution, could thus see the modern world with its abolition of the distinction between clergy and laity, its spread of the doctrine of universal human rights, and its recognition of "reason as the rose in the cross of the present" (*Die Vernunft als die Rose im Kreuze der Gegenwart*) as the realization of the Christian principle of freedom.[21]

Yet alongside the concept of secularization as a return to the roots of the biblical tradition was another, more radical idea of secularization, which was viewed not as the heir to but as the replacement of the Bible. Thinkers of the radical Enlightenment, of whom Spinoza was a preeminent example, saw history as a progressive process of secularization, by which they meant the gradual and steady substitution of reason for superstition and science for religion, along with the moral and intellectual emancipation of the individual from "self-incurred tutelage." Kant himself established the "motto" for the radical enlightenment: *Sapere aude*, "Have the courage to use your own understanding."[22]

Those spearheading the Enlightenment saw themselves as engaged in a life and death struggle with the adherents of religion or orthodoxy, who continued to believe in such supernatural phenomena as miracles, the creation of the world ex nihilo, and particular providence. Voltaire's famous *écrasez l'infâme* was nothing short of a battle cry against all ecclesiastical institutions. Reduced to a primitive or prelogical *mentalité,* biblical orthodoxy had to disappear to make room for its replacement by science and the rational apprehension of truth. The older "kingdom of darkness" would have to be replaced by the new "century of light" and "age of criticism."[23]

In Spinoza's conception of a secular political time the Enlightenment was not just a process but a progress. This progress represented a war waged on two fronts. The two poles of moral and intellectual progress are imagination and reason. In the *Ethics* and the *Treatise* alike Spinoza presents an essentially progressive account of the transition from a life dominated by fear, passion, and superstition to one based on autonomous, self-governing reason. A life dominated by the passions is one of servitude and weakness due to our ignorance of causes, whereas the rational life is one of action, a life in which the more we reflect on the order and coherence of our ideas, the greater becomes our awareness of our power and free agency.

The control of the passions is for Spinoza a progressive activity in both the life of the individual and the collective life of nations. Progress takes place at both the ontogenetic and phylogenetic levels of development. It takes place in the life of individuals as they struggle to control the ill effects of the passions of hatred, anger, envy, and so on. These passions are assimilated to aspects of their bodily nature, which, like the forces of external nature, are subject to rational mastery and control through the new theoretical science contained in the *Ethics.* This new science is regarded as a mental hygiene or therapeutic that can purge the mind of the causes of superstition in order to increase self-mastery. This project is conceived along the lines of the famous "quarrel between the ancients and the moderns," in which scientific and rational knowledge generally come to replace mythical and religious beliefs based on revelation and prophecy.[24]

Moral and intellectual progress has an important counterpart in Spinoza's account of social and political progress in the central books of the *Treatise.* Here terms like "barbarism" and "civilization" recapitulate those like "imagination" and "reason." Spinoza sets out an account of the transition from the early Hebrew theocracy to the modern democratic-republican state. A crucial part of this theory of historical progress concerns the secularization or desacralization of the state. "Sacred history," as André Tosel remarks, "loses its sacrality."[25] The ancient theocracy corresponds to a world dominated by religious passions and superstition; the modern republic, to the free use of reason, maximum scope being granted to the expression of heterodox religious and political views in the public arena. In the course of history no value is attached to "ancient times," which are seen not as a golden age but as a period of ignorance and poverty, when life was "solitary, poor, nasty, brutish, and short."

The modern state is no longer associated with charismatic leaders like Moses and the prophets who claim to speak for God; rather, it is the product of the *libera multitudo,* who join together in a social contract for the sake of protecting their natural rights and liberties. On this view, the social contract is not an act completed in the distant past but a goal yet to be accomplished in historical time. The republic figures for Spinoza much like one of Kant's "regulative ideals."[26] According to Spinoza, the *libera respublica* cannot be grasped by reference to any existing state of affairs, although it has been most closely approximated in the Holland of de Witt's administration. It figures instead as an ideal of reason that can point or guide the way to action even when those ideals seem to be at odds with experience. In this respect, the *Treatise* itself becomes an agent for progress, an intervention in the historical process that it would otherwise attempt to describe and explain.

These two forms of progress do not represent two different histories but one. Political changes do not occur after or following moral and intellectual advances; nor is morality dependent on changes in political structures and institutions. In keeping with Spinoza's dictum that the "order and connection of ideas is the same as the order and connection of things" (*ordo et connexio idearum idem est, ac ordo et connexio rerum*) there can be no changes in morality without corresponding social and political changes, because morality is embedded in, indeed partially constitutive of, social and political institutions.[27] To describe the one is to describe the other. Spinoza's account of moral progress from superstition to enlightenment begins with the biblical conception of prophecy. The critique of prophecy is the basis of the critique of revealed religion as such. Only after discrediting the claims of prophecy and revelation can Spinoza present a new set of purely secular or rational principles on which to ground the democratic-republican state.

The Critique of Prophecy

The *Treatise* begins with two chapters entitled "Of Prophecy" and "Of the Prophets." It is not immediately evident why Spinoza presents this subject first. One possibility is that the belief in prophets was a cardinal pillar of the old orthodoxy and that Spinoza repeats or imitates this orthodoxy. In this respect, the *Treatise* would seem to be more a traditional than a revolutionary work. It very quickly becomes clear, however, that Spinoza starts with this traditional theme in order to cut the ground out from under orthodox belief. He attacks the traditional understanding of prophets and prophecy for two reasons. First, he denies that prophets are endowed with a supra-rational knowledge or revelation, and, second, he disputes that there is anything miraculous or mysterious about the phenomenon of prophecy. The intention informing this twofold attack is to liberate reason from what Spinoza regards as its subservience to theological dogma and to substitute a new rational ethic of self-rule and autonomy. Let us see how the *Treatise* attempts to accomplish this end.

The first sentence of the first chapter of the *Treatise* reads as follows: "Prophecy, *or* Revelation, is the certain knowledge of some thing revealed, by God to men" (*Prophetia sive Revelation est rei alicujus certa cognitio a Deo hominibus revelata*).[28] The Hebrew word for "prophet" is *navi*, which means "speaker" or "interpreter." In the context of Scripture, the word applies only to those to whom God has spoken. So far, then, Spinoza's definition of prophecy stays within the bounds of tradition. But in virtually the same breath that he defines "prophecy" as *certa cognitio* Spinoza remarks that prophecy includes "natural knowledge" (*cognitionem naturalem*) acquired through the "natural light."[29] From this he infers that natural knowledge achieved through experience is to be considered the equal of prophecy obtained through communication with God.[30]

After identifying prophetic insight with ordinary knowledge, Spinoza then denies that knowledge of nature deserves to be called prophecy.[31] Natural knowledge can be taught to others, but prophecy cannot. Whereas a scientist or a philosopher can teach others how to become scientists or philosophers, a prophet cannot teach someone else how to be a prophet. Prophecy is a special gift that can be neither learned nor taught. In a footnote Spinoza suggests that "if the men who listened to prophets became prophets," prophecy itself would lose its special status, for "hearers would rely, not on the testimony and authority of the prophet himself, but on divine revelation itself, and internal testimony [*interno testimonio*] as he does."[32]

But after identifying prophecy with natural knowledge in chapter 1, Spinoza argues in chapter 2 that prophecy is in fact inferior to natural knowledge. Prophecy requires an external "sign" to vouchsafe its authenticity, whereas natural knowledge contains its own protocols of verification.[33] The statement that prophecy requires a sign to authenticate it is implicated in Spinoza's judgment that prophecy pertains to moral rather than speculative truth. A truth in physics does not require some additional sign or mark to guarantee its credibility. Nor is a scientific truth guaranteed because of the personal testimony or authority of a particular scientist. The theory of relativity is not true because Einstein stated it. Prophecy, in contrast, is dependent on some additional sign or omen for its credibility. The inferiority of prophecy to natural knowledge is now related to the fact that prophecy is unable to give a rational explanation of itself but requires some additional authority to verify it. The sign in question is the moral goodness or reputation of the prophet.[34] This need for additional corroboration signifies a deficiency in prophetic knowledge.

Spinoza now prepares the reader for the conclusion toward which the discussion has been tending, namely, that prophetic knowledge is a function of the imagination rather than the rational intellect. The source of prophecy is not God but the psychological imaginings of the prophet. To ascribe prophetic insight to the power of God is merely a way of expressing one's ignorance about the psychological mechanisms that control the human mind. It is "the nature of the mind" that is the "first cause" of divine revelation.[35] Statements like "God spoke to a prophet" and "God commanded a prophet" are to be explicated by a series of natural causes, including the prophet's own mental state and emotional disposition.

It is of great importance for Spinoza that in every instance the prophets' teachings were given in accordance with "the opinions and capacity of each prophet," so that what one prophet found convincing would be unconvincing to another:

> Prophecy varied, finally, according to differences in the opinions of the prophets. To the Magi, who believed in the trifles of astrology, Christ's birth was revealed through the imagination of a star rising in the east (see Matthew 2). To the augurs of Nebuchadnezzar the destruction of Jerusalem was revealed in the entrails of animals (see Ezekiel 21:26). The same King also understood this from oracles and from the direction of arrows which he hurled up into the air. Again, to those prophets who believed that men act from free choice and from their own power, God was revealed as indifferent, and as unaware of future human actions. We shall demonstrate all these things separately from Scripture itself.[36]

The identification of prophecy with the imaginative faculty has the function of turning it into a purely natural or psychological phenomenon. While admitting that prophets were endowed with a "singular virtue, beyond what is ordinary" (*virtutem singularem et supra*), not bestowed on others, Spinoza adds in a footnote that their virtue does not transcend "the limits of human nature." He compares prophetic power to the art of composing poetry extempore, a gift that is rare but still human.[37] The implication is that prophecy was not a sign of divine election, nor was it confined to the land of Israel or to speakers of the Hebrew language. Rather, all nations possessed prophets, even if they were called by different names.[38] The prophets Isaiah and Jeremiah were no different in kind from the soothsayers, shamans, and magicians reported by other ancient peoples.[39]

Spinoza explains the superstitious belief in the miraculous power of prophecy by means of a philological point. Biblical Hebrew, he says, lacked a language for expressing the proximate or mediate causes of events. He provides an extensive catalogue of uses of the biblical term *ruach,* frequently translated as "spirit" or "spirit of God," to demonstrate the number of commonplace events ascribed directly to the will of God.[40] The term is translated variously as "breath" (Pss. 135:17), "life" (1 Sam. 30:12), "courage" (Josh. 2:11), "disposition of mind" (Num. 14:24), and "will" (Ezek. 1:12) to explain the causes of events associated with prophetic inspiration. For example:

> And in this sense, the Jews used to refer everything which surpassed their power of understanding, and whose natural causes they did not, at that point in time, know, to God. So, a storm was called *ge'arat yehowah,* God's rebuke, and thunder and lightning were called God's arrows, for they thought that God kept the winds shut up in caves, which they called God's treasuries. In this opinion they differed from the Pagans in that they believed that it was not Aeolus, but God, who was their ruler. For this reason also, miracles are called works of God, i.e., works to be astonished at. . . . Therefore, when unusual works of nature are called works of God, and trees of unusual size are called trees of God, it is no wonder that in Genesis the strongest men, and those of great stature, are called sons of God, even when they are immoral robbers and libertines.[41]

Spinoza's naturalistic reduction of prophecy and prophetic knowledge to the facts of human psychology is clearly an attack on the canonical treatment of that subject by Maimonides, who is mentioned in the *Treatise* for the first time in chapter 1.[42] Maimonides treats the topic of prophecy in a number of places in both his *halakhic* and his philosophic works. In the *Mishneh Torah* he asserts that "it is one of the basic principles of religion that God inspires men with the prophetic gift."[43] In the same text he refers to the prophet as distinguished by "great wisdom and strong moral character" and as one who "by his rational faculty always has his passions under control, and possesses a broad and sedate mind."[44]

In the *Guide,* Maimonides takes up this theme again, asking whether prophets and prophecy are purely natural phenomena or whether they contain some element of the mysterious.[45] Here as elsewhere Maimonides canvasses a variety of opinions before stating his own. Among the "multitude" of the pagans, as well as "the common people professing our Law," there are those who profess a belief in the wholly miraculous character of prophecy. On this view, the prophet is singled out arbitrarily by God for reasons beyond human comprehension. Among "philosophers" a wholly different opinion prevails. On this view, prophecy is produced by "a certain perfection in the nature of man"; that is, an individual "who is perfect with respect to his rational and moral qualities . . . will necessarily become a prophet." Far from being mysterious and beyond the rational intellect, prophecy is understood here as "a perfection that belongs to us *by nature*."[46]

After considering the case that prophecy is either against nature or according to nature, Maimonides states his own opinion, which, he says, is "the opinion of our Law and the foundation of our doctrine." This opinion is "identical with the philosophic opinion except in one thing": that an individual may be perfect in his natural capacities and may still be denied the gift of prophecy.[47] The natural prerequisites of prophecy include a perfect intellect, perfect morality, a perfect power of the imagination, courage, and the power of leadership. But in addition to all our natural capacities, prophecy requires the intervention of the divine will, which Maimonides likens to something miraculous. Prophecy, then, is neither wholly natural nor wholly against nature; rather, it "enters into what is natural."[48] Whereas there must be a certain "natural preparedness in [a prophet's] original constitution," the gift of prophecy is ultimately a gift from God.[49]

In the *Guide*, II, 36, Maimonides states his conception of prophecy as follows: "Know that the true reality and quiddity of prophecy consist in its being an overflow overflowing from God, may He be cherished and honored, through the intermediation of the Active Intellect, toward the rational faculty in the first place and thereafter toward the imaginative faculty. This is the highest degree of man and the ultimate term of perfection that can exist for his species; and this state is the ultimate term of perfection for the imaginative faculty."[50] Prophecy is said here to be "the highest degree of man" and "the ultimate term of perfection" for the species. In what, then, does this perfection consist?

What distinguishes the prophet is more than the degree of moral and intellectual perfection. In this respect, he would be the equal of, but no better than, the philosopher whose classical representative was described in Plato's *Republic* and Aristotle's *Ethics*. Both the prophet and the philosopher have achieved the perfection of the rational faculty, or "Active Intellect," which Maimonides describes as an "overflow" from God. What distinguishes the prophet from the philosophers is, above all, the perfection of the "imaginative faculty."

The imagination is described in the first instance as a bodily faculty. It is thus dependent on "the best possible temperament, the best possible size, and the purest possible matter."[51] But although the imagination depends on a perfect body and a perfect character, it is not equivalent to them. The imagination is the source of "vision" through which God communicates his revelation. The prophet is, then, superior to the philosopher because he has everything that the philosopher has and in addition a kind of "X" imparted by the power of the imagination. It is the faculty of the imagination that allows its possessor to communicate God's revelation in images to others in language that each can understand. One might almost say that it is the imagination that enables the prophet to communicate directly to each according to his ability and his needs.[52]

Now we can begin to see what is at stake in Spinoza's psychological explanation of prophecy. The prophets, he everywhere maintains, were not philosophers but ignorant and passionate men who spoke according to their imaginings. In particular he denies the Maimonidean equation of the prophet with the philosopher plus the power of a perfect imagination. The power of prophecy implies not "a more perfect mind, but only a more vivid imagination [*vividiore imaginatione*]," Spinoza declares at one point, adding later that "prophets were endowed not with a more perfect mind [*perfectiore mente*], but instead with a power of imagining unusually vividly."[53] What the prophets variously said with regard to God was flagrantly contradictory and must accordingly be understood by their individual psychologies:

> [A prophecy] varied according to his temperament in this way: if the prophet was cheerful, victories, peace, and things which move men in turn to joy were revealed to him; for such men usually imagine things of that kind more frequently; on the other hand, if the prophet was sad, wars, punishments, and all evils were revealed to him; and thus, as the prophet was compassionate, calm, prone to anger, severe, etc., to that extent he was more ready for one kind of revelation than for another. It varied also according to the disposition of his imagination, in the following way. If the prophet was refined, he perceived the mind of God in a refined style; but if he was confused, then he perceived it confusedly. It varied similarly concerning those revelations which were represented through images. If the prophet was a countryman, bulls and cows were represented to him; if he was a soldier, generals and armies; if he was a courtier, the royal throne and things of that kind.[54]

Even "more important," what the prophets said about the nature and attributes of God is utterly unreliable except as a residue of their own opinions and prejudices. There is no reason to believe that prophets had great speculative powers or were bearers of profound philosophic truths. Instead, "the prophecies *or* representations also varied according to the opinions of the prophets," who in turn held "various, indeed contrary, opinions and . . . prejudices."[55]

The conclusion that Spinoza draws is emphatic. "Prophecy never rendered the prophets more learned [*doctiores*]," but "left them with their preconceived opinions, that for that reason we are not at all bound to believe them concerning speculative matters [*res mere speculativas*]."[56] In all matters relating to the speculative employment of the intellect, the prophets maintained "quite ordinary opinions about God" (*admodum vulgares de Deo habuerunt opiniones*).[57] From all of this, Spinoza concludes that the prophets were not to be praised for "the loftiness and excellence of their understanding" (*ingenii sublimitatem*) but for their "piety and constancy of heart (*pietatem, et animi constantiam*)."[58]

Spinoza's critique of prophecy is intended to serve two ends. In the first place, the belief in the authority of prophets is evidence of the continuing dominance of the imaginative-affective life over the individual. The imagination is understood here not as the perfection of the intellect but as its antithesis. Imagination begins where reason leaves off. The imagination is the source of intellectual confusion and is thus the seedbed of revealed religion. The critique of prophecy is thus intended to substitute a life of rational planning and autonomy for one of dependence on the passions and emotions.

Second, the critique of prophecy is intended to effect our liberation not just from the internal yoke of the passions but from external political control and authority. The gist of Spinoza's difference with Maimonides is that prophets are not philosophers but something like charismatic political leaders.[59] These leaders, like Moses, may be at times functionally necessary; once their particular historical function is complete, however, they are responsible for maintaining their people in a condition of political tutelage and immaturity. Prophecy may have been a necessary stage in the historical drama of human emancipation, but it now stands as a barrier to self-government and autonomy. The *imaginatio*, then, is more than the source of epistemic confusion; it is the basis of mankind's continuing reliance on external authority. A thoroughgoing critique of prophecy is a necessary first step toward the emancipation of the individual.

Prophecy, Politics, and Law

Spinoza's attack on the authority of prophecy was a thinly veiled attack on the authority of Maimonides. Behind that attack, however, is nothing short of a critique of Moses himself. According to Maimonides and the tradition for which he spoke, Moses was not simply another prophet but the bearer of divine legislation. It is a principle of the Jewish religion that there never has been, and never will be, a prophet the like of Moses again (Deut. 34:10). Maimonides repeats in the *Guide*: "It is a fundamental principle of our Law that there will never be another Law . . . [that] there will never be a Law except the one that is the Law of Moses our Master."[60]

The unique legislative character of Mosaic prophecy is developed in the

Guide, where Maimonides argues as follows. Man is by nature a political animal intended for life in society. But owing to the "manifold composition" of the species, human beings are more unlike one another than are the members of any other species. It is the sheer variety of human "moral habits" that makes us peculiarly dependent on law and therefore lawgivers. Laws are, however, of two kinds. The first kind consists of those laws that aim at the health, protection, and security of the body; Maimonides refers to this type by the Greek word *nomos* to indicate a human law or convention. The second is that whose purpose is the health of the soul, chiefly our moral and intellectual perfection. This type of law is, properly speaking, a divine law, and its harbinger is a prophet. It is the aim of the prophet to bring all human beings to the peak of moral and speculative perfection or to the level of "the man who is perfect among the people."[61]

The summary of the two kinds of law further indicates two very different kinds of political communities. Corresponding to the first type of law are communities whose chief ends are securing peace and political stability. A nomocratic community is a city whose legislation is intended to obtain "the abolition in it of injustice and oppression," as well as attain "a certain something deemed to be happiness." The bringer of this type of law may be a prophet, but only one who has a developed imaginative faculty.[62] A second type of community is based on the divine law, which is brought by a prophet in the truest sense of the term, that is, one who is perfect in both intellect and imagination. The type of community governed by divine law is a theocracy insofar as its legislation is concerned with bringing about the highest degree of perfection in its citizens. A theocracy, then, is a regime which controls for both "the soundness of the circumstances pertaining to the body" and also "the soundness of belief" and the giving of "correct opinions with regard to God."[63]

The two kinds of regimes correspond to the two orders of human perfection. The first order of perfection consists of "the welfare of the body," which is acquired through one of two means: (1) through the abolition of wrongdoing by giving up claims to unlimited power and "being forced to do that which is useful to the whole"[64] and (2) through the acquisition of those "moral qualities that are useful for life in society" so that the community may be well ordered. The second order of perfection, which is "indubitably greater in nobility" than the first, is the "welfare of the soul." Bodily health is a precondition for the health of the soul. Perfection of the second order consists in the acquisition of "correct opinions" concerning "all the things that it is within the capacity of man to know."[65] This perfection in the strictest sense refers neither to actions nor to moral qualities but to "opinions toward which speculation has led and that investigation has rendered compulsory."[66] Maimonides notes in passing that the second order of perfection cannot be achieved at the expense of the first because "a man cannot represent to himself an intelligible even if he has been taught to understand it . . . if he is in pain or is very hungry or is thirsty or is hot or is very cold." Once these needs have been satisfied, "it is possible to achieve the ultimate, which is indubitably more noble and is the only cause of permanent preservation."[67]

It is only the law of Moses that provides for both perfections. In the *Guide*, III, 27, we read:

> The true Law, then, which we have already made clear is unique — namely, the Law of Moses our Master — has come to bring us both perfections, I mean the welfare of the states of people in their relations with one another through the abolition of reciprocal wrongdoing and through the acquisition of a noble and excellent character. In this way the preservation of the population of the country and their permanent existence in the same order become possible, so that every one of them achieves his perfection; I mean also the soundness of the beliefs and the giving of correct opinions through which ultimate perfection is achieved.[68]

This is not the end of the matter, however. The law of Moses may aim at the ultimate perfection of human nature, namely, "the giving of correct opinions," but these opinions are also of two kinds. There are, first, "necessary beliefs," which exist "for the sake of political welfare."[69] Among these politically useful beliefs are, for example, the belief that God is angry with those who disobey him and that he responds instantly to the prayers of those who have been wronged.[70] Maimonides refrains from drawing the cynical conclusion that these beliefs are like the "noble lies" of Plato's *Republic,* but he does remark that such beliefs have a "clear cause" and a "manifest utility."[71]

Opinions in the second class consist of true beliefs concerning "ultimate perfection" which the law has communicated "in a summary way."[72] These opinions concern such things as the existence of the deity and his unity, knowledge, power, and eternity. These are clearly the speculative issues alluded to in the introduction to the *Guide* about which Maimonides said he would reveal only "the chapter headings." These are the kinds of opinions that have no obvious utility or whose utility is hidden by their "external meaning."[73] The correct opinions are those which concern "the whole of being" and which include all "the theoretical sciences," such as physics and metaphysics. Maimonides notes that the Mosaic law does not directly communicate the correct opinions regarding the "ultimate ends," but communicates them in a summary or elliptical way by commanding people to love God "with all thy heart, and with all thy soul, and with all thy might" (Deut. 6:5).

Spinoza attacks the Maimonidean conception of the Mosaic law at precisely the point where it seems most vulnerable, that is, in its claim to divinity. Even here, we can see a certain equivocation in his opening pages. To some degree, Spinoza respects the traditional understanding of Mosaic prophecy. Unlike the other prophets discussed in the *Treatise,* Moses is singled out out for having heard a real voice and for communicating directly with God.[74] This uniqueness makes it possible to conceive of prophecy as the revelation of truths that surpass the capacity of human reason.

Yet just as Spinoza prepares the reader to accept the authority of Moses, he turns the scriptural account against itself. Moses is presented not as the bearer of an absolute, unchanging, and eternal Torah but as a political leader whose sole function was to establish a national sovereignty for his people. Spinoza takes the legislative character of Mosaic prophecy and gives it an unequivocally political interpretation. Moses is to be understood as a statesman and national leader in much the same way as any political founder is to be so understood. Implicitly Moses is assimilated to the other founders of classical antiquity — Theseus, Cyrus, Romulus — as, in fact, Machiavelli had already done.[75]

Several features in Spinoza's treatment of Mosaic prophecy suggest that his target is Maimonides. The first is the repeated assertion that Mosaic prophecy was a purely political legislation intended to achieve only the transition from bondage in Egypt to nationhood. Moses appears in the *Treatise* as the bringer of a new national *nomos,* but scarcely as the bearer of a divine law. Spinoza takes an almost malicious glee in showing how Mosaic prophecy emerged out of a background of slavery and social degradation:

> Nor is it credible that men accustomed to the superstitions of the Egyptians, unsophisticated and worn out by the most wretched bondage, would have understood anything sensible about God, or that Moses would have taught them anything other than a way of living [*modum vivendi*] — and that not as a Philosopher, so that after some time they might be constrained to live well from freedom of mind [*ex animi libertate*], but as a Legislator [*Legis*], so that they would be constrained by the command of the Law [*ex imperio Legis*] to live well. So the way of living well, *or* true life, and the worship and love of God were to them more bondage than true freedom, and the grace and gift of God.[76]

Spinoza draws a number of striking, even startling conclusions from his assertions. Even though prophecy, we have seen, was a universal phenomenon of the ancient world, common to Jews and Gentiles, Spinoza now maintains that the Mosaic prophecy is radically particularist. In the third chapter of the *Treatise,* Spinoza argues that the divine "election" or "chosenness" of the

Jewish people applied only during the period of their political sovereignty. "The Laws God revealed to Moses were nothing but the legislation of the particular state of the Hebrews" at that time; no one else was obliged to accept them, and "even the Hebrews were bound by them only so long as their state lasted."[77] In a passage reminiscent of Machiavelli, Spinoza maintains that the ancient Hebrews were chosen only with respect to their political success; in regard to matters concerning true happiness "they were equal to the other nations."[78]

In suggesting that the belief in divine election is a fundamentally political designation historically binding only for the period of national sovereignty, Spinoza does much to undermine the biblical view which holds that the Jewish people have a special and absolutely unique mission (Deut. 4:7, 8, 32; Deut. 10:15). This mission, according to the book of Exodus, is to live as "a kingdom of priests and a holy nation" (Exod. 19:6), that is, to live by the entire body of Mosaic law. The Jewish people were chosen to serve as a model for all humanity in terms of righteousness and justice. But Spinoza denies that the biblical view of chosenness has anything at all to do with moral, to say nothing of intellectual, perfection. There is no such thing as a people chosen in respect of their moral and intellectual attributes.[79] These qualities are more or less randomly distributed among the human race, so to say that one nation is chosen over another is simply a way of expressing the desire for that nation to be superior to or to rule over the other. The belief in election is nothing less than a mark of vanity or national pride.[80]

In the *Treatise* Spinoza devastatingly reduces the promise of God's election to the question of political success. God, like nature, apparently favors the rule of the powerful. Thus the law of Moses is said to promise no other reward for obedience than "the continual prosperity of their state [*imperii continua felicitas*] and the other conveniences of this life [*vitae commoda*]."[81] Basing his evidence on a New Testament source (Mark 10:21), Spinoza denies that the Mosaic law ever promised eternal life; at most, it offered security and its attendant advantages, which he interprets to mean political or military hegemony.[82]

Two passages among many in the *Treatise* suggest that the Mosaic law had nothing to do with any special intellectual or "priestly" qualities: "It is only by this, then, that the nations are distinguished from one another: by reason of the social order and of the laws under which they live and by which they are directed. Therefore, the Hebrew nation was not chosen by God before others by reason of its intellect or of its peace of mind, but by reason of the social order and of the fortune by which it acquired a state and by which it kept [a state] for so many years."[83] Spinoza adds: "Since God is equally well disposed to all and chose the Hebrews only with respect to their social order and their state, we conclude that each Jew, considered alone and outside that social order and state, possesses no gift of God which would place him above other men and that there is no difference between him and a gentile."[84]

Not only does Spinoza deny any special providence for the Jewish people, he maintains that the Mosaic law is coercive and paternalistic. It spoke "according to the Hebrews' power of understanding" (*ad Hebraeorum captum locutum*) rather than to the truth.[85] Moses is thus said to have treated his fellow Jews "in the same way parents customarily do children who are lacking in all reason," that is, by holding out rewards for obedience and threats for transgressions.[86] Even the image of God as a "lawgiver or prince" who is alternately harsh and merciful represents a concession to popular understanding, for people generally were unable to develop any elevated sense of the deity.[87] Judaism is presented as the archetypal religion of fear. In Kantian terms, we could say that it is a form of heteronomy aimed at keeping its adherents in a perpetual state of tutelage and immaturity rather than elevating them to a condition of moral autonomy.

This consolidation of political and ecclesiastical power serves two functions in Spinoza's rewriting of scriptural history. In the first place, it had the function of insulating and to some degree protecting the Jewish people at the time of their liberation. It helps account for the survival of the Jews even after the loss of the state. The question posed by Spinoza at the end of chapter 3 is, How did the Jews, unique among the nations, manage to sustain themselves as a people even in the absence of a state? The traditional explanation was, By particular providence. God had chosen the Jewish people to fulfill a special historical mission. It is important to note in this context that Spinoza was almost an exact contemporary of Sabbatai Zevi, who brought Jewish messianic hopes to their apex, proclaiming himself messiah in 1666.[88]

Moreover, we know from Spinoza's correspondence that he took a keen interest in the possibility of a Jewish return to the land of Israel. In a letter from Henry Oldenburg, in Oxford, written about the time of the messianic frenzy surrounding Sabbatai Zevi we read: "Everyone here is talking of a report that the Jews, after remaining scattered for more than two thousand years, are about to return to their country. . . . I should like to know what the Jews of Amsterdam have heard about the matter, and how they are affected by such important tidings which, if true, would assuredly seem to harbinger the end of the world."[89] We do not know Spinoza's answer, if any. It seems likely, however, that the final paragraphs of chapter 3 of the *Treatise* constitute his response to the upsurge in messianic expectations even after Sabbatai's announced apostasy.

In these paragraphs Spinoza suggests a purely political explanation for the phenomenon of Jewish survival. Like the Chinese, who have "most scrupulously" adopted a distinguishing mark that they wear on their heads (the pigtail) in order to keep themselves apart, so have the Jews ensured their survival by adopting a peculiar set of laws and customs that have set them off from the rest of the nations.[90] Jewish history obeys the same rules as the history of other nations. These customs and such "external rites" as circumcision have marked off the Jews, but they have also drawn the resentment of the other nations, and it is Gentile hatred more than anything else that has preserved the Jewish nation through the centuries.[91]

Spinoza goes on to suggest a second and far more damaging consequence of Mosaic law. Adherence to the law has made the Jews into an unwarlike, unaggressive people unable to regain their political sovereignty. The belief in the divine character of Mosaic prophecy has encouraged a messianic politics that has prompted either passivity or an impotent longing for an imagined world-to-come.[92] The messianic dimension of Judaism has enfeebled it and kept it in a position of political weakness. The Latin verb that Spinoza uses to describe this condition is *effeminare,* "to effeminate." The crucial passage runs: "I think the sign of circumcision is also so important in this matter that I am persuaded that this one thing will preserve this nation to eternity. Indeed, if the foundations of their religion did not effeminate their hearts, I would absolutely believe that some day, given the opportunity, they will set up their state again, and that God will choose them anew, so changeable are human affairs."[93]

This passage recalls the famous discussion in Machiavelli's *Discourses* where the same word, *effiminare,* is used to describe the impact of Christianity on the moral and political practices of pagan antiquity.[94] Here Machiavelli describes how the advent of Christianity has slowly undermined the taste for political freedom by turning men's attention away from worldly goods and toward the afterlife. What Machiavelli calls "our religion" has glorified "humble and contemplative men" (*uomini umili e contemplativi*), with the result that one sees fewer republics in the world today than in ancient times. Citizenship has been rendered a relic of the past. This is all due to a radical transformation of education brought about by biblical religion, which has taught a contempt for the things of this world.

The effect of this transformation of moral education has been the kind of "effeminization" that makes men unfit for political life. He attributes this, however, not to Christianity as such but to those who have interpreted it in an "indolent" manner:

> This pattern of life, therefore, appears to have made the world weak, and to have handed it over as a prey to the wicked, who run it successfully and securely since they are well aware that the generality of men, with paradise for

their goal, consider how best to bear, rather than how best to avenge, their injuries. But, though it looks as if the world were become effeminate [*effeminato il mondo*] and as if heaven were powerless, this undoubtedly is instead owing to the pusillanimity of those who have interpreted our religion in terms of indolence [*l'ozio*] rather than virtue [*virtù*]. For, had they borne in mind that religion permits us to exalt and defend the fatherland, they would have seen that it also wishes us to love and honor it, and to train ourselves to be such that we may defend it.[95]

The idea present in both Machiavelli and Spinoza that revealed religion is inimical to the spirit of liberty is picked up again later with increasing passion by Rousseau. In *On the Social Contract* he contrasts the ancient republics based on an austere subordination of the private interest to the public good with modern cosmopolitan societies where the social bond is much weaker.[96] This transition from the ancient republic to the modern state was prepared by Christianity, which directed attention away from the particular community to the general society, which is a community of the entire human race, of "humanity" as a whole.[97] "Christianity," he remarks, "is a totally spiritual religion, uniquely concerned with heavenly matters."[98] If the Christian obeys the laws of the state, it is with a sense of "profound indifference" for the consequences of his acts. Unlike Machiavelli, who attributes this indifference to the "pusillanimity" of the interpreters, Rousseau regards it as the very essence of Christianity. "Christianity preaches nothing but servitude and dependence," he writes. "Its spirit is so favorable to tyranny that tyranny always profits from it. True Christians were made to be slaves."[99]

The same criticism that Machiavelli and Rousseau level against Christianity, Spinoza with somewhat less rhetorical zeal brings against Judaism. Judaism has induced a sense of passivity and self-abasement rather than providing a framework for political action. But Spinoza's critique does not end here. Combined with the idea that God's election of the Jewish people extended only to the period of their political sovereignty is the thought that God's favor may once again be granted if they cease their pious passivity and take affairs into their own hands. That the Jews could be elected a second time (*de novo*) is not outside the realm of possibility. To win election, however, it is not enough to rely on divine promises. One must have the courage to rely on one's own strength.

How seriously Spinoza took the possibility of a restoration of a Jewish state in the modern world can only be a matter of speculation.[100] We know for certain that he believed that the restoration of Jewish sovereignty would be possible only after a profound alteration of historical Judaism, especially its belief in the divinity of the Mosaic law and the injunction to live as a "kingdom of priests and a holy nation." Judaism, to the extent that it would have a future today, would no longer be based on the community established by the Jewish faith and a distinctively Jewish way of life. Rather, it would be an entirely secular faith in which a national and political identity had come to take the place of the older theological one. More to the point, however, in the *Treatise* Spinoza championed a solution whereby Jews could continue to live as Jews in a condition of political equality with their non-Jewish neighbors within a framework of secular law. Not political Zionism but the democratic republican state is the option most consistently favored in the *Treatise* as a replacement for historical Judaism.

How Jewish Is the Treatise?

Every reader of the *Treatise* is confronted with the problem of Spinoza's religion and its relation to the work as a whole. Is the *Treatise* a Jewish book, a Christian book, a philosophical text, or something else altogether? The earliest readers of the work were perplexed about its author's religious identity and believed that he was being less than candid in his professions of belief. Even though the *Treatise* was published anonymously, the preponderance of Jewish materials and Old Testament sources made it evident that its author was a Jew, even if not a practicing one. Of the first fifteen chapters of the book, only one is devoted to problems specific to the New Testament. Even here Spinoza begs off a discussion of Christianity for the surreptitious reason that he lacks "so exact a knowledge of the Greek language that I might dare to undertake this task" and that criticism of the New Testament has already been performed by certain unnamed individuals "most expert in the sciences and especially in the languages" (*Viris cum scientiarum, tum maxime linguarum*).[101]

Acknowledging the paucity of his knowledge of the Christian Scripture does not prevent him from presenting the New Testament as morally superior to the Old and the apostles as superior to the prophets. Most notably, he presents Jesus, invariably called Christ, as the messiah and, as such, the successor of Moses. Further, he continually attributes to Jesus, while denying to Moses, many of the attributes that Maimonides had ascribed to the true prophet, in particular the qualities of the philosopher. Spinoza's philosophical interpretation of Jesus and the apostles as the bringers of a true universalist religion of reason stands in stark contrast to his depiction of Moses and the prophets as men of limited intellect and vivid imagination. Indeed, one of the not so subtle ironies of the *Treatise* is that Spinoza adopts Maimonides' idea of Moses as the supreme philosopher in order to create his own Christology.[102]

Given Spinoza's generally favorable treatment of Christianity in comparison to his treatment of Judaism, the question naturally arises, Why did the *Treatise* elicit such extreme skepticism, if not outright hostility, even from its Gentile readers? One possible answer is that theologically thoughtful readers of the *Treatise,* such as Leibniz, Oldenburg, and Henry More, saw that Spinoza had a habit of taking back with one hand what he had given with the other.[103] Consider the following. It is not self-evident that Spinoza believes Judaism to be particularistic and Christianity to be universalist. Spinoza's own approving reference to the universalism of Isaiah would appear to contravene this view.[104] Nor is it clear that he maintains consistently that Judaism is a merely political legislation, whereas Christianity is a private, transpolitical faith. Spinoza knows full well that there are Christian states and empires and that Judaism has survived for millennia even in the absence of a state.[105]

The contradictions do not end here. Spinoza does not clearly uphold the view that Christianity is a religion of love whereas Judaism appeals to fear. Spinoza admits that with respect to the teaching of virtue, the doctrine of Paul is "exactly what we require"; in the context the "we" refers to Spinoza's own beliefs.[106] A common way of reading the *Treatise* is to accept Spinoza's professions of faith at face value, but another suggests that he attacked Judaism in order to make possible the critique of Christianity in the name of a new secular teaching. Thus although he characterizes the Hebrew Scripture as "the prejudices of the common people of long ago" (*antiqui vulgi praejudicia*)[107] and depicts Christianity as more spiritual and hence closer to philosophy than carnal Judaism, he nevertheless identifies Solomon, "who surpassed everyone else in his age in the natural light" (*lumine naturali omnes sui saeculi superavit*), as a "philosopher."[108]

Even more damaging, he speaks of Hebrew prophecy as a function of the imagination and of the prophets' diverse and contradictory opinions of the deity but appears to remain agnostic about the Christian doctrine of the Resurrection. Regarding "those things which certain Churches maintain about Christ," Spinoza says, "I freely confess that I do not grasp them."[109] His apparent modesty here barely conceals his belief that the doctrine in question is patently absurd. The evidence for this assertion is provided in a letter to Oldenburg written subsequent to the *Treatise.* Spinoza reaffirms his point about the unintelligibility of the doctrine of the Resurrection in exactly the same language, then adds a stinging comparison: "The doctrines added by certain churches, such as that God took upon Himself human nature, I have expressly said that I do not understand; in fact, to speak the truth, they seem to me no less absurd than would a statement that a circle had taken upon itself the nature of a square."[110] He concludes by telling Oldenburg that "you will know better than I" whether his explanation of certain disputed points in the *Treatise* will be satisfactory to Christians.[111]

Despite these admissions and in full awareness of what he was doing, Spinoza refuses to match his excoriation of Judaism with an equally vitriolic attack on Christianity. This is not because he accepts the Gospels as an authentic report of divine revelation, but because he intends to "soften up" (*mollire*) his audience to make possible the critique and ultimate rejection of revealed religion as such. "Spinoza's motives in this matter may have been complex and overdetermined," Shlomo Pines has remarked, but there can be little doubt that so far as his teachings on Christ are concerned, he "practiced the gentle art of deliberately contradicting oneself."[112] Spinoza's contradictions were partly dictated by matters of personal prudence; more importantly, by a theologico-political purpose, that is, the creation of a civil religion that could serve as a basis for peace and the elimination of persecution. His decision to cast Jesus in the role of philosopher was dictated not by the methods of historical philology but by the need to gain Gentile support for his universal religion of tolerance and obedience to the laws of a secular democratic state.

From the Old to the New Dispensation

Spinoza's careful and studied ambiguities with regard to Judaism and Christianity are frequently overshadowed by the broad and perspicuous contrasts that he suggests between the prophets and the apostles. At issue is the depiction of Moses as the bringer of a purely national law or political legislation and Jesus as the founder of an apolitical religion of reason. Moses is the virtual archetype of the *politici* discussed at the outset of the unfinished *Political Treatise* who have followed the Machiavellian advice to be as wise as serpents, who know that evils will exist as long as human nature remains constant. By contrast, Jesus belongs to the tribe of *theoretici* or *philosophi*, who see men not as they are but as they ought to be and who stand convicted of building their principalities in the air. In the *Political Treatise* Spinoza leaves no doubt that he prefers the shrewd politicians to the naive philosophers.[113] In the *Theologico-Political Treatise*, however, he presents each of these positions as dangerously one-sided and in need of correction by the other. By setting up the contrasts between the conflicting prophecies of Moses and Jesus, Spinoza prepares the way for a religion that will combine or synthesize the practical realism of the prophets with the rationalism and universalism of the apostles.

The prophecy of Moses is everywhere said to be a purely political legislation; that of Jesus and the apostles, a teaching of universal moral principles. Thus Moses, "who did not write at a time of oppression but—note this—worked for the institution of a good state" (*bona respublica*),[114] is contrasted with Christ, who "did not institute laws as a legislator [*legislator*], but taught doctrines as a teacher [*doctor*], because . . . he did not want to correct external actions so much as the heart."[115] The reason for the distinction between the Old and New Testaments is that "before the coming of Christ the prophets were accustomed to preach religion as the law of their own country [*legem Patriae*] and by the force of the covenant entered into in the time of Moses; but after the coming of Christ the apostles preached the same religion to everyone as a universal law [*legem catholicam*], solely by the force of the suffering of Christ."[116]

The distinction between the law of Moses and the teachings of Christ runs through the *Treatise*. Whereas the legislator seeks to bring about obedience through social control, the teacher is an inculcator of moral norms and principles. Spinoza leaves no doubt as to which of the two he considers superior. "For example, Moses does not teach the Jews as a teacher or prophet that they should not kill or steal, but commands these things as a lawgiver and prince. For he does not prove these teachings by reason, but adds a penalty to the commands, which can and must vary according to the temperament of each nation."[117] As evidence for this proposition, Spinoza claims that the Mosaic injunction against adultery is given merely with reference to "the advantage of the body politic and the state"; Jesus, however, is concerned with "the peace of mind and true blessedness of each person." Moses condemned the "external action," leaving the intention or "consent of the mind" untouched, whereas Christ, who promised a spiritual rather than a temporal reward, "was sent, not to preserve the state and institute laws, but only to teach the universal law."[118]

The unequal status accorded to Judaism and Christianity is ascribed directly by the *Treatise* to the carnal and materialist character of the Mosaic law. Spinoza plays dangerously upon certain anti-Jewish prejudices with regard to the concern for success and material well-being. The sole ends of the Mosaic legislation are said to be the "security of life and its conveniences" (*vitae securitas ejusque commoda*), which were held out as the only conceivable reward for obedience to the law.[119] The election of the Jews entailed "only their state and the conveniences of the body" (*imperium et corporis commoditates*)" and had nothing to do with the moral and intellectual virtues with respect to which no nation can be distinguished from another.[120] The same is true for "those five books which are commonly said to be the books of Moses" (the Torah), where nothing is promised beyond "temporal prosperity, i.e., honors *or* reputation, victories, wealth, pleasures, and health."[121]

Likewise, throughout the *Treatise* Spinoza speaks of the "Pharisees," using the long-standing term of Christian opprobrium for Jews in general. The Pharisees, in their "ignorance," are said to have believed that "the one who lived blessedly was the one who observed the legislation of the body politic," and after the destruction of the Temple they continued to perform their rites less to please God than to oppose the Gentiles.[122] The Pharisees "bitterly maintain that the divine gift [prophecy] was peculiar to their nation only" and that others divined the future by means of "I know not what diabolical power" (*ex virtute nescio qua diabolica*).[123] In one of his more outrageous anachronisms Spinoza refers to Maimonides as "the first person among the Pharisees," in full knowledge that the Pharisees had ceased to exist centuries before the time of Maimonides.[124]

While Judaism is made carnal and material, Christianity is elevated and spiritualized. Unlike Moses, Jesus prophesied without the aid of the imagination. Whereas Moses spoke to God "face to face," Jesus communed "mind to mind" (*mente ad mentem*).[125] "God revealed himself immediately to Christ, *or to his mind*," not through the medium of "words and images" (*verba et imagines*).[126] One result of this difference is that while Moses received his revelation not as eternal truth but as "precepts and things instituted," Christ is said to have "perceived things truly and adequately" (*vere et adaequate percepisse*), for he was not so much a prophet as the very "mouth of God."[127] From the fact that Christ received his revelation without the aid of an intermediary, it follows that he, unlike Moses, possessed a "common and true" (*communibus et veris*) philosophical knowledge of God.[128] He possessed a certain *scientia intuitiva*, much like the Spinozist philosopher.[129]

These differences apply to the various rituals and ceremonies observed by the two religions, as well as to the forms of prophecy. Spinoza routinely says that Jewish ritual observances "make no contribution to blessedness and virtue" but were instituted for the sake of "the temporal prosperity of the state" (*imperii temporaneam foelicitatem*).[130] Their function was to ensure that "men should do nothing by their own decision, and everything according to the command of someone else."[131] Christian ritual practices, in contrast, are accorded a relatively benign treatment: "As for the ceremonies of the Christians, viz., Baptism, the Lord's Supper, the festivals, public prayers, and whatever others there may be in addition which are and always have been common to all Christianity, if Christ or the apostles ever instituted these (which so far I do not find to be sufficiently established), they were instituted only as external signs of the universal Church, but not as things which contribute to blessedness or have any holiness in them. So although these ceremonies were not instituted with respect to a state, still they were instituted only with respect to a whole society."[132]

The most surprising difference Spinoza draws between the Mosaic and apostolic prophecies concerns the role of reason. Moses issued his injunctions like a general or commander. Unlike Maimonides, who depicted Moses as a philosopher-king or philosopher-priest, Spinoza portrays him as a "visionary realist" not above using force and guile to impose his will upon an often recalcitrant people.[133] Moses was principally a lawgiver, who, like a Machiavellian *principe,* used his *virtù* to gain power over a bedraggled *multitudo:*

> When they first left Egypt, [the Jews] were no longer bound by the legislation of any other nation, so they were permitted to enact new laws as they wished, *or* to ordain new legislation, and to maintain their dominion wherever they wished, and to occupy what lands they wished. Nevertheless, they were quite incapable of ordaining legislation wisely and retaining the dominion in their own hands, as a body. Almost all of them were crude in their understanding and weakened by wretched bondage. Therefore, the dominion had to remain in the hands of one person only, who would command the others and compel them by force, and who would prescribe laws and afterwards interpret them. But Moses was easily able to retain this dominion, because he excelled the others in divine power [*virtute supra caeteros excellebat*], persuaded the people that he had it, and showed this by many testimonies.[134]

This depiction of Moses is all the more surprising when we compare it to the depiction of Christ in the *Treatise.* The preaching of Jesus and the apostles is presented as the foundation of a universal rational morality. Where the prophets presented God's decrees issuing from "bare authoritative judgments and decisions" that do not admit of discussion, the apostles "reason everywhere [*ratiocinantur*], with the result that they seem not to prophesy, but to debate [*disputare*]."[135] The apostles spoke to one another in a spirit of "brotherly advice, mixed with politeness," as would be found in conversation rather than prophecy. They wrote their Epistles by the light of "natural judgment" (*naturali judicio*), far removed from the sound and fury of "prophetic authority."[136] The prophets spoke in terms of "authoritative judgments *or* decrees" (*dogmata et decreta*), while the apostles, especially Paul, made arguments that approached "natural knowledge," which appeared to have little to do with supernatural revelation.[137] Their arguments were drawn from "the storehouse of reason," whereas those of the prophets sought to instill the products of the prophets' own overheated imaginations.[138]

The transition from Judaism to Christianity is presented as more than as a set of stylized juxtapositions; it is also presented as a progress in human rationality. This progress marks a new stage in human history where prophecy ceases to be a "peculiar mandate" of a "specified nation" and becomes an expression of universal human reason. The laws of God were no longer binding because they were written down on tablets (*lex scripto*); rather, they were binding because they were "inscribed by divine agency in the hearts of men, i.e., in the human mind [*humanae menti divinitus inscriptam*]," which is "the true original text of God."[139] Thus in the time of the prophets the words of God needed to be "written in ink" or "set in stone tablets," whereas the apostles were able to find the "spirit of God" within the heart.[140] The result was a gain not only in our powers of rationality but also in our capacity for moral autonomy and self-direction.

Spinoza draws particular attention to the teachings of Paul, the most self-consciously philosophical of the apostles. Early in the *Treatise* Spinoza cites the Epistle to the Romans as evidence for the proposition that "God is the God of all Nations" (Rom. 2:25, 26) and that "God sent to all nations his Christ, who would free all equally from bondage to the law, so that they would no longer act well because of the commandement of the Law, but because of a stable decision of the heart."[141] Spinoza credits Paul for introducing notions of personal accountability and responsibility into his teachings.[142] Paul thus spoke to his hearers openly as a teacher rather than adapting himself to the prejudices of his audience. None of the apostles "philosophized" more than Paul when called to preach to the Gentiles, although they changed tactics when speaking to the Jews, who, as such, "disdained" philosophy.[143]

Nothing would be easier than to read these passages as evidence of Spinoza's anti-Semitism, his deep-seated antipathy to Jews and Judaism. His statement that the Jews disdained philosophy concludes with the exclamation: "How happy our age would surely be now, if we saw religion again free of all superstition!"[144] Yet even as the *Treatise* appeals to an age blessedly free of superstition, it appeals to those very prejudices and superstitions from which it would ostensibly liberate us! Spinoza surely knew that his frequent distortions and caricatures of Judaism played to some of the worst forms of anti-Jewish bigotry. His continual depiction of Judaism as a legalistic, carnal, and authoritarian religion helped to lay the basis for Kant's later conception of Judaism as a "statutory" religion, Hegel's attack on religious "positivity," and Marx's invidious assaults on Jewish "egoism" and "materialism."[145] Why, then, does he do it?

One answer is that the contrasts between Judaism and Christianity represent something more than anti-Semitism or Spinoza's desire to seek revenge for his excommunication. They were intended as markers of historical progress. Spinoza sets up the figures of Moses and Jesus to mark the change from an ethic of law and external authority to one of love and individual moral autonomy. Judaism and Christianity are way stations on the road from sacred to secular history. Both are theologically *aufgehoben* in Spinoza's own dialectical synthesis.[146]

But Spinoza does more than prepare the reader for the overcoming of Judaism by Christianity. As I suggested earlier, he prepares the reader for the overcoming of both Judaism and Christianity by the secular democratic state. After depicting Christ as the teacher of a universal rational morality (a kind of Spinoza *avant la lettre*),[147] he shows how Christianity did not possess the true moral teaching. In particular, he shows that Christianity, not Judaism, became the cause of the persecution and intolerance to which the *Treatise* takes itself to be the answer. In Spinoza's recasting of sacred history, if Christ takes the place that Maimonides had accorded to Moses, Spinoza now assumes the place that had previously been accorded to Christ. He is the bringer of a new theologico-political dispensation every bit as far-reaching as the historical religions that he claims to overcome.[148]

Before showing how Spinoza intends to accomplish this feat of legerdemain, I need to show how he deconstructs Christianity as the alleged foundation of rational morality. The first and most serious weakness of Christianity stems precisely from what Spinoza had previously appeared to praise as its chief virtue. The apostles, we are told, reasoned more freely than the prophets and expressed their own opinions and beliefs on their own initiative. Spinoza draws once again on the authority of Paul to indicate that the apostles took upon themselves the responsibility not only for teaching and exhorting but for admonishing whenever and whomever it pleased them to do so (1 Tim. 2:7; 2 Tim. 1:11).[149] Each apostle, then, developed his own method and style of teaching, with the result that these differences came to affect the very "foundations" of religion. The apostles soon became like the wrangling dogmatists of different philosophical sects, each attempting to initiate people into the inner workings of his private creed. Paul, for example, maintained that faith, not works, is necessary for salvation (Rom. 3:27–28), whereas James upheld precisely the opposite, that man is justified by works and not by faith alone (James 2:24).[150]

The differences between the apostles over the teachings of Christ were thus the cause of the schisms and quarrels within the early church. These conflicts were traceable directly back to the authority of the individual apostles in propagating the new faith: "Finally, there is no doubt but what the fact that the apostles built religion on different foundations [*diversis fundamentis religionem*] gave rise to many disputes and schisms, which have tormented the church incessantly from the time of the apostles to the present day, and will surely continue to torment it forever, until at last someday religion is separated from philosophic speculations and reduced to those very few and very simple tenets [*paucissima et simplicissima dogmata*] Christ taught to his followers."[151]

The quarrels and schisms supplied the ideological grounds for the later policies of religious persecution and intolerance. Paul here ironically bears the greatest share of blame for turning "the very few and very simple tenets" taught by Christ into a scholastic system based on "philosophic speculations." Christianity is held responsible for inaugurating an era of confusion about philosophy and religion, which is the peculiarly modern form of superstition. Christianity ceased to offer a few simple truths regarding justice and charity and was turned into a pseudo-philosophy. With the multiplication of religious dogmas and creeds, the interpretation of religion became the preserve of professional ecclesiastics with the skills of a philosopher and leisure for "a great many useless speculations."[152] The result was a grotesque mélange that confused the moral truths of religion with the rational truths of philosophy.

The second and equally damaging fallibility of Christianity is traced back to its circumstances of origin. Without nearly the detail of his account of the Hebrew Scripture, Spinoza provides a political etiology of Christianity designed to situate the Gospels in secular historical time. While still affirming the superiority of the teachings of Jesus to the Mosaic law, Spinoza traces the origins of Christianity back to the internal decomposition of Judaism during the period of the Second Temple. The dissolution of political life under Roman social hegemony had a profound impact on the character of original Christianity.

The most important impact produced by historical circumstances is that Christianity emerged as a preeminently apolitical sect taught by "private men" (*viri privati*):

> For it was not kings who first taught the Christian religion, but private men who — against the will of those who had political authority and whose subjects they were — were accustomed, for a long time, to address meetings in private Churches, to establish and administer sacred functions, to arrange everything by themselves, and to make decrees without any consideration of the political authority. . . . But among the Hebrews the situation was very different. For their Church began at the same time their state did, and Moses, who had absolute political authority, taught the people religion, ordained sacred ministries, and chose the ministers for them. That is why royal authority was valued very highly among the people, and why the Kings had a very great right concerning sacred matters.[153]

Although Christianity may have developed outside the formal institutions of the state, it was not without political consequence. The private character of Christianity meant that it was no longer adapted to citizens of a particular state; instead, it was adapted to human beings in the abstract. Its teachings were not addressed to members of a specific national identity but were applicable to citizen and noncitizen alike, Jew as well as Gentile. The moral universalism of Christianity gave rise in turn to a universal church that assumed responsibility for teaching its precepts to kings and emperors, that is, setting itself over and above the political sovereign proper. The apostles, like the prophets before them, even claimed the right to censure royal authority. The apostles were, then, ministers of rebellion whom even "pious Kings" found "intolerable" for their constant badgering and rebukes.[154]

The privatization of religion is the nerve of the theologico-political problem that Spinoza confronts in the *Treatise* . This privatization, he suggests, is the cause of the "intense civil wars" to which he and his contemporaries have been subject.[155] The great struggles between church and state to which the history of the Christian West has been peculiarly prone grew directly out of the effort to transform the law of Moses into a "universal divine law" immediately applicable to all persons regardless of time, place, and circumstance. Spinoza's answer to the problem posed by the privatization of religion is to propose a new dispensation that incorporates the moral dogmas common to Judaism and Christianity but that transcends both. The *Treatise* thus points to a new kind of religion and a new kind of cultivated or cultured individual.

In the short term, however, the practical task that Spinoza attempts to accomplish is to reappropriate political control of religion from a clergy that has set itself up as independent of and even in opposition to the state. For Spinoza, like Hobbes, a religion that culminates in a teaching of disobedience cannot be morally desirable. What he calls in the *Treatise* the true or "universal faith" (*fides universalis*) is, properly speaking, a religion of obedience to the secular authority, which is the democratic-republican state. As we have already seen, in the preface, Spinoza attributes to this state ultimate power in matters of religion and education. The task that he set himself in the *Treatise* was to find a way of reconciling the requirements of religion with the needs of civil society without fostering rebellion.

Spinoza's New Dispensation

Spinoza's reconstruction of sacred history culminates in chapter 14 of the *Treatise* with his announcement of the universal or catholic religion (*religio catholica*) which might serve as a civil theology for citizens of the modern democratic-republican state. This universal religion is distinguished from two other kinds of religion discussed in the *Treatise*. The first is the religion of the masses (*vulgi religio*), identified with superstition and belief in supernatural revelation. It is a religion of the imagination, maintaining its adherents in a condition of fear and credulity. The second is the religion of the philosophers. This religion is circumscribed by what Spinoza in the fourth chapter of the *Treatise* calls the "natural divine law" that dictates the one best way of life for a human being. Qualifying "divine law" with the expression "natural" indicates that this religion is not dependent on the truth of any historical narrative or the performance of any particular ceremony. It is a religion of unaided human reason and hence is accessible only to the few, not the many.

Between these two religions we find Spinoza's formulation of the universal or catholic religion, which is intended to lay the grounds for civil peace. The purpose of this religion is to compel obedience to the law. Because this kind of religion makes minimal epistemic demands on its adherents, it can serve as the basis for harmony between philosophers and nonphilosophers, as well as between Jews and Gentiles. Unlike the religion of the philosophers, the *religio catholica* is based not on reason alone but on a kind of distillation or condensation of the teachings of the prophets and apostles in both Testaments. By basing this religion on precepts allegedly common to both Judaism and Christianity, Spinoza intended it to support the new democratic political order, with Spinoza himself serving as the new Moses.

The central problem that the *religio catholica* is designed to solve is the issue of obedience to the law. Faith, Spinoza avers, consists entirely in obedience to God. The main object of both Testaments is nothing other than obedience.[156] Spinoza maintains here, in what might be called his *profession de foi*, that faith consists entirely in obedience to God. This outward assertion of faith conceals the radically novel conception of piety that is in fact being proposed. For Spinoza, like Hobbes, obedience to law means primarily obedience to the laws of the sovereign.[157] In a conflict between the welfare of the state, which requires obedience to its laws, and the welfare of the individual, one's obligation is to obey the civil authority. Unlike revealed or scriptural religion with its belief in prophets who may put themselves above the law or may rebuke the civil sovereign, Spinoza's new civil theology teaches a doctrine of fidelity to the law. Trading on an ambiguity in his use of the term "faith," Spinoza wants to make obedience to the laws of the republic into a sacred or absolute duty.[158]

The universal religion of the *Treatise* is intended, then, as the foundation of civil peace rather than as a cause of political conflict, which has all too often been the case with the established historical religions. To achieve this end, Spinoza enumerates seven "dogmas," or tenets of faith, which he believed were necessary to instill correct behavior and obedience to the law.[159] These dogmas may be summarized as follows:

1. God or a Supreme Being exists who is just and merciful.
2. God is one.
3. He is omnipresent and all-knowing.
4. He has absolute dominion over all beings, and his actions are the result not of compulsion, but of freedom and grace.

5. The correct worship of God consists in performing acts of justice and charity, which are understood to mean love of one's neighbor.
6. Salvation may be achieved through obedience to God's law as specified in dogma 5.
7. God forgives those who sincerely repent of their sins.[160]

Several commentators have drawn attention to the affinity between Spinoza's seven dogmas and the fundamental principles of religion discussed by Maimonides in the *Guide,* III, 27–28.[161] In these chapters, as we have seen already, Maimonides distinguishes between "the correct opinions" that convey certain truths about the nature and attributes of God and those "necessary beliefs" that conduce to political welfare. By those true opinions concerning God, Maimonides means such things as belief in God's unity, knowledge, power, and eternity, while necessary beliefs are those propositions required for the regulation and control of social behavior, such as the abolition of reciprocal wrongdoing and the acquisition of sound moral character.

Two important, even fundamental, differences separate Spinoza from Maimonides. First, for Maimonides these principles were the principles of Judaism only. Maimonides never undertook the task of legislating the principles of a religion that would encompass both Jews and Gentiles. Spinoza's dogmas, however, are intended as an amalgam taken from both Judaism and Christianity. The first four dogmas about the attributes of God seem to be taken from a predominantly Jewish intellectual tradition.[162] But the last three dogmas concerning the proper manner of worship and faith are indebted more to Christian sources. In addition to affirming a belief in the existence, unity, and omnipotence of God, as well as a belief in his mercy and justice, Spinoza says that the person who firmly believes in God's forgiveness can be said to "know Christ according to the Spirit [*revera Christum secundum Spiritum novit*] and Christ is in him."[163]

Despite an appearance of a balance between the two religions, Spinoza weights the *religio catholica* in favor of Christianity. The first four dogmas are in fact common both to Christians and Jews, and the last proposition is specific to Christians only. Further, Spinoza's designation of his new theology as "universal" or "catholic" gives it a greater resemblance to Christianity than to Judaism, which is routinely designated in the *Treatise* as particularistic. There is considerably less onus on Christians to accept and assimilate to this universal faith than there is on Jews. Yet in at least one crucial respect, Spinoza's universal faith takes its cue from Judaism. In claiming that all true religion commands only actions, not beliefs, Spinoza to some degree "Judaizes" his religion of humanity. As we shall see later, he takes over certain features from the religion of the Hebrew theocracy while adapting them to the needs of the modern democratic state.

Second, Maimonides' distinction between "true" and "necessary" opinions leaves open the question of whether the necessary propositions contained any share of truth or were merely convenient fictions. For Spinoza, however, all seven dogmas are put forward as necessary beliefs. "Faith," he remarks, "does not require tenets which are true as much as it does tenets which are pious" (*Sequitur denique fidem non tam requirere vera, quam pia dogmata*).[164] The greatest virtue of these dogmas, then, is that they can be held and yet in no way infringe upon the greatest freedom, the freedom of mind. "Faith requires piety more than it does truth," Spinoza avers.[165] The greatest piety is not necessarily possessed by "the one who displays the best arguments, but by the one who displays the best works of Justice and Loving-kindness."[166] Because the dogmas of this religion compel actions rather than beliefs, Spinoza confidently states that there can be no doctrines in the catholic or universal religion to which "honest men" (*honestos*) cannot in good conscience subscribe.[167]

Spinoza leaves intentionally ambiguous whether the dogmas of his universal faith are intended to have any share in truth. To say that a belief is necessary is by no means to say that it is false, and although the *religio catholica* may be designed with the end of obedience in mind, it may still be composed of some true opinions. For example, Spinoza clearly believes that the principles of this religion are superior to the superstitious beliefs that he analyzes elsewhere in the *Treatise,* thus indicating that he is operating with some conception of differing degrees of truth. A true belief may be held for the wrong reasons. Thus the unenlightened person may believe in the existence and unity of God because that belief has the support and authority of Scripture behind it, whereas the philosopher may arrive at the same belief because reason leads to that conclusion.

At the same time Spinoza maintains that philosophers can assent to the propositions of his religion because religion compels obedience, not truth. The universal religion makes no epistemic demands on its adherents and therefore may receive the full consent of philosophers. Thus philosophers, like all "honest men," may subscribe to this religion because it leaves untouched their freedom of thought. Among other things, we know that Spinoza himself could not have subscribed literally to the seven dogmas of his religion because they explicitly contradict his teachings about God in the *Ethics*. The God of the *Ethics* does not love charity and justice or punish the wicked. The dogmas of religion set out in the *Treatise,* then, represent not Spinoza's true conception of

God but rather those beliefs that are salutary for the purpose of political life. The *Treatise* leaves its readers with the irony that if there is a true religion, it is entirely agnostic as to the question of truth.

The key to Spinoza's new religion is the command to practice acts of justice and charity, which he interprets to mean religious toleration. Spinoza's doctrine of toleration is presented as if it were the common core of both Judaism and Christianity. This interpretation represents a remarkable transubstantiation. From two revealed religions that make extraordinarily stringent moral demands on their adherents, Spinoza derives a nonrevealed liberal religion of universal tolerance. His claim to be doing nothing more than laying bare the moral teachings of the prophets and apostles is belied by his replacement of the old Decalogue with a new septalogue. Whatever may have led the prophets of old to declare that one should love one's neighbor as oneself, they most assuredly had nothing to do with the freedom to philosophize, which is declared to be the most important subject of the *Treatise*.[168] The apparent theological modesty of this new religion notwithstanding, Spinoza regards it as marking a turning point in the sacred history of the West, the crowning moment of a new dispensation with a new messiah.

This new dispensation, announced in chapter 14, takes the form of a democratic civil theology. The essence of the new theology is the separation of reason and faith. Faith in the dogmas of religion requires obedience, not belief. Faith means not adherence to any particular set of opinions but performance of acts of justice and charity. Because faith teaches nothing but obedience to the law, it follows that true religion "grants everyone the greatest freedom to philosophize, so that without wickedness he can think whatever he wishes *about anything*."[169] In a remarkable sleight of hand, Spinoza turns freedom of thought and universal toleration into the essence of piety. If true faith allows the maximum freedom of thought, then intolerance is blasphemy. "Those who love Justice and Loving-kindness we know by that fact alone to be faithful," Spinoza writes, and "whoever persecutes the faithful is an Antichrist."[170]

The *Treatise* attempts to provide this unprecedented liberationist theology with a sheen of traditional respectability by citing the apostle James to the effect that "faith without works is dead" (James 2:17).[171] In the same passage he cites the verse that is used on the title page of the *Treatise* itself: "Hereby we know that we dwell in God and He in us, because He has given us of his Spirit" (I John 4:13).[172] Spinoza nowhere indicates that when seen in context, these passages have nothing whatever to do with teaching toleration of heterodox beliefs.

If there is an analogue to Spinoza's *religio catholica*, it is the *religion civile* of Rousseau's *Social Contract*. Here Rousseau applauds "the philosopher

Hobbes," who "of all Christian authors" was "the only one who correctly saw the evil and the remedy, who dared to propose the reunification of the two heads of the eagle, and the complete return to political unity."[173] Rousseau's characterization of Hobbes as a "Christian author" is scarcely fortuitous. Rousseau knew that Spinoza was not a Christian author and that the bitter pill he was trying to tempt his readers to swallow would go down more easily if he could sweeten it with reference to an authority — if not a respectable authority, at least a Christian one.[174]

Rousseau's solution to the theologico-political problem, then, is the subordination of religion to the civil authority. In place of "the dominating spirit of Christianity," Rousseau proposes a "purely civil profession of faith," which is to be considered less a revealed religion than the "sentiments of sociability."[175] The dogmas of this theology "ought to be simple, few in number, stated with precision, without explanations or commentaries" and include such things as a belief in the existence of a powerful, intelligent, beneficent, and foresighted deity, the happiness of the just and the punishment of the wicked, and the sanctity of the social contract and its laws.[176] The only absolute prohibition in this theology is intolerance. Rousseau demands ostracism for anyone declaring that salvation is the monopoly of any one particular church. Theological intolerance is the root of all other kinds of intolerance. Wherever theological intolerance exists, it is only a matter of time until priests demand to rule. Consequently, one should tolerate only those religions that tolerate others.[177]

For both Rousseau and Spinoza, civil religion serves as the minimal basis for obedience to the law. Because obedience is itself an act of faith, some kind of civil theology is necessary to maintain respect for the law. Thus although Rousseau avers that "it matters greatly to the state that each citizen have a religion that causes him to love his duties," he also says that the precise "dogmas of that religion are of no interest either to the state or its members" and that "everyone can have whatever opinion he pleases . . . without the sovereign having to know what [those opinions] are."[178]

This highly liberal profession of faith follows more or less exactly the lines laid down in Spinoza's *Treatise.* Although Spinoza's dogmas are "before all things necessary to be believed," he also realizes that everyone will interpret them in his own way, according to his individual capacity. The idea that God exists, that he is one and indivisible and has dominion over all things will be interpreted variously. Whether one understands God to be a legislator-judge or equivalent to the laws of nature, whether one believes that God rules by fiat or by necessity, or whether one accepts that salvation is due to supernatural or to natural causes is a personal matter and bears not at all on the principles of religion. Spinoza goes so far as to conclude this part of his discussion with the observation that "each person is bound to accommodate these tenets of faith to his own power of understanding [*ad suum captum accommodare*]" in order "to accept them without any hesitation" and "obey God with full agreement of the heart [*integro animi*]."[179]

By making the practice of toleration the essence of religion, Spinoza hopes to lay the basis for the kind of state that will be theoretically neutral concerning the various creeds and sects under its jurisdiction. The sovereign will be prepared to tolerate all religions that do not challenge his authority. Like Hobbes and Rousseau, Spinoza knew that establishing toleration would be no easy task. Those who take their religion seriously would never willingly cede religious authority to the sovereign. The way to accomplish this was to present the case not as a usurpation but as a mandate of true religion. True religion compels obedience, and obedience means obedience to the rules of a purely secular sovereign. The danger of Spinoza's solution is that it appears to replace one form of servitude with another, the priestly class with a new secular clerisy. The task of combining theological with political liberty is the burden of the last five chapters of the *Treatise*.

5

A Democratic Turn

Chapter 16 marks a new beginning in the *Treatise*. The first fifteen chapters deal with theological matters broadly understood. There Spinoza sets out the guidelines for scriptural interpretation and applies them to the study of the Hebrew and Christian Testaments. Working on the principle that "knowledge of Scripture must be looked for in Scripture only," Spinoza reconfigures sacred history along the lines of a progressive philosophy of history. Starting with the discussion of prophets and prophecy in the opening chapters of the *Treatise,* Spinoza uses a combination of erudition and dizzying speed to lead the reader through treatments of the law of Moses, the order and composition of the books of the Torah, and the status of the Gospels, culminating in the announcement of the universal or catholic religion. Basing this religion on principles allegedly common to and thus purportedly neutral vis-à-vis Judaism and Christianity, Spinoza creates a *fides universalis* that is intended to serve as a foundation for the new democratic state, open to Jew and Christian, pagan and Muslim, alike.

Beginning with the Mosaic prophecy, Spinoza shows how this law was historically adapted to men living in the earliest, most barbarous times, who were rude and uncultivated (*rudis ingenii*), prone to fear and superstition, economically oppressed (*miserrima*), and altogether lacking in any experience of freedom and self-government. Under these circumstances, Moses could do little more than act as a legislator to create conditions favorable to political autonomy. The result of the Mosaic legislation was an almost perfect "sacralization of the political" and "politicization of the sacred" such that the laws of the state and the laws of religion were effectively the same laws.[1] This condition remained more or less intact even after the Babylonian exile. Then came the destruction of Jerusalem for Jewish resistance to Roman imperial rule. With the destruction of the Temple, the symbol of Jewish political independence, in the year 70, the Diaspora became an irreversible fact, thus rendering the law of Moses a historical anachronism. According to Spinoza, stubbornness and resistance to Gentile hatred account for the survival of the Jews even after the loss of their state.

The law of Moses is presented in the *Treatise* as both related to and fulfilled by the new law enunciated in the Christian Gospels. This law grew out of historical factors internal and external to Judaism. Internally the law was the result of an ongoing and unresolved feud between the Levites, the priestly class, and the political rulers, and externally it was the product of the conditions imposed by the Roman conquest. Christianity was initially a private religion taught by private persons and directed not toward any particular people but to all humankind. The teachings of Christ and the apostles were, moreover, not political but moral, aimed not at the flesh but at the spirit, and were not given as arbitrary commands but offered in the spirit of reason and persuasion. Partly because of the conditions of persecution under which Christianity arose, the religion came to acquire the trappings of a philosophy or quasi philosophy, with a distinctive set of creeds, doctrines, and catechisms required for membership. Paul, it will be recalled, "philosophized" more than the other apostles, and it was only a matter of time until the purely moral teachings of Christ took on the character of a sect in competition with other schools of Hellenistic thought.

The problem, diagnosed in the *Treatise,* emerged once Christianity ceased to be an apolitical sect adhered to by a subject people and became the official religion of the Roman state. The very universalism of Christianity uniquely adapted it to conditions of a multicultural imperial state. Unlike Judaism, which was tied to a particular state, Christianity, with its teaching of "render unto Caesar," could serve as the basis for a universal empire. In the attempt to extirpate the remnants of paganism, Christianity itself became a persecutory religion. Directed at transforming opinions and beliefs as well as actions, Christianity bequeathed to the West a legacy of intolerance and inquisitorial zeal. The lesson that Spinoza bids us draw concerns the danger of turning an essentially private creed into a public dogma.

Not until the fourteenth and fifteenth chapters of the *Treatise* does Spinoza define the proper role of faith and the true relation of philosophy to theology. The rational or "catholic" religion is said to be nothing more than a distillation or synthesis of the moral teachings of the prophets and apostles culled from both Testaments. The seven dogmas of this new creed should in principle be acceptable to adherents of both faiths. The essence of the *Treatise*'s new moral theology is an unprecedented doctrine of charity and justice interpreted to mean toleration and noninterference with the beliefs of others. The first three-quarters of the *Treatise* culminate in the declaration of a new theology for a modern democratic age and the presentation of Spinoza himself as a new secular messiah.

Spinoza begins the sixteenth chapter of the *Treatise* with the following announcement: "So far our concern has been to separate Philosophy from Theology and to show the freedom of philosophizing which [Theology] grants to everyone. Now it is time for us to ask how far this freedom of thinking, and of saying what each person thinks, extends in the best State [*optima Respublica*]."[2] Having spent fifteen chapters defending the necessity of freedom of opinion and belief, Spinoza proposes spending the next five showing the limits of that freedom, if any. The question of the limits of liberty is more properly a political than a theological issue.

The last five chapters of the *Treatise* do more than announce a new subject matter. They set out a new method to replace the method of scriptural interpretation and exegesis followed hitherto. Until now, Spinoza has followed (more or less faithfully) the principle of *sola Scriptura*, reading Scripture by itself alone. But the purpose of this method of reading, we can now see, has not been to restore or fulfill the biblical prophecies but to undermine and replace them. Spinoza's reading of Scripture has the purpose of replacing Scripture with reason as the ultimate ground of both theological and political authority. Spinoza's new beginning is meant to substitute for the "hieroglyphic" morality of the Bible a new rational or "intelligible" ethics of the scientist-philosopher.

Once Spinoza has completed his reconstruction of biblical history in the first part of the *Treatise*, he can turn to a new method of establishing the legitimacy of his own teachings in the second part. This new intelligible morality would find its home in a new kind of political regime. This regime is neither the virtuous republic of classical antiquity nor the holy city of the Bible but the commercial metropolis of modernity. The *optima Respublica* of the *Treatise* is, above all, a democracy. Spinoza's defense of democracy needs to be distinguished from two widely held apologias in the history of political theory. Ironically, Spinoza, the first avowed defender of democracy, did not hold any great confidence in the wisdom, actual or potential, of the people as a whole. The multitude are, and will remain, prone to superstition and credulity, so the purpose of politics is to find a means, both institutional and psychological, of restraining the passions. Because rulers and ruled alike are governed by the same passions, democracy is the regime most likely to subordinate the interests of both subjects and rulers to the interests of the whole state.

Second, unlike Hobbes, Bodin, and the *politiques,* Spinoza did not regard the achievement of peace and the avoidance of conflict as the chief goals of political life.[3] As important as these ends are, the *Treatise* held out a more positive role for politics than the avoidance of the *summum malum.* Spinoza endorses the democratic republic because it is the regime most consistent with the autonomous individual or liberated self. Democracy is desirable because it fosters the conditions for reason and the expression of individual faculties. This democracy bears an uncanny resemblance to seventeenth-century Amsterdam. One can say, with perhaps only slight exaggeration, that Amsterdam is for Spinoza the new Jerusalem, a commercial republic based on freedom of trade, freedom of religion, and freedom of opinion. Indeed, he could almost have subtitled the *Treatise* "From Jerusalem to Amsterdam."

Hobbes and Spinoza on the Derivation of Natural Right

The new foundation announced in chapter 16 of the *Treatise* takes its point of departure not from Scripture or revelation but from a new set of "scientific" categories, like the state of nature, natural right, and the social contract. There is no basis whatsoever in either the Jewish or Christian theological traditions for any of these. To the extent that Spinoza has a predecessor in this effort to establish politics on a new rational foundation, that predecessor is his most illustrious (and notorious) contemporary Thomas Hobbes, who not long before the publication of the *Treatise* declared with characteristic bravado that "civil philosophy" was born with his book *De cive* of 1642.[4] Because Spinoza and Hobbes are often considered together and because Spinoza is almost as often regarded as derivative of Hobbes, it is important to emphasize the real differences between them.[5]

Hobbes and Spinoza both attempt to establish a foundation for the state on a new doctrine of natural right. Where they differ, at least initially, is in their derivation of this right. Hobbes derives natural right from an analysis of individuals in the state of nature, by which he means a condition of putative equality prior to or outside the constraints of civil society.[6] Equality is derived by Hobbes not from the presence of any positive features or attributes of human beings but from the power that anyone has to kill anyone else "either by secret machination or by confederacy with others." Because "the weakest has strength enough to kill the strongest," the natural condition emerges as one of maximum distrust and enmity.[7] Hobbes hopes to verify this hypothesis by reference not to nature but to human opinion. In the preface to *De cive* he remarks that it is "by experience known to all men and denied by none" that "every man will distrust and dread each other" and so, by natural right, "will be forced to make use of the strength he hath, toward the preservation of himself."[8]

From his account of the state of nature, Hobbes establishes his idea of the right of nature, which is nothing more than the liberty that each person has to use his own power for the preservation of life and limb.[9] In the state of nature the right of nature is not restricted by any reciprocal duties or obligation. The right of nature grants virtually unlimited liberty to take whatever measures are necessary to ensure survival. Because nature gives each person a right to "all things," it follows that the state of nature is "a war of all against all" in which competition for scarce resources, diffidence or a desire for security, and love of distinction or glory become the three most important causes of conflict.[10] Because the state of nature is an ultimately absurd situation, with human beings torn between conflicting desires — to harm others and to escape violent death — those human beings seek peace and form civil society. The laws of nature are those rules derived from the more fundamental right of nature, which lead men to compromise their liberty for the sake of peaceful and secure cohabitation.

Spinoza presents a very different derivation of natural right. Anticipating by roughly a century Rousseau's criticism that Hobbes had projected the qualities of civil man (diffidence, vanity, competition) back onto the state of nature, Spinoza derives natural right not from a meditation on human nature but from the power and articulation of nature as a whole:

> By the right and established practice of nature I mean nothing but the rules of the nature of each individual, according to which we conceive each thing to be naturally determined to exist and act in a certain way. For example, fish are determined by nature to swim, and the large ones to eat the smaller; so it is by the supreme right of nature that fish are masters of the water, and that the large ones eat the smaller. For it is certain that nature, considered absolutely, has the supreme right to do everything in its power, i.e., that the right of nature extends as far as its power does. For the power of nature is the very power of God, who has the supreme right to do all things.[11]

Spinoza explains himself here in a related passage from the *Political Treatise*.[12] By "the right and established practice of nature," Spinoza means nothing more than "the eternal power of God" (*Dei aeternam potentiam*).[13] By the power of God, however, he certainly does not mean the intending or providential deity of Scripture. God, as Spinoza understands him (or it), is simply the power of nature. When we speak about God or nature, we are in fact speaking of a perfectly homogenous system that can nevertheless be articulated into two parts: (1) extension (*res extensa*) and (2) thought (*res cogitans*). Matter and thought are not two different substances, as Descartes believed; rather, they are two "modes" or "attributes" of the Substance that Spinoza calls God or nature (*Deus sive natura*).[14]

From this initial identification of natural right, Spinoza goes on to declare that the right of nature is equivalent to the power of nature. Might equals right. By natural right is understood "the actual laws or rules of nature in accordance with which all things come to be; that is, the actual power of nature."[15] Spinoza's description of natural right as the power according to which "everything" takes place is intended to divest nature of all normative purpose. Because all things exist under the hegemony of nature, there is no reason to believe that nature can serve as the basis for morality. "But since we are dealing at present with the power or right of nature," Spinoza writes, "we can admit no distinction here between desires which are engendered in us by reason, and those which arise from other causes. . . . For man, whether enlightened or unenlightened, is part of nature."[16] On the evidence of this passage nature alone can no longer be said to favor a condition of war to peace, of superstition to reason, of slavery to freedom.

It is by the right of nature, then, that "each thing strives to persevere in its state, as far as it can, by its own power," and therefore "each individual has the supreme right to do this."[17] When Spinoza says "each individual," he does not mean each human being but rather something like each natural kind or species, because he does not wish to grant any special priority or privilege to the human order within the natural order. Hobbes attempts to derive natural right from reflection on human nature. "Read thyself" is the motto by which the author of *Leviathan* exhorts his readers to see whether "the similitude of the thoughts and passions of one man" are not identical to "the thoughts and passions of another."[18] For Spinoza, human nature is made coextensive with the comprehensive order of nature. There is simply nothing very special about the human vantage point. Each species — of dogs, mice, and human beings — has an inner drive or urge (*conatus*) that impels it to seek its own preservation and do whatever is necessary to maintain itself.[19] The natural right of human beings, rather than being a mark of distinction, is no loftier or more dignified than that of fish.

The virtually complete naturalization of right in the *Treatise,* though completely amoral, has moral consequences. By right, individuals act according to the laws appropriate to their diverse natures. This right also applies to the different types of human beings:

Nor do we recognize here any difference between men and other individuals in nature, nor between men endowed with reason and those others who are ignorant of true reason, nor between fools and madmen and those who are sound. For whatever each thing does according to the laws of its own nature, it does with supreme right, because it acts as it has been determined to do according to nature, and cannot do otherwise. . . I.e., as the wise man has the supreme right to do everything which reason dictates, *or* to live according to the laws of reason, so also the ignorant and weak-minded have the supreme right to do everything appetite urges, *or* to live according to the laws of appetite.[20]

Prior to Spinoza natural right had meant something like the life of human excellence or virtue. Reason was generally accorded a special place in determining the rules circumscribing the character of the good life. Aristotle in the *Nicomachean Ethics* establishes that the good life is life according to the natural order of the human soul, with reason controlling and directing the passions toward virtue. The virtues are in turn determined by right reason (*orthos logos*) or the habit of choosing actions wisely.[21] Natural right is thus intrinsically bound up with the virtuous life as practiced by the citizen of a well-ordered city. Aristotle's famous statement near the beginning of the *Politics* to the effect that man is "by nature" (*kata physein*) a political animal (*zōon politikon*) and that the polis exists by nature merely completes the virtuous circle.[22] Nature favors reason, which favors human sociability because sociability creates conditions favorable to reason.

The thesis that the life according to nature is the life of virtue was expounded as well by Cicero and the Stoics and even became an expressed belief of Christian Aristotelians. Thomas Aquinas argued that the precepts of natural law are embedded in practical rationality and, as such, can be promulgated and understood by all whose reason has not become corrupted.[23] Not even Hobbes, for all of his anti-Aristotelian and anti-clerical ire, managed to distinguish fully between nature and reason. By the laws of nature Hobbes means those rules of prudence that lead men to prefer peace to war. These laws are described variously as "convenient articles," "precepts," or "conclusions" that reason "suggesteth" in order to obtain peace.[24] Hobbesian natural right, like Aristotle's, has an ineluctably teleological component. It presupposes and thus helps rational beings see the necessity, and therewith the goodness, of society.

Spinoza's derivation of natural right from the more general operations of nature presupposes no special dispensation for human reason within the whole. This is not because Spinoza was oblivious to the differences between virtue and vice, the lives of "fools, madmen, and those who are sound." Rather, from the standpoint of nature these distinctions have no meaning at all. These are human judgments intended and created for human convenience and do not reflect the natural order and articulation of things. The statement that the state of nature is a state of war (Hobbes) or a condition of peace (Rousseau) is at best a *façon de parler* and at worst a misleading projection of human ends and purposes onto nature. Such statements may have metaphorical value but absolutely no rational or scientific value. Just as Maimonides divested the biblical God of all anthropomorphic qualities and attributes, so does Spinoza divest nature of all preferences for reason, peace, and virtue to unreason, war, and vice. All of these are equally ways of being human and thus equally legitimate qualities when seen from the perspective of God or nature. The practical moral consequence of Spinoza's thoroughgoing naturalism is neither pessimism nor despair. Spinoza takes a naturalist's delight in, and celebrates, the sheer variety of distinctive types and their diverse means of preserving themselves.[25]

The teaching of natural right leads Spinoza to the conclusion that from the standpoint of nature all things are permitted. Necessity takes away the need for judgments of praise and blame. This is, again, because judgments of good and bad are human distinctions and are of no consequence to the eternal order of nature. Nature may be the ultimate source of human moral distinctions insofar as everything refers back to nature, but for Spinoza nature in and of itself is morally neutral. Nature is neither good nor evil but, in Nietzsche's phrase, "beyond good and evil." Spinoza writes:

> From these considerations it follows that the right and established practice of nature, under which all are born and for the most part live, prohibits nothing except what no one desires and what no one can do: not disputes, not hatreds, not anger, not deception; and without qualification, it is not averse to anything which appetite urges. This is not surprising, for nature is not constrained by the laws of human reason, which aim only at man's true advantage and preservation, but [is governed] by infinite other [laws], which are related to the eternal order of the whole of nature, of which man is only a small part. . . . So when anything in nature seems to us ridiculous, absurd, or evil, that is because we know things only in part, and for the most part are ignorant of the order and coherence of the whole of nature, and because we wish everything to be directed according to the usage of our reason, even though what reason dictates to be evil is not evil in relation to the order and laws of nature as a whole, but only in relation to the laws of our nature.[26]

The Social Contract as the Rational Basis of Legitimate Authority

The question that Spinoza has yet to raise is how in such a naturalistically determined world is politics, and hence political philosophy, possible. If the human order is as perfectly integrated into the determined order of nature as are fish and birds, how is it that human beings alone among the species think in terms of good and evil, just and unjust? Why did Spinoza write the *Ethics* rather than *On the Origin of Species*? Here, Spinoza's answer is roughly that human nature, unlike leonine or canine nature, requires human beings to live under the hegemony of laws and government. Human nature, to be sure, exists within the overall order of nature. Spinoza denies that the human can escape or evade the comprehensive order of nature. Yet within the whole there is a certain heterogeneity of the parts that makes the good for a human being different from the good of all other species or creatures. What, then, is that good?

The good for human beings is to live in society because only society makes self-preservation and hence liberation from fear a positive reality. Reason enjoins men to seek peace, and peace cannot be maintained except in the context of a commonwealth (*respublica*).[27] In one of his rare direct references to Hobbes, Spinoza says: "No matter what state a man is in, he can be free. For certainly man is free insofar as he is led by reason. But (contrary to Hobbes) reason urges peace in all circumstances; moreover, peace cannot be obtained unless the common rights of the state [*civitatis*] are maintained without infringement. Therefore, the more a man is led by reason, i.e., the more he is free, the more will he steadfastly maintain the rights of the state and carry out the commands of the supreme power of which he is a subject."[28]

Hobbes's view seems to have changed over time. In *Leviathan* he makes it nothing short of "the first and fundamental law of nature" that men ought to strive for peace whenever they have a hope of attaining it.[29] Make peace, not war, is the foremost "suggestion" of reason. But Spinoza is here probably thinking of that passage in *De cive* where Hobbes identifies reason with the desire for honors and glory, for "man scarce esteems anything good, which hath not somewhat of eminence in the enjoyment, more than that which others do possess."[30] Reason, rather than being a cause of civic harmony, is, in *De cive,* the unique source of human disorders. Unlike the beasts who use their voices "to signify their affections to each other," humans use their reason to signal "a contestation for honor and preferment." Whereas the other species are able to live in peace without envy and hatred, "the tongue of man is a trumpet of war and sedition."[31]

The difficulty immediately recognized by Spinoza is that while reason is a part of human nature, even the best part, it is still only a part. Indeed, Spinoza goes further than Hobbes in emphasizing the rarity of reason. Hobbes maintained that even though human beings may be vain, competitive, and superstitious, there was still a common propensity toward rationality that experience bestows on all. "Reason," Hobbes wrote in the *Elements,* "is no less of the nature of man than passion, and is the same in all men."[32] Reason here is not a faculty of intuiting the essences of things but a capacity of calculation. "Reason," he states, "is nothing but Reckoning," that is, discovering which means are the most appropriate to attain desired ends.[33] For Spinoza, however, reason remains a more difficult attainment. Unlike Hobbes, Spinoza seeks to recapture some of the classical dignity of reason as the *ens perfectissimum*. Reason is not just the ability for making sound calculations but is connected to the highest good, which is contemplation. There is no room for the contemplative ideal in Hobbes's understanding, but for Spinoza the highest virtue is connected to the exercise of the rational intellect.[34]

For Spinoza the problem remains: How can political life can be possible for human beings, who are far from perfectly rational and whose capacity for reason may even be deeply impaired? The issue is posed as follows. Everyone wishes to live securely, as far as possible from the reach of fear, and this would be impossible if everyone obeyed his own desires or if reason was lowered to the level of passions, like hatred and envy. As evidence, Spinoza refers the reader back to a passage that he says was "proved" in chapter 5 of the *Treatise*:

> Now if men were so constituted by nature that they desired nothing except what true reason indicates, then of course the social order would require no laws, but it would be enough, absolutely, to teach men true moral lessons, so that they would do spontaneously, wholeheartedly, and in a manner worthy of free men, what is really useful. But human nature is constituted very differently from that. Everyone, indeed, seeks his own advantage, but people want things and judge them useful, not at all by the dictate of sound reason, but for the most part only from immoderate desire and because they are carried away by affects of the mind which take no account of the future and of other things. That is why no social order can subsist without dominion and force, and hence, laws which moderate and restrain men's immoderate desires and unchecked impulses.[35]

Spinoza adds, as a possible rejoinder to the Hobbesian sovereign, that he does not favor giving the government arbitrary power over the lives of its subjects. "Human nature," he assures the reader, "does not allow itself to be compelled absolutely"; and with reference to the "tragic poet," Seneca, he observes that the violent regimes perish while "moderate ones last" (*moderata durant*).[36]

This passage brings to mind another from book IV of the *Ethics,* where Spinoza gives a succinct but powerful statement of the problem. In the second scholium to proposition 37, Spinoza briefly reviews his doctrine of natural right. Every person, he affirms, exists by sovereign natural right and, by that right, judges what is good or bad according to his own advantage.[37] Now if everyone exercised his natural right in accord with his reason, there would be no need for government, for reason mandates peace, and peace entails mutual respect.[38] But because a central thesis of Spinoza's psychology is that human beings are prone to superstition and emotion, then the exercise of our natural right puts us directly at variance with one another. Thus if we are to live together in peace, it is necessary to forgo the exercise of our natural right to all things for a more limited share of the right to some things. This condition of mutual forbearance, whereby we agree to limit our natural right, is the legitimate origin of society. Only within the context of society is the exercise of natural right transformed into a moral right. Nothing in the state of nature is either good or bad, because nature can be neither good nor bad. Terms of moral distinction have meaning only within society, because it is only for the sake of social convenience that they are created at all.[39] "There is in the state of nature," Spinoza avers, "nothing which by universal consent is pronounced good or bad," for "such ideas are only possible in society when it is decreed by common consent what belongs to one man and what to another."[40]

The problem that Spinoza here addresses is not how to make rational persons submit to political authority. This, he believes, is no problem, for reason dictates peace and security. The problem is how to make the irrational submit, for such persons are perforce deaf to the ministrations of reason. To construct a regime governed by an omnicompetent philosopher-king is no longer an option. Even if such a person were available, who would listen? For Spinoza, this is at best an ersatz solution to a real problem. The trick is to create a lasting and stable society even in the absence of reason or wisdom. Absent the efficacy of reason, what can motivate men to submit to political authority?[41]

Spinoza's solution to this problem was to become a standard stratagem of liberal political theory.[42] Reason may well enjoin peace and self-preservation, but not everyone, Spinoza believes, is rational. Human beings are prone to have powerful emotions, chief among them hope and fear. Reason is rare: a goal to be attained rather than a premise from which to begin. If reason is powerless to constrain the passions, what must be found is another emotion sufficiently powerful to do so. If no one can be compelled to listen to reason, one might at least be persuaded by the promptings of the desire for self-preservation. If men cannot be induced to seek peace through their reason, they might still be called to do so through their fear, especially fear of abuse at the hands of others. By playing off one passion against another, Spinoza offers a solution to the problem of political authority even in the absence of a controlling intellect.[43]

The desire for self-preservation is a passion powerful enough to offset the passions for gain, honor, or power over others. It is a "universal law of human nature," Spinoza tells us, that everyone acts either to achieve some good or avoid some evil.[44] So long as we remain unprotected by the collective power of law, we are subject to arbitrary treatment and possibly "very great injury" at the hands of others. Outside the bounds of society these injuries are not impermissible. In the state of nature every person retains full power over his natural right to seek his own preservation, a power coextensive with his natural power to do so.[45] No one may legitimately complain of harm any more than the zebra has the right to complain against the lion.

This new authority is not established by a prophetic founder bearing divine rewards and punishments but by a social contract maintained by fear of the evil consequences of failing to attend to individual promises.[46] This solution to the problem of civil authority seems, once again, to come straight out of Hobbes. But here, too, the differences seem almost as powerful as the similarities. According to Hobbes, on at least one important interpretation, the social contract is made possible by virtue of a prior moral obligation that promises be kept.[47] Even in the state of nature there is a moral law that ought to be respected and that provides the foundation for all civil law. The contract comes into being, then, only because in the state of nature the moral law is ineffective. In Hobbes's terms, it is binding *in foro interno* but not *in foro externo*.[48] Civil power exists to make it possible to fulfill peacefully and securely our obligations to the natural law.

For Spinoza, the contract derives from no preexisting moral obligation; it springs from the convenience of the parties seeking security from conditions of uncertainty. "No contract," he writes, "can have any force except by reason of its utility" (*pactum nullam vim habere posse, nisi ratione utilitatis*).[49] Spinoza compares the compact as the foundation of society with an act of usurpation. A person who hands over his wallet to a robber does so because he believes the loss of his money is a lesser evil than the loss of his life. Similarly, one hands over the exercise of one's natural right to society because one expects more good than harm to come through the transfer. The contract is not a moral relationship but a relationship of power. As soon as anyone finds it advantageous to break the terms of the agreement, he may well do so—there is no reason to believe that he will not—unless, that is, they are restrained by fear of some greater evil.[50] The state is the product of a necessity of human nature and should not therefore be endowed with a sacred status. This secularization of the state is Spinoza's ultimate answer to the Mosaic theocracy.

Democracy as the Most Rational Constitution

Chapter 16 of the *Treatise* is the locus classicus of modern democratic theory.[51] Unlike the Hobbesian contract, which begins from egalitarian premises only to arrive at radically inegalitarian conclusions, and unlike the Lockean compact, which was intended to limit the power of the sovereign and to preserve the individual's prepolitical rights, Spinoza's contract is a defense of democracy. Not only was Spinoza the first modern thinker to defend democracy as such, but he did so on the principle that might makes right. Spinoza was by no means the first person to adopt the view that right equals the interest of the stronger. One needs only to recall Thrasymachus, Callicles, and several unnamed speakers in Thucydides.[52] Spinoza is, however, the first to draw avowedly democratic policies from the grim fact that big fish eat little fish.

Spinoza introduces the idea of democracy not from any idealization of the people but as a conclusion drawn from the doctrine of sovereignty strictly understood: "In this way, then, a society can be formed without any conflict with natural right, and every contract can always be preserved with supreme reliability: if each person transfers all the power he has to the society, which alone will retain the supreme right of nature over all things, i.e., the supreme authority, which each person will be bound to obey, either freely, or from fear of the supreme punishment. The right of such a society is called Democracy, which is defined, therefore, as a general assembly of men which has, as a body, the supreme right to do everything it can."[53]

The doctrine of sovereignty was Hobbes's answer to the question of how to reduce the state of war and conflict, which we find in the absence of civil authority, to a condition of peace. The Hobbesian sovereign is the creation of a compact or "covenant" between individuals who, being equal to one another, agree to transfer their natural right to an "artificial person" who can act on behalf of the contracting parties.[54] This artificial person, the leviathan, like the biblical sea monster for which he is named, is entrusted with a grant of absolute power for the sake of establishing and maintaining peace.[55] By virtue of the Hobbesian "covenant of union," the sovereign becomes "the absolute representative of all the subjects" in everything that he does.[56] Although one "artificial person" is not, for Hobbes, the same thing as one "natural person," his reference to the sovereign in the singular indicates an unmistakable preference for monarchy.[57] Once established, the sovereign has the absolute authority to determine the laws of property, to declare war, to establish forms of religion, and to decide which doctrines are fit to be taught.[58]

Democracy is Spinoza's answer to what he regarded as an unresolved problem in the Hobbesian theory of sovereignty: the problem of arbitrary rule that follows from the investiture of absolute power in one person or body of persons. To be sure, Hobbes was not oblivious to the issue of the abuse of power, but he thought it a danger more incident to democracies than to monarchies. He denies, for instance, that the crimes of Nero or Caligula belong properly to monarchies. He asserts instead that "in a popular dominion, there may be as many Neros as there are orators who soothe the people."⁵⁹ Hobbes suggests that under a Nero only the ambitious who are "offensive and contumelious" live in danger, and in what is almost certainly an autobiographical reference he remarks that in a monarchy whoever would lead a "retired life" has nothing to fear, "let him be what he will that reigns."⁶⁰

Spinoza's reply is, surprisingly, not that the Hobbesian sovereign is too strong but that he is not strong enough. He suggests as much in his only other published reference to Hobbes: "With regard to politics, the difference between Hobbes and me . . . consists in this: that I ever preserve the natural right intact so that the Supreme Power in a State has no more power over a subject than is proportionate to the power by which it is superior to the subject. This is what always takes place in the state of nature."⁶¹ In this admittedly cryptic formulation Spinoza seems to be struggling to articulate the following thought. The Hobbesian sovereign is not a party to but a creation of the original covenant. No matter how complete the transfer of right may be, the sovereign remains to some degree limited by, and thus dependent on, the terms of the agreement. Hobbes's own language shows an ambiguity in prescribing precisely how far the sovereign is able to compel obedience. At times he suggests that the sovereign's power is virtually absolute; elsewhere, however, he acknowledges certain fundamental liberties that not even the sovereign may abridge.⁶²

The problem to which Spinoza is alluding is the difference between the sovereign's right to command and his power to do so. This problem is solved in a democracy, where people transfer their right to all things not to a third party but to nothing other than the collective power of a united people. For reasons that Rousseau would develop at length in the *Social Contract*,⁶³ Spinoza argues here that everyone may give over all his rights unstintingly to the sovereign. Indeed, there is an important affinity between Rousseau's conception that each person alienates himself entirely to the "general will" or "common self" and Spinoza's view that the social contract produces "one mind" (*una mente*) such that individuals have only those rights that the public law permits.⁶⁴ In both cases, individuals must give up their rights absolutely or unconditionally so that the power of the sovereign will encounter no restrictions. The terms of the contract being the same for everyone, no one need fear putting himself under the arbitrary control of another. There is no unequal division between the power of the people and that of the sovereign. This is what Spinoza means when he says that, unlike Hobbes, he preserves the natural right of the individual "intact."

Spinoza is not unaware of the classical objection that even Hobbes echoes regarding the capriciousness of democratic majorities. Democratic rule was traditionally thought to be inimical both to the rights of minorities and to the freedom of the individual.[65] Furthermore, democracies were thought to be peculiarly susceptible to the power of demagogues, who could use populist rhetoric to cloak their private agendas. Spinoza thus has to assure the reader that democracies are not vulnerable to this abuse of power:

> Moreover, everyone was able, without hesitation, to run the risk of submitting himself absolutely to the authority and will of another. For, as we have shown, this right of commanding whatever they wish belongs to the supreme powers only so long as they really have supreme power. If they should lose that power, they also lose, at the same time, the right of commanding all things, and [the right] falls to him or those who have acquired [the power] and can retain it. So only very rarely can it happen that the supreme powers command the greatest absurdities. For to look out for their own interests and to retain their authority, it is incumbent on them most of all to consult the common good, and to direct everything according to the dictates of reason. As Seneca says, no one continues a violent rule for long.[66]

The dangers traditionally associated with democratic rule, then, are considerably abated according to the *Treatise* because in obeying the laws of the sovereign, we do no more than obey ourselves.[67] Because the sovereign is the power of the people in their collective capacity, there is little likelihood that a people would knowingly harm itself. Spinoza does not consider the force of the Socratic objection that a sovereign, like an individual, might mistake its own interests and therefore unwittingly do itself harm. Rather, he confidently proposes that especially if the majority of a people be sufficiently large, there is no reason to fear "absurdities."[68] At one point he comes dangerously close to maintaining that the will of the majority is infallible. Because questions of right and wrong come to light only in society, the sovereign alone has the authority to establish the rules of justice. Justice is no more, but also no less, than whatever the sovereign says it is.[69]

The ultimate justification of democracy in the *Treatise* is its enhancement of human freedom. To a degree developed later by Rousseau and then the German idealists, freedom becomes the true end and purpose of political life. But freedom is understood by Spinoza not as negative but as positive liberty.[70] Negative liberty has come to mean essentially the absence of constraints or impediments to action. This kind of liberty, as Hobbes defined it in *Leviathan*, is the freedom to act or forbear from acting when the laws are silent (*silentium legis*).[71] Law and liberty are regarded from this perspective as mutual antitheses. The purpose of the law is not to enhance liberty but to restrain it and to protect persons from its destructive effects. This is not to say that even Hobbes believed that it was the business of the sovereign to abolish liberty. The sovereign has the right to do only what he has the power to do, and no power on earth is sufficient to eradicate the human desire for freedom. "The liberty of man," Hobbes writes, "consisteth in this, that he finds no stop in doing what he has the will, desire, and inclination to do."[72] So long as we breathe, we cannot stop willing and desiring. Human life is a progress from one desire to another that ceases only with life itself.[73]

The *Treatise* offers a very different idea of liberty, one that is more than the absence of impediments to action: liberty as obedience to one's own reason. Freedom is, for Spinoza, a supremely ethical goal. The call to freedom in this ethical sense means the power to be self-determining, to act according to the laws of reason alone. Freedom, then, is the very opposite of lawlessness, which means allowing oneself to be determined by impulses and passive affects; a lawless person is not his own master but a slave to the vagaries of chance and circumstance. The free individual, by contrast, "complies with no one's wishes but his own, and does only those things he knows to be the most important in life and therefore desires very greatly."[74]

Spinoza's conception of ethical freedom and his distinction between slavery and freedom anticipates the theories of Rousseau and Kant. When Rousseau writes that "the impulse of appetite alone is slavery, and obedience to the law one has prescribed for oneself is freedom," he virtually recapitulates Spinoza's viewpoint that the free person is one "who is led by reason alone" and whose actions derive not from anything outside himself but from "adequate ideas."[75] It follows for Spinoza, as well as for Hobbes and Rousseau, that the free man, who lives according to reason, will not isolate himself but will join others in peace and society. This does not represent a limit on the power of self-determination but an enhancement of it, for we can accomplish things in cooperation with others that we could not accomplish by ourselves.[76] Moral freedom is possible once we have decided to forgo the lawlessness of the state of nature and live under laws of our own making. Thus, if reason mandates peace, and peace requires society, then freedom consists in obedience to the laws of society. Spinoza is aware of the paradox of this formula that seems to identify freedom with obedience. By obeying the government we become free, for the alternative would be chaos and hence a complete loss of freedom. But it is one thing to say, as he suggests at one point, that obedience to the law, even "absurd" laws, is the lesser of two evils.[77] It is something else to say, as Rousseau does, that obedience to the law makes one free.[78]

What Spinoza proposes is the classic recipe for positive liberty. In the *Treatise* he attempts to restore something like the classical conception of freedom as the rule of reason but a rule based on an entirely new conception of natural right:

But perhaps someone will think that in this way we make subjects slaves, because they think that a slave is one who acts according to a command, whereas a free man is one who indulges his own disposition. But this is not true without qualification. For really the one who is drawn by his own pleasure, and can neither see nor do anything advantageous to himself, is most a slave. Only he is free who lives wholeheartedly according to the guidance of reason alone. Now, an action according to a command, i.e., obedience, does, in some manner, take away freedom; but it is not that aspect which makes the slave, it is the reason for the action. If the end of the action is not the advantage of the agent himself, but that of the person commanding, then the agent is a slave, and useless to himself. But in a state and under a government [*Republica et imperio*] where the supreme law is the well-being of the whole people, not that of the ruler, one who obeys the supreme power in everything should not be called a slave, useless to himself, but a subject. And therefore, that state is most free whose laws are founded on sound reason [*sana ratione*]. For there each person, when he wishes, can be free, i.e., live wholeheartedly [*integro animi*] according to the guidance of reason.[79]

Where Spinoza most clearly differs from Hobbes and the negative libertarian tradition is in his understanding of the relation between freedom and rationality. Rationality is not simply a means to the satisfaction of desires and inclinations. It is not and ought not to be a slave to the passions, as David Hume said it was. Reason is, rather, essential for and internally related to the full development of individual liberty. Among other things, reason provides a way to understand why we have the kinds of desires that we have. When we understand the causes of our desires, we can become in a sense liberated from them. Not that our desires disappear. As embodied creatures, we can never be free of our desires, nor does Spinoza believe, as did the Stoics, that the ruthless minimization of our desires contributes to our happiness. His point is that when we understand the causes of our desires, these desires no longer unconsciously determine our behavior. Our increase in self-understanding is crucial to our freedom.

Reason, then, could be said to be a therapy for desire. Only by understanding the causes of our desires do we gain power over them. This power in turn enhances our sense of freedom. Spinoza did not go as far as Rousseau and his German followers, who espoused the belief that reason could somehow alter the fundamental structure of our desires. For Spinoza, as for Hobbes, the fundamental desire, the desire of all desires, remains the desire for self-preservation.[80] But even the bare desire for "persistence" comes to have a new meaning for Spinoza. Persistence means not the sustaining of mere life, nor even the maintenance of a comfortable or "commodious" life, but the support of the rational life, the life of free self-understanding. Only the life devoted to reason can be fully or completely free.

It has been suggested that Spinoza's ethic of positive liberty contains dangerous authoritarian, if not totalitarian, implications.[81] Liberal politics has generally rested uneasily with the suggestion that there is a *summum bonum,* a single best way of life. The idea that there is one supreme end for human life has often gone together with the idea that politics should work to force the attainment of that end. Liberalism has generally been thought to work better with an idea of a *summum malum,* a highest evil, making the work of politics the more modest business of avoiding harm rather than maximizing good.[82] This issue is raised, obliquely but significantly, at the end of chapter 16.

Spinoza frames the question in terms of a quarrel between the right of the sovereign and divine right. The right of the sovereign is itself derivative from natural right. The natural right of any class or species is its endeavor (*conatus*) to preserve itself. The natural right of an organism originates in its power to persist. Spinoza's definition of natural right is so far intended to be indifferent to the differences between human and nonhuman species. Operating within a severely naturalistic metaphysics, he articulates the laws of human nature within the comprehensive order of nature. By nature, human beings have the same right as the members of every other species, that is, the right to preserve themselves by whatever means are at their disposal. Natural right is perfectly coextensive with natural powers.

Given the equal right of all persons to exercise their power, Spinoza advocates the doctrine of democratic sovereignty as "the most natural" form of regime and "the one which approached most nearly the freedom nature concedes to everyone" (*maxime naturale videabtur, et maxime ad libertatem*).[83] Democracy is the most natural regime for the crude but compelling reason that the majority in any community contains a greater share of power, and therefore right, than does the minority. Democracy is, therefore, the most natural form of sovereignty; all other forms derive from it. Democracy is also the freest regime because Spinoza believes that the majority would never impose any law that would oppress itself. In a democratic republic, in which everyone freely agrees to transfer his rights to the sovereign, no one gains an unfair advantage over anyone else. Democracy is, then, the *optima Respublica* because each person retains an equal share of the right that he possesses by nature.

The *Treatise* does not answer the question of how people who are described as naturally credulous and prone to superstition can be made rational. By what leap of faith could Spinoza maintain that men who are driven by nothing other than "desire and power" could conclude an agreement to curb their passions and "live wholeheartedly according to the guidance of reason?"[84] Unlike Plato or Maimonides, Spinoza does not advocate the rule of a philosopher-king or a prophet who might educate his subjects to a lofty vision of human perfection. Spinoza's politics are, by contrast, starkly anti-perfectibilian. He is not bereft of an idea of human perfection, but he does doubt that politics or law is the appropriate means by which to achieve it. The distinction between the philosophic few and the unphilosophic many runs like a thread through the *Treatise*. It is precisely Spinoza's awareness of this difference that prevents him from straining to overcome it. The task of politics consists not in raising the many to the level of the few but in creating laws and institutions to prevent the multitude from giving free vent to their passions.

Given what has just been said, no one should confuse Spinoza's democratic politics with his conception of the highest good. The highest good for an individual is not life, nor even the life of the democratic citizen, but the rational life. But Spinoza now maintains that no regime, however constituted, can make people become rational. Although the rational life cannot flourish outside society, no society can compel its members to become rational. Rationality remains an intensely private commitment transcending, even as it arises from, regime politics. Not for nothing have readers often found it difficult to square Spinoza's defense of democracy with his passionate commitment to the radical autonomy of the rational life. Spinoza recognizes that the relationship between the rational individual and the ordinary run of mankind is deeply problematic. He therefore wants to assure his readers that society has nothing to fear from this type of individual while at the same time retaining his emphasis on the utterly solitary character of the philosophic life.[85]

Divine Law and the Problem of Individual Perfection

On the basis of Spinoza's teachings on natural right, a new conception of rationality begins to appear that is at least potentially at odds with the requirements of society. In order to preserve ourselves, Spinoza claims that it is reasonable to seek out others in friendship and society. As with Hobbes, the edicts of natural right lead not to isolation but to joining others for the sake of mutual preservation. We need the help of others if only better to protect ourselves. But this "model" (*examplar*) of human nature is not Spinoza's last word on the subject.[86]

Our rational need for others appears to conflict with the demand for complete rationality. The rational person of whom "we desire to form an idea" is not merely one who can figure out the most efficient means to safety and security but one who is "led by reason alone."[87] Rationality thus entails the control of the passions, for freedom requires that we be the cause of our actions, that we act rather than be acted upon. But the control of the passions is possible only when we know the causes of the passions. Thus there is a hierarchy in Spinoza's conception of rationality, going from the need for sociability to the control of the passions to the knowledge of causes. The ordering of the various goals of reason are presented in serial form in the third chapter of the *Treatise*:

> Whatever we can honorably desire [*honeste cupimus*] is related above all to these three things:
>
> 1. to understand things through their first causes;
> 2. to gain control over the passions, *or* to acquire the habit of virtue;
> 3. to live securely and healthily.[88]

This list indicates that what is of ultimate importance for Spinoza is not the preservation of life as such but the preservation and enhancement of freedom, especially inner freedom, the freedom of mind that comes with knowledge of and hence control over natural causes. Beginning from premises similar to Hobbes's, Spinoza arrives at conclusions that are radically different. We are told that the free or rational person "thinks of nothing less than death," avoids danger, and "always acts honestly, not deceptively."[89] What is more, the rational person who seeks knowledge of the adequate causes of all things is ultimately led to reflect upon God, who is the totality of those causes. The exemplary life culminates in the life of the free person engaged in the solitary and virtually continual contemplation of God and the world, an individual whose thoughts and actions stem not from envy or fear but from feelings of love and friendship.[90]

Spinoza's view of human perfection, though self-regarding, is not necessarily inimical to the social virtues. In chapter 5 of the *Treatise* he presents a compelling account of the social order as arising out of the "useful" and "necessary" things but serving the end of human perfection:

> A social order is very useful, and even most necessary, not only to live securely from enemies, but also to spare oneself many things. For if men were not willing to give mutual assistance to one another, they would lack both skill and time to support and preserve themselves as far as possible. Not all men are equally capable of all things, nor would each one be able to provide those things which, alone, he most needs. Everyone, I say, would lack both powers and time, if he alone had to plow, to sow, to reap, to grind, to cook, to weave, to sew, and to do the many other things to support life, not to mention now the arts and sciences, which are also supremely necessary for the perfection of human nature and its blessedness.[91]

Society may grow out of our common weakness and need for security. We need others to compensate for our lack of strength and ability. But if life in society is a necessary means for self-preservation, it is also conducive to "the perfection of human nature and its blessedness." This perfection is not diminished but enhanced by the presence of others, who make up for our weaknesses and supplement our strengths. "The foundation of virtue," Spinoza writes in the *Ethics,* may be in "this striving to preserve one's own being," but we seek out the aid, comfort, and even love of others for the sake of enhancing our well-being.[92] Nothing is more excellent "than those that agree entirely with our own nature." Because "there is nothing more useful than man to man," when two individuals are joined, "they compose an individual twice as powerful as each one" taken separately and thereby, we expect, more capable of achieving human perfection.[93]

The rules circumscribing the exemplary way of life are set out in the fourth chapter of the *Treatise* in Spinoza's account of philosophical theology or the Divine Law. Even to attribute a doctrine of philosophical theology to Spinoza might appear to be an oxymoron. In the preface to the *Treatise* he urges the strongest possible separation between truth or philosophy and faith or religion. A philosophical theology would seem to be premised on a fundamental confusion, a category mistake, as it were, between the realms of truth and obedience. On the basis of later statements, however, a new or at least different teaching emerges. What Spinoza means by the separation of religion and philosophy turns out to be the separation of philosophy from scriptural theology. Only scriptural religion, not religion as such, is inimical to truth. At the highest level, philosophy and religion, far from being incompatible, are identical. Perhaps no thinker — with the possible exception of Plato — has endowed religion with a higher claim to truth, or philosophy with a greater share in the redemption of mankind. It is no exaggeration to say that Spinoza's divine law lays the basis for a new kind of religion and a new kind of church: the church of reason and the cult of the rational individual.

Spinoza begins his treatment of the divine law with an account of law in its "absolute" sense: "The word *law* [*Legis*], taken absolutely, means that according to which each individual, or all or some members of the same species, act in one and the same certain and determinate manner. This depends either on a necessity of nature or on a decision of men. A law which depends on a necessity of nature is one which follows necessarily from the very nature *or* definition of a thing. One which depends on a decision of men, and which is more properly called a rule of right, is one which men prescribe for themselves and others, for the sake of living more safely and conveniently, or for some other reasons."[94] Law, in other words, seems to be of two kinds. *Lex* follows from the nature or definition of the thing, while *jus* depends on a "decision of men" (*ab hominum placito*), which one person lays down for another. As examples of the first kind of law Spinoza cites the "universal law of all bodies" to lose as much of their motion as they impart to others and certain laws of human psychology that lead us to associate like things with one another. For *jus* he cites the necessity of persuading or compelling men to give up some portion of their natural right for the sake of living in a convenient manner with others (*commodius vivendum*).[95]

Like every theorist who confronts the possibility of a natural law, Spinoza is compelled to note an ambiguity in the use of the term. The word "law" seems to apply to natural phenomena only "figuratively" (*per translationem*).[96] It is commonly applied to commands that can be obeyed or disobeyed depending on human resolve. Only by analogy, then, is the term "law" applicable to natural phenomena, which exhibit no rational understanding or will of their own. If natural laws are laws in the strict sense, who is it that decreed such laws, and what are the penalties for disobedience? For a law to be a law, there must be a lawgiver with the power to compel obedience. If natural laws are laws, they are not laws in this sense, then, for nature does not give decrees or have the power of enforcement. From this it would seem to follow that human law with its notions of command and agency is paradigmatic of law, whereas natural law is law only by analogy.

Spinoza does not want to give up altogether on the possibility of a natural law or divine law. In the first place, divine law is simply Spinoza's term for the power of nature as a whole.[97] Insofar as human beings are themselves a part of nature, the laws governing and regulating their behavior can be called a part of the divine law. Divine law does not supervene upon or contradict the ordinary operations of nature but conforms to them. Spinoza's positive theology, such as it is, depends entirely on the radical identification of God with the extended order of nature.[98] Second, Spinoza denies that human beings occupy a special *imperium,* or place of privilege within the natural order, but are part of a single, unitary system of laws. To say that these laws are the product of divine decree or universal necessity is the same thing. In either case, these laws set out a "manner of living" (*ratio vivendi*) that restrains human nature within certain limits and beyond which it cannot go.[99]

Spinoza uses the term "natural divine law" (*legis divinae naturalis*) to describe "the highest good" for a human being, which includes "the true knowledge and love of God."[100] This law is called natural because it is "universal *or* common to all men" (*universalem, sive omnibus homnibus communem*).[101] That is to say, the natural divine law does not rely on any specific historical revelation, or on the truth of any particular historical narrative, or on the fulfillment of any ceremonial functions. The law is called divine because it teaches us our highest end, which is intellectual perfection. Spinoza explains that he means by intellectual perfection the knowledge of God. But the God that emerges in these pages of the *Treatise* is not the God of mercy and forgiveness but rather the philosophical God of the *Ethics,* an infinitely extended Substance accessible not through prayer or supplication but through the study of the general causal processes of nature. "The more we know natural things," Spinoza writes, "the more perfectly do we know God's essence, which is the cause of all things."[102] The implication of this statement is that because we ourselves are a part or mode of nature, knowledge of God entails a degree of self-knowledge. One could almost say that the injunction to know God is the Spinozist equivalent of the Socratic dictum "Know thyself."

The statement that the highest good of an individual is knowledge of God is intended to effect not just an intellectual but a moral and psychological emancipation of the knower. The knowledge of God is expressed in the closing propositions of the *Ethics* by the phrase *amor Dei intellectualis,* "the intellectual love of God."[103] "The sum total of the divine law, and its highest precept, is to love God as the highest good . . . not from fear of some punishment or penalty, nor from love of some other thing, in which we desire to take pleasure," but rather to love him as "the ultimate end toward which all our actions are to be directed."[104] The perfection of the intellect for no other reason than a desire to know God is said to lead to a condition of genuine happiness or blessedness (*beatitudo*).[105] To speak of the knowledge of God is another way of speaking about the causes of things. In understanding the causes of our actions and desires, we cease to submit passively to them but instead submit them to the control of our intellectual powers. This knowledge brings in turn the redemption of the individual attainable only through the development of individual reason. Such knowledge is redemptive because it liberates the knower from dependence on and submission to unrefined passions and emotions; it is secular because the love of God means essentially a kind of higher self-love.[106]

Spinoza probably took over the idea of the intellectual love of God from Maimonides.[107] The term is introduced near the end of the *Guide of the Perplexed* in the context of a discussion of the "four perfections."[108] Having established to his satisfaction that the highest good for a human being consists in the imitation of God (*imitatio Dei*), Maimonides proffers a text that registers considerable ambiguity over what this imitation requires of us.[109] Is the *imitatio* in question primarily a moral or a theoretical concept? Earlier in the *Guide* Maimonides proposed that the imitation of God is best achieved through the performance of certain actions or the accomplishment of certain deeds.[110]

Because God's nature is inaccessible to us except through the so-called attributes of action, the imitation of God is best revealed through the acquisition of those moral virtues that most closely approximate God's acts of mercy, justice, and loving-kindness. And because the moral virtues are intrinsically bound up with the life of society, human perfection can be achieved only through loving obedience to the commandments of religious law and communal life. Citing Jeremiah 9:22–23 as his proof text, Maimonides suggests that the intellectual love of God entails the imitation of God's actional attributes.[111]

The view that the imitation of God is necessary for correct moral practice is at least partially undercut in the final chapter of the *Guide* where Maimonides presents the ultimate terms of perfection along radically solitary and individualist lines. The perfect individual was characterized earlier as one who lives alone.[112] Maimonides reads the scriptural verse "They shall by thine own . . ." (Prov. 5:17), as suggesting that perfection "pertains to you alone, no one else being associated in it with you in any way."[113] The highest order of perfection, then, must be achieved in solitude, apart from the duties and responsibilities of the moral and communal life. Not only is the imitation of God interpreted here as radically private, but Maimonides gives it a severely intellectualist gloss. Knowledge of God is best acquired not through the imitation of divine actions but through the study of the divine sciences — physics and metaphysics, referred to metaphorically in the *Guide* as the Account of the Beginning and the Account of the Chariot, respectively.[114] Knowledge of God is acquired through a correct knowledge of the workings of nature or through solitary reflection on the divine governance of the world. Such a conception of the love of God does not require the perfect individual to disavow the moral virtues but instead to regard them as subordinate to the acquisition of intellectual excellence. Even Moses, the greatest of all the prophets, returned from Sinai to the practical affairs of his community with his "limbs only" — his mind was elsewhere.[115]

Spinoza identifies the intellectual love of God exclusively with the contemplative ideal. In perhaps this sense alone, he remains a Maimonidean *malgré lui*. The fourth perfection of Maimonides is virtually identical to what Spinoza in the *Ethics* calls "knowledge of the third kind."[116] This knowledge is not a mystical intuition uncommunicable by ordinary discourse, although such an interpretation may be what led to the rehabilitation of Spinoza by the German romantics.[117] Instead, as we have seen, Spinoza is notorious for using traditional religious language and imagery to mask his new, fundamentally irreligious teachings. Even while he says that this third kind of knowledge entails "an adequate idea of the absolute essence of certain attributes of God," it is clear from the immediate context and elsewhere that he means nothing more than a rational knowledge of the natural processes in which we are embedded.[118] The intellectual love of God is not intended to effect the mystical obliteration of the self in some kind of *unio sacra* with the divine. Rather, it lends itself to an ever more intense awareness of one's own individuality. The intellectual love of God is complete only when knowledge of nature contains the intensely held feelings of personal satisfaction, even joy, that come from the exercise of individual reason.[119]

Knowledge of the third kind does not derive, then, from some type of mystical insight different from and inaccessible to the ordinary forms of knowledge acquired through reason and the senses. Toward the end of the *Ethics* Spinoza makes a point of reinforcing the claim that knowledge of this kind is "intellectual," not emotional or imaginative: "From the third kind of knowledge, there necessarily arises an intellectual love of God. For from this kind of knowledge there arises joy, accompanied by the idea of God as its cause, i.e. love of God not insofar as we imagine him as present, but insofar as we understand God to be eternal. And this is what I call intellectual love of God."[120]

Knowledge of the third kind grows out of an intellectual synthesis in which the confused and inadequate ideas that we already possess are made more coherent by being placed within a single comprehensive system of knowledge. This system is the metaphysics of Substance of which everyone and everything is a part. Only when we begin to see ourselves as part of the comprehensive order of nature can the psychology of fear be replaced by a psychology of love. Metaphysics, Spinoza's preferred form of mental therapy, is also, then, a form of erotics in which feelings of love replace fear, envy, and hatred as the dominant motives of human life.[121]

In describing the intellectual love of God, then, Spinoza posits a model of individual perfection that concerns at most a few rare human beings. Although anyone with a moral sense can be supposed to follow the precepts of Spinoza's civil religion, only those endowed with an exceptional rational capacity can love God according to the divine law. Even if this law is "universal or common to all men," invariably only a few follow it.[122] Like Maimonides, Spinoza makes clear that this difference between the few and the many is not merely a contingent fact of society or history to be overcome at some future end point. It is a necessity of nature expressing the psychological and intellectual difference between the wise, who live according to *ratio*, and the vulgar, who live according to *appetitus*.[123]

Perhaps not surprisingly, then, Spinoza has remained a lonely and neglected voice within the democratic tradition. His ruthlessly naturalistic psychology that identifies might with right has found few vocal adherents. His belief that the rule of the stronger — that is, popular sovereignty — is most likely to ensure freedom of opinion and a "liberal spirit" (*liberum ingenium*) has been met with more skeptical views of the power of democratic majorities. The idea that the ultimate terms of perfection are the province of a few scientist-philosophers has inevitably brought with it the charge that Spinoza's model of human excellence is aristocratic and elitist, not to say inconsistent with the premises of his democratic politics.[124]

Spinoza's model of human perfection is elitist, but it is also deeply antipolitical. For this reason it need not contradict his commitment to democracy as the *optima Respublica*. The divine law issues in a command to love God, not to lord it over men. The intellectual love of God cannot be imposed on others but must be practiced by each individual according to his or her own abilities. Spinoza's is a deeply private or solitary idea of the philosophic life, for which the requirements of political rule are inappropriate. As the prophet of the newly liberated self, Spinoza exhorts his readers to rely on their own powers of reason and judgment for the attainment of this ideal. Such a self is likely to seek not domination of, but freedom from, the community in order to pursue this all-consuming passion. The *amor Dei intellectualis* is an intensely private model of human perfection, for "all things excellent are as difficult as they are rare."[125]

6

From Jerusalem to Amsterdam

In the final chapters of the *Treatise* Spinoza turns from the problems of the *optima Respublica* and the best way of life to the real world of politics and history. Chapter 17 begins with the following observation: "In the last chapter we contemplated the right of the supreme powers to do everything, and the natural right which each person has transferred to them. But though the view expressed there agrees in no small measure with practice, and a practice could be established so that it approached more and more closely to the condition contemplated, still, it will never happen that this view should not remain, in many respects, merely theoretical [*mere theoretica*]."[1]

Throughout chapter 17 and the remainder of the work, Spinoza's account of the political history of the Bible is significantly mediated by his reading of Tacitus and the Roman historians whose works are frequently cited in support of his "conclusions" (*concluduntur*).[2] In fact, he immediately moves from the level of high theory to the plane of historical generalization when he notes that no one ever so completely transfers his natural right to the sovereign that he does not retain some portion of it for his own private use. This being the case, even the best regime will exhibit some tension between the power of the sovereign and the rights of the subjects. As a result, every government has always had more to fear from the disaffection of its citizens than from the animosity of its neighbors. The "task and toil" (*hoc opus, hic labor est*) of government, Spinoza now avers, is "to so establish everything that everyone, no matter what his mentality, prefers the public right to private advantage."[3]

In the final chapters of the *Treatise* Spinoza reads the current Dutch debates over church and state back into the Hebrew Scripture.[4] The Dutch had already used the image of themselves as a "chosen" people in the context of the war of independence from Spain. Throughout the sixteenth and seventeenth centuries numerous comparisons between the history of Holland and the history of the Jews were made to justify the existence of an independent nation whose model could be drawn from the very words of Scripture. The Calvinist clergy had used Scripture to interpret the Dutch republic as the "new Israel" and their own position as akin to that of the ancient prophets. They claimed for themselves the sole right of scriptural interpretation and the eradication of heresy. Like the Puritans in England, the Dutch Calvinist church leaders considered themselves the equal of the prophets of ancient Israel and saw themselves, like the prophets, as seeking to create a kingdom of priests and a holy nation.

Spinoza reverts here to the scriptural narrative of the ancient Hebrews not least because of its place within the emergent Dutch national consciousness. To be sure, he uses the example of ancient Israel in order to subvert the Calvinists' use of it. The story of Israel functions in the *Treatise* very much the way the model of ancient Rome did in Machiavelli's *Discourses,* that is, as a reflecting mirror held up to the present. The influence of Machiavelli's republicanism is immediately evident throughout these chapters in the appeal to classical sources and texts, the praise of the virtues of liberty and self-government, the denunciations of clericalism and the abuses of monarchical rule, and the search for laws that promote the common good.[5] Spinoza's republicanism is mediated by a scriptural inheritance that most clearly separates his work from Machiavelli's. To a far greater degree than his Florentine predecessor, Spinoza realizes the role played by the language of Scripture for instilling obedience to the law. Although Spinoza viewed Machiavelli as a kindred spirit, at least in his opposition to royal authority and the power of the clergy, he regarded the purpose of the republic as guaranteeing the freedom of individuals to believe what they like in matters of religion and to speak about their beliefs. An important strand of individualism, especially the freedom of conscience and belief, runs through the *Treatise* but is muted in the *Discourses.*

Spinoza refers to the rise and fall of the Hebrew state in order to convey a teaching about the signal importance of obligation. Whereas the Calvinist clergy use the prophetic teachings of Scripture to appeal over and above the head of even an existing monarch, Spinoza uses the image of Moses as lawgiver to reassert the primacy of the law. Indeed, it is the primacy of law in Judaism that makes the Judaic state, for Spinoza, a paradigm for the kind of state he wants to recommend.[6] Judaism's emphasis on actions and behavior, the entire realm of the *mitzvot,* makes it an ideal source for a model of the liberal state that grants freedom of opinion and belief. Earlier in the *Treatise,* Spinoza castigated Judaism as a purely political legislation void of higher ethical purposes, but he now invokes a nontranscendent civil religion that is virtually identical with the public political interest. The legal and practical character of Judaism is now rehabilitated as the basis for obligation to the secular authority. Spinoza wants to enlist Scripture in the service of a democratic republic rather than using it to exacerbate existing tensions between church and state. Addressing his audience in the only language they would understand, Spinoza uses the story of Moses at Sinai to urge both the subordination of the clergy to secular control and the toleration of religious heterodoxy as necessary for the welfare of the state. The *Treatise* went beyond the standard debates between Remonstrants and Counterremonstrants in defending toleration not simply as a necessary evil but as a positive good contributing to the peace and prosperity of the state.[7]

The Hebrew Theocracy: Paradise Lost

At the center of the secular history in the *Treatise* stands Spinoza's account of the Hebrew commonwealth, or "theocracy."[8] By theocracy Spinoza means a form of political organization in which the civil and ecclesiastical authorities are one and the same. Anyone who betrayed the law was guilty of impiety, and anyone who broke with the religion ceased to be a citizen of the state.[9] Spinoza's reasons for investigating the theocracy were not just antiquarian. Maimonides and traditional Jewish sources made theocracy into the perfect regime. If Spinoza could demonstrate that theocracy contained internal defects that led to its collapse, he would go a long way toward calling this form of governance into question. Indeed, theocracy was not merely an ancient political constitution with no relevance to the present. Spinoza's biblical history was in part a commentary on those Calvinist sects that sought to use the Hebrew Bible as a source of political authority.[10]

The *Treatise* provides two quite different accounts of the Hebrew commonwealth, which correspond roughly to the two methodologies employed in the work. In the fifth chapter, as we have seen, he presents the theocracy not as the perfect or divine order but as an order appropriate to the rudest and most primitive times, to human beings sunk in ignorance and superstition. Under these circumstances it was relatively easy for Moses, who "excelled the others in divine power," to maintain his position of political leadership. Because of "the divine power in which he was pre-eminent," Moses, like a Machiavellian prince or a Rousseauian legislator, was able to impose a code of laws on a disorderly multitude.[11]

Later in the *Treatise,* after introducing the concepts of natural right, the state of nature, and the social contract, Spinoza describes the origins of the Hebrew state in the following terms:

> After the Hebrews escaped from Egypt, they were no longer bound by any law to another nation, but were permitted to institute new laws for themselves as they pleased, and to occupy whatever lands they wanted to. For after they had been freed from the intolerable oppression of the Egyptians, and had not attached themselves to any mortal by any contract, they again acquired their natural right to do everything they could, and each of them could decide anew whether he wanted to keep it, or to surrender it and transfer it to someone else. So when they had been placed in this natural condition, they decided, on the advice of Moses, in whom they had the utmost trust, to transfer their right only to God, not to any mortal. Without further delay they all promised equally, in one voice, to obey God in absolutely all his commands, and not to recognize any other law except what he would establish by prophetic revelation. And this promise, *or* transfer of right to God, was made in the same way as above we have conceived it to be done in ordinary society, when men decide to surrender their natural right. For by an explicit covenant and an oath they freely surrendered their natural right and transferred it to God, without being compelled by force or terrified by threats (Exod. 24:7).[12]

In this passage from chapter 17 Spinoza presents the Jewish commonwealth as a theocracy in name only.[13] Unlike in the earlier account, where Moses is seen as a lawgiver and prince, he is here treated as an advisor in whom the Hebrews put "the utmost trust." Spinoza now maintains that the Jewish state was based on the free transfer of rights as in "ordinary society." Even though the people had "in opinion" transferred all their rights to God, in fact they "absolutely" maintained the right of sovereignty for themselves "as in a democracy."[14] All remained bound by the same covenant and all retained an equal right to consult the deity. Only after the Hebrews heard the voice of God and replied that "all that the Lord hath spoken we will do" did they abrogate their rights to Moses (Exod. 19:8).

Far from excoriating the fact that the Jewish state was based on a theoretically false idea of God as a legislator, judge, and king who has a special relationship to one particular nation as he had earlier in the *Treatise,* Spinoza now goes out of his way to praise the theocracy for the considerable strengths that it possessed. Taking a page from Machiavelli's *Prince,* Spinoza praises the Hebrews' use of citizen armies. The army was composed of citizens between the ages of twenty and sixty, with no exceptions, who formed an important check on "the unbridled lust of the leaders [*Principum libidinem*]."[15] Writing with an eye to the present, he drolly observes that if the citizen-soldiers of a theocracy were able to control the ambition of leaders who were fighting for the glory of God, it must be much easier to restrain contemporary monarchs who are out for their own glory and who use mercenaries to suppress popular liberty.[16] It was the citizen-soldiers who "by their virtue, work, and great expense of blood" (*virtute, labore, et magno sui sanguinis*) contributed more than any other institution to "the freedom and glory of the state" (*imperii libertas et gloria*).[17]

In addition, Spinoza praises the Hebrew state for the security of property and person that it bestowed on all citizens. Even poverty was endurable, he maintains, in a state where "loving-kindness towards your neighbor, i.e., towards your fellow citizen, had to be cultivated with the utmost piety," even if doing so is but a means of gaining the favor of God the King.[18] Finally, Spinoza singles out those "causes" that helped to "strengthen the hearts" (*animos firmare*) of the Jews and allowed them to maintain their sovereignty "with special constancy and virtue" (*singulari constantia et virtute*). Among these were a devotion to country, a healthy capacity for hatred and contempt, the singularity of their religious laws and rituals, and a firm belief in their own "election" over other nations.[19]

Spinoza admits that the Hebrew theocracy might have been "eternal" had it not been for certain fateful steps that led to its decline. The most significant of these was the creation of a priestly caste, the Levites, who assumed the sole right of interpreting the law. Spinoza traces the emergence of the Levites back to the incident of the golden calf (Exod. 32:25–28; Deut. 10:8).[20] According to the account given in Exodus, when Moses was away in Sinai the people beseeched Aaron, his brother, to fashion an idol that they might worship. Aaron complied, and when Moses got word from God that the people had relapsed into idolatry, he argued with God until he won their ultimate forgiveness. Nevertheless, when Moses returned from the mountaintop and entered the camp, he smashed the idols and declared, "Who is on the Lord's side? Let him come unto me." On that day, according to the Torah, three thousand of the idol worshipers were slain.[21]

The account in the *Treatise* of the downfall of the Jewish commonwealth is traced directly back to this incident. Spinoza cites Ezekiel to the effect that the duties of the priesthood had been originally intended for the firstborn.[22] But when all except the Levites worshiped the golden calf, the firstborn were rejected and the Levites were substituted in their place. Being the only tribe that remained pure of idolatry, they took upon themselves the task of reproaching the others for their moral failings and claimed for themselves the sole right of consulting the deity. Over time the priests, "who were idle [and] envied . . . especially when food was expensive," became hateful to the people. Had this fateful step not occurred and had everyone retained the rights of priesthood, all the subsequent problems could have been avoided, but as it happened, the Levites, the distant ancestors of the rabbis who ordered Spinoza's excommunication, hastened the disintegration of the state from within.[23]

Spinoza is so struck by this development that he introduces a comment by way of a passage from Tacitus: "At that time God's concern was not with their security, but with punishment" (*illo tempore non fuisse Deo curae securitatem illorum, fuisse ultionem*).[24] "And I cannot sufficiently wonder," he writes, "that there was so much anger in the heavenly heart that he established the laws themselves, which always aim only at the honor, well-being and security of the whole people, with the intention of taking vengeance and punishing the people, with the result that the laws seemed not to be laws, i.e., the salvation of the people, but rather penalties and punishments."[25]

The idea that the Hebrew state was under a divine malediction flies directly in the face of Spinoza's oft-repeated denials of a particular providence. As we have seen, the idea that God could act vengefully or angrily is a piece of anthropomorphism that grows out of the very human propensity toward superstition. Just as it is absurd to believe that the Jewish nation was "elected" by divine providence, so is it false to think that the destruction of the state was a sign of God's displeasure.[26] When Spinoza here speaks of God's anger, he is using traditional language to make a secular point. He showed earlier that the chosenness of a people referred exclusively to the excellence of their laws and institutions, but he now uses God's malediction to indicate the establishment of the Levites as the cause of all the later conflicts that plagued the Jewish state.[27]

Spinoza uses this chapter from biblical history to illustrate the origins and dangers of an independent clergy. It is equally evident that the example of subsequent clerical abuses of power was never far from his mind:

> For all the gifts they were bound to give the Levites and priests, as well as the fact that the first-born were obliged to be redeemed and to give money to the Levites on a per capita basis, and finally, the fact that only the Levites were permitted to approach the sacred things — all these things continuously accused them of defilement and rejection. And again, the Levites had the opportunity to continually reproach them. For there is no doubt that among so many thousands there were many relentless and foolish theologians. As a result the people were anxious to keep an eye on the Levites' deeds — no doubt they were men — and as happens, to charge them all because of one person's offense.[28]

Spinoza concludes his account with the observation that "there was continual murmuring."[29]

The elevation of the Levites to priestly status was the prototype for all later theologico-political conflicts. The "murmuring" against the Levitical aristocracy eventually extended to Moses himself, whom the people began to suspect of arbitrarily elevating his own tribe to the priesthood (Num. 8:17). The assumption of ecclesiastical authority by the Levites destroyed the semblance of equality of all those who had shared in the Sinai experience. The ensuing resentment of the Levites produced a spirit of rebelliousness and an extended period of political disorder (Deut. 31:21). We do not know what Moses replied to the "murmurers," but Spinoza states in the *Treatise* that Moses, being unable to convince them with reasons (*nec eos ulla ratione sedare*), instituted another massacre to subdue the rebels.[30] Spinoza adds the ominous statement that rebellion failed; he does not say that harmony was reestablished.[31]

After the death of Moses things went from bad to worse. The establishment of an independent clergy led to the demand for an election of a king in order to offset the power of the priests. It was hoped that the institution of a monarch might normalize the political situation by reinstating some semblance of the equal citizenship that had existed before the priests gained the upper hand. The establishment of a king created "a great inducement to new rebellions," which resulted eventually in "the complete ruin of the whole state" (*imperii totius ruina*).[32] The first kings, recruited from the ranks of "private citizens," ruled moderately, but their sons, ruling precariously, felt unable to tolerate the priestly aristocracy, who had become a "state within a state" (*imperium in imperio*). The result was a usurpation of power by the monarchs, who conspired to get all the sovereign rights into their own hands. The ensuing conflict between kings and priests was the final nail in the coffin of the original theocracy. "There was no end to dissension and civil wars," Spinoza concludes.[33] The rest, one could say, is history.

The Secularization of the Sacred

The last three chapters of the *Treatise* are devoted to a single proposition, namely, that the political control over religion is necessary for the sake of civil peace and for the sake of political, intellectual, and even religious liberty. The striking paradox of the *Treatise* is that Spinoza argues for the sharpest possible separation of philosophy and theology only to settle in the end on the radical subordination of theology to political control. This conclusion raises the issue of whether Spinoza's politics results in some form of absolutism, denying, as it must, the sacred liberal separation of church and state.

Before turning to this main theme, Spinoza observes that the Hebrew polity contained many excellent features that are "well worth noting" and even today "would be highly advisable to imitate."[34] Among the principles or "political dogmas" that recommend themselves are, first, the need to choose a sovereign authority, like Moses during his lifetime, endowed with sole responsibility for the creation and administration of law and, second, the need to prevent the theologians ("the ministers of sacred affairs") from using their power to judge and excommunicate citizens.[35] Be this as it may, Spinoza notes that re-creating the biblical polity in the present would be difficult, not to say impossible. Doing so would require a whole new covenant between God and those who wished to transfer their right to him, and this, God has revealed through the apostles, he is no longer willing to do. The basis for any future covenant must be found not in "stone tablets" but in "the heart with the spirit of God" (*Dei spiritu in corde scribi*).[36]

Spinoza goes on to adduce a second, more political reason for the inadvisability of imitating the biblical theocracy: "Moreover, such a form of state could be useful, perhaps, only for those who are willing to live by themselves, alone, without any foreign trade [*externo commercium*], shutting themselves up within their own boundaries, and segregating themselves from the rest of the world. It could not be at all useful for those to whom it is necessary to have dealings with others. So it could be useful only for a very few people."[37] The theocracy was possible only in a world where "commerce" between peoples was expressly prohibited and each nation strove for the greatest possible self-sufficiency. The idea of commerce in the sense of both trade and the exchange of ideas that leads to the cultivation of the arts, science, and philosophy is, as we shall see, a vital component of the modern republic. The regime endorsed in the *Treatise* is not the ancient republic, with its austere moralism and self-sacrificing devotion to the common good, but the modern commercial republic, with its openness to popular enlightenment, travel, and the freedom of the individual.

The main positive lesson that Spinoza learned from the study of history was the necessity of political control over religious authority. In chapter 19 of the *Treatise* he deduces political control over religion from the nature of sovereign power. The right of the sovereign, we recall, is itself derivative from natural right. The natural right of any class or species is simply its endeavor (*conatus*) to preserve itself. The political sovereign, then, has the right to control whatever he can control for the sake of self-preservation. This right entails control not only over civil law but also over the law concerning "sacred matters."[38] By sacred matters Spinoza means only the external forms (*cultum externum*) of religious worship, that is, its practices and institutions, not its opinions and beliefs. "The internal worship of God [*internus enim Dei cultus*]" belongs inalienably to the individual.[39] What he demands is that the external forms of religion and piety (*Religionis cultus et pietatis*) "be accommodated to the peace and utility of the state" (*republicae paci et utilitati accommodari*).[40]

What Spinoza means by the outward forms of piety clearly harks back to the seven dogmas of religion enumerated in the fourteenth chapter of the *Treatise*. Above all else, these dogmas commend acts of charity and justice toward one's neighbors, which means an absolute prohibition against intolerance. Spinoza now claims that the command to practice justice and charity acquires the force of right only within the state.[41] The state, or "supreme power," may have no power, and hence no right, to control the contents of our minds, but it may legitimately control our deeds. In what is perhaps the most remarkable piece of secularization in the entire work, Spinoza suggests that the correct worship of God is the highest form of patriotism or civic duty. "It is certain," he avers, "that religious duty towards a person's country is the supreme religious duty he can render."[42] As evidence for this last proposition he cites the example of Manlius Torquatus, a pagan hero esteemed by both Plutarch and Machiavelli, whose devotion to the public welfare outweighed even his devotion to family and children. The public welfare is that to which all law, both human and divine, should be made to conform.[43]

The assimilation of "spiritual rights" to the "temporal rights" of the sovereign might seem to destroy both the autonomy and spirituality of true religion, as well as the liberty of the individual to practice what religion he likes. Spinoza's statements that "the supreme powers are the interpreters of religion" and that "no one can obey God rightly if he does not accommodate to the public advantage the practice of religious duty" appear to reduce all religion to a species of civil theology.[44] Such statements also directly contradict the earlier thesis that "the supreme right of thinking freely, *even concerning religion*, is in the hands of each person" and "it is *inconceivable* that anyone can abandon his claim to this right."[45] Therefore, Spinoza says, "the supreme authority to explain religion and to judge regarding it will be in the hands of each person, because it is a matter of the right of each person."[46] How, then, to explain this contradiction? Is the individual or the state to have ultimate authority in matters of religion?

This startling paradox cuts to the very core of the *Treatise*. After earlier seeking to liberate the individual from the power of ecclesiastical interpreters, Spinoza now seeks to subordinate the same individuals to political authority. A "Machiavellian" reading of the *Treatise* might even suggest that Spinoza seeks to coax individuals to leave the protective cocoons of their particular theological traditions precisely to create a new kind of dependency, dependence on the modern secular state. This type of state has been called totalitarian because it fails to recognize any legal or political institution to which the sovereign is accountable. The only limit to sovereign power is the fear of armed insurrection.[47]

To be sure, Spinoza is an absolutist if by that is meant that he brooks no limitations on the powers of the sovereign. However, the expansion of state power is necessary precisely in order to protect the rights of individuals from the ambitions of powerful and highly mobilized groups. His aim is not to create a version of Orwell's *Animal Farm,* but to prevent the Balkanization of society into warring factions where the strong eat the weak.[48] He does not share anything like Montesquieu's or Tocqueville's later enthusiasm for the mediating function of civil associations as the seedbed of liberty over and against an all-powerful state. Nor does he share contemporary liberalism's pluralistic image of the peaceful competition of rival groups for access to political power and scarce resources. Spinoza's form of liberalism is individualist but not pluralist. He sees in the power of groups not a source of liberty but bands of conspirators organized against the interests of both individuals and the state.[49] Only a unified national sovereignty can defend the interests of the individual from clerical strongmen and bullies.[50]

The logic of Spinoza's position is not difficult to ascertain. His strategy of strengthening the power of the state has as its correlate the weakening of the power of the clergy. Indeed, his assimilation of spiritual to temporal rights is based not only on a reading of biblical history but on an assessment of the current political situation. The dispute over who had the ultimate right of scriptural interpretation was part of a bitter controversy over the primacy of church or state. The Calvinist sects often identified themselves with the prophets of ancient Israel, then on that basis claimed the right to establish and enforce norms of conduct befitting a holy people.[51] But whereas the Calvinist divines identified themselves with the prophets, Spinoza sought to rehabilitate the image of Moses as a lawgiver who not only brought his people from the state of nature to civil society but also subordinated the Ahronide priests to political control.

The task of the *Treatise,* then, is not to create a new dependency on the state but to use the state as an instrument for the liberation of the individual from the power of the clerics. Spinoza seeks to forge an identity of interests between the newly liberated individual and the democratic republic. Only a powerful state can protect the rights and liberties of the individual against tyrannical religious majorities with their power to punish and ostracize. At one point Spinoza even asks rhetorically, What if the sovereign uses his power to tyrannize and oppress? He adds, unconvincingly, that because both sovereign and clergy are equally fallible in matters of scriptural interpretation, the state will go to ruin more quickly if private citizens take upon themselves authority over "divine right" (*jus divinum*).[52]

Spinoza is aware of these difficulties and seeks to allay the concerns of his readers by offering two kinds of arguments. He affirms that whoever would deny the public power authority over religion is attempting to divide the sovereign by stirring up "quarrels and disagreements" between kings and priests "which can never be restrained."[53] For evidence he draws again from an array of historical examples. Returning to the previous chapter, he rebukes the prophets, who as "private men," irritated rather than reformed humanity by their incessant rebukes and censures.[54] As outspoken critics of even pious kings, the prophets were a perpetual cause of dissension and agitation. Spinoza draws also on the recent history of the conflict between the German emperors and the pope, which he says will be a "paradigm" for all. Every effort to curtail the power of the papacy even by the least bit failed to make a dent. What no monarch could accomplish with "iron and fire," the popes of Rome were able to achieve with "the might of their pens." The lesson that Spinoza draws in this chapter is the necessity for the civil authority to retain a monopoly on "force and power."[55]

Spinoza thus puts the argument for the secular control of religion in terms of a stark either-or. Either the sovereign controls spiritual rights or the ecclesiastics will control temporal rights. There is no third way. Power abhors a vacuum, and "anyone who wants to take this authority away from the supreme power is trying . . . to make himself sovereign."[56] In speaking of reasons for the seemingly endless (*semper*) disputes over the control of sacred matters in Christian states, Spinoza offers a diagnosis: "Surely it could seem very unnatural that there has always been a question about something so evident and necessary, and that the supreme powers never had this right without controversy, indeed, never had it without great danger of rebellions and harm to religion. Undoubtedly, if we could not assign any definite cause for this, I might be easily persuaded that everything I have shown . . . is only theoretical, *or* an example of that kind of speculation which could never have any use. But anyone who considers the origins of the Christian religion will find the cause of this completely clear."[57]

The cause of the dispute over spiritual power derives originally from the emergence of Christianity as a religion independent of and in opposition to the state. This opposition eventually hardened into a conflict between the emperors and the church that has persisted up to the present. How, over time, ecclesiastics and men of the pen came to acquire power over kings and emperors, who had fire and the sword at their command, is a story that Nietzsche would later tell. From the outset the church set itself up as a tribunal or protector of the faith concerned to monitor opinions and beliefs. Lacking any political authority, the church set about reforming the opinions of men, which is the precise opposite of the ancient Hebrew condition; in that case, the temple and the state were inseparable, and "the kings had a very great right concerning sacred matters."[58]

Freedom of Speech and the Liberated Individual

Although Spinoza grants virtually unlimited authority to the state to control religion in the penultimate chapter of the *Treatise,* he makes a significant alteration in the direction of individual liberty and freedom of speech in the final chapter. He begins the penultimate chapter, chapter 19, with the bold assertion that "those who hold political authority have a right to do *everything* and that all law depends solely on their decision," but now it appears that "everything" does not necessarily mean everything.[59] The sovereign may control only what it is in his power to control; for practical as well as theoretical reasons there are important limitations to what a sovereign may do. Although Spinoza said earlier that the "internal worship" of God was inalienable and within everyone's private right, he now extends this right beyond the inner theater of people's private beliefs and feelings to a considerably wider realm of speech and opinion. The final chapter of the *Treatise* takes its title from a passage in Tacitus's *History*: "In a free state everyone is permitted to think what he likes and to say what he thinks."[60] This classical republican sentiment sets the stage for much of what is to follow.

Spinoza produces several arguments in favor of allowing the maximum latitude for freedom of opinion. The first follows from the very definition of natural right as the liberty to do whatever one's individual power permits. This argument is addressed to sovereigns who may be tempted to use their power to crush freedom of thought and discussion. Rather than using the argument from natural right to enlarge the scope of sovereign power, Spinoza focuses instead on the limitations of that right.

His awareness of the limitations on sovereign power begins from the recognition that human actions are easier to control than the mind, for "it cannot happen that a mind should be absolutely subject to the control of someone else."[61] The difficulty stems from the fact that although governments may be effective at controlling behavior, including public speech, they have been much less successful at finding ways of controlling the mind. The attempt to extend sovereign power to the control of thought and judgment, "to prescribe to each person what one must embrace as true and what reject as false," is condemned in the *Treatise* as tyrannical and violent (*imperium violentum*).[62] Questions of truth and falsity, as opposed to moral issues of good and bad, belong to natural right, which a person cannot abdicate "even if he wishes to."[63]

At this point Spinoza continues to speak in the language of hard-boiled realism. His arguments so far have been couched solely in terms of the power that the sovereign has at his disposal. The emphasis is not on the rights of the subject but on the power of the sovereign. Note that Spinoza's judgment about the limitation of sovereign power does not derive from any belief in the sacred or privileged status of the mind but from the definition of sovereignty strictly understood. Actions can be controlled, but what is going on in the mind cannot be seen and is therefore less susceptible to coercion. Spinoza does not here consider the possibility that truly tyrannical regimes may and in fact often do control the minds of their subjects to a considerable extent. Presumably, had he known of or contemplated the possibilities for mind control posed by propaganda and modern advertising, he would have seen nothing to prohibit the sovereign from using these techniques to enhance his power.

These considerations were not altogether beyond Spinoza's ken. Earlier in the *Treatise* he remarks that "though hearts cannot be commanded in the same way tongues can, still hearts are *to some extent* under the command of the supreme power."[64] Spinoza acknowledges that emotions do not arise at the express command of the sovereign, but "experience abundantly testifies to" (*experientia abunde testatur*) the extent to which the authority of the office may influence subjects so that "the great majority of men believe, love, and hate whatever [the sovereign] wills."[65] How far Spinoza believed that the thoughts and the passions (loves and hates) of one's subjects can be shaped is not clear. By the end of the *Treatise*, however, Spinoza emphasizes less what the sovereign can control than what evades his power. The attempt to control the contents of the mind is wrong not because it is immoral but because it is inherently self-defeating.

The limitations on the natural right of the sovereign do not constitute Spinoza's only argument in favor of toleration. Bound to this is the pragmatic or political argument that policies of persecution tend to backfire. Attempts to control the content of thought, far from producing consensus and harmony, breed conflict and ultimately revolution. The reasons are woven into the very fabric of human nature. There is, to begin with, the sheer diversity of human judgment. Spinoza admits that judgment can be biased in many ways. As he states in the preface, what leads one person to piety and religion leads another to laughter and contempt.[66] This difference of opinion may be carried to "almost incredible lengths." That "there are as many differences between men's heads as there are between their palates" militates against any policy of uniformity.[67] Next, though conceding that sovereigns have the right to brand all speech that does not accord with their own as criminal and "can rightly consider as their enemies anyone who does not think absolutely as [the sovereigns do] in every matter," Spinoza counsels that he is discussing not just the strict rights of the sovereign but "what is advantageous" (*quod utile est*).[68] A doctrine of natural right and sovereignty needs to be supplemented with one of political prudence and restraint, that is, knowing when enough is enough.

It follows from the above that any attempt to control speech must fail. Not only are our faculties diverse, but we also have a misplaced confidence in our own opinions. From the "most knowledgeable" to the unlearned, it is a "common vice of men to entrust their plans to others, even if there is need for secrecy." Human beings are almost uncontrollable chatterboxes, so any government that proscribes the right of a person "to say and teach what he thinks" to be true would be considered harsh and, further, would violate a universal tendency of human nature.[69]

It is the very "obstinacy" of human beings that militates against a policy of uniformity. People do not like being told what to think and generally "endure nothing with greater impatience than that opinions they believe to be true should be considered criminal."[70] Resistance is less likely to come from the greedy, the sycophantic, and the "weak-minded" (*impotentes animi*) than from those whose appetite for liberty (*virtus liberiores*) has been whetted by good education (*bona educatio*), moral integrity (*morum integritas*), and virtue. The very constitution of human nature is such that laws made about opinions invariably do less to restrain the wicked than "to aggravate the honorable" and alienate "those who act in a manner worthy of a free man."[71] Criminalizing opinions will invariably make it appear honorable to take up the mantle of revolution.[72]

Spinoza may have been a radical, but he was not a political revolutionary.[73] He follows Machiavelli here in maintaining that the effort to alter government by changing its original principles is always a mistake.[74] Because modes of government are rooted in custom, history, or what might otherwise be called "national character," Spinoza opposes efforts to abolish and transform them by force. The imposition of new political forms can lead only to disaster, a lesson that Spinoza applies to the Puritan revolution in England. The effort of Cromwell and the protectorate to establish a republic ended in reproducing a monarchy in all but name:

> The English people have given us a deadly example of this truth, when they sought reasons for removing a monarch from their midst under a pretext of right. When they had removed him, they were completely unable to change

the form of government. After much blood had been spilled, they reached the point where they hailed a new monarch under another name, as if the whole issue had only been about the name! The new monarch could survive only if he completely destroyed the royal family, killed the king's friends, or anyone suspected of friendship, and upset the tranquility of peace, so suitable for generating murmurings, with a war, so that the common people, intensely preoccupied with new crises, would turn their thoughts about royal slaughter in a different direction. Too late the people realized that the only thing they had accomplished for the well-being of their country was the violation of the right of a legitimate king and change things from bad to worse. So as soon as they could, they decided to retrace their steps; they did not rest until they saw things restored to their original condition [*statum restaurata vidit*].[75]

Spinoza's judgment of Cromwell tells us something about the prudence needed to complete any doctrine of natural right. Considerations of natural right dictate only the peace and preservation of the state. But the means that the legislator has at his disposal to effect those ends will vary widely and depend on the circumstances and the moral habits and disposition of particular peoples and states. What is wrong is to believe that one can remake political institutions and the moral disposition that sustains them from scratch. Thus monarchical institutions may be appropriate to England, but they are inappropriate for Holland, where republican sentiments and habits of mind have long been established. In a pointed reference to the ambitions of the House of Orange, Spinoza warns:

As for the Estates of Holland, so far as we know, they never had kings, but only counts, to whom the right of command was never transferred. For as the Most Powerful Estates of Holland themselves made generally known in the document they published at the time of Count Leicester, they have always reserved for themselves the authority to advise the counts of their duty, and retained for themselves the power to defend this authority of theirs and the freedom of the citizens, to avenge themselves if the counts degenerated into tyrants, and to check them in such a way that they could accomplish nothing without the permission and endorsement of the estates.[76]

Spinoza finishes his discussion of revolution confirmed in the belief that "the form of each state must necessarily be retained and that it cannot be changed without a danger that the whole state will be ruined."[77]

So far, all of Spinoza's reasoning in support of the extension of the liberty of opinion derives from the danger of attempting to impose uniformity. Governments, he acknowledges, may be hurt by words as well as deeds, but to maintain political stability and ward off dissent, free speech is a necessary evil the right to which the prudent sovereign will do well to respect. But if this were

Spinoza's last word on the subject, the *Treatise* would be indistinguishable from *Leviathan*. Above all, the exaltation of liberty is what differentiates Spinoza from Hobbes. The dominant view in the *Treatise,* a view by no means current in its time, is not a grudging toleration of freedom but a celebration of the advantages to both the individual and the polity that are derived from it. "So the end of the state," Spinoza boldly declares, "is really freedom."[78] The boldness of Spinoza's conception is that not the individual alone but society as a whole will benefit from a policy of maximum liberty of opinion and belief.

The *Treatise* is perhaps the first work in Western political theory that defends the proposition that the exercise of free speech is the goal of social policy. Free speech is not, for Spinoza, an end in itself, however; rather, it is instrumental to the attainment of other goods. Freedom of speech is desirable because it allows for the development of individual judgment or personal autonomy, which is the true end of government. "The end of the state," Spinoza proclaims, "is not to change men from rational beings into beasts or automata, but rather that their mind and body should perform all their functions safely, [and] that they should use their reason freely."[79] Freedom of speech is desirable because it fosters in turn a certain type of human being with a certain kind of character. This kind of person could be called the autonomous or liberated self. In what does this person consist?

The type of liberated self that Spinoza helped to create is now a familiar feature of our moral landscape, the hero of many books of moral philosophy and works of imaginative literature.[80] Such a person strives, so far as possible, to be free of tradition and external sources of authority. Knowing himself to be a creature of passions, he neither blindly submits to nor vainly rejects them but takes an active pleasure in understanding their causes. The liberated self is a master of his passions, especially those arising from the fear of death and the terrors of the hereafter. Above all, this person thinks of life and the means necessary to its enhancement.[81] While the liberated self has certain classical precedents in the works of Plato and the Stoics, he remains to a considerable extent a characteristically modern phenomenon. To a greater degree than in the past, the individualism posited by Spinoza is based on the notions of personal autonomy, self-mastery, and courage.[82]

More than anything else, the free individual values the *vita activa* and the virtues necessary to sustain it. In the *Ethics* Spinoza acknowledges that all human life is subject to the emotions (*affectus*), but some of the emotions are passions (*passiones*), and others are actions or activities (*actiones*). Passions control us, and we submit to them, but actions contribute to our sense of power and autonomy.[83] All the emotions necessarily refer back to feelings of pleasure and pain, but some of these feelings diminish our freedom while others enhance it.[84] The central life-enhancing virtue Spinoza calls by the comprehensive name *fortitudo*:

> All actions that follow from affects related to the Mind insofar as it understands I relate to Strength of character [*fortitudo*], which I divide into Tenacity [*animositas*] and Nobility [*generositas*]. For by Tenacity I understand the desire by which each one strives, solely from the dictate of reason, to preserve his being. By Nobility I understand the Desire by which each one strives, solely from the dictate of reason, to aid other men and join them to him friendship. Those actions, therefore, which aim only at the agent's advantage, I relate to Tenacity, and those which aim at another's advantage, I relate to Nobility. So Moderation, Sobriety, presence of mind in danger, etc., are species of Tenacity, whereas Courtesy, Mercy, etc., are species of Nobility.[85]

Strength of character, then, is the primary characteristic of the free individual. The free individual *is* the *vir fortis*.[86] But *fortitudo* has a two-dimensional quality. There is an inner-directed part, or *animositas*, which Spinoza calls courage and defines as "the desire whereby every man strives to preserve his own being," and an outer-directed part, or *generositas*, which is the desire to help other men and to join with them in friendship. *Generositas*, so understood, is the Spinozist equivalent of the Aristotelian virtue of greatness of soul (*megalopsychia*), which unifies all the virtues into an ordered whole and which indicates a freedom from pettiness and small-spirited calculation.[87] The free individual seeks to benefit others not because he feels pity or harbors any affect with a residue of hatred but because he feels the joy that comes with a proper self-regard.

The courage and high-mindedness of Spinoza's free individual has a counterpart in Descartes's idea of generosity. In the *Passions of the Soul* Descartes treats generosity as part of his "physiology" of the passions. He lists "wonder" as the first of the passions, the one from which the phenomena of esteem and disdain are derived.[88] Esteem and disdain are species of wonder defined by the value or lack of it that the soul attaches to an object. Thus esteem and contempt are dispositions of the soul to wonder at the value or insignificance excited in us by some object or experience. Because knowing whether we should esteem or despise ourselves is one of the "principal parts of wisdom," Descartes turns his attention to the reasons for self-evaluation. Self-esteem is in part justified by our possession of a free will but even more importantly by the use we make of it.[89] Courage, or resolution of the will, is the legitimate basis for self-esteem because "in a certain measure [it] renders us like God in making us masters of ourselves."[90]

Nobility of soul is, then, identified as that "which causes a man to esteem himself as highly as he can."[91] "True generosity," as Descartes calls it, contains elements of both knowledge and feeling: "True generosity . . . consists alone partly in the fact that he knows that there is nothing that truly pertains to him but this free disposition of his will, and that there is no reason why he should be praised or blamed unless it is because he uses it well or ill; and partly in fact that he is sensible in himself of a firm and constant resolution to use it well, that is to say, never to fail of his own will to undertake and execute all the things which he judges to be the best — which is to follow virtue perfectly."[92]

Cartesian generosity has a dual structure. It proceeds from that "firm and constant resolution" of the will to master the passions. Like the Stoics before him, Descartes emphasizes self-control and restraint as the core of moral virtue. But generosity also has a more political or public dimension. It manifests itself as a desire to find new and more useful ways of benefiting the public. Among these ways Descartes proposes "an infinity of arts and crafts," which are the fruits of modern science. The new science of which Descartes is the bearer promises as its principal goal "the preservation of health, which is without doubt the chief blessing and the foundation of all other blessings in this life."[93] The same firmness and resolution employed in the mastery of the passions is to be set to work in the conquest or mastery of nature. It is through the mastery of nature that "the fruits of the earth and all the good things which are to be found there" can be shared by all.[94] The scientific control of nature is the highest kind of generosity that the Cartesian wise man can bestow upon humanity.

Spinoza's Liberal Republicanism

Spinoza follows Descartes's example of presenting his findings as beneficial to humanity as a whole. The model of *fortitudo* in the *Ethics* is put forward as a new kind of humanitarianism. In the *Treatise* he explicitly links the virtues of toleration and freedom of speech to the free flow of information both within and between nations. The exchange of ideas and opinions across borders contributes to the safety, prosperity, and prestige of the few scientists and philosophers who benefit most directly and to the intellectual, moral, and material welfare of society. The humanitarianism of Spinoza consists in his demonstration or assertion that there is a harmony of interests between reason and society, between the intellectual class and the many.

Spinoza's ethic of freedom thus displays his marked preference for universal, cosmopolitan, and "open societies" at the expense of purely local, traditional, or particularistic moralities. Believing that reason should be allowed to develop freely, Spinoza in the *Treatise* presents the liberal case for intellectual progress and popular enlightenment in its purest form:

He who wants to set limits to everything by laws will aggravate vices more than he will correct them. What cannot be prohibited, must necessarily be conceded, even if it frequently leads to harm. For how many evils do extravagant living, envy, greed, drunkenness, and the like give rise to? Still, we endure these things, because the authority of the laws cannot prohibit them, even though they are all really vices. So much the more must we grant freedom of judgment, which not only cannot be suppressed, but is undoubtedly a virtue. Moreover, it does not lead to any disadvantages which cannot be avoided by the magistrates' authority . . . not to mention the fact that this freedom is especially necessary to promote the sciences and the arts [*scientias et artes promovendum*]. For these can be cultivated only by those who have a free and uncontrolled judgment.[95]

The progress of the arts and sciences is invariably linked to issues of trade and commerce. Intellectual freedom is possible and flourishes only in an environment of commercial freedom. The enlightened society is necessarily a commercial society or commercial republic with a combination of economic, political, and religious liberties. The commercial republic was not exactly a creation of Spinoza's, but he saw in this model of society a more humane and practical alternative to the two great alternatives under whose dispensation European civilization had previously labored, namely, the regimes of civic and Christian virtue.[96]

Spinoza's commercial republic has both a positive and a negative component. It is defined primarily by what it rejects: monarchical or aristocratic ambitions; a disdain of the mundane and the useful; a vision of human perfection attainable only by the few. More positively, it has a number of distinct features. It is possessed of a unitary sovereign with the power to arbitrate religious disputes affecting public life. Like Hobbes, Spinoza opposes the classical mixed or balanced constitution because a divided sovereignty is an open invitation to civil war.[97] In this republic the urban commercial patriciate is favored over the older rural squirearchy. Commercial capital, rather than landed property, should be encouraged for its beneficial impact on relations between citizens. In particular, movable property, so Spinoza believes, would equalize itself over time, thus avoiding the factitious and contentious influences of the landed nobility. A society in which everyone is engaged in commerce is, further, more likely to promote peace than destructive wars of ambition.[98] A century before the argument for commerce became fashionable, Spinoza understood the attractions of *doux commerce*.[99]

In contrast to the classical tradition of republicanism with its emphasis on civic virtue, frugality, self-sacrifice, and suspicion of trade, Spinoza's republic is a markedly liberal one. This may seem an odd juxtaposition; the liberal and republican traditions in modern thought have often developed in quite different directions. The republican "paradigm," which is said to go back to Aristotle and extend through Machiavelli, Harrington, and the radical Whig opposition party in the eighteenth century, has emphasized virtue (or *virtù*), which arises from man's political nature and is achieved through patriotic devotion to the common good. The liberal paradigm, by contrast, which begins with Locke, has emphasized individual rights and defines government as an instrument, and a limited one at that, for the protection of such private goods as peace and property. Whereas in republican language, freedom meant the freedom to participate in a *vivere civile,* in liberal or jurisprudential language it meant freedom from the arbitrary use of power along with security of life and property under the protection of law. The republican tradition is centered on the concept of *virtus*; the liberal tradition is a tradition of law.[100]

The discord between these alleged republican and liberal paradigms was not as great for Spinoza as it appears to be in the works of subsequent interpreters. In the *Treatise* Spinoza is certainly republican in his championing of popular government as opposed to monarchy, in his defense of the rights and powers of secular as opposed to ecclesiastical authority, and in his use of civil religion as an instrument for achieving social solidarity and respect for the laws. At the same time, the work is decidedly liberal given his skepticism about the language of civic virtue, the contractual and interest-based model of civil association, his openness to issues of trade and commerce, and his unqualified preference for individual liberty and tolerance of heterodoxy as the goals of the state. In addition to self-government, a cardinal ingredient of liberty is the freedom of conscience and belief. The addition of this ingredient represents an important shift in the language of liberty from the civic humanist conception of freedom as political participation to a conception based on the individual's right to believe what he wants and to speak openly about his beliefs.[101] Arguably, this view of liberty testifies to the profound influence of the Protestant Reformation, but it is at least as likely that it stems from Spinoza's experience as a Jew living under conditions of persecution. Perhaps the most notable feature of the *Treatise* and its author is their resistance to any easy typological classification.[102]

Spinoza indicates his preference for the modern commercial republic in two key respects. First, he evinces none of the fears of "corruption" by the new commercial classes that exercised many of his contemporaries. As we have seen, he warns against imitating the ancient biblical polity precisely because of its lack of trade with its neighbors. For the civic republicans, commerce would bring economic dependence and moral decay, but for Spinoza, commerce was a source of enlightenment and an enlarged sphere of liberty. Second, unlike the classical republicans, who favored often harsh sumptuary legislation to control luxury, Spinoza denies that such laws can be effective in controlling the forms of private vice. He even encourages the propagation of avarice (*avaritia*) as beneficial to society.[103] Although avarice was strictly prohibited by the ancient moral tradition as *pleonexia,* "the vice of wanting more," and the biblical tradition as *cupiditas,* or "greed," Spinoza, like Mandeville and Adam Smith, regards it as having beneficial consequences for the welfare of the nation.[104]

Most important, the commercial republic is characterized by liberty in its many dimensions. Liberty brings with it not only the progress of the arts and sciences but the refinement and improvement of moral behavior.[105] Free trade is both a cause and a consequence of this liberty. The *Treatise* concludes with ringing praise of the commercial metropolis of Amsterdam as the regime where the effects of liberty are the most fully available for all to see:

> Take the city of Amsterdam, which knows by experience the fruits of this liberty, among them great growth and the admiration of all nations. For in this most flourishing Republic, this most outstanding city, all men, of whatever nation or sect, live in the greatest harmony. In deciding to entrust their goods to someone, they are concerned to know only whether the person is rich or poor, and whether he is accustomed to acting in good faith or deceptively. They don't care at all what his religion or sect is, for that would do nothing to justify or discredit their case before a judge. There is, without exception, no sect so hated that its followers are not protected by the public authority of the magistrates and their forces, provided that they harm no one, give each person his due, and live honorably.[106]

Only in the following century would Spinoza's commercial republic bear fruit in the works of Montesquieu, Hume, Smith, and others.[107] There, increasing trade was offered as something that "polishes" and "refines" manners, fosters peace and toleration, and discourages ferocity and xenophobic zeal.[108] Everywhere the commercial republic was proposed as a more humane alternative to the regimes of virtue that had dominated Europe and much of its colonial periphery. Such a regime would favor commercial over rural interests, the city over the country, and the rule of interest and utility over devotion to intangible goods and "lofty ambition."[109] The enjoyment of life rather than its mortification, a disposition to cultivate freedom rather than regret it, the celebration of the civilized pleasures of fine food, the appreciation of beauty, and music—all of these are the ends of the commercial republic that Spinoza hoped to make possible.[110]

7

The Legacy of the Treatise

Spinoza has been marked out by posterity as the very symbol of the emancipated Jew. As such, he represents the embodiment of the Jewish Question. In the century or so after his death, Spinoza's reputation as a materialist and atheist was more than sufficient to put him beyond the pale of respectability, even among those of liberal opinion. Yet even though the author of the *Ethics* was almost universally reviled by liberals and anti-liberals alike, the author of the *Treatise* penetrated even the most "enlightened" circles of European thought.[1] It was the influence of the *Treatise* that made it possible for defenders of the Enlightenment to advocate toleration of Jews while simultaneously holding Judaism in contempt. At issue is more than the personal anti-Semitism of some of the Enlightenment's most notable figures.[2] The doctrine of toleration scarcely mandated extending equal recognition and respect to all beliefs and practices. Rather, toleration of Jews was seen as a first step toward the eventual absorption of Judaism into the main current of European culture.

The rehabilitation of Spinoza marked a new stage in the development of the relation between Judaism and the Enlightenment. The early Enlightenment, as we have seen, disowned Spinoza for his radicalism and irreverence, whereas the later Enlightenment, or *Spätaufklärung*, adopted him as one of their own. Nowhere was this rehabilitation of Spinoza more vividly illustrated than in Germany. The *Pantheismusstreit* of the mid-1780s played a decisive role in this process. But even for those who formally disavowed Spinoza's system of metaphysics and theology, he came to represent a victim of religious persecution and a martyr to the cause of intellectual freedom, a kind of Jewish Jean Calas. His excommunication was seen not as his just deserts for defying properly constituted religious authority but as an act of vindictive cruelty enacted upon an otherwise blameless individual. This posthumous vindication of Spinoza at the expense of the Jewish community can be seen as a virtual litmus test for the dilemma faced by European Jewry at the outset of the age of emancipation.[3]

Enlightenment and Emancipation

The Enlightenment's conception of emancipation posed an unprecedented challenge to Judaism. At the normative level, the Enlightenment's ideal of *Bildung* as a process of self-formation and personal autonomy was the veritable antithesis of Jewish communal ethics and law (*Halakah*). The values of the Enlightenment, though in principle open to all regardless of social status and ethnicity, were in practice deeply hostile to the traditions and practices of Judaism. Jews might be welcomed into the new liberal order, but only on condition that they abandon their collective culture and ancient traditions. Emancipation through *Bildung* thus represented a double offer. It meant liberation from medieval social restrictions and discrimination, but it also entailed emancipation from Judaism. At the institutional level, the emergence of modernizing political structures gradually undermined the autonomy previously accorded to local Jewish communities. The power of ecclesiastical authorities to compel religious observance through the use of the *herem* was no longer recognized by the state. Without the institutional means to enforce conformity with the law, obedience to ritual practice became increasingly "Protestantized," that is, consigned to the precincts of individual conscience and personal belief.[4]

Spinoza's bequest to the Enlightenment is most evident in the framing of the terms of the Jewish Question. The Jewish Question was not an incidental or peripheral aspect of the Enlightenment but an integral part of it. The Jews were, even for the most advanced thinkers of the *Aufklärung*, the quintessential "Other," the exotic or "Oriental," a vestige of the East within the West.[5] The capacity to assimilate this Other would be the true test of the program of emancipation through *Bildung*. At the same time, however, the onus was shifted to the Jews to prove that they were morally and intellectually prepared to accept this offer of emancipation. This offer was accepted with enthusiasm by some, with ambivalence by others, and with hostility by still others. Toleration meant that Jews would have to render themselves tolerable to their Gentile neighbors, which usually meant some form of assimilation or, in the most extreme cases, conversion.

Although Heinrich Heine could regard his conversion as an entrance ticket to the modern world, as the nineteenth century wore on such tickets ceased to guarantee admission. Partly owing to secularization, new forms of discrimination were created. If religion ceased to be a criterion of exclusion, new secular categories like "culture" and later "race" were invoked to establish barriers to emancipation. The sociologist Zygmunt Bauman has brilliantly captured the "Catch-22" plight of the Jews: the more they played by the rules of the game, the more quickly the rules were changed from under them.

> Thus the assimilating Jews did not cheat or otherwise fail to play the game according to the rules. Rather, the rules kept changing, so that every gain the hapless players made promptly became a loss. Having agreed at the start never to challenge the exclusive right of the casino owners to set the rules, and concerned with demonstrating above all their appreciation of the opportunities such rules create, converts to assimilation made themselves hostages to the same house managers whose unquestionable authority they swore to accept to legitimate their own success. They could not challenge that authority without sapping the foundation of their redemptive hopes. The project of assimilation turned out to be a trap. Without control over the rules, it was impossible to win. The closer success came, the more elusive it became. The currency of emancipation tended to be devalued or withdrawn from circulation faster than it could be hoarded.[6]

The case of Spinoza was never far from the thinking of those who gave the Jewish Question its most notable expressions: Mendelssohn, Lessing, Kant, and Hegel. This is not to say that Spinoza's legacy ended with Hegel. Spinoza exerted a powerful, even profound, influence on subsequent thinkers as diverse as Marx, Nietzsche, and Freud. But to varying degrees and for different reasons, these thinkers developed their views in opposition to the Enlightenment. They belong more properly to the anti- or counter-Enlightenment tradition.[7] It was the Enlightenment, above all, that made the case for Jewish emancipation and *Bildung* that is the theme of this book. Moreover, it was in Germany, more than in any other nation, where the belief in the modernization and hence liberalization of Judaism became a fervid, almost religious faith, especially among Jews themselves. Emancipation through *Bildung* became the new form of secular liberal piety. That the possibility of a "German-Jewish dialogue" proved later to be chimerical demonstrates, as vividly as anything could, the limits of the Enlightenment faith.[8]

The immediate ground for the assimilation of Spinoza into the main current of German-Jewish (and later, arguably, American-Jewish) thought was prepared by Moses Mendelssohn. The father of the Jewish Enlightenment (*Haskalah*), Mendelssohn was deeply moved by the image of Spinoza as a Jewish outcast and sought to reform Judaism to make it compatible with liberal politics. By way of example Mendelssohn showed how it was possible to negotiate the slippery slope between fidelity to Judaism and identification with the highest aspirations of the German Enlightenment. Borrowing the the claim in the *Treatise* that Judaism is not a theology but a body of revealed law, Mendelssohn hoped to demonstrate that although Judaism possessed certain codes of right conduct, it contained no creeds or dogmas that could otherwise encumber the mind. From this it followed for him that neither state nor church has the authority to excommunicate any of its members, for no one has the right to coerce others to hold certain opinions.

Spinoza's reception into the German Enlightenment was furthered by Mendelssohn's friend Gotthold Ephraim Lessing, who, a year before his death in 1781, confessed his Spinozism in a series of conversations with the young Friedrich Jacobi.[9] Although the reports of the Spinoza conversations between Lessing and Jacobi are short on specifics, it is clear that Lessing relied heavily on Spinoza's account of prophetic history, which he transformed into a full-fledged program for the "education of the human race." Using the plan in the *Treatise* for a non-revealed religion of reason, Lessing theorized about the possibility of a final age of humanity, an end of history, as it were, when a purified moral religion would at last reveal mankind as one. The publication of the philosophical correspondence between Jacobi and Mendelssohn formed the immediate philosophical backdrop to German Idealism and its belief in the unity and divinity of nature.

Kant accepted Spinoza's and Mendelssohn's depictions of Judaism as a supremely political legislation but used it to deny moral status to Judaism. For Kant, the paradigmatic Enlightenment rationalist, pure moral theology stems from our own "autonomy." Consequently, Judaism, as a body of authoritative commandments, represented the archetypal religion of coercion and force, utterly lacking in moral content. All religious practices, ceremonies, and rituals that derive from either history or revelation are rejected as forms of "heteronomy" that bind and enslave the will. Kant's goal, like that of many of the *Aufklärer*, was less to welcome Judaism than to purge Christianity of its vestigial Jewish characteristics. Finally, Hegel saw both Judaism and Kantianism as variations on the same theme. The Kantian moral law was no different in kind from the commands of Moses: both were equally coercive and authoritarian and had to be dialectically *Aufgehoben* in order to realize human freedom. By situating Judaism within the dialectics of world history, Hegel hoped to render it anachronistic.

For each of these thinkers, Spinoza's depiction of Judaism represented a way station on the road to modernity. For all concerned, the case of Spinoza represented a harbinger of what was yet to come. Are Judaism and liberalism compatible, as Mendelssohn seems to have believed, or is the promotion of the new liberal order at odds with Judaism as a set of moral beliefs and a way of life, as Kant and Hegel argued? I do not mean to say that the role of Spinoza was singularly determinative in shaping the debate over the Jewish Question in the eighteenth and nineteenth centuries. Rather, as Pierre Birnbaum and Ira Katznelson have reminded us recently, there are multiple "paths of emancipation."[10] They all at least begin with Spinoza.

Mendelssohn's Defense of Toleration

There is a paradox involved in viewing Mendelssohn as an heir or even successor to Spinoza. Mendelssohn is best remembered in the history of philosophy as the man who died while attempting to clear his friend Lessing's name of the charge of Spinozism.[11] While Spinoza is known as perhaps Judaism's foremost, or at least most learned, critic from within the camp of the Enlightenment, Mendelssohn remains its greatest defender. His one explicit reference to Spinoza in his *Jerusalem* is directed to his metaphysics rather than his ethics and is entirely in keeping with the negative judgment of the early Enlightenment. As Mendelssohn drolly remarks: "His ingenious errors have occasioned inquiry."[12]

The more than obvious differences between Spinoza and Mendelssohn may tend to obscure their strong affinities.[13] Mendelssohn appropriated what was perhaps the leading thesis of the *Treatise,* that Judaism is a revealed legislation and not a revealed religion. Even here, however, the different uses to which this insight is put are revealing. Whereas Spinoza treats the ceremonial laws of Judaism as abrogated with the end of the ancient theocracy, for Mendelssohn the law remains binding on all Jews everywhere. Whereas Spinoza sees pre-Diaspora Judaism as so many *antiqui vulgi praejudicia,* Mendelssohn sees its kinship to the Enlightenment's version of a natural or rational religion. In spite of these differences, as deep and far-reaching as they are, Spinoza and Mendelssohn converge on one essential end: the absolute necessity for toleration and liberty of conscience, or what Mendelssohn calls "the noblest treasure of human felicity."[14]

Unlike Spinoza, a heretic and excommunicant, Mendelssohn was the acknowledged leader of enlightened European Jewry during the 1770s and 1780s. He served as the model for the saintly Nathan in Lessing's play *Nathan the Wise* (1779) and at the same time remained deeply committed to the cause of Jewish autonomy and community.[15] He was a friend of Kant's, a contributor to the influential *Berlinische Monatsschrift,* and a participant in the weekly *Mittwochsgesellschaft.*[16] He was admirably suited to bridge the gap between the worlds of German *Bildung* and Jewish law and ethics. His major work of political philosophy, entitled *Jerusalem; or, On Ecclesiastical Power and Judaism,* was published in 1783 and bore a striking resemblance to the *Treatise.* It was, in the words of Julius Guttmann, "a first attempt to justify Judaism before the cultural consciousness of modernity."[17]

Mendelssohn wrote *Jerusalem* in response to an earlier treatise by Christian Wilhelm von Dohm, *On the Civil Improvement of the Jews* (1781), whose author defended the cause of Jewish emancipation while still supporting the traditional right of ecclesiastical institutions to excommunicate members for nonconformity.[18] In *Jerusalem* Mendelssohn took up this issue but put it within the broader context of the relations between church and state. His aim was to accomplish two, not wholly consistent ends. In the first part of the work he denied that religious communities retain the right of excommunication even against heretics and other nonconformists. In the second part he defended his commitment to Jewish separatism while denying to the Jewish community its long-standing right to command ritual observance of its laws. Mendelssohn's work is even today the most compelling statement of the modern Jew caught between the appeal of emancipation and fidelity to tradition.[19]

Mendelssohn's argument for toleration begins with an account of church-state relations that is derived partially from Locke and the English Deists. In the *Letter on Toleration* Locke had argued for the separation of church and state on the grounds that true religion is a matter of "the inward persuasion of the mind" and is, as such, impervious to threats or force.[20] Because only what is sincerely and conscientiously believed can be pleasing to God, policies of persecution are not only self-defeating but impious.[21] The state may be justified in using force for the sake of protecting such "civil goods" as person and property, but it must refrain from seeking to compel religious belief. Toleration is thus nothing other than the absence of force used for religious ends.[22]

Mendelssohn accepts Locke's conclusions that religion not be subject to political control but disagrees with his reasons for arriving at them. The doctrine of the strict separation of church and state is "neither in keeping with the truth nor advantageous to man's welfare."[23] Temporal and eternal, state and church, are not as opposed to one another as Locke's theory implies. By divesting the state of any role in what contributes to our "eternal felicity," Mendelssohn accuses Locke of depriving the state of all moral justification. According to *Jerusalem,* religion and politics are two paths to the same end. The difference between them is one of means, not ends. The state may employ force and coercion to achieve its goals, the church only persuasion and education.

The consequence of insisting on the absolute separation of church and state is to turn the state into an instrument of force, whereas Mendelssohn hoped that the church, as well as the mosque and synagogue, could assist the government in inculcating moral reasons for obeying the law.[24]

Mendelssohn's brief for liberty of conscience begins with an account of the natural law and an elaborate discussion of the rights and duties incumbent upon men in the state of nature.[25] The natural condition is not, pace Hobbes and Spinoza, one of unmitigated exercise of power but one of perfect and imperfect duties. Duties, like the obligation to help the needy, are imperfect if they depend entirely on the goodwill of the individual to carry them out. Duties, like the injunction not to harm others or give offense, are perfect if they have sanctions attached. In the language of Hobbes, imperfect duties bind the agent *in foro interno*; perfect duties are obligatory *in foro externo*.[26] Or, in modern language, imperfect duties bind the intention of the agent; perfect duties control the action. Because of a conflict or "collision" of rights we agree to leave the natural state and enter civil society. Typically for Mendelssohn, he thinks of the state as coming into being to make it easier for us to fulfill our natural obligations, as well as to secure peace and stability. The state cannot create new classes of duties, but it can transform duties that were only imperfectly held in the state of nature into perfect ones by putting the force of law behind them. Man thus enters civil society "in order to transform his fluctuating rights and duties into something definite."[27]

Mendelssohn's use of a fairly traditional natural law vocabulary should not obscure the novelty of his theory. The purpose of the state as a "moral person" is to adjudicate between conflicts of rights. For this very reason, he asserts, the state must refrain from interfering in matters of religion. In *Jerusalem* he offers several reasons in defense of this conclusion. First, he argues that the social contract applies only to those rights and duties that are enforceable by law. Like Spinoza in the *Treatise*, Mendelssohn argues that the state has the right to do only what it has the power to do. It follows that because our principles and beliefs are ours alone, they cannot be alienated to the state. "Convictions by their very nature permit no coercion or bribery."[28] Hence the state has no coercive power over religious beliefs. Second, Mendelssohn defends liberty of conscience on eudaimonist grounds. "Man's natural liberty," he asserts, "makes up a great portion of his felicity."[29] Human well-being consists in large part in the exercise of individual discretion to confer or withhold benefits on whom the individual chooses. Because man is "the master . . . of the free use of his powers and capacities," it would be wrong for the state to deprive citizens of this source of happiness.[30] Finally, Mendelssohn proposes that the social contract is an agreement among equals to resolve conflicts of rights. But between man and God there are and can be no conflicts, and the relationship is scarcely one of equality. Coercive power cannot then apply to matters of religion, which belong properly to the conscience of every individual.[31]

Similar views had, no doubt, been set forth before by Locke and Spinoza, but Mendelssohn takes them a step further. The radical conclusion that he wants the reader to draw is a teaching of virtually unlimited toleration. Part I of *Jerusalem* concludes with a passionate denunciation of the power of excommunication as a means of enforcing religious conformity. "Neither church nor state has a right to subject men's principles and convictions to any coercion whatsoever."[32] Excommunication is "diametrically opposed to the spirit of religion," which cannot enforce sanctions but only make appeals of persuasion and example.[33] Unlike Locke, who maintained that religious organizations retain the right to expel heterodox members, Mendelssohn claims that excommunication cannot be done without incurring at least some civil disabilities.[34] "But how is it possible to separate excommunication from all civil consequences?" he asks.[35] By denying the legitimacy of the *herem* as a form of social control, Mendelssohn hoped to facilitate the Jewish transition from the medieval to the modern world.

But just as the church is denied the power of excommunication, so is the state denied the right to discriminate against any citizen on the basis of religion. "The smallest privilege which you publicly grant to those who share your religion and convictions is to be called an indirect bribe, and the smallest liberty you withhold from dissidents an indirect punishment."[36] The admission of the Jews to full rights of citizenship could hardly have been stated more completely. The state must remain scrupulously indifferent to all religions, although it need not be neutral with respect to all beliefs. Unlike Locke, Mendelssohn did not say that atheists should be excluded from the social contract but that some beliefs, like "atheism and Epicureanism," are clearly contrary to "the felicity [on which] social life is based."[37] But even here Mendelssohn does not advocate the exclusion of atheists. Such beliefs are more to be monitored than controlled: "The state, to be sure, is to see to it from afar that no doctrines are propagated which are inconsistent with the public welfare. . . . But it is only from a distance that the state should take notice of this, and only with wise moderation should it favor even those doctrines upon which its true felicity is based. It should not interfere directly in any dispute or wish to decide it through the use of its authority. For it evidently acts contrary to its own purpose when it directly forbids inquiry, or allows disputes to be decided in any other manner than by rational arguments."[38]

In part I of *Jerusalem* Mendelssohn makes the case for the liberal state and the civil equality of all beliefs. Even here, however, it might be wondered whether Mendelssohn is fully consistent in applying his principle of toleration. Although he flatly denies that ideas can be coerced, he leaves open the possibility that some opinions are to be watched, if only from "afar," by the civil authorities. His suggestion that the state might favor — albeit with "wise moderation" — some opinions at the expense of others seems to contradict his earlier thesis that this kind of civic privileging constitutes an unjust form of discrimination. Furthermore, he leaves entirely unstated what measures the state might adopt to discourage the views that it deems run contrary to "true felicity." To be fully consistent with his initial premises, Mendelssohn would have to reject even these partial qualifications and extend a doctrine of full equality to all groups, independent of creed.

The contradiction may not be as glaring as has sometimes been thought. Mendelssohn is not necessarily concerned to extend unrestricted equality to all beliefs, but rather to all religious beliefs. An important, perhaps central, teaching of *Jerusalem* is the elimination of civil discrimination based on religion alone. Thus atheists are not systematically excluded from Mendelssohn's social contract, but they are not given full immunity to propagate their views, either. Mendelssohn does not regard the liberal state as a neutral state if that means indifference to all doctrines. The state is to be neutral with respect to religion alone. Secular doctrines ("atheism and Epicureanism") still remain indirectly under civil control. The more difficult problem created in *Jerusalem* concerns the relation between parts I and II of the work. For it is one thing to say that the state should be neutral regarding religion; it is something quite different to say that such a state is compatible with Judaism. But this is precisely what Mendelssohn sets out to do. The tour de force of part II of *Jerusalem* is the effort to demonstrate that liberalism is compatible with the claims of Jewish particularity.

Having delimited the scope of ecclesiastical power and the state in part I of *Jerusalem,* Mendelssohn sets out to establish in part II the congruity of Judaism with the liberal state so defined. The main obstacle to proving this point is the objection that Judaism is nothing other than "a system of religious government, of the power and right of religion."[39] Remove from Judaism the power of law and you have nothing left. The implication is that by denying to Judaism the right of excommunication, Mendelssohn cuts the ground out from under it. "This objection," Mendelssohn admits, "cuts me to the heart."[40]

The core of Mendelssohn's answer to this objection is the claim that Judaism is not a revealed religion but a revealed legislation (*Gesetzgebung*). The same claim was, it will be recalled, the basis of Spinoza's treatment of Judaism in chapters 3 and 5 of the *Treatise.* This distinction between a revealed religion and a revealed legislation constitutes, according to Mendelssohn, "a characteristic difference" between Judaism and Christianity: "I believe that Judaism knows of no revealed religion in the sense in which Christians understand this term. The Israelites possess a divine *legislation* — laws, commandments, ordinances, rules of life, instruction in the will of God as to how they should conduct themselves in order to attain temporal and eternal felicity. Propositions and prescriptions of this kind were revealed to them by Moses in a miraculous and supernatural manner, but no doctrinal opinions, no saving truths, no universal propositions of reason. These the Eternal reveals to us and to all other men, at all times, through *nature* and *thing*, but never through *word* and *script*."[41]

Judaism, as both Spinoza and Mendelssohn contend, consists of actions and rules of conduct, not prescribed beliefs and opinions. It is for both of them predominantly orthopractic, concerned with ritual and practice rather than creed. But if Spinoza and Mendelssohn are in agreement about the difference between Judaism and Christianity, they disagree as to what they mean by Judaism's revealed law. For Spinoza, the Mosaic law was an exclusively political legislation intended to maintain "security of life and its conveniences."[42] The election of the Hebrew nation applied not to its wisdom or tranquillity but only to its "social order and of the fortune by which it acquired a state, and by which it kept it for so many years."[43] The law of Moses was the political law governing the Hebrew commonwealth during the period of its sovereignty and had no validity outside or beyond the spatial and temporal limitations of the state. For Mendelssohn, however, the Mosaic legislation was more than a set of political statutes; it had genuine moral content. In making the case for the binding character of the ceremonial law, Mendelssohn is arguing with Spinoza and against the Enlightenment's general derogation of Judaism.

In response to Spinoza's depiction of the Mosaic law as a strictly political legislation, Mendelssohn draws a distinction between two kinds or classes of truth, each with its own manner of validation. Eternal or necessary truths are those like the laws of logic or the means required for the attainment of human felicity.[44] These truths depend on reason alone for their verification and are independent of any divine revelation or supernatural gift. Historical or temporal truths, in comparison, are those "which occurred once and may never occur again."[45] These truths, like the narratives in Scripture, are dependent on the testimony of witnesses for their credibility. Reason is not sufficient to guarantee the truth of Scripture, for in historical matters, "the authority and credibility of the narrator constitute the only evidence."[46]

Mendelssohn departs from Spinoza in seeing primordial Judaism as composed of both a set of rational or eternal laws and a set of revealed or historical laws. The rational laws are the rules deemed necessary for us to attain intellectual and moral perfection. The rules are not specific to Judaism but are "as widespread as mankind itself, as charitably dispensed as the means of warding off hunger and other natural needs."[47] Like the "dogmas" of Spinoza's *fides universalis,* Mendelssohn's religion of reason is available to all peoples, however historically situated:

> I therefore do not believe that the powers of human reason are insufficient to persuade men of the eternal truths which are indispensable to human felicity, and that God had to reveal them in a supernatural manner. Those who hold this view detract from the omnipotence or the goodness of God, on the one hand, [and] what they believe they are adding to his goodness on the other. . . . If, therefore, mankind must be corrupt and miserable without revelation, why has the greater part of mankind lived without *true revelation* from time immemorial? Why must the two Indies wait until it pleases the Europeans to send them a few comforters to bring them a message without which they can, according to this opinion, live neither virtuously nor happily?[48]

The truths of rational theology, however necessary, are hardly a sufficient condition of Judaism. In addition to the truths of reason, Judaism consists of a body of revealed law received through the historical events occurring on Mount Sinai. Mendelssohn makes clear that the laws revealed at Sinai contain no truths that could not be grasped by reason alone; rather, they constitute a code of conduct binding only on the Jews. Hence these laws are impervious to the kind of rational proof or demonstration required by philosophers. The proof of revelation is the authority of Scripture itself, which testifies to the miracles and other "extraordinary signs."[49] Unlike Spinoza, Mendelssohn does not question the veracity of the narrative account contained in Scripture. He appears to assume that all the events have been reliably witnessed and recorded therein. All the events contained in Scripture "are historical truths which, by their very nature, rest on historical evidence."[50]

The specificity of Judaism, then, consists not in its possession of religious truth, which it shares with "the righteous of all nations." It consists in a body of historically authenticated revealed law that was given exclusively to the Jewish people. These laws are ceremonial and ritual commands intended not, as Spinoza argued, as a means of instilling obedience to authority, but as an inducement to reflection and the practice of moral virtue.[51] The ceremonial laws of Judaism were the means of attaining both individual and national perfection.[52] But whereas Spinoza argued that the ceremonial laws lost their obligatory power with the end of the Hebrew polity, Mendelssohn maintains that just because the ancient theocracy no longer exists, that does not mean that a fundamental alteration in the law is required. The ceremonial precepts and commands of Judaism are as binding now as in the time of Moses. Even though the connection between civil and ecclesiastical law no longer obtains, the justification for the ritual law remains intact. Thus even though Mendelssohn recognizes that the "burden of civil life" has been made heavier during the Diaspora, he can advise his readers to "hold fast to the religion of your fathers."[53]

Jerusalem provides two reasons for defending a continued adherence to traditional Judaism. These reasons express the internal tension within the book between orthodoxy and emancipation. First, Mendelssohn contends that ceremonial laws remain intact until they are expressly revoked by the lawgiver. "I cannot see how those born into the House of Jacob can in any conscientious manner disencumber themselves of the law."[54] If civil emancipation requires the Jews to forgo their ancient traditions, then so much the worse for emancipation.[55] Mendelssohn staunchly believed, however, that there was no contradiction between adherence to the ceremonial law and the discharge of one's duties as citizen.

The second reason is developed in the final paragraph of *Jerusalem* and is based on an appeal to religious diversity. Religious pluralism is "evidently the plan and purpose of Providence," Mendelssohn asserts.[56] The cultivation of diversity became one of the central features of the German idea of *Bildung*, which meant more than the development of reason in the narrow sense of the term. Indeed, *Bildung* represented an ideal of social and psychological harmony achieved through the cultivation of the most diverse experiences and situations. In Alexander Altmann's terms, *Bildung* meant for Mendelssohn nothing less than "the harmonious development of all psychic faculties" and "the accord between reason [*Vernunft*] and sensibility [*Sinnlichkeit*]."[57] The emphasis on *Bildung* as an education in diversity led Mendelssohn to warn against assimilation. "A union of faiths," Mendelssohn declares, "is not tolerance but the very opposite of true tolerance!"[58] No one thinks or feels exactly like his neighbor, so the demand for religious uniformity seems at odds with human nature. In *Jerusalem* Mendelssohn demands more than mere toleration: a genuine respect for humanity in all of its diversity.[59]

In *Jerusalem* the case for toleration goes beyond anything found in the *Treatise*. How much the differences reflect matters of fundamental philosophical principle or different rhetorical adjustments and accommodations cannot be settled here.[60] The *Treatise* was written with the express aim of freeing the state from ecclesiastical interference. Spinoza's intention was to provide the secular democratic state with the means necessary to regulate the public exercise of religion, although he still maintained that "the internal worship of God and piety itself . . . are subject to each person's control, which cannot be transferred to another."[61] Further, Spinoza was more interested in urging toleration of Jews than in pleading on behalf of Judaism. He saw no contradiction between the establishment of a secular state and the abrogation of Judaism as a body of particular or political law. Politics, like nature, cannot tolerate an *imperium in imperio*. Extending toleration to Jews or other religious minorities does not require respect for their particular theologico-political identities, which is why Spinoza was anxious to demonstrate that the Mosaic law was nullified with the loss of the ancient theocracy.

By contrast, in *Jerusalem* Mendelssohn is less concerned with defending the power of the secular state than with guaranteeing the free exercise of religion. He is far more favorable to the genuine separation of church and state than was Spinoza, who still favored a national church. There is some evidence to believe that Mendelssohn was influenced here by events unfolding on the other side of the Atlantic.[62] In a footnote at the very end of *Jerusalem* he notes with an air of disappointment: "Alas, we already hear the Congress in America striking up the old tune and speaking of a *dominant religion*."[63] From the context it seems clear that he finds this talk of a "dominant religion" at odds with the liberal, secular spirit of the American Constitution. His concern here and throughout *Jerusalem* is with more than the individual's right to practice the religion of his choice; his concern is that Judaism not be made the basis of social ostracism or political exclusion.

Mendelssohn, who seems to have been an admirer of the American example, would have been encouraged by Jefferson's views on religious pluralism expressed in his *Notes on the State of Virginia,* penned the same year as *Jerusalem*.[64] Had Mendelssohn but lived, he no doubt would have appreciated George Washington's views on religious diversity, presented to the members of the Hebrew congregation of Newport: "It is now no more that toleration is spoken of, as if it was by the indulgence of one class of people, that another enjoyed the exercise of their inherent natural rights. For happily the government of the United states, which gives to bigotry no sanction, to persecution no assistance, requires only that they who live under its protection should demean themselves as good citizens, in giving it on all occasions their effectual support."[65] Washington adds his variation on the traditional Hebrew blessing: "May the children of the stock of Abraham who dwell in this land continue to merit and enjoy the good will of the other inhabitants, while every one shall sit in safety under his own vine and fig-tree, and there shall be none to make him afraid."[66]

In spite of the manifest and important differences between Mendelssohn's and Spinoza's conclusions, Mendelssohn is forced to make his case on the grounds laid down by his distinguished predecessor. Like Spinoza, he saw

Judaism as constituted by a body of revealed law; unlike Christianity, it carries no doctrines or creeds (for instance, the Trinity) that must be believed. His denial that religious authority has the power of excommunication is based on Spinoza's belief that ideas cannot be coerced and that to try to force an individual to change his convictions is a violation of natural right. But even though Mendelssohn clearly draws on and incorporates many of Spinoza's chief insights, *Jerusalem* remains an admixture of elements taken from both orthodoxy and Enlightenment. Mendelssohn hoped to prove that continued adherence to the ceremonial law of Judaism was fully consistent with the Enlightenment's idea of freedom of conscience. He hoped to synthesize fidelity to Judaism, on the one hand, and identification with the highest aspirations of the modern liberal state, on the other. More than a century before Hermann Cohen, he was the consummate mediator of *Deutschtum* and *Judentum*.[67] The synthesis did not survive. That it survived as long as it did is testimony in large part to the power of Mendelssohn's example.

Lessing, Kant, and the "Pure Moral Religion"

Mendelssohn has been called a part of the "consolatory Enlightenment" (*Trostvolle Aufklärung*) for good reason.[68] He attempted to soften the harsh, unpalatable teachings of Spinoza. Like other champions of this moderate Enlightenment, he sought to synthesize or harmonize both fidelity to orthodoxy and membership in the modern world. Such thinkers as Mendelssohn, Leibniz, and Wolff sought a compromise between revealed religion and a belief in the self-sufficiency of reason, but this view came under increasing attack by those radical Enlighteners who sought a once-and-for-all victory of modernity. Mendelssohn's views on the value of religious diversity were not, to begin with, shared by all his fellow *Aufklärer*. The *Spätaufklärung* was not so much concerned with the toleration of religious diversity as with the transformation of revealed religion into a new religion of reason that could serve as the basis for a new cosmopolitan social order.[69]

The radicalization of the Enlightenment was due in part to Lessing, who was widely held to have become a crypto-Spinozist at the end of his life. In his short work *The Education of the Human Race* (1780), Lessing takes over the sacred story of the fall and redemption of humanity and turns it into a secular drama of mankind's progressive education.[70] The transformation of sacred history into the story of mankind's secular education was typical of the effort during the *Spätaufklärung* to turn *Heilsgeschichte* into *Bildungsgeschichte*. What in earlier times could be conveyed only by means of Scripture and revelation could now be apprehended through reason and education.[71] In the

Education, as well as in his dialogue *Ernst and Falk,* Lessing depicts the future development of humanity from its current condition of divisiveness and despotism to a state of harmony and self-government. The path from past to present to future is not easy or straight ("it is not true that the shortest line is always straight"), but it is necessary.[72]

Lessing's account of the three stages of human development in the *Education* reads like a compendium of Spinoza's *Treatise.* Lessing adopted Spinoza's legacy by treating Judaism as equivalent to the spiritual childhood of humanity. The Jews were "the rudest and most ferocious" of peoples.[73] Unlike Mendelssohn, who insisted that religious truth is accessible to all peoples at any time, Lessing maintains that the Mosaic law was given only to "the people of Israel *of that time,* and his commission was perfectly adapted to the knowledge, capacities, inclinations of the *then existing* people of Israel."[74] The Hebrew Bible, rather than being a repository of divine revelation, was no more than a "primer" for a people who were "rough" and "incapable of abstract thoughts" and therefore intellectually unprepared to receive such doctrines as the immortality of the soul and the existence of an afterlife.[75] To the extent that the Jews were capable of religious progress, credit can mainly be given to their captivity in Babylon, where they first came into contact with the Chaldeans and Persians, as well as "the schools of the Greek philosophers in Egypt."[76]

In the *Education* Lessing thus gave the Enlightenment's views of Judaism a new historical grounding. The methodological teaching in the work is presented at its precise center. "Every primer," Lessing writes, "is only for a certain age."[77] Having outgrown the older book of instruction, humanity had to await a new and better teacher with a new and better text.[78] Like Spinoza, Lessing presents the new dispensation in terms of moral and intellectual progress, but, even bolder than Spinoza, he applies this progressivist doctrine to Christianity itself. Lessing's story does not conclude, therefore, with the conquest of Judaism by Christianity but with the conquest of both historical religions by a "new covenant" that will usher in the "third stage of the world."[79] This age will be home to a new kind of religion, a religion of humankind; the New Testament will become as antiquated as the Old.[80] The *Education* culminates with a vision not of tolerance and religious diversity but of a universal religion of reason that would transcend the particularistic, historical religions of the past. It is not the past or the present but the future that gives meaning and dignity to human beings.[81]

Lessing gave his picture of a universal religion vivid expression in his play *Nathan the Wise,* which has often been regarded as a tribute to his friendship with Mendelssohn.[82] Upon examination it turns out to be an ambiguous tribute. Unlike Mendelssohn, who thought defending Judaism and the Enlightenment was possible, Lessing's hero is less concerned with defending Judaism than with attacking revealed religion. Nathan's heroism consists less in his fidelity to his ancient faith — "Are Jew and Christian rather Jew and Christian than men?" he asks — than in his alleged ability to transcend his faith by espousing a religion of humanity and good will.[83] Whatever the particular differences between Christian, Muslim, and Jew, these are secondary to their humanity. "All lands bear good men," he assures the Templar Kurt.[84]

The core of *Nathan*'s argument is the potential of all revealed religions to suffer abuse at the hands of political authority. If Judaism has any comparative advantage, it is that, unlike Christianity and Islam, it is altogether lacking in political power and cannot be so abused. Like Spinoza's *fides universalis,* Nathan's is a universal religion of good will and benevolence. "What makes me for you a Christian, makes you for me a Jew," he tells the befuddled friar Bonafides.[85] Nathan's virtue consists in his independence from the historical religion of Judaism; in Franz Rosenzweig's judgment, Nathan was a disembodied Jew, "abstracted" from the concrete realities of Judaism.[86] The most revealing scene in the play occurs when Nathan, a merchant, instructs the sultan, Saladin, on the benefits of commerce and religious tolerance.[87]

It would be inconceivable to discuss the Enlightenment's appropriation of Spinoza without some mention of Kant, whose *Religion Within the Limits of Reason Alone* (1793) reads like a summary of the *Treatise.*[88] Kant lifts almost verbatim the distinction between an "ecclesiastical faith" and the "pure moral theology."[89] Whereas ecclesiastical religions are historical and "merely statutory," moral theology derives from the universal imperatives of practical reason. Whereas ecclesiastical religions are based on obedience to external authority ("heteronomy"), only moral theology respects human autonomy. By autonomy Kant does not mean doing what we like; he means acting in accordance with the moral law. This law is nothing other than reason, which indicates our moral duty regardless of our personal inclinations. Kant does not say — indeed, he emphatically denies — that we are the creators of the moral law. The moral law is discovered, "primordially engraved in our hearts."[90] What is important, however, is that we act as if we were the authors of this law. Human autonomy means submitting to the moral law not because it is the will of God but because it is the right thing to do.[91]

This distinction between an ecclesiastical faith and a moral theology is the hook on which Kant hangs his entire treatment of Judaism and Christianity. Throughout the *Religion* Judaism serves as the virtual ur-type for a purely heteronomous religion of force and coercion. Accordingly, Judaism is maligned as "a collection of mere statutory laws upon which was established a political organization."[92] It is further described as "not a religion at all," for it makes no claims upon conscience but is "merely a union of a number of people who, since they belonged to a particular stock, formed themselves into a commonwealth under purely political laws."[93] Following Spinoza's view that the laws of Moses were the laws of only the Hebrew theocracy, Kant avers that Judaism "was intended to be merely an earthly state" with "theocracy as its basis." Even the Ten Commandments do not attest to any "moral disposition" within Judaism, because they "are directed to absolutely nothing but outer observance." It follows that the God of Israel is not the God of practical reason but "an earthly regent making absolutely no claims upon, and no appeals to, conscience."[94] Consequently, obedience to the laws and rituals of this God is deemed a "pseudo service," just as Judaism itself, rather than being a moral faith, is nothing more than a political regime.[95]

This entirely negative depiction of Judaism is nearly a mirror image of Kant's treatment of Christianity. Though not unrelated to Judaism, Christianity inaugurated "a wholly new principle" that "effected a thoroughgoing revolution in doctrines of faith."[96] The revolution to which Kant here alludes is the doctrine of the pure moral law. This law is not based on ritual or ceremony, much less on any body of sacred texts, but on "the pure faith of reason," which "stands in need of no documentary authentication."[97] Even though Christianity has over time become encrusted with ecclesiastical dogma, Kant contends that in its pure form it contains nothing inimical to reason. The "great advantage" of Christianity over Judaism is that from its beginning it emerged *"from the mouth of the first Teacher* not as a statutory but as a moral religion, and as thus entering into the closest relation with reason so that, through reason, it was able of itself, without historical learning, to be spread at all times and among all peoples with the greatest trustworthiness."[98] Even though Kant is a determined critic of clericalism of whatever denominational variety, Christianity in its pristine form comes closest to "the universal religion of pure reason," because it is based on nothing more than "the pure moral disposition of the heart," which alone "can make men pleasing to God."[99]

To his credit, Kant is fully aware that his highly selective, indeed, positively distorted, depiction of religion is not historically accurate. This does not particularly worry him. The purpose of the *Religion* is not to present a literal interpretation of biblical texts but to explicate Scripture in accordance with the requirements of morality. In Spinozist terms Kant, like Maimonides, is a "dogmatist" for his efforts to make Scripture speak the language of reason.[100] "The moral improvement of men," he confidently avers, "will comprise the highest principle of all Scriptural exegesis."[101] In a revealing passage he notes that the *Religion* "must not be read as though intended for Scriptural exegesis which lies beyond the limits of the domain of pure reason."[102] In other words,

the task of scriptural hermeneutics is not simply to acquire one more "unfruit-
ful addition to our historical knowledge." Historical knowledge is not the
point. Knowledge of the history of Scripture belongs to "the class of *adia-
phora*" that by the very nature of the case has no bearing on the moral improvement of mankind.[103]

In the *Religion* Kant distinguishes the art of scriptural interpretation from
mere biblical scholarship (*Schriftgelehrsamkeit*).[104] The interpreter is concerned with the moral meaning of Scripture, the scholar in establishing the
historical credibility of the text. To a considerable degree, these two activities
presuppose each other, because the interpreter needs to have knowledge of the
original language as well as knowledge of the conditions, customs, and opinions of the times in question. But what to do when the historical meaning of a
text is in conflict with morality? In the case of a conflict the answer is clear:
The text must be harmonized or interpreted to fit the needs of morality. If it
cannot be, so much the worse for the text. As an illustration of this point Kant
takes Psalm 59:11–16 and asks "whether morality should be expounded according to the Bible or whether the Bible should not rather be expounded
according to morality."[105] He answers emphatically that one must always try
"to bring the New Testament passage into conformity with . . . self-subsistent
moral principles."[106] In cases where this cannot be done, it is permissible to
interpret the passage in a historical sense "as applying to the relation in which
the Jews conceived themselves to stand to God as their political regent."[107]

Kant's hermeneutic principle of reading Scripture according to "self-
subsistent moral principles" is entirely of a piece with his conception of the
Enlightenment as man's emergence from a condition of self-imposed immaturity. Perhaps more than any other thinker, Kant invested the Enlightenment
with a moral and religious idealism. The Enlightenment is understood here as
deeply rooted in certain long-range historical trends. Like Lessing, Kant regards the Enlightenment as a process of moral and intellectual education, even
transformation. Its aims are both the negative one of clearing up the detritus of
the old historical religions and the constructive one of establishing a new
moral religion of reason. The *Religion* amounts to an attack on or critique of
revelation as such.[108] The only morality, and hence the only religion, worthy of
the name is one based on the autonomy of human reason. Religious diversity is
thus not a value for Kant except insofar as diversity hastens an awareness of
the genuine morality. His goal is a world, not unlike Lessing's "third age," in
which the revealed religions of the past are rendered anachronistic once and
for all.

Kant was hopeful that the "revolution" he aspired to was being confirmed
by mounting evidence. In a letter to Mendelssohn, he expressed admiration for

"the penetration, subtlety, and wisdom" of *Jerusalem*.[109] He goes on to draw the following lesson:

> I regard this book as the proclamation of a great reform that is gradually be-
> coming imminent, a reform that is in store not only for your own people but
> for other nations as well. You have managed to unite with your religion a
> degree of thought that one would hardly have thought possible and of which
> no other religion can boast. You have at the same time thoroughly and clearly
> shown it necessary that every religion have unrestricted freedom of thought,
> so that finally even the Church will have to consider how to rid itself of
> everything that burdens and oppresses man's conscience, and mankind will
> finally be united with regard to the essential point of religion. For all re-
> ligious propositions that burden our conscience are based on history, that is,
> on making blessedness contingent on belief in the truth of those historical
> propositions.[110]

These encouraging words written to Mendelssohn are, however, belied by Kant's published views in the *Religion*. In a footnote Kant refers snidely to Mendelssohn's "ingenious" attempt to show the internal relatedness of Christianity to Judaism.[111] Responding to the view that he should abandon Judaism because his denial of the ecclesiastical right of excommunication brought him near Christianity, Mendelssohn said that the abandonment of Judaism would have devastating consequences for Christianity. "Now Christianity," he writes, "is built upon Judaism, and if the latter falls, it must necessarily collapse with it into *one* heap of ruins."[112] Kant was unpersuaded. In keeping with the thrust of the argument in the *Religion*, he denies to Judaism any status as a moral religion and hence any intrinsic connection to Christianity. This is not to say that Judaism is completely without historical interest. It will continue to be preserved as a relic of an ancient civilization. "The sacred books of this people," Kant says, "will doubtless always be preserved and will continue to possess value for scholarship even if not for the benefit of religion."[113]

This statement is consonant with Kant's views as expressed in his last published work, *The Conflict of the Faculties* (1798). Here he offers his moral religion as the basis for the moral improvement of humanity. Considering the proposition whether the multiplication of sects is a desirable sign of liberty of opinion, Kant answers that although diversity is to some degree inevitable, it is by no means desirable.[114] Different sects with different ceremonies are bound to appear, but this should not affect the view that there is but one moral theology. Whereas Mendelssohn looked forward to an age of diversity and increasing tolerance, Kant saw "the unity and universality of religion" as the ground of liberty. Thus Kant finds reasons for optimism in the current rapprochement between "enlightened Catholics and Protestants" who, "while still holding to their own dogmas, could thus look upon each other as brothers in faith."[115] He holds open the possibility that this enlightenment may yet spread to the Jews: "Without dreaming of a conversion of all Jews (to Christianity in the sense of a *messianic* faith), we can consider it possible even in their case if, as is now happening, purified religious concepts awaken among them and throw off the garb of the ancient cult, which now serves no purpose and even suppresses any true religious attitude."[116]

Kant offers this possibility as a way to open the question of the civil emancipation of the Jews. Both here and in the *Anthropology from a Pragmatic Point of View* (1798) he presents the Jews as belonging to a separate and distinctive nation. Their devotion to "the garb of the ancient cult" remains the cause of Jewish isolation and particularism. But where Mendelssohn saw fidelity to the rudiments of this "cult" as binding until revoked by the lawgiver, Kant regards such fidelity as an act of stubbornness and defiance. Kant was not an anti-Semite, so it is somewhat surprising to find him engaging in purely ad hominem attacks to make his case. "The Palestinians who live among us," he says in the *Anthropology,* are a "nation of cheats"; they are addicted to "the spirit of usury," have no "civil honor" and live "at the expense of one another as well as those who grant them protection."[117] As if this were not enough, Kant speaks of an entire "nation of merchants" who have turned the maxim "buyer beware" into "the supreme principle of morality." Regardless of what he said above about the awakening of "purified religious concepts," Kant despairs here of "vain plans to make this people moral."[118]

The hostility of these remarks seems to go against the belief that the moral reform and improvement of Judaism is already under way. Thus in *Conflict* Kant refers favorably to Lazarus Bendavid ("a highly intelligent Jew"), who advocated the adoption of the religion of the Gospels. Conversion on a large scale, Kant predicts, would "quickly call attention to [Jews] as an educated and civilized people who are ready for all the rights of citizenship and whose faith could also be sanctioned by the government."[119] In any case, Jewish emancipation will only be possible with prior evidence of moral and religious reform. The price of admission to civil society is nothing so crude as forced conversion; what is required is the "purification" of belief and an abrogation of the ceremonial laws. "The euthanasia of Judaism is the pure moral religion" is Kant's final word on the Jewish Question.[120]

Hegel on Judaism and Religious Positivity

Kant's views on religion in general and Judaism in particular were historically influential in the nineteenth and twentieth centuries but played a relatively minor role in his system as a whole. Not until approximately the last decade of his life did Kant devote any sustained attention to the religious question, and even then his writings came as something of an afterthought to the main outlines of his ethics. In fact, a good case could be made that the *Religion* served a largely defensive and rhetorical purpose. Kant's aim in writing the book was principally to enlist the muscle of religion in the service of rational morality. The *Religion* adds no new principles to our understanding of morality but contributes to it a sense of "awe," "admiration," "dignity," and "respect" that reason alone might be unable to compel.[121]

The same could not be said of Hegel, for whom the religious question was never far from the forefront of his thinking. Hegel, like most of the generation of post-Kantian idealists, began as a theologian, whereas Kant started out as a student of the physical sciences. In addition, Hegel gave sustained and weighty attention to the Jewish Question. He was, in the words of Emil Fackenheim, "the only non-Jewish modern philosopher of the first rank to take Judaism seriously in its own right."[122] His choice of subject invariably raises the question of his attitudes toward Judaism and the prospects of Jewish emancipation. Was he an anti-Semite, as some of his critics have contended, or was he an advocate of emancipation and the elimination of civil restrictions on Jews?[123] Clearly, Hegel harbored many of the same negative judgments against Judaism that were characteristic of such classical Enlightenment figures as Lessing and Kant, but to a greater extent than either Lessing or Kant, he makes the idea of civil emancipation a benchmark of the modern liberal-Protestant state. Yet at the same time that he adopted broadly liberal views on the Jewish Question, his general philosophical framework put Judaism at the margins of society. Henceforth Judaism was to be consigned to the status of a historical relic, a vestige of a once vital but now superseded civilization.

I think it is fair to say that Hegel's writings on the Jewish Question underwent a considerable change — one could almost say a paradigm shift. His earliest works express a typical Enlightenment conception of Judaism as a religion of force and coercion, of mere external observance, a religion to be contrasted with a religion of natural reason. These writings were themselves deeply indebted both to Kant's *Religion* and Mendelssohn's *Jerusalem.* But even within these writings we can see the beginnings of a rebellion against Kant and a movement toward a more characteristically "Hegelian" position. His later writings, especially the *Philosophy of History* and the *Philosophy of Right,* are attempts to remove from Judaism the stigma of a purely "statutory" or "positive" religion and to situate it within a larger dialectic of history and culture. The Hegelian philosophy of history should be seen from this angle not as the antithesis of but as an appendage to Spinoza's treatment of the religious question in the *Treatise.*

In his early writings Hegel adhered to the Enlightenment's belief in a religion of reason and human autonomy. In one of the first of the so-called *Early Theological Writings*, an essay entitled "On the Positivity of the Christian Religion" (1795), Hegel set out to show in largely Kantian terms how Christianity, which appeared initially as religion of pure inwardness, was transformed into a "positive" religion, that is, a system of statutory laws that must be held as truths independently of the convictions of the believer.[124] By a positive religion Hegel means one based on authority and coercion, not an individual's free consent and practical rationality. Throughout these writings Judaism is presented as the religion of blind obedience to externally imposed command.[125]

A part of Hegel's explanation for the corruption of Christianity centers on the Judaic context of early Christian belief. The following passage merely confirms the hoary Enlightenment view of Judaism as a "barren legalism" void of all life-affirming qualities: "The Jews were a people who derived their legislation from the supreme wisdom on high and whose spirit was not overwhelmed by a burden of statutory commands which pedantically prescribed a rule for every casual action of daily life and gave the whole people the look of a monastic order. As a result of this system, the holiest of things, namely the service of God and virtue, was ordered and compressed in dead formulas, and nothing save pride in this slavish obedience to laws not laid down by themselves was left to the Jewish spirit."[126] Hegel speculates that "there must have been Jews of a better heart and head who could not renounce their feeling of selfhood or stoop to become lifeless machines."[127] Thus when Jesus confronted "the contagious sickness of his age and his people" and "undertook to raise religion and virtue to morality," he found himself thwarted by "the hatred of the priesthood and the mortified national vanity of the Jews."[128]

These remarks should be kept in perspective. The essay containing them is "On the Positivity of the *Christian* Religion." Far from singling out Judaism for abuse, Hegel is hostile to revealed religion as such. The young Hegel, like the old Kant, was a partisan of the French Revolution and its religion of reason and saw revealed religion as one with the abusive social and political practices of the ancien régime. In a fragment from 1795 entitled "The Earliest Program for a System of German Idealism," he wrote: "Religion and politics have played the same game. The former has taught what despotism wanted to teach: contempt for humanity and the incapacity of man to realize the good and achieve something through his own efforts."[129] Given passages like this, some historians have even wondered whether the compendium *Early Theological Writings* should not have been called Hegel's *Early Anti-Theological Writings*.[130]

Even here, not everything Hegel says about Judaism is completely negative. These early essays, written under the influence of the French Revolution, are marked by a burning desire to see Germany transformed into a republic. Ancient Judaism could serve here as an example. The ancient Jews, unlike the modern Germans, had a state of their own. They valued their independence above all else and had recourse to messianic hopes only when their political sovereignty came under attack. When the promise of messianism turned out to be a chimera, the Jews took up arms with "the most enthusiastic courage" and later endured "the most appalling of human calamities" in their struggle to restore their state.[131] Hegel's judgment is that the Jews stand in history among those nations "whose cities outlived their polities" and whose example Hegel exhorts his countrymen to follow if only "the sense of what a nation may do for its independence were not too foreign to us."[132]

If "The Positivity of the Christian Religion" was directed not against Judaism but against revealed religion in all its varieties, the same cannot be said of a slightly later work called "The Spirit of Christianity and Its Fate" (1798–99). In the earlier work both Judaism and Christianity stand condemned; in the later essay Judaism has become the "villain" of the piece.[133] Throughout, Judaism is depicted as the religion of sheer externality, as opposed to Christianity, which is described as the religion of divine love. The soul of Judaism is portrayed as the "*odium generis humani*" from which all other nations recoil in horror.[134]

Hegel's depiction of Judaism here proceeds from a lengthy discussion of Abraham, "the true progenitor of the Jews," who is said to "regulate the entire fate of their posterity."[135] The central feature of Jewish history, which has its source in Abraham, is its sense of estrangement not only from the community but from nature and God. This quality of "disseverance" characterizes the "fate" (*Schicksal*) of Judaism. "The first act which made Abraham the true progenitor of the Jews," Hegel writes, "is a disseverance which snaps the bonds of communal life and love."[136] From a desire to be "a wholly self-subsistent, independent man" Abraham, and through him the entire Jewish people, was destined to be as "a stranger on the earth," among men yet "so far removed from them and independent of them that he needed to know nothing of them whatever."[137]

Abraham's separation from the ongoing life of his community had a metaphysical dimension in the separation from God. Unlike the pagan gods, who were anthropomorphic projections of men's own passions, Abraham's jealous God stood outside the world altogether. "The whole world Abraham regarded as simply his opposite. . . . Nothing in nature was supposed to have any part in God; everything was simply under God's mastery."[138] Abraham's "infinite Ideal" was the antithesis of everything human; it could not even be represented in a concrete shape or image.[139] This condition whereby man was reduced to the level of something "made" brought about a slavelike demeanor incompatible with a free people. By depriving themselves of "living" spirituality, the Jews could do nothing but curry favor from a despotic deity who ensured their national survival in times of crisis.

It was only with Jacob and Moses, "an isolated enthusiast for the liberation of his people," that the Jewish state gained reality. The principle of this state was law (*Gesetz*). The Mosaic law was not characterized by relations among political equals, as Hegel imagines law in the Greek polis.[140] It was, rather, characterized by a relation between the Jews and their "infinite Object," who is represented as "the sum of all truth and relations."[141] Hegel sees in this relation between the human and the infinite not free self-determination but a retreat into passivity in which "the nullity of man and the littleness of an existence maintained by favor was to be recalled in every enjoyment, in every human activity."[142] Even at the time of Jewish independence Hegel depicts Judaism as typified by a "thoroughgoing passivity" whose only concern was physical sustenance. Moses thus became the founder of an Eastern despotism who concluded his legislation with "an orientally beautiful threat" to all who disobeyed his commands.[143]

It was against the lawlike character of Judaism that Hegel expressed his theological ire. This attitude marks a new point of departure in his thinking. In "The Positivity of the Christian Religion" he drew a sharp distinction between Kantian and Jewish ethics. Jewish law was depicted by Hegel, as by Kant before him, as having its source in a transcendent or revealed deity wholly outside mankind. On the face of it, this appears to be the direct antithesis of Kantian ethics, in which the moral law is said to have its source in practical reason, so that in obeying the law we do no more than obey ourselves. In "The Spirit of Christianity," however, Hegel turns Kant on his head. Far from congratulating Kant for overcoming traditional theological ethics, Hegel shows that he has remained an unwitting captive of it. Kant contrasted the slavery of obedience to ritual law with the freedom of the agent who obeys his own self-imposed commands of duty. But on Hegel's reading now, this analogy only partially removes the problem. Kant did not eliminate slavery; he internalized it. So long as morality is conceived, as it is in both Judaism and Kantianism, as obedience to law, it can never succeed in overcoming the problem of slavery. It merely relocates the source of slavery from the outside to the inside, from a social relationship to a psychological one. Kantianism is now merely Judaism's alter ego.[144]

Hegel attacks both Judaism and Kantianism from a position that comes close to theological antinomianism. Kantianism and Judaism are both said to embody a morality of rules; Christianity, the ethic of love. By a morality of rules, or law, Hegel means at least two things. First, rules express general commands that do not treat persons and their circumstances as unique but as instances or cases. Second, because rules always express an "ought-to-be" (*Sollen*), they stand in opposition to what is, to life itself. Against a morality of law, Hegel now tells us that Christianity offered a morality of love, a morality of "the subjective in general."[145] Rather than judging persons or actions as instances of general laws, Christianity proposed examining the merits of each case on its own terms. The new dispensation of love, then, represented "a spirit raised above morality" which sought "to strip the laws of . . . their legal form."[146]

Hegel's judgment on Judaism in "The Spirit of Christianity," then, is that it is the religion of sheer legalism. This legalism was expressed in Abraham's separation from the community, from nature, and from God. His separation impressed itself upon Judaism as an ineluctable fate that the Christian teaching of love could not overcome. Such a view, like others we have seen, fails to account for the dignity of Jewish life, the gravity of Abraham's sacrifice, and the moral, not merely political, quality of Mosaic prophecy. Hegel thus describes the fate of the Jews not as a Greek but as a Shakespearean tragedy: "The great tragedy of the Jewish people is no Greek tragedy; it can rouse neither terror nor pity, for both of these arise only out of the fate which follows from the inevitable slip of a beautiful character; it can arouse horror alone. The fate of the Jewish people is the fate of Macbeth who stepped out of nature itself, clung to alien Beings, and so in their service had to trample and slay everything holy in human nature, had at last to be forsaken by his gods (since these were objects and he their slave) and be dashed to pieces on his faith itself."[147] Only in his later writings would Hegel try to comprehend Judaism within the larger dialectic of world history.

Hegel: From "The Religion of Sublimity" to the "Protestant Principle"

Hegel's later conception of Judaism is not treated in any one place but needs to be culled from a number of different texts.[148] All of his writings contribute to what could be called his new dialectical or historical paradigm. From this standpoint, Judaism is no longer seen as a static system of coercive laws but as part of the development of the human spirit in its movement toward freedom. Unlike the *Early Theological Writings*, Hegel's mature works emphasize Judaism's positive contribution to the development of *Geist*. Thus even while Hegel's considered views on the Jewish Question may have certain omissions and distortions, there is an effort to do greater justice, even if not complete justice, to the contribution of Judaism to history.

In the *Philosophy of History* Hegel treats Judaism as part of the Oriental World. By this geographical designation Hegel means a condition of mind as well as a place on the globe. World history is depicted here as the struggle of the human spirit to realize freedom, a struggle carried out across various world cultures and civilizations. These cultures are ranked and organized around their collective embodiments of freedom. The Oriental World knew that only one was free; the Greco-Roman world knew that a few were free; the world of modern Protestant Europe, finally and for the first time in human history, recognized that all men are free. History becomes, then, an immense process of *Bildung,* of the moral education of humanity, toward an awareness of freedom and rights.[149]

Hegel's initial statement that the Jews were simply one of the wide circle of nationalities composing the Persian Empire sounds at least superficially similar to many of his early remarks. Here Judaism opens a break or fissure with nature that "forms the point of separation between the East and the West."[150] Yet rather than regarding this separation and the corresponding Jewish emphasis on exclusivity as an alienation from God and nature, Hegel treats it as a decisive advance in the development of self-conscious spirit. In a brief methodological aside that typifies his new position, he says that every religion contains a "divine presence" and that the task of the philosophical historian is "to seek out the spiritual element even in the most imperfect forms."[151]

Later in the same text Hegel returns to Judaism in his treatment of the causes of the emergence of Christianity in the Roman world. Unlike in "The Spirit of Christianity," he does not treat Judaism as the antithesis of Christianity but as its basis. In a passage that calls to mind Kierkegaard's later religious anguish or even Joseph Soloveitchik's "lonely man of faith," Hegel describes the biblical Jew as a "divided and discordant being" for whom "the pain occasioned by our individual nothingness . . . and the longing to transcend this condition of soul" constitutes "the world historical importance and weight" of the Jewish people.[152] Rather than disparaging the "cold," "dead," and "lifeless" formalism of Judaic law, Hegel now seems almost to go out of his way to take cognizance of the wellsprings of Jewish spirituality. The Psalms of David and the prophetic books of the Tenach "most purely and beautifully" reveal "the thirst of the soul after God, its profound sorrow for its transgressions, and the desire for righteousness and holiness."[153]

The same attitude is expressed in Hegel's analysis of the Jewish Bible, "a canonical book" that is now said to contain a "deep truth." This truth is the account of the origins of moral knowledge in Genesis, which Hegel interprets philosophically as "consciousness occasion[ing] the separation of the ego in its boundless freedom as arbitrary choice."[154] In other words, far from expressing a slavish and passive demeanor, biblical Judaism expresses the essential freedom of man, his capacity to choose good as well as evil, as a result of his fall away from nature. This fall, "the disannulling of the unity of mere nature," is itself paradigmatic of "the eternal history of spirit." Here, too, this fall is not just a moral tragedy; it is a necessary stage in the development of humanity. "Paradise," Hegel says in a striking, almost aphoristic passage, "is a park where only brutes, not men, can remain."[155]

One can also discern a major change in Hegel's attitude toward the fate of the ancient Jews. He forgoes the harsh and uncharitable judgment of the *Early Theological Writings,* where he presented Jewish suffering as the result of some deep-seated character flaw, and instead traces it back to purely secular or political causes. The Roman Empire under Hadrian annulled this "God-serving nation" with its destruction of the Temple.[156] Not until then, when "every source of satisfaction was taken away" and the people themselves "scattered to the winds," did the Jews return to "the standpoint of that primeval mythos," namely, the need for divine mercy and love. Even here, the Jews did not experience their suffering as "the stupid immersion in a blind fate" but confronted it head on with "a boundless energy of longing" for reconciliation with God.[157] Hegel believes that only Christianity developed a language adequate to express this longing, but what is of note is that he now regards Christianity not as the negation but as the fulfillment of what was originally a Jewish need.

The treatment of Judaism in Hegel's lectures on the philosophy of religion merely fills out the account given in the *Philosophy of History*. His classification and evaluation of the major world religions in the later lectures parallels his presentation of the sweep of the major world cultures in the *Philosophy of History* and the development of the forms of moral self-awareness in the *Phenomenology*. In these lectures Hegel develops what could be called a phenomenology of religious experience. He describes religious belief both as an experience of the believer and as part of an evolution from superstition and idolatry to higher levels of religious and speculative truth. Within this bold and original schema, Judaism corresponds to what Hegel calls "the religion of sublimity [*Erhabenheit*]."[158]

The central feature of the religion of sublimity is its conception of God as "infinite Power." Sublimity implies here the remoteness and distance of God, as it did in the early works, but it also entails a conception of God as spirit, freed "from the natural and consequently [from] what is sensuous," whose actions are both rational and moral. No longer is Hegel contrasting the "positivity" of Judaism with the "beauty" of natural theology. Now Judaism is praised for combining "the rational characteristics of freedom, the moral characteristics," into one determinate end, namely, the idea of holiness.[159]

Hegel remarks that although this conception of God is still "formal," it is nonetheless of "infinite importance," so it is "not to be wondered at that the Jewish people put such a high value upon it." For the first time anywhere in his writings, Hegel admits the Jewish conception of the deity into the domain of moral and religious truth. The conception of the infinite power of God is now said to contain "the essential character of absolute truth" and the beginning of wisdom.[160]

A major feature of the sublime is defined here by the radical separation of the human and the divine, the finite and the infinite. The religion of sublimity is religion as grasped by the power of *Verstand,* the intellectual faculty of division and separation by which men treat God as separate from and sovereign over divine creation.[161] Hegel remarks that it is a "defect" of this religion that while God is apprehended as "the universal and irresistible power," the entire world of nature becomes empty of divine purpose. In relation to God, the sublime creator, the world becomes prosaic or, to use a Weberian term, "disenchanted." The principle of division, the root of Judaism, also characterizes "the view taken by the modern 'enlightenment,'" which says "*Il y a un être suprême* and lets the matter rest." The God of the Enlightenment becomes, then, "only a bare name, a mere *caput mortuum* of abstract understanding."[162]

Here again Hegel's perspective on the meaning of God's power in the *Philosophy of Religion* is entirely different from that in the early works. Rather than instilling in the Jews a slavelike manner, Judaism became the basis for an admirable self-assurance, which he calls the most "fundamental and praiseworthy trait of the Jewish people."[163] Hegel uses the Book of Job to express this insight. In spite of Job's protest against his unjust sufferings, it is ultimately his recognition of God's power that restores his happiness. Judaism is not defined in terms of an external conformity to law. Instead, Job's inner determination to do what is right, to love God and practice justice despite his misfortunes, typifies Judaism's strength and greatness. It is precisely the Jews' "examination into and anxiety about what is wrong," this "crying of the soul after God . . . and this yearning of the spirit after what is right," that marks this form of religious experience.[164]

Even if Hegel shows a greater appreciation for Judaism in his later works, the "religion of sublimity" occupies only a "moment" in the progress of *Geist* through history. Every historical people has its peak moment of creativity, and by now the Jewish moment is long since past. Following a line of argument that is traceable back to chapter 5 of Spinoza's *Treatise,* Hegel regards the fundamental Jewish contribution as the idea of theocracy. Moses was "the lawgiver of the Jews," the bearer of a divine legislation. Hegel criticizes the legislation for failing to distinguish between divine revelations and the wealth of particular commands regulating the conduct of daily life. "All law," he writes, "is given by the Lord and is thus entirely positive commandment."[165] This fusion of civil and ecclesiastical power is what most clearly differentiates the ancient Hebrew theocracy from the modern liberal Protestant state, besides constituting the strongest possible contrast between the God of Abraham, Isaac, and Jacob and "the conception which we have of God."[166] Within the world of liberal Protestant modernity, Jews may find a home, but at the cost of social and spiritual marginality.[167]

Hegel's idea of historical progress came to fruition in the *Philosophy of Right,* where he treats the modern state as the actuality of "substantive freedom."[168] The modern state with its protection of the right of property, its separation of the social and political spheres, and its complex role differentiation is itself the institutionalization of what could be called the Protestant idea of liberty. Central to the "Protestant principle" is, of course, the idea of subjective or inner freedom. With Christianity came the introduction of the idea that "the individual *as such* has an infinite value" and that "man is implicitly destined to supreme freedom."[169] Not until the Protestant Reformation, that "all-enlightening Sun," however, can we can begin to see the outlines of a civilization entirely shaped by the culture of subjectivity.[170]

The Reformation stands at a pivotal moment in Hegel's understanding of freedom. For the Protestant idea of liberty, what counts is "the subjective feeling and the conviction of the individual . . . as equally necessary with the objective side of truth."[171] This inner liberty is in turn regarded not as the monopoly of some ecclesiastical or spiritual elite but as "the common property of all mankind."[172] It is, then, "the essence of the Reformation" that "man is in his very nature destined to be free."[173] To be sure, this freedom remains an inner freedom, the liberty of conscience, which Hegel takes to be the unique contribution of the "Germanic nations," by which he meant more than Germany or even the German-speaking countries but something like the culture of Protestant Europe. It is the "pure inwardness of the Germanic nations," their "inward-looking tenderness," that made them "the proper soil for the emancipation of the spirit."[174]

The whole period of modern history from the Reformation to the French Revolution has witnessed the gradual spread and secularization of the principle of Protestant liberty.[175] This freedom has received its most advanced form in the modern state, with its constitutional structure and public recognition of rights. It is the recognition of the "I," the "will," the "free infinite personality," that distinguishes the modern state from both the ancient polis and the Hebrew theocracy. "This 'I will,'" Hegel writes, "constitutes the great difference between the ancient world and the modern, and in the great edifice of the state it must therefore have its appropriate objective existence."[176] Like many later social theorists, Hegel even remarks on the kinship between the Christian principle of subjectivity and the development of the modern market economy where individuals "in their capacity as burghers" are free to pursue their own interests.[177]

We can now begin to see the deep affinity between Hegelian history and a certain kind of Protestant religiosity. A central feature of this conviction is its toleration of religious heterodoxy. Hegel does not defend religious toleration because he is indifferent to matters of religious truth. In fact, he regards as a "monstrous blunder" the belief that the spheres of politics and theology are "mutually indifferent" to one another.[178] Instead, Hegel can extend toleration to Jews and other religious minorities because of his assurance of the truth of Protestant Christianity. For him it is the "absolute" religion. Protestantism alone accords primacy to the role of the I or the self in the determination of truth. Thus for the state to attempt to coerce belief would be both self-defeating and offensive to true religion. It is, paradoxically, in Protestantism's recognition of religious freedom that "the divine spirit" is said "to interpenetrate the entire secular sphere" and the state and religion become "reciprocal guarantees of strength."[179]

Nevertheless, on the issue of the place of Judaism in the modern state, Hegel is emphatic. In two passages from the *Philosophy of Right* he finds that whatever the remaining differences between Christians and Jews, the extension of equal rights for Jews remains a focal point of the modern state. "It is a part of education [*Bildung*], of thinking as the consciousness of the single in the form of universality, that the ego comes to be apprehended as a universal person. . . . A man counts in virtue of his manhood alone, not because he is a Jew, Catholic, Protestant, German, Italian, etc."[180]

The second, and perhaps even more decisive, passage reads as follows: "But the fierce outcry raised against the Jews . . . ignores the fact that they are, above all, men; and manhood, so far from being a mere superficial abstract quality . . . is, on the contrary, itself the basis of the fact that what civil rights rouse in their possessors . . . is the feeling of selfhood, infinite and free from all restrictions, the root from which the desired similarity in disposition and ways of thinking comes into being."[181] Hegel argues that to exclude Jews from civil rights would only confirm the separatism for which they have been reproached. A state that does not guarantee rights for all its citizens has "misunderstood its own basic principle, its nature as an objective and powerful institution."[182]

Hegel's case for emancipation rests not on a belief in the inherent dignity of

Jewish identity but on a confidence that history has finally rendered Judaism obsolete. Resistance to persecution is what has made possible Jewish survival over centuries of Diaspora. Hegel's answer to the Jewish Question, then, is the one that has been adopted by virtually every liberal society. In the modern state, toleration will achieve what hitherto persecution has failed to accomplish. Not ghettoizing but "emancipating" Jews is the best means of achieving their assimilation and even disappearance within the liberal Protestant state.

The liberal solution to the Jewish Question has been both a blessing and a curse. Liberalism could promise that there would be no more pogroms, no more state-sponsored wars of religious genocide. Liberal regimes could provide havens of safety and security, where Jews and other peoples could live and practice their religion free from the worst forms of bigotry and intolerance. But tolerance came at a price. Liberalism is inseparable from, indeed, scarcely intelligible without, the Protestant belief that the claims of conscience are inviolable and ought not to be subject to either political or ecclesiastical control. Religions are tolerated to the extent that their adherents are willing to become members of a voluntary association, like every other group in society, free to come and go from their group as they please. Religious affiliation, like consumer loyalty, becomes a matter of individual choice and conscience. But this recognition of free choice as the core of religion has no basis in Jewish experience. To the extent that Judaism and liberalism remain compatible, it is partly because of the recognition of the hegemony of a largely Protestant culture.

8

The Jewish Question Reconsidered

The *Theologico-Political Treatise* is one of the great documents of Enlightenment liberalism. The aim of the work is to liberate the individual from bondage to superstition and ecclesiastical authority. Spinoza's ideal is the liberated individual who uses the power of reason to conquer fear and achieve mastery over the passions. As if this were not ambitious enough, the work culminates in an exhilarating vision of a democratic republic where citizens live in peace and security and where all have the freedom to speak their mind without fear or favor. The foundation for this republic is a universal religion of human reason that transcends the historical differences between the revealed faiths and that can serve as an ethical basis for a free, open, and tolerant society. In historical perspective, Spinoza was successful beyond his wildest dreams. What must have appeared to be an almost unapproachable ideal in 1670 gradually came to acquire the force of law in countries like Holland, England, and later the United States.

In spite of his advocacy for freedom, a number of barriers, not to say prejudices, stand in the way of regarding Spinoza as a founding father of modern liberalism. In the first place, his unified conception of the political sovereign may seem more characteristic of an age of absolutism than an age of liberalism. His view that the sovereign must be one and indivisible seems radically opposed to the Lockean notion of limited government or the *Federal-*

ist's scheme of constitutional checks and balances. Further, Spinoza's pronounced elitism and condescension toward the "multitude" may seem an unfortunate relic of a premodern age. His skepticism of the many, coupled with his use of coded language, can make him appear less than a wholehearted defender of liberal government and institutions. Finally, Spinoza's belief in the necessity for a public religion to ensure political obligation may seem evidence of insufficient liberality. His insistence on the right of the sovereign to determine which religious practices and observances conform to the public good is not sufficient to persuade constitutional lawyers for whom "the great wall of separation" between church and state is one of the few modern absolutes.

The common view is that Spinoza sacrificed the individual on the altar of an absolutist state in which right is identical to power. To function properly, the state must have absolute power over the life, personal feelings, and emotions of the individual. But this view projects contemporary fears about the modern totalitarian state back onto Spinoza and his time. The defining characteristic of modern totalitarianism is not so much its absolutism as the presence of technology and the use of an ideology of terror. Both of these features are absent in the *Treatise*. Not for an instant does Spinoza allow the strength of the sovereign to obliterate the will of the individual. Part of the failure to see the liberalism of the *Treatise* comes from the misidentification of its argument. The threat to liberty in Spinoza's time came not from the danger of an all-powerful state but from those very groups and authorities who profited from the absence of such a state. The danger to freedom stemmed from the organized power of the clerics, who appealed to a spurious right to prophecy in order to impose their particular mandates. Spinoza's theory of sovereignty is absolutist, but not totalitarian. The instrumentality of the state is used to protect the individual from the pressures exerted by organized groups and collectivities. It is the very absoluteness of the sovereign that makes it the proper guardian of the individual.

Nor is Spinoza's liberalism compromised by his use of coded speech. Like virtually every early modern thinker, Spinoza had a robust vocabulary for distinguishing the few from the many. The *Treatise* is itself addressed to those relatively few "prudent" readers who had achieved a certain degree of emancipation from popular prejudice and superstition and who could serve as political allies in Spinoza's struggle against orthodoxy. Indeed, the history of liberalism is replete with examples of this kind. For Kant, the great apostle of "the public use of reason," the project of Enlightenment was better entrusted to those rare individuals who have the courage to think for themselves than to "the great unthinking mass," who are prone to prejudice. Similarly, John Stuart Mill put the struggle between the exceptional individual, or genius, and the majority of society at the very center of *On Liberty*. Even today, many constitutional lawyers prefer to see such politically sensitive issues as abortion and school prayer taken away from the volatile public and given over to the more enlightened judges and the courts.

Spinoza did not believe that the gap between the few and the many could ever be eliminated but did think that it might in time be narrowed. Even his division of humanity into the wise and the unwise did not prevent him from championing democracy as the *optima Respublica*. The chief obstacle to the creation of a stable democratic republic was not the multitude as such but the power of the divines, who used their authority to inflame popular passion and make it appear honorable for men to fight for their enslavement with the same zeal as if it were their freedom.[1] Eliminating distrust of philosophy and skepticism of "intellectuals" may never be possible; still, a democratic republic is the best guarantor of freedom of speech and opinion and the regime most likely to provide philosophy with a secure status in the community.

It is in his treatment of the religious question — the theologico-political problem — that Spinoza's liberalism is put most vividly on display. In the *Treatise* he sets himself the task of domesticating religious intolerance and the zeal for persecution. In the history of political liberalism only Locke and Milton rival Spinoza as advocates of religious liberty. However, Spinoza believed that if liberty of opinion is to be more than a philosopher's wishful thinking, it must have the public weight of religion behind it. Religion must be reinterpreted so that it will at least appear to teach the liberal virtues of toleration, respect for rights, and freedom of expression. Thus Spinoza helped to prepare the way for a new kind of rational religion, a new understanding of the divine law, that would arise out of but ultimately transcend the historical religions of Judaism and Christianity. The *fides universalis* would stress not divisive doctrinal beliefs but rather acts of "justice and charity," interpreted to mean toleration and nonpersecution. The Bible must be shown to contain nothing offensive to society, and, in fact, its highest teachings are reworked to support the requirements of the new liberal state. The tenets of the universal creed, like those of the rational theologies expounded by the other framers of constitutional democracy, were intended to frustrate the power of ecclesiastics, who have a professional stake in multiplying the obscurities of religion. The result would be a new liberal civil theology that would lay the basis for a truce between the warring religious sects of Europe and perhaps even beyond.

Spinoza's plan to resolve once and for all the theologico-political problem may seem today to have costs that he either overlooked or did not foresee. In particular, his proposal for a universal faith that could serve as the basis for civil obligation appears in hindsight to be the weakest and least sustainable part of the *Treatise*. The *fides universalis* stands somewhere between traditional forms of religious belief and a wholly rational ethic. It teaches obedience to the liberal state for reasons ostensibly drawn from the very words of Scripture. But to those for whom the biblical God — the God of Abraham, Isaac, and Jacob — is an indispensable part of the moral life, Spinoza's proposal for a religion of reason seems to lack the power to compel real obligation. Its very "reasonableness" is devoid of the biblical elements of sacred awe and divine mystery. At the same time, contemporary liberalism finds Spinoza's advocacy of a common civil faith an unacceptable halfway house on the road to a more radically secularized society. His belief in the necessity for some kind of civil religion, if only to underwrite intellectual freedom and toleration, is apparently at odds with the Enlightenment's imperative of rational autonomy and responsibility.

Spinoza's solution to the theologico-political problem can be summarized in a single word: assimilation. The assimilation he has in mind does not mean conversion to Christianity or any of the revealed faiths but assimilation to a secular society that is, formally, neither Christian nor Jewish but liberal. The idea of the *fides universalis,* the common civil faith, seems to embody the liberal idea of the "melting pot," where all the old religious and ethnic particularities of a people are refined in order to produce a new universal human identity. This new identity can trace its beginnings back to the early modern wars of religion and the need to put an end to the continual conflict between the contending sects of Christian Europe. Thus it was not uncommon to find the framers of liberal democracy arguing that allegiance to a common creed was necessary to both ensure civil peace and guarantee religious freedom. The purpose of such a creed was to find a common ground for a shared civic identity while still allowing ample room within which individual and group differences could be given free expression. Inevitably, the kind of culture that came to dominate took on a largely Protestant hue. America may not have been a Christian nation, but it was a nation composed overwhelmingly of Christians, as has been noted by the most astute observer of our civil creed.[2] The image of the melting pot, though in principle open to all, was far from neutral. An amalgam of liberal political institutions and cultural Protestantism virtually defined the uniquely American version of this civic ethos well into this century.

Ironically, the dominance of this kind of liberal civil theology has come under fierce attack at just the moment when it has gone into abeyance, if not irretrievable decline. The idea that human beings can shed their particularistic loyalties and identifications like old suits of clothes has been criticized as both psychologically and sociologically naive. The very terms "individual" and "individualism" are invariably preceded by the modifier "abstract" and are said to express the values of patriarchy and domination. The older model of individualism based on the virtues of self-reliance and independence (the "rugged individualism" of so much of American folklore) has been replaced with terms like "identity" and "difference." These terms are not understood as properties of individuals but of groups or collectivities, which are in turn said to determine individual identity. According to some identity theorists, because individuals are fundamentally shaped by their group loyalties and commitments, the claims for a common culture or universal citizenship, even within a single nation-state, are inherently oppressive and exclusionary. In place of the older assimilationist version of liberalism, we have been offered a new vision of a multiculturalist society where the cultivation of group identities is not merely tolerated but encouraged and where a politics of "difference" takes priority over a politics of the common good.

The issue of identity and difference has recently dominated much of contemporary public discourse in the United States. We live in the age of the hyphenated American; many consider the older idea of a common citizenship to be neither possible nor desirable. Instead of focusing on what unites us as a people, we are increasingly told that authenticity, empowerment, and self-esteem are bound up with our sense of ethnic, racial, or cultural identity. These issues were not unknown to Spinoza. He lived in an age of what might be called identity politics. Were he alive today, he would no doubt see this universal human phenomenon in a different set of historical circumstances. In the seventeenth century identity was conferred not so much as it is today by race, ethnicity, or even gender but by religious affiliation. One was defined by one's religion, period. Exit, except on rare occasions, was not yet considered a viable option. This is why Spinoza's decision to leave the synagogue looked like both a profound anomaly and a paradigm for the new liberated individual. Spinoza was, and to some degree remains, the prototype of the emancipated secular Jew.

In the *Treatise* Spinoza offers a strategy for dissolving group identities and differences, not accommodating them. The problem of diversity — regarding religion and various conceptions of the human good — was for Spinoza the natural state of human affairs. The question that he posed was not how to enhance diversity but how best to control and contain it. He sought ways of increasing the power of the individual in order better to resist the coercive power of group identities. Identity politics was not for him a source of empowerment but a means of imposing narrow orthodoxies and conformity. The threat to freedom was less likely to stem from the imposition of a common culture than from the tyranny of group differences, when, for example, clerical enthusiasts and other putative leaders arrogate to themselves power over the individual. Furthermore, Spinoza regarded a politics of group difference as more likely to produce lasting enmities and hatreds than a pleasing diversity and mutual respect. Did he not say with brutal candor that what leads one person to piety and religion leads another to laughter and contempt?[3]

Spinoza's solution to the theologico-political dilemma poses a set of special problems, at least so far as Judaism is concerned. Jews do not need to convert to acquire their "passport" to Western civilization, as Heinrich Heine put it. They can subscribe to the very latitudinarian civil religion to gain full rights of citizenship. In providing for the liberal state, Spinoza helped to provide for a liberal civil religion. The chief difficulty has been the assimilation of Judaism, not to Christianity, but to the universalistic norms and principles of the liberal state. Indeed, for many, Judaism has become virtually inseparable from support for liberal causes like freedom, equality, and universal human rights. Liberalism's emancipation of the Jews has been widely reciprocated in the Jewish attachment to liberalism. The expression "Jewish liberalism," rather than the statement of a paradox, has become a commonplace. The result of this identification of Judaism with the Enlightenment values of autonomy and liberation from tradition has been the transformation of Judaism from a body of revealed law into something like a modern cultural or political identity. The transformation of Jewishness, once considered a mark of God's election, into a modern sociological category of group identity has raised powerful and profound problems for the survival of Judaism in the secular liberal state.

Leo Strauss remarked that "the Jewish problem is the most manifest symbol of the human problem insofar as it is a social or political problem."[4] I take it that "the human problem" to which this statement refers is the problem of managing unity and diversity, the one and the many. How can we balance the claims of individual and group difference within the requirement of social unity? How can one be faithful to the traditions and customs of Judaism and fulfill one's obligations as a citizen of a constitutional democracy? The Jewish Question seems to be the most emblematic expression of this problem in modern politics. There is an almost natural affinity between the Jewish Question and the language of modern identity politics.

An answer to the problem of unity and diversity that has become the dominant one in contemporary politics has been to think of Jews as just one of several racial or ethnic groups vying for equality and acceptance in the modern liberal state. This was not exactly Spinoza's preferred solution to the theologico-political problem. He preferred to see the withering away of the revealed religions, both Judaism and Christianity, and their replacement by a rational faith that would form the basis of a common culture. This Enlightenment hope for the secular transformation of religion has been only partially or imperfectly fulfilled. Some aspects of the Enlightenment's solution to this problem have been captured by aspects of Reform Judaism and certain of the mainstream Protestant denominations in the United States. But, as the return of the religious question has demonstrated, not everyone has been willing to sign on. Religious and other forms of ethnic identification seem to be as intractable today as in the sect-ridden Holland of the seventeenth century. The persistence of strong identity claims would not necessarily have surprised Spinoza. He would have been saddened, but not shocked, by recent events in Bosnia, to say nothing of the reemergence of religious extremism in Israel and throughout the Middle East.

For Spinoza, the fact of Jewish survival over centuries of dispersion was the textbook case of the persistence of identity. In the *Treatise* he sought to dissolve the notion of a specifically Jewish identity by denying the divine election of Israel and confining the Mosaic law to the period of the ancient Hebrew theocracy. Unlike today's advocates of multiculturalism and diversity, however, Spinoza did not idealize the sense of communal solidarity deriving from the experience of shared identitarian commitments. To the contrary, his own experience led him to believe that the politics of group identity were destructive of the values of individual freedom and intellectual independence, which he deeply cherished. One may, of course, on Spinoza's view, continue to practice Judaism as a religion, just as one may, under the liberal state, pursue any self-chosen goal compatible with the freedom of others to do likewise. Judaism, so understood, is entirely consistent with the modern conception of a religion that one is free to adopt or reject as one chooses. Indeed, it would be tempting to view the Jewish Question as the ur-form of the identity problem in modern politics except for this fundamental difference: Judaism claims to be derived from a revealed law based on explicit divine promises. Making Judaism a case of modern identity politics is thus to deny or undercut its own self-understanding.

That liberalism has provided the only decent solution to the theologico-political problem is defensible. The liberal state is based on the separation of the public and the private and the subsequent privatization of religious faith. Religion, as understood by liberalism, is deprived of all public power to compel and coerce. As thinkers like Locke and Mendelssohn were to argue, the scope of religion should be confined to the precincts of private disposition and belief. The result has been to free not only Jews but all religious minorities from the worst forms of state-sanctioned bigotry and exclusion from civil rights. To be sure, liberalism has not meant the end of what is commonly called discrimination. One aspect of the separation of public and private is that although policies of religious persecution are prohibited by the state, they may continue to exist in muted form in the private sphere of civil society. Liberalism has not proved to be entirely neutral to the differences between Christians and Jews. Political emancipation has been granted, but full social equality remains to be achieved and is probably incompatible with the existence of a robust private sphere.

The view of Spinoza as a prophet of emancipation is not diminished but enhanced if we bear in mind his reputation for over a century as a precursor of political Zionism. Spinoza, as we have seen, was perhaps the first modern thinker to consider the restitution of Jewish sovereignty in an independent state.[5] Yet Spinoza defends the institution of a state run on secular, liberal lines insofar as he defends the possibility of the restitution of Jewish sovereignty in the *Treatise*. The premise of Spinoza's Zionism is the rejection of the "foundations" of Judaism, understood as belief in the divine revelation of the Torah and the expectation of redemption. Spinoza deemed these beliefs responsible for Jewish weakness and passivity and incompatible with the imperatives of political self-rule. His solution would protect Jews as individuals, not as Jews, and would certainly not give any special credence to Judaism. Such an answer to the Jewish Question is detached from Jewish custom and heritage, understood as a connection to the land of Israel and the Hebrew language. Spinoza may have eloquently defended freedom for Jews, but at the cost of what was specific to Judaism.

Spinoza's treatment of the Jewish Question is consistent with, even the precondition for, liberalism's attempt to create a new civic identity out of the traditional religious particularities. This new identity, though not neutral, has still yielded greater inclusivity and toleration of individual differences than has the multiculturalist politics of identity. Under liberal regimes Judaism has flourished, even proliferated, in ways Spinoza could hardly have imagined. For all of the claims of identity politics to increased sensitivity to the diverse needs of different groups, it has tended to foster narrow forms of groupthink and ethnocentric intolerance.[6] It is incompatible with the liberal priority of recognizing the worth of each individual. Liberalism, by contrast, has demonstrated a greater readiness to welcome Jews; the politics of difference has historically and sociologically been associated with an anti-Jewish animus. Group identities are formed not only around the affirmation of a common set of values and beliefs but in opposition to others. Multiculturalists may pay lip service to the equal worth and dignity of all groups, but invariably some groups turn out to be more equal than others in the game of moral one-upsmanship. The intensification of group loyalties has typically gone together with suspicion, if not hatred, of things Jewish. The liberal solution to the

Jewish Question, despite its manifest imperfections, is, I believe — echoing Winston Churchill — the worst solution except for all the alternatives.

To assert that liberalism is the last best hope for Judaism is still a far cry from asserting that Judaism and liberalism are fully compatible. The spiritual core of Judaism remains a belief in the reality of a supernatural revelation. The fundamental Jewish experience in history was the revelation of the Torah on Mount Sinai. This revelation had the function, to some degree, of insulating and protecting the Jews from the cultures and customs of other nations. Unless it can somehow be demonstrated that this revelation demanded the unification of all humankind through the abandonment of each particular faith, Jews are justified in remaining attached to their own particularity. To the extent that the liberal Enlightenment urges the abolition of a particular providence, it will always be at odds with Judaism.

Notes

The following abbreviations are used in citations. Translations from the *Theologico-Political Treatise* are by Edwin Curley (unpublished MS); other references to the same text are provided for convenience.

Cor   *The Correspondence of Spinoza*, ed. and trans. A. Wolf. New York: Dial Press, 1927.

CW   Spinoza, *Collected Works*, ed. and trans. Edwin Curley. Princeton: Princeton University Press, 1985. Vol. 1.

Elwes   Spinoza, *Theologico-Political Treatise*, trans. R. H. M. Elwes. New York: Dover, 1951.

Ethics   Spinoza, *Ethics Demonstrated in Geometrical Order*, in CW. "*Ethics*, IV, P 37, p. 550" is a reference to book IV, Proposition 37, page 550. In the citations P stands for Proposition, S for Scholium, C for Corollary, and D for Demonstration.

G   *Spinoza Opera*, ed. Carl Gebhardt. Heidelberg: Carl Winter, 1925. "G, 2: 238 (23–27)" is a reference to this Gebhardt edition, volume 2, page 238, lines 23–27.

PT   Spinoza, *Political Treatise*, in Spinoza, *The Political Works*, ed. and trans. A. G. Wernham (Oxford: Clarendon, 1958).

TEI   Spinoza, *Treatise on the Emendation of the Intellect*, in CW.

TTP   Spinoza, *Tractatus Theologico-Politicus*, in G, vol. 3. "*TTP*, 77 [37–38] (11–19)" is a reference to this edition, page 77, lines 11–19; the bracketed figures refer to the section numbers used in the Bruder edition of the work.

Chapter 1. The Return of the Theologico-Political Problem

1. Peter Berger, *The Sacred Canopy: Elements of a Sociological Theory of Religion* (New York: Doubleday, 1967); Thomas Luckmann, *The Invisible Religion: The Problem of Religion in Modern Society* (New York: Macmillan, 1967); Will Herberg, *Protestant, Catholic, Jew: An Essay in American Religious Sociology* (New York: Doubleday, 1955). Many of these views derive from Weber's arguments about the "disenchantment" of the world; see *From Max Weber,* ed. H. H. Gerth and C. W. Mills (New York: Oxford University Press, 1967), pp. 139–41, 350, 357.

2. For exceptions to this view see the splendid work by George A. Kelly, *Politics and Religious Consciousness in America* (New Brunswick, N.J.: Transaction, 1984); William A. Galston, *Liberal Purposes: Goods, Virtues, and Diversity in the Liberal State* (Cambridge: Cambridge University Press, 1991); James Davison Hunter and Os Guinness, eds. *Articles of Faith, Articles of Peace: The Religious Liberty Clauses and the American Public Philosophy* (Washington, D.C.: Brookings Institution, 1990). For some of the best pages ever written on the subject see Alexis de Tocqueville, *Democracy in America,* trans. George Lawrence, ed. J. P. Mayer (New York: Doubleday, 1969), pp. 286–301, 442–49.

3. Claude Lefort, "The Permanence of the Theologico-Political?" in *Democracy and Political Theory,* trans. David Macey (Minneapolis: University of Minnesota Press, 1988), pp. 213–55.

4. Amos Funkenstein, *Theology and the Scientific Imagination: From the Middle Ages to the Seventeenth Century* (Princeton: Princeton University Press, 1986), pp. 3–9.

5. Thomas Hobbes, *Leviathan,* ed. Michael Oakeshott (Oxford: Blackwell, 1955), part IV.

6. John Locke, *First Treatise,* in his *Two Treatises of Government,* ed. Peter Laslett (Cambridge: Cambridge University Press, 1960), par. 58, p. 219.

7. John Locke, *A Letter on Toleration,* ed. Raymond Klibansky, trans. J. W. Gough (Oxford: Clarendon, 1968), pp. 65–67.

8. Pierre Bayle, *Pensées diverses,* in his *Oeuvres diverses,* ed. Elisabeth Labrousse (Hildesheim, Ger.: Georg Olms, 1966), vol. 3, pp. 86–87, 103–04, 109–10, 110–12.

9. See Voltaire, *Philosophical Letters,* trans. E. Dilworth (New York: Macmillan, 1961), p. 26: "If there were only one religion in England, there would be danger of tyranny; if there were two, they would cut each other's throats; but there are thirty, and they live happily together in peace."

10. Thomas Jefferson, Letter to Dr. Thomas Cooper, November 2, 1822, in *Writings,* ed. Merrill Peterson (New York: Library of America, 1984), p. 1464: "The diffusion of instruction to which there is now so growing an attraction will be the remote remedy to the fever of fanaticism; while the more proximate one will be the progress of Unitarianism. That this will, ere long, be the religion of the majority from north to south, I have no doubt."

11. See Leon Weiseltier, "Two Concepts of Secularism," in *Isaiah Berlin: A Celebration,* ed. Edna and Avishai Margalit (London: Hogarth Press, 1991), pp. 80–99, esp. 86–94.

12. Locke, *Letter on Toleration,* pp. 133–35.

13. See Leo Strauss, *Philosophy and Law: Essays Toward the Understanding of Maimonides and His Predecessors,* trans. Fred Baumann (Philadelphia: Jewish Publication

Society, 1987), p. 18: "The last and purest basis of justification for the revolt against the tradition of revelation in the end turns out to be a new form of bravery. . . . This new bravery, understood as the readiness to hold firm while gazing upon the abandonment of man, as the courage to endure fearful truth, as hardness against the inclination of man to deceive himself about his situation, is called probity."

14. For some of the better-known statements of the American framers see Jefferson, "Notes on the State of Virginia," in *Writings,* pp. 283–87; James Madison, "Memorial and Remonstrance Against Religious Assessments," in *The Writings of James Madison,* ed. G. Hunt (New York: Putnam, 1900–10), vol. 2, pp. 183–91; George Washington, "Letter to the Hebrew Congregation of Newport," in *The Writings of George Washington,* ed. John C. Fitzpatrick (Washington, D.C.: Government Printing Office, 1939), vol. 31, pp. 93–94.

15. Joseph Cropsey, "Religion, the Constitution, and the Enlightenment," in *Understanding the United States Constitution, 1787–1987: Three Bicentennial Lectures,* ed. Timothy Fuller, no. 24 of *The Colorado College Studies* (College Springs: Colorado College, 1988), pp. 25–35. This view does not preclude the possibility of a nonsectarian civil religion, as argued in Robert Bellah, "Civil Religion in America," in *American Civil Religion,* ed. Russell Richey and Donald Jones (New York: Harper and Row, 1974), pp. 21–44.

16. For the meaning of the term "enthusiasm" see John Locke, *An Essay Concerning Human Understanding,* ed. Alexander Campbell Fraser (New York: Dover, 1959), vol. 2, chap. 19, pp. 428–41; see also David Hume, "Of Superstition and Enthusiasm," in *On Religion,* ed. Richard Wollheim (Cleveland, Ohio: Meridian, 1969), pp. 246–51.

17. See two recent works: Barry Shain, *The Myth of American Individualism: The Protestant Origins of American Political Thought* (Princeton: Princeton University Press, 1994); Jon Butler, *Awash in a Sea of Faith: Christianizing the American People* (Cambridge, Mass.: Harvard University Press, 1990).

18. Hobbes, *Leviathan,* chap. 11, p. 69.

19. Stephen Carter, *The Culture of Disbelief: How American Law and Politics Trivialize Religious Devotion* (New York: Basic Books, 1993).

20. Carter, *Culture of Disbelief,* pp. 35–36, 134. Carter here cites Tocqueville as an authority.

21. Carter, *Culture of Disbelief,* pp. 48–49, 227–29.

22. For a provocative reply to Carter's thesis see Stephen Macedo, "Multiculturalism for the Religious Right? Defending Liberal Civic Education," in *Multiculturalism in a Democratic Society,* ed. Yael Tamir (Oxford: Blackwell, forthcoming).

23. Richard Neuhaus, *The Naked Public Square: Religion and Democracy in America* (Grand Rapids, Mich.: W. B. Eerdmans, 1984).

24. The best biography remains Jacob Freudenthal, *Spinoza: Leben und Lehre* (Heidelberg: Carl Winter, 1927). For a more accessible English study see Lewis Feuer, *Spinoza and the Rise of Liberalism* (New Brunswick, N.J.: Transaction, 1984).

25. The documents surrounding Spinoza's excommunication have been gathered in I. S. Revah, *Spinoza et le Dr. Juan de Prado* (Paris: Mouton, 1959).

26. Jean M. Lucas, *The Oldest Biography of Spinoza,* trans. and ed. A. Wolf (New York: Dial Press, 1928), pp. 48, 53.

27. Johannes Colerus, "The Life of B. De Spinosa," in Frederick Pollock, *Spinoza: His Life and Philosophy* (London: Duckworth, 1899), p. 389.

28. For a full account of the Marrano underground during the time of Spinoza see Yosef Kaplan, *From Christianity to Judaism: The Story of Isaac Orobio de Castro,* trans. Raphael Loewe (Oxford: Oxford University Press, 1989); see also Freudenthal, *Spinoza: Leben und Lehre,* vol. 1, pp. 16, 26, 56–58, 67–68.

29. Feuer, *Spinoza and the Rise of Liberalism,* pp. 4–5.

30. Colerus, "Life," p. 399.

31. Isaac Bashevis Singer, "The Spinoza of Market Street," in *An Isaac Bashevis Singer Reader* (New York: Farrar, Straus and Giroux, 1971), pp. 71–92. Flaubert is perhaps the greatest novelist who pays explicit homage to Spinoza; see his letter to Georges Sand of April 29, 1870: "I know Spinoza's *Ethics,* but not the *Tractatus theologico-politicus,* which bowls me over. It's dizzying! I'm in transports of admiration! *Nom de dieu!* What a man! What a brain! What learning and keenness of mind!" (in *Flaubert-Sand: The Correspondence,* trans. Francis Steegmuller and Barbara Ray [New York: HarperCollins, 1993], pp. 196–97; see also pp. 201, 269). *Madame Bovary* as a whole can be seen as embodying much of the spirit of Spinoza's ruthless critique of religion.

32. Freudenthal, *Spinoza: Leben und Lehre,* vol. 1, pp. 150–56, 240–44.

33. *Cor* #48, pp. 266–67: "Since . . . it was never my intention to give public instruction, I cannot be induced to embrace this glorious opportunity, although I have debated the matter with myself so long . . . I think that I do not know within what limits that freedom of philosophizing ought to be confined in order to avoid the appearance of wishing to disturb the publicly established religion. . . . I have already experienced these things while leading a private and solitary life, much more then are they to be feared after I shall have risen to this degree of dignity."

34. Colerus, "Life," pp. 397, 398; for a full account of the incident see Freudenthal, *Spinoza: Leben und Lehre,* vol. 1, pp. 243–48; Feuer, *Spinoza and the Rise of Liberalism,* pp. 141–42.

35. Freudenthal, *Spinoza: Leben und Lehre,* vol. 1, pp. 177–78.

36. See Leo Strauss, *Persecution and the Art of Writing and Other Essays* (Glencoe, Ill.: Free Press, 1952). More recently, interest in esoteric or censored speech has been pursued by literary scholars; see Frank Kermode, *The Genesis of Secrecy: On the Interpretation of Narrative* (Cambridge: Harvard University Press, 1979); Annabel M. Patterson, *Censorship and Interpretation: The Conditions of Writing and Reading in Early Modern England* (Madison: University of Wisconsin Press, 1984). For the application of similar views to the study of early modern political thought see Perez Zagorin, *Ways of Lying: Dissimulation, Persecution, and Conformity in Early Modern Europe* (Cambridge: Harvard University Press, 1990); Antoine Faivre, *Access to Western Esotericism* (Albany: State University Press of New York, 1994); Paul Bagley, "On the Practice of Esotericism," *Journal of the History of Ideas* 53 (1992): 231–47.

37. Leszek Kolakowski, *Chrétiens sans église: La conscience religieuse et le lien confessional au XVIIe siècle* (Paris: Gallimard, 1969).

38. Freudenthal, *Spinoza: Leben und Lehre,* vol. 2, p. 179: "Die philosophische Weltanschauung ist es, die hier den Kampf aufnimmt gegen bestimmte Richtungen des staatlichen und kirchlichen Regiments, wie es in den Niederlanden zu Spinozas Zeit in Geltung war. Der *theologische-politische Traktat* ist eine Tendenzschrift."

39. Yirmiyahu Yovel, "Bible Interpretation as Philosophical Praxis: A Study of Spinoza and Kant," *Journal of the History of Philosophy* 11 (1973): 189–212.

40. *TTP,* 77 [37–38] (11–19): "quod si quis doctrinam aliquam integram nationem, ne dicam, universum humanum genus docere, et ab omnibus in omnibus intelligi vult, is rem suam solā experientiā confirmare tenetur, rationesque suas, et rerum docendarum definitiones ad captum plebis, quae maximam humani generis partem componit, maxime accommodare, non autem eas concatenare, neque definitiones, prout ad rationes melius concatenandum inserviunt, tradere; alias doctis tantum scribet, hoc est, a paucissimis tantum hominibus, si cum reliquis comparentur, poterit intelligi"; *Elwes,* chap. 5, p. 77.

41. Gilles Deleuze, *Spinoza: Practical Philosophy,* trans. Robert Hurly (San Francisco: City Lights, 1988), p. 10.

42. John Aubrey, *Brief Lives,* ed. Andrew Clarke (Oxford: Clarendon, 1898), vol. 1, p. 357.

43. John Locke, "Second Reply to the Bishop of Worcester," in Locke, *Works* (London: Tegg, 1823), vol. 4, p. 477. Locke's remark may be taken as slightly disingenuous given that he had a copy of Spinoza's *Treatise* in his library; see Laslett, "Introduction," in Locke, *Two Treatises,* appendix B. In addition, it seems unlikely that Locke would not have run across some of Spinoza's ideas during his years of exile in Holland. For English and Dutch intellectual exchanges during this period see Rosalie L. Colie, *Light and Enlightenment: A Study of the Cambridge Platonists and the Dutch Arminians* (Cambridge: Cambridge University Press, 1957). For some speculations on the influence of Spinoza on Locke see Michael Hoffheimer, "Locke, Spinoza, and the Idea of Political Equality," *History of Political Thought* 7 (1986): 341–60.

44. Pierre Bayle, "Spinoza," in his *Historical and Critical Dictionary,* trans. Richard Popkin (Indianapolis: Hackett, 1991), p. 293.

45. Bayle, "Spinoza," pp. 301–02.

46. Freudenthal, *Leben und Lehre,* vol. 2, p. 216.

47. Denis Diderot and Jean le Ronde d'Alembert, eds., *Encyclopédie ou dictionnaire raisonné des sciences, des arts, et des métiers* (Geneva: Jean-Leonard Pellet, 1750), vol. 3, pp. 811–29.

48. David Hume, *A Treatise of Human Nature,* ed. L. A. Selby-Bigge (Oxford: Clarendon, 1980), book I, part IV, pp. 240–41.

49. Montesquieu, "Defense de l'esprit des lois," in his *De l'esprit des lois,* ed. Robert Derathé (Paris: Garnier, 1973), vol. 2, pp. 414–17: "Il n'y a donc point de spinosisme dans *l'Esprit des Lois.*"

50. Jean-Jacques Rousseau, *Discourse on the Sciences and Arts,* in his *First and Second Discourses,* trans. and ed. Roger D. Masters and Judith R. Masters (New York: Saint Martin's, 1964), pp. 61–62.

51. *The Spinoza Conversations Between Lessing and Jacobi,* ed. Gerard Vallée; trans. G. Vallée, J. B. Lawrence, and C. G. Chapple (Lanham, Md.: University Press of America, 1988). The Spinoza controversy has been discussed in David Bell, *Spinoza in Germany from 1670 to the Age of Goethe* (London: Institute of Germanic Studies, 1984), pp. 71–96; Sylvain Zac, *Spinoza en Allemagne: Mendelssohn, Lessing et Jacobi* (Paris: Meridiens-Klincksieck, 1989); Frederick Beiser, *The Fate of Reason: German Philosophy from Kant to Fichte* (Cambridge: Harvard University Press, 1987).

52. Colerus, "Life," pp. 393–95. For a contemporary statement of this view see Alfred

Gottschalk, "Spinoza — A Three Hundred Year Perspective," in *Spinoza: A Tercentenary Perspective,* ed. Barry S. Kogan (Cincinnati: Hebrew Union–Jewish Institute of Religion, 1979), p. 4. Gottschalk speaks of Spinoza's "utter sublimity," "divine serenity," and "incorruptible purity," making him comparable only to Socrates.

53. Johann Wolfgang von Goethe, *Dichtung und Wahrheit,* in *Goethes Werke* (Hamburg: Christian Wegner, 1959), vol. 10, pp. 76–78.

54. Samuel Taylor Coleridge, *Biographia literaria,* in his *Collected Works,* ed. James Engell and W. Jackson Bate (Princeton: Princeton University Press, 1983), vol. 1, p. 152.

55. Coleridge, *Biographia literaria,* vol. 2, p. 245.

56. Matthew Arnold, "Spinoza and the Bible," in *Lectures and Essays in Criticism,* ed. R. H. Super (Ann Arbor: University of Michigan Press, 1962), vol. 3, pp. 158, 182.

57. Arnold, "Spinoza and the Bible," p. 182.

58. Stuart Hampshire, *Spinoza* (New York: Penguin, 1975), p. 11.

59. Hampshire, *Spinoza,* pp. 233–34.

60. An important exception is Antonio Negri, *The Savage Anomaly: The Power of Spinoza's Metaphysics and Politics,* trans. Michael Hardt (Minneapolis: University of Minnesota Press, 1991).

61. See Edwin Curley, "Notes on a Neglected Masterpiece (II): The 'Theologico-Political Treatise' as a Prolegomenon to the 'Ethics,'" in *Central Themes in Modern Philosophy,* ed. J. A. Cover and Mark Kulstad (Indianapolis: Hackett, 1990), p. 152: "Whatever we may think of the primacy of the *Ethics* in the Spinozistic corpus, the *TTP* is, among other things, an important document for the study of Spinoza's development."

62. Deleuze, *Spinoza,* pp. 28–29.

63. For the debate over the Jewish Question in Germany see Paul Lawrence Rose, *Revolutionary Antisemitism in Germany: From Kant to Wagner* (Princeton: Princeton University Press, 1990), pp. 61–69; Julius Carlebach, *Karl Marx and the Radical Critique of Judaism* (London: Routledge and Kegan Paul, 1978), pp. 9–90; Jacob Toury, "'The Jewish Question': A Semantic Approach," *Leo Baeck Institute Year Book* 11 (1966): 85–106.

64. Pierre Birnbaum and Ira Katznelson, eds. *Paths of Emancipation: Jews, States, and Citizenship* (Princeton: Princeton University Press, 1995).

65. See Ernst Kantorowicz, *The King's Two Bodies: A Study in Medieval Political Theology* (Princeton: Princeton University Press, 1957); see also Lefort, "The Permanence of the Theologico-Political?" pp. 249–54.

66. The importance of the state has been observed even by semi-Marxists; see Perry Anderson, *The Lineages of the Absolutist State* (London: NLB, 1974), pp. 15–42; Gianfranco Poggi, *The Development of the Modern State: A Sociological Introduction* (Stanford, Calif.: Stanford University Press, 1978), pp. 60–85. For a brilliant discussion of the difference between medieval corporations known collectively as *universitas* and the modern juridical state understood as a *societas,* see Michael Oakeshott, "On the Character of a Modern European State," in his *On Human Conduct* (Oxford: Clarendon, 1975), pp. 185–326, esp. 199–206.

67. See Jacob Katz, "A State Within a State: The History of an Antisemitic Slogan," in his *Emancipation and Assimilation: Studies in Modern History* (Westmead, Eng.: Gregg International Publishers, 1972), pp. 47–76.

68. Cited in Pierre Birnbaum, *Anti-Semitism in France,* trans. Miriam Kochan (Oxford: Blackwell, 1992), p. 30; see also Arthur Hertzberg, *The French Enlightenment and the Jews: The Origins of Modern Anti-Semitism* (New York: Columbia University Press, 1968), pp. 359–61.

69. Jacob Katz, *Out of the Ghetto: The Social Background of Jewish Emancipation, 1770–1870* (Cambridge: Harvard University Press, 1973).

70. For the *Bildung* literature see Rudolf Vierhaus, "Bildung," in *Geschichtlicher Grundbegriffe, Historisches Lexikon zur Politisch und Sozialen Sprache in Deutschland,* ed. O. Brunner, W. Conze, and R. Koselleck (Stuttgart: Klett-Cotta, 1978), vol. 1, pp. 508–51; Alexander Altmann, "Moses Mendelssohn on Education and the Image of Man," in *Studies in Jewish Social Thought: An Anthology of German Jewish Scholarship,* ed. Alfred Jospe (Detroit, Mich.: Wayne State University Press, 1981), pp. 387–403; George Mosse, "Jewish Emancipation: Between 'Bildung' and Respectability," in *The Jewish Response to German Culture: From the Enlightenment to the Second World War,* ed. Juhuda Reinharz and Walter Schatzberg (Hanover, N.H.: University Press of New England, 1985), pp. 1–16.

71. Hannah Arendt, "The Jew as Pariah," in *The Jew as Pariah: Jewish Identity and Politics in the Modern Age,* ed. R. H. Feldman (New York: Grove, 1978).

72. Yosef H. Yerushalmi, *Freud's Moses: Judaism Terminable and Interminable* (New Haven: Yale University Press, 1991), p. 10.

73. Yerushalmi, *Freud's Moses,* p. 10.

74. Franz Rosenzweig, "Lessings Nathan," in *Gesammelte Schriften,* ed. Reinhold Mayer and Annemarie Mayer (Dordrecht, Neth.: Martinus Nijhoff, 1984), vol. 3, p. 450.

75. *TTP,* 56 [53] (20–21); *Elwes,* chap. 3, p. 56. On the place of Spinoza in the emergence of modern Jewish historiography see Yosef H. Yerushalmi, *Zakhor: Jewish History and Jewish Memory* (New York: Schocken, 1989).

76. See Emil Fackenheim, *To Mend the World: Foundations of Future Jewish Thought* (New York: Schocken, 1982), pp. 38–58; Isaac Franck, "Spinoza's Onslaught on Judaism," *Judaism* 28 (1979): 177–93; Franck, "Was Spinoza a 'Jewish' Philosopher?" *Judaism* 28 (1979): 345–52.

77. *TTP,* 12 [32] (1–2); *Elwes,* pref., p. 11.

78. Hermann Cohen, "Spinoza über Staat und Religion, Judentum und Christentum," in *Jüdische Schriften,* ed. Bruno Strauss (Berlin: Schwetschke, 1924), vol. 3, pp. 290–372. For useful studies of the role of Spinoza in Cohen's thought see Hans Leibeschütz, "Hermann Cohen und Spinoza," *Bulletin des Leo Baeck Instituts* 12 (1960): 225–38; Franz Nauen, "Hermann Cohen's Perceptions of Spinoza: A Reappraisal," *AJS Review* 4 (1979): 111–24.

79. Cohen, "Spinoza über Staat und Religion," pp. 298, 360.

80. Cohen, "Spinoza über Staat und Religion," p. 361.

81. Emmanuel Levinas, "The Spinoza Case," in *Difficult Freedom: Essays in Judaism,* trans. Séan Hand (London: Athlone, 1990), pp. 106–10.

82. Levinas, "Spinoza Case," p. 107.

83. Leo Strauss, "Cohens Analyse der Bibelwissenschaft Spinozas," *Der Jude* 8 (1924): 295–314.

84. Strauss, "Cohens Analyse," pp. 309–11.

85. Leo Strauss, *Spinoza's Critique of Religion,* trans. E. M. Sinclair (New York: Schocken, 1965), pp. 1–31. For a useful discussion see Michael Morgan, "Leo Strauss and the Possibility of Jewish Philosophy," in his *Dilemmas in Modern Jewish Thought* (Bloomington: University of Indiana Press, 1992), pp. 55–67; Steven B. Smith, "Leo Strauss: Between Athens and Jerusalem," *Review of Politics* 53 (1991): 75–99, reprinted in *Leo Strauss: Political Philosopher and Jewish Thinker,* ed. Kenneth Deutsch and Walter Nicgorski (Lanham, Md.: Rowman and Littlefield, 1994), pp. 81–105.

86. Strauss, *Spinoza's Critique of Religion,* p. 21.

87. Strauss, *Spinoza's Critique of Religion,* p. 19.

88. Strauss, *Spinoza's Critique of Religion,* pp. 19, 21.

89. Yirmiyahu Yovel, *Spinoza and Other Heretics,* vol. 1: *The Marrano of Reason* (Princeton: Princeton University Press, 1989); see also Zagorin, *Ways of Lying,* pp. 38–62.

90. Yovel, *Spinoza and Other Heretics,* vol. 1, pp. 15–39.

91. Yovel, *Spinoza and Other Heretics,* vol. 1, pp. 26–27.

92. Yovel, *Spinoza and Other Heretics,* vol. 1, pp. 29–32.

93. Yovel, *Spinoza and Other Heretics,* vol. 1, pp. 36–38.

94. *TTP,* 57 [55] (1–6); *Elwes,* chap. 3, p. 56; see Ze'ev Levy, *Baruch or Benedict: On Some Jewish Aspects of Spinoza's Philosophy* (New York: Peter Lang, 1989), pp. 69–76.

95. To be sure, Strauss was not unmindful of the broader political purposes of the *Treatise*; see his *Spinoza's Critique of Religion,* p. 20: "The liberal society with a view to which Spinoza has composed the *Treatise* is then a society of which Jews and Christians can be equally members. . . . In providing for the liberal state, Spinoza provides for a Judaism that is liberal in the extreme."

96. See Julius Guttmann, "Mendelssohn's 'Jerusalem' and Spinoza's 'Theologico-Political Treatise,' " in *Studies in Jewish Social Thought,* pp. 361–85; Sander Gilman, " 'Ebrew and Jew': Moses Mendelssohn and the Sense of Jewish Identity," in *Humanität und Dialog: Lessing und Mendelssohn in neuer Sicht,* ed. E. Bahr, E. P. Harris, and L. G. Lyon (Detroit, Mich.: Wayne State University Press, 1982). pp. 67–82.

97. Isaac Deutscher, "The Non-Jewish Jew," in his *Non-Jewish Jew and Other Essays* (Oxford: Oxford University Press, 1968), pp. 25–41.

98. Deutscher, "Non-Jewish Jew," p. 26.

99. Deutscher, "Non-Jewish Jew," p. 27.

100. Deutscher, "Non-Jewish Jew," p. 30.

101. Hampshire, *Spinoza,* p. 192

102. Steven B. Smith, "Spinoza's Democratic Turn: Chapter 16 of the 'Theologico-Political Treatise,' " *Review of Metaphysics* 48 (1994): 359–88; Feuer, *Spinoza and the Rise of Liberalism,* pp. 101–07; Stanley Rosen, "Benedict Spinoza," in *History of Political Philosophy,* ed. Joseph Cropsey and Leo Strauss (Chicago: Rand McNally, 1972), pp. 431, 433, 441–42.

103. Tocqueville, *Democracy in America,* p. 288: "Most of English America was peopled by men who, having shaken off the pope's authority, acknowledged no other religious supremacy; they therefore brought to the New World a Christianity which I can only describe as democratic and republican; this fact singularly favored the establishment of a temporal republic and democracy."

104. Joel Schwartz, "Liberalism and the Jewish Connection: A Study of Spinoza and the Young Marx," *Political Theory* 13 (1985): 58–89.

105. Shlomo Pines, "Spinoza's 'Tractatus Theologico-Politicus' and the Jewish Philosophical Tradition," in *Jewish Thought in the Seventeenth Century,* ed. Isadore Twersky and Bernard Septimus (Cambridge: Harvard University Press, 1987), pp. 499–521.

106. See Walter Eckstein, "Rousseau and Spinoza: Their Political Theories and Their Conception of Ethical Freedom," *Journal of the History of Ideas* 5 (1944): 259–91; Franck Tindal, "Hobbes, Spinoza, Rousseau et la formation de l'idée de democratie comme mesure de la legitimité du pouvoir politique," *Revue philosophique de la France et de l'étranger* 110 (1985): 195–222; Paul Vernière, *Spinoza et la pensée française avant la révolution* (Paris: Presses Universitaires de France, 1954), vol. 2, p. 494: "L'influence de Spinoza sur Rousseau, limitée mais précis, ne peut faire oublier que leurs voies divergeront, l'une vers Kant, l'autre vers Goethe."

107. *TTP,* 7 [12] (23–24); *Elwes,* pref., p. 6.

108. *Ethics,* III, P 59, p. 529; *G,* 2: 188 (21–25).

109. *TEI,* par. 15, p. 1: "Because Health is no small means of achieving this [education] . . . the whole of Medicine must be worked out. And because many difficult things are rendered easy by ingenuity, and we can gain much time and convenience in this life . . . Mechanics is in no way to be despised"; *G,* 2: 9 (4–9).

110. For the influence of Dutch republicanism on Spinoza see Eco O. G. Haitsma Mulier, *The Myth of Venice and Dutch Republican Thought in the Seventeenth Century* (Assen, Neth.: Van Gorcum, 1980), pp. 170–209; Hans Blom, "Virtue and Republicanism: Spinoza's Political Philosophy in the Context of the Dutch Republic," in *Republiken und Republikanismus im Europa der Frühen Neuzeit,* ed. Helmut G. Koenigsberger (Munich: R. Oldenbourg, 1988), pp. 195–212. Neither of these works appreciates sufficiently Spinoza's defense of the modern commercial republic as part of his general quarrel with and rejection of ancient republican models; on this point see André Tosel, "Y-a-t-il une philosophie du progrès chez Spinoza?" in *Spinoza: Issues and Directions. The Proceedings of the Chicago Spinoza Conference,* ed. Edwin Curley and Pierre-François Moreau (Leiden, Neth.: E. J. Brill, 1990), pp. 306–26.

111. On the cultural transformation of Judaism see Michael Meyer, *The Origins of the Modern Jew: Jewish Identity and European Culture in Germany, 1749–1824* (Detroit, Mich.: Wayne State University Press, 1967), pp. 85–114; Paul Mendes-Flohr, *Divided Passions: Jewish Intellectuals and the Experience of Modernity* (Detroit, Mich.: Wayne State University Press, 1991), pp. 67–76; Zygmunt Bauman, "Exit Visas and Entry Tickets: Paradoxes of Jewish Assimilation," *Telos* 77 (1988): 45–77.

Chapter 2. Spinoza's Audience and Manner of Writing

1. *TTP,* 240 [11–12] (33)–241(8); *Elwes,* chap. 20, p. 259; *Cor,* #30, p. 206.

2. Quibus ostenditur libertatem philosophandi non tantum salva pietate, et reipublicae pace posse concedi: Sed eandem nisi cum pace reipublicae, ipsaque pietate tolli non posse.

3. 1 John 4:13: "But this we know that we abide in him and he in us, because he has given us of his own Spirit" (*The New Oxford Annotated Bible with Apocrypha* [New York: Oxford University Press, 1977]). For Spinoza's later use of this passage see *TTP,* 175 [17] (34)–176(1); *Elwes,* chap. 14, p. 185.

4. *TTP,* 179 [33] (30–32); 184 [21] (19–21): "So we have . . . established unshakably both that Theology is not bound to be the handmaid of reason, and that reason is not bound to be the handmaid of Theology, but that each remains in charge of its own domain"; *Elwes,* chap. 14, p. 189; chap. 15, p. 194.

5. *TTP,* 10 [27] (31)–11(1); 184 [21–22] (22–23): "Surely . . . reason is the domain of truth and wisdom, whereas Theology is the domain of piety and obedience . . . the power of reason does not extend to the point of being able to determine that men can be blessed by obedience alone, without understanding things, whereas Theology teaches nothing beyond this, and does not command anything beyond obedience, and neither wills nor can do anything against reason"; *Elwes,* pref., p. 10; chap. 15, p. 194.

6. *TTP,* 10 [24] (16–18); *Elwes,* pref., p. 9.

7. *TTP,* 7 [11] (11–21); *Elwes,* pref., p. 6.

8. Immanuel Kant, *Critique of Pure Reason,* trans. Norman Kemp Smith (New York: Saint Martin's, 1965), p. 9: "Our age is, in especial degree, the age of criticism (*Kritik*), and to criticism everything must submit." See Ernst Cassirer, *The Philosophy of the Enlightenment,* trans. Fritz Koelln and James Pettegrove (Princeton: Princeton University Press, 1951), pp. 275–78; Reinhart Koselleck, *Critique and Crisis: Enlightenment and the Pathogenesis of Modern Society* (Cambridge, Mass.: MIT Press, 1988), pp. 98–123.

9. Roy Porter and Mikulas Teich, eds. *The Enlightenment in National Context* (Cambridge: Cambridge University Press, 1981).

10. Jean le Rond D'Alembert, "Discours preliminaire," in *Encyclopédie ou dictionnaire raisonné des sciences, des arts, et des métiers* (Geneva: Jean-Leonard Pellet, 1750), 1: xliii–xlvii; Thomas Jefferson, Letter to John Trumbull, February 15, 1789, in *The Portable Thomas Jefferson,* ed. Merrill Peterson (Harmondsworth, Eng.: Penguin, 1975), pp. 434–35: "I consider them [Bacon, Locke, and Newton] as the three greatest men that have ever lived, *without any exception,* and as having laid the foundation of those superstructures which have been raised in the Physical and Moral sciences" (emphasis added); Jean-Jacques Rousseau, *Discourse on the Sciences and the Arts,* in his *First and Second Discourses,* trans. Roger D. Masters and Judith R. Masters (New York: Saint Martin's, 1964), p. 63.

11. Hans-Georg Gadamer, *Truth and Method* (New York: Seabury, 1975), pp. 239–40.

12. Immanuel Kant, "What Is Enlightenment?" in *Political Writings,* ed. Hans Reiss (Cambridge: Cambridge University Press, 1970), p. 54.

13. *TTP,* 5 [1] (1–9); *Elwes,* pref., p. 3.

14. *TTP,* 6 [5] (1); *Elwes,* pref., p. 4.

15. Thomas Hobbes, *Leviathan,* ed. Michael Oakeshott (Oxford: Blackwell, 1955), chap. 6, p. 35: "*Fear* of power invisible, feigned by the mind, or imagined from tales publicly allowed, RELIGION: not allowed, SUPERSTITION."

16. *Ethics,* IV, P 54, p. 576: "The mob is terrifying, if not afraid. So it is no wonder that the Prophets, who considered the common advantage, not that of the few, commended Humility, Repentance, and Reverence so greatly"; *G,* 2: 250 (17–19).

17. *Ethics,* I, appendix, pp. 439–40; *G,* 2: 77 (28)–78 (12); see Leo Strauss, *Spinoza's Critique of Religion,* trans. E. M. Sinclair (New York: Schocken, 1965), pp. 215–16; André Tosel, *Spinoza ou le crépuscule de la servitude* (Paris: Aubier, 1984), pp. 28–35.

18. *Ethics,* V, P 34, D, p. 611: "An imagination is an idea by which the mind considers a

thing as present, which nevertheless indicates the present constitution of the human body more than the nature of the external thing"; *G,* 2: 301 (17–21).

19. Hobbes, *Leviathan,* chap. 2, p. 9.

20. Hobbes, *Leviathan,* chap. 8, pp. 43–44.

21. Friedrich Nietzsche, *Beyond Good and Evil,* trans. Walter Kaufmann (New York: Random House, 1966), par. 187, p. 100.

22. *TTP,* 6 [7] (18–23); *Elwes,* pref., p. 5.

23. *TTP,* 5 [4] (32–34); *Elwes,* pref. p. 4.

24. Hobbes, *Leviathan,* chap. 2, pp. 12–13: "If this superstitious fear of spirits were taken away, and with it, prognostics from dreams, false prophecies, and many other things depending thereon, by which crafty ambitious persons abuse the simple people, men would be much more fitted than they are for civil obedience."

25. *TTP,* 8 [16–17] (23–24, 28–29); *Elwes,* pref., p. 7.

26. *TTP,* 7 [10–11] (12–18); *Elwes,* pref., pp. 5–6.

27. For the influence of Lucretius on Spinoza and the Enlightenment see Strauss, *Spinoza's Critique of Religion,* pp. 37–52; Peter Gay, *The Enlightenment: An Interpretation,* vol. 1: *The Rise of Modern Paganism* (New York: Vintage, 1966), pp. 98–104; Frank Manuel, *The Eighteenth Century Confronts the Gods* (New York: Atheneum, 1967), pp. 145–46.

28. *Cor,* #56, p. 290; see also *TTP,* 9 [19] (5–6); *Elwes,* pref., p. 7, where Spinoza speaks of the "insanity" (*insanire*) of the Greeks.

29. Lucretius, *The Way Things Are (De rerum natura),* trans. Rolfe Humphries (Bloomington: Indiana University Press, 1969), I.66–71, III.1–6.

30. Lucretius, *De rerum natura,* III.15–18: "For, once your reason, your divining sense / Begins its proclamation, telling us / The way things are, all terrors of the mind / Vanish, are gone."

31. Lucretius, *De rerum natura,* III.982–83.

32. Lucretius, *De rerum natura,* V.106–10: "It's like this always, isn't it, when you bring / Something the ears have never heard before / And eyes can't visualize, or fingers grasp, / Where only the paved highway of belief / Is the short boulevard to heart and mind?"

33. Hobbes, *Leviathan,* chaps. 34, 39, 42.

34. For the seventeenth-century reaction to Hobbes see Samuel I. Mintz, *The Hunting of Leviathan* (Cambridge: Cambridge University Press, 1962). Contemporary writers are apt to take Hobbes's professions of piety more seriously; see, for example, W. B. Glover, "God and Thomas Hobbes," in *Hobbes Studies,* ed. K. C. Brown (Oxford: Blackwell, 1965), pp. 141–68; J. G. A. Pocock, "Time, History, and Eschatology in the Thought of Thomas Hobbes," in his *Politics, Language, and Time: Essays on Political Thought and History* (New York: Atheneum, 1971), pp. 148–201; see also H. W. Schneider, "The Piety of Thomas Hobbes" and P. J. Johnson, "Hobbes' Anglican Doctrine," both in *Thomas Hobbes in His Time,* ed. R. Ross, W. H. Schneider, and T. Waldmann (Minneapolis: University of Minnesota Press, 1974).

35. John Aubrey, *Brief Lives,* ed. Andrew Clark (Oxford: Clarendon, 1898), vol. 1, p. 357.

36. Hobbes, *Leviathan,* chap. 37, p. 285.

37. Hobbes, *Leviathan,* chap. 37, p. 285.

38. Hobbes, *Leviathan,* chap. 37, p. 288.

39. See Edwin Curley, "Spinoza on Miracles," *Spinoza nel 350 anniversario della nascita,* ed. Emilia Giancotti (Naples: Bibliopolis, 1985), pp. 421–38.

40. *TTP,* 84 [15] (11–13); *Elwes,* chap. 6, p. 84.

41. *TTP,* 81 [1] (5–9); *Elwes,* chap. 6, p. 81.

42. *TTP,* 82 [6] (13–15); *Elwes,* chap. 6, p. 82.

43. *TTP,* 84 [17–18] (33)–85(5); *Elwes,* chap. 6, p. 85.

44. *TTP,* 7 [10] (6–9); *Elwes,* pref., p. 5.

45. *TTP,* 7 [9] (2–5); *Elwes,* pref., p. 5.

46. *TTP,* 7 [12] (21–28); *Elwes,* pref., p. 6.

47. Hobbes, *Leviathan,* chap. 29, p. 214: "From the reading of such books, men have undertaken to kill their kings, because the Greek and Latin writers, in their books, and discourses of policy, make it lawful, and laudable, for any man so to do; provided, before he do it, he call him a tyrant."

48. For Spinoza's indebtedness to the classical historians see Chaim Wirszubski, "Spinoza's Debt to Tacitus," *Scripta Hierosolymitana* 2 (1955): 176–86; see also Strauss, *Spinoza's Critique of Religion,* pp. 312–14.

49. Colerus attributes Spinoza's view to the Talmudic injunction regarding the necessity of learning a trade; see Johannes Colerus, "The Life of B. De Spinosa," in Frederick Pollock, *Spinoza: His Life and Philosophy* (London: Duckworth, 1899), p. 391: "This Rabbin Gamaliel does positively say in the Treatise of the Talmud *Pirke avoth,* chap. 2, where he teaches that the study of the Law is a very desirable thing when it is attended with a Profession or a Mechanical Art: . . . And Rabbi Jehuda adds that every Man who does not take care that his children should learn a Trade does the same thing as if he taught them how to become Highway men" (punctuation was modernized).

50. Of the few commentators to note this connection see Eco O. G. Mulier, *The Myth of Venice and Dutch Republican Thought in the Seventeenth Century* (Assen, Neth.: Van Gorcum, 1980), pp. 170–81; Robert A. Duff, *Spinoza's Political and Ethical Philosophy* (Glasgow: James Maclehose and Sons, 1903), pp. 9–10, 26–27. See also Claude Lefort, *Le travail de l'oeuvre de Machiavel* (Paris: Gallimard, 1972), pp. 100–01; Edwin Curley "Kissinger, Spinoza, and Genghis Khan," in *Cambridge Companion to Spinoza,* ed. Don Garrett (Cambridge: Cambridge University Press, 1996), pp. 315–42.

51. *PT,* chap. 1, par. 1, p. 261; G, 3: 273 (9–25).

52. *PT,* chap. 1, par. 4, p. 263; G, 3: 274 (26–28).

53. *Ethics,* III, pref., p. 492; G, 2: 138 (26–27).

54. Efraim Shmueli, "The Geometrical Method, Personal Caution, and the Idea of Tolerance," in *Spinoza: New Perspectives,* ed. Robert Shahan and J. I. Biro (Norman: University of Oklahoma Press, 1978), p. 209.

55. *Ethics,* III, P 6, p. 498: "Each thing, as far as it can by its own power, strives to persevere in its being"; G, 2: 146 (7–8). See Emilia Giancotti, *Lexicon Spinozanum* (The Hague: Martinus Nijhoff, 1970), vol. 1, pp. 195–96.

56. *Ethics,* III, P 59, S, p. 529; G, 2: 188 (21–28).

57. *PT,* chap. 1, par. 1, p. 261; G, 3: 273 (9–25).

58. *PT,* chap. 1, par. 2, p. 261; G, 3: 273 (26)–274(9).

59. Machiavelli, *The Discourses,* trans. Leslie J. Walker (London: Routledge and Kegan Paul, 1950)), book I, chap. 58, pp. 341–45.

60. Machiavelli, *Discourses,* book I, chap. 58, p. 342.

61. Machiavelli, *Discourses,* book I, chap. 58, p. 345.

62. *PT,* chap. 5, par. 7, p. 313; G, 3: 296 (30)–297(11).

63. This paradox is explored in Etienne Balibar, "Spinoza: La crainte des masses," in *Spinoza nel 350 anniversario della nascita,* pp. 293–320.

64. *Ethics,* V, P 42, p. 617; G, 2: 308 (26–27).

65. *PT,* chap. 1, par. 6, p. 265; G, 3: 275 (26–34).

66. *TTP,* 8 [14] (1–5): "I have often wondered that men who boast of their allegiance to the Christian religion — i.e., to love, gladness, peace, continence, and honesty towards all — would contend so unfairly against one another, and indulge daily in the bitterest hate toward one another, so that each man's faith is known more easily from his hatred than from his love"; *Elwes,* pref., p. 6. See Gilles Deleuze, *Spinoza: Practical Philosophy,* trans. Robert Hurley (San Francisco: City Lights, 1988), p. 10.

67. The best account of the Marrano community in Amsterdam at the time of Spinoza is Yosef Kaplan, *From Christianity to Judaism: The Story of Isaac Orobio de Castro,* trans. Raphael Loewe (Oxford: Oxford University Press, 1989). For the details of Spinoza's excommunication see I. S. Revah, *Spinoza et le Dr. Juan de Prado* (Paris: Mouton, 1959), which draws in turn on Carl Gebhardt, "Juan de Prado," *Chronicon Spinozanum* 3 (1923): 269–91. For a recent retelling of the story see Yirmiyahu Yovel, *Spinoza and Other Heretics,* vol. 1: *The Marrano of Reason* (Princeton: Princeton University Press, 1989), pp. 40–84.

68. Colerus, "Life," p. 390: "M. Bayle tells us, that he [Spinoza] happened one day to be assaulted by a Jew, as he was coming out of the Playhouse, who wounded him in the face with a knife, and Spinoza knew that the Jew designed to kill him though his wound was not dangerous. . . . He kept still the coat that was run through with the dagger, as a memorial of that event. Afterwards, not thinking himself to be safe at Amsterdam, he resolved to retire somewhere else." The story that Colerus refers can be found in Pierre Bayle, "Spinoza," in his *Historical and Critical Dictionary,* trans. Richard Popkin (Indianapolis: Hackett, 1991), pp. 291–92.

69. The most impressive is Annabel Patterson, *Censorship and Interpretation: The Conditions of Writing and Reading in Early Modern England* (Madison: University of Wisconsin Press, 1984). Patterson develops a theory that she calls the "hermeneutics of censorship" which is applied principally to literary texts. Edwin Curley, in " 'I Durst Not Write so Boldly' or How to Read Hobbes' Theologico-Political Treatise," in *Hobbes e Spinoza: Scienza e politica,* ed. Emilia Giancotti (Naples: Bibliopolis, 1988), pp. 497–593, esp. 511–20, finds ample uses of irony and coded speech in Hobbes's *Leviathan.*

70. This reading is most widely associated with Leo Strauss; see "How to Study Spinoza's 'Theologico-Political Treatise,' " in his *Persecution and the Art of Writing* (Chicago: University of Chicago Press, 1988), pp. 142–201. For a contrary point of view — an argument that Spinoza neither contradicts himself nor writes deceptively — see Errol Harris, "Is There an Esoteric Doctrine in the 'Tractatus Theologico-Politicus'?" in *Mededelingen XXXVIII: Vanwege Het Spinozahuis* (Leiden, Neth.: E. J. Brill, 1978), pp. 1–19; see also Alan Donagan, *Spinoza* (Chicago: University of Chicago Press, 1988), pp. 14–15.

71. Harris, in "Is There an Esoteric Doctrine?" p. 1, asks rhetorically why Spinoza should have bothered to simulate orthodoxy — after all, he had already been excommunicated from the synagogue — unless, he muses, his youthful frankness had taught him to become devious. Harris then says: "If this were so, however, we should either have to interpret his ethical teaching as hypocritical, or to believe that he failed to practice what he preached." He continues to see the problem through moral, not political, lenses and hence cannot believe that an honest man might speak cautiously. "Had Spinoza believed it morally acceptable to insinuate his true beliefs under a mask of appeasive presentation, that in itself would affect our judgement of his intellectual integrity" (p. 2).

72. *Ethics,* IV, P 72, p. 586; G, 2: 264 (10).

73. For evidence of Maimonidean influences on Spinoza see Shlomo Pines, "Spinoza's 'Tractatus Theologico-Politicus,' Maimonides, and Kant," *Scripta Hierosolymitana* 20 (1968): 3–54; Warren Zev Harvey, "A Portrait of Spinoza as a Maimonidean," *Journal of the History of Philosophy* 19 (1981): 151–72.

74. On religious esotericism in the Middle Ages see Miriam Galston, *Politics and Excellence: The Political Philosophy of Alfarabi* (Princeton: Princeton University Press, 1990), pp. 22–54; Gershom Scholem, *Major Trends in Jewish Mysticism* (New York: Schocken, 1961), pp. 18–25.

75. Bayle, *Historical and Critical Dictionary,* p. 290.

76. *TTP,* 6 [8] (26–34), 29 [2] (31)–30(4), 114 [79] (24–31), 244 [33–35] (20)–245(9); *Elwes,* pref., p. 5; chap. 2, p. 27; chap. 7, p. 116; chap. 20, pp. 262–63.

77. Robert McShea, in *The Political Philosophy of Spinoza* (New York: Columbia University Press, 1968), pp. 4–7, speaks of "the danger of persecution" and motives of "personal safety" as the reasons behind Spinoza's "tactfulness." Nevertheless, McShea believes that Spinoza's attempted concealments were fairly obvious and can be easily penetrated by "any sufficiently motivated student." Lewis Feuer, in *Spinoza and the Rise of Liberalism* (New Brunswick: Transaction, 1988), p. 117, writes about an air of "conspiratorial secrecy" hovering over all of Spinoza's political writings, but attributes this to a "strain of defeatism" in his thought that always vied unsuccessfully with the striving toward liberation. Leo Strauss, in "How to Study Spinoza's *TPT,*" pp. 183–84, suggests that Spinoza's caution was dictated less by issues of personal safety than by a belief that religion was indispensable to society, and therefore his claim to speak *ad captum vulgi* was imposed by what he believed were the legitimate claims of society. Tosel, in *Spinoza ou la crépuscule de la servitude,* pp. 55–60, follows Strauss on this issue. See also Elmer E. Powell, *Spinoza and Religion* (Boston: 1941), pp. 60–61; Powell thinks that "excessive prudence" is what led Spinoza to "veil" his religious opinions.

78. Stuart Hampshire, *Spinoza* (New York: Penguin, 1975), p. 231.

79. CW, p. 207; G, 4: 63 (16).

80. CW, p. 207; G, 4: 63 (24–25).

81. CW, p. 229; G, 1: 131 (25–35); emphasis added.

82. See Strauss, *Persecution and the Art of Writing,* p. 17.

83. CW, p. 207; G, 4: 64 (3–6).

84. CW, p. 208; G, 4: 64 (9–10).

85. Powell, *Spinoza and Religion,* p. 61.

86. Shmueli, "Geometrical Method," pp. 208–09; Yovel, *Spinoza and Other Heretics,* vol. 1, pp. 139–40.

87. Giancotti, *Lexikon Spinonzanum*, vol. 2, pp. 728–79

88. *Cor,* #29, p. 204.

89. *Cor,* #30, p. 206.

90. *TTP,* 12 [33] (11–13); *Elwes,* pref., p. 11.

91. For Spinoza's political involvement see Feuer, *Spinoza and the Rise of Liberalism,* pp. 76–80, 137–38; McShea, *Political Philosophy of Spinoza,* pp. 20–27. For a comprehensive study of Dutch politics during the time of Spinoza see Pieter Geyl, *The Netherlands in the Seventeenth Century* (London: Dernest Benn, 1961); Herbert H. Rowen, *John de Witt, Grand Pensionary of Holland, 1625–1672* (Princeton: Princeton University Press, 1978); Simon Schama, *The Embarrassment of Riches: An Interpretation of Dutch Culture in the Golden Age* (Berkeley: University of California Press, 1988).

92. *TTP,* 7 [12] (22–23); *Elwes,* pref., p. 6.

93. For the gruesome details of the murder of the de Witts and Spinoza's response see Rowen, *John de Witt,* pp. 875–82, 885–86.

94. Rowen, *John de Witt,* pp. 398–99, 410–11. Rowen maintains that there is no reason to believe that de Witt even knew Spinoza; he maintains that "there is neither evidence nor reason to believe that he was particularly concerned with the thought of the apostate Jew and lens grinder." In the absence of evidence, the relation between de Witt and Spinoza is likely to remain unresolved, although Rowen is wrong to label Spinoza an "apostate."

95. For De la Court's influence see Eco O. G. Haitsma Mulier, *The Myth of Venice,* pp. 120–69; Feuer, *Spinoza and the Rise of Liberalism,* pp. 66–67; Rowen, *John de Witt,* pp. 391–98. See also Hiram Caton, *The Politics of Progress: The Origins and Development of the Commercial Republic, 1600–1835* (Gainesville: University of Florida Press, 1987), pp. 228–40.

96. See Joyce Appleby, *Economic Thought and Ideology in Seventeenth-Century England* (Princeton: Princeton University Press, 1978), pp. 73–98.

97. See Karl Marx, *Capital,* trans. Samuel Moore and Edward Aveling, vol. 1 (London: Lawrence and Wishart, 1970), p. 81: "By classical Political Economy, I understand that economy which, since the time of W. Petty, has investigated the real relations of production in bourgeois society, in contradistinction to vulgar economy, which deals with appearances only."

98. William Petty, *Political Arithmetick,* in *Economic Writings,* ed. Charles Henry Hull (Cambridge: Cambridge University Press, 1899), vol. 1, p. 262.

99. Petty, *Political Arithmetick,* p. 262.

100. Petty, *Political Arithmetick,* p. 263.

101. Petty, *Political Arithmetick,* p. 264.

102. For an interesting account of Temple's life and career see T. B. Macaulay, *Literary Essays* (Oxford: Oxford University Press, 1923), pp. 411–97, esp. 434–41, on his services in Holland.

103. William Temple, *Observations upon the United Provinces of the Netherlands,* in *The Works of Sir William Temple* (Edinburgh, 1754), vol. 1, pp. 119–20.

104. Temple, *Observations upon the United Provinces,* p. 123.

105. Temple, *Observations upon the United Provinces,* p. 125.

106. Temple, *Observations upon the United Provinces,* pp. 112–13.

107. Temple, *Observations upon the United Provinces,* pp. 116–17.

108. Temple, *Observations upon the United Provinces*, p. 117.

109. Rowen, *John de Witt*, pp. 412–14; Feuer, *Spinoza and the Rise of Liberalism*, pp. 76–80.

110. For the reception of Cartesianism in the Netherlands see Theo Verbeek, *Descartes and the Dutch: Early Reactions to Cartesian Philosophy, 1637–1650* (Carbondale: Southern Illinois University Press, 1992).

111. On the notion of atheism in early modern Europe see Lucien Febvre, *The Problem of Unbelief in the Sixteenth Century: The Religion of Rabelais*, trans. Beatrice Gottlieb (Cambridge: Harvard University Press, 1982); John Redwood, *Reason, Ridicule, and Religion: The Age of Enlightenment in England, 1660–1750* (London: Thames and Hudson, 1976); Michael J. Buckley, *At the Origins of Modern Atheism* (New Haven: Yale University Press, 1987).

112. See Paul Dibon, "Scepticisme et orthodoxie reformée dans la Hollande du siècle d'or," in *Scepticism from the Renaissance to the Enlightenment*, ed. Richard H. Popkin and Charles Schmitt (Wiesbaden, Ger.: Wölfenbuttler, 1987), pp. 55–81.

113. Verbeek, *Descartes and the Dutch*, pp. 10–11, 22–23, 32–33.

114. Rosalie Colie, *Light and Enlightenment: A Study of the Cambridge Platonists and the Dutch Arminians* (Cambridge: Cambridge University Press, 1957), pp. 49–65; Ernestine van der Wall, "Orthodoxy and Scepticism in the Early Dutch Enlightenment," in *Scepticism and Irreligion in the Seventeenth and Eighteenth Centuries*, ed. Richard Popkin and Arjo Vanderjagt (Leiden, Neth.: E. J. Brill, 1993), pp. 121–41.

115. Van der Wall, "Orthodoxy and Scepticism in the Early Dutch Enlightenment"; Verbeek, *Descartes and the Dutch*, p. 77.

116. Leszek Kolakowski, *Chrétiens sans église: La conscience religieuse et le lien confessional au XVIIe siècle* (Paris: Gallimard, 1969).

117. The fullest account of Spinoza and his contemporaries is K. O. Meinsma, *Spinoza et son cercle* (Paris: J. Vrin, 1983). See also Madeleine Frances, *Spinoza dans le pays néerlandais de la seconde moitié du XVIIe siècle* (Paris: Alcan, 1937); Colie, *Light and Enlightenment*, chaps. 5 and 6.

118. Kolakowski, *Chrétiens sans église*, pp. 166–77.

119. Kolakowski, *Chrétiens sans église*, pp. 210, 217.

120. See Sarah Hutton, "Reason and Revelation in the Cambridge Platonists and Their Reception of Spinoza," in *Wölfenbutteler Studien zur Aufklärung: Spinoza in der Frühzeit seiner Religiosen Wirkung*, ed. Karlfried Grunder and Wilhelm Schmidt-Biggemann (Heidelberg: Lambert Schneider, 1984), pp. 181–200.

121. *Cor*, #61, p. 302; *G*, 4: 272 (5–7).

122. *Cor*, #61, p. 302; *G*, 4: 272 (7–16).

123. *Cor*, #61, p. 302; *G*, 4: 272 (20–21); emphasis added.

124. *Cor*, #61, p. 303; *G*, 4: 273 (9–11).

125. *Cor*, #68, p. 334; *G*, 4: 299 (12–17).

126. *Cor*, #68, p. 335; *G*, 4: 299 (26–31).

127. *Cor*, #71, p. 340; *G*, 4: 304 (7–9): "Non possum non probare institutum tuum, quo illustrare, et mollire te velle significas, quae in Tractatus Theologico-Politico crucem Lectoribus fixere."

128. *G*, 4: 304 (9–18); *Cor*, #71, p. 340.

129. Cited in Colie, *Light and Enlightenment*, p. 73.

130. Cited in Colie, *Light and Enlightenment*, p. 94.

131. Colerus, "Life," p. 403.

132. Cited in Colie, *Light and Enlightenment*, p. 96.

133. Cited in Colie, *Light and Enlightenment*, p. 99.

134. Colie, *Light and Enlightenment*, p. 114.

135. Etienne Balibar, *Spinoza et la politique* (Paris: Presses Universitaires de France, 1985), p. 34.

136. *TTP*, 11 [29–30] (13–23); *Elwes*, pref., p. 10.

137. *TTP*, 12 [35] (21–25); *Elwes*, pref., p. 11.

138. *TTP*, 12 [35] (25–27); *Elwes*, pref., p. 11.

139. Feuer, in *Spinoza and the Rise of Liberalism*, pp. 115–16, maintains that passages like these are evidence of the strain of defeatism and pessimism that beclouded Spinoza's progressivist liberal vision; for a critique of the assumptions upon which this reading rests, see Christopher Norris, *Spinoza and the Origins of Modern Critical Theory* (Oxford: Blackwell, 1991), pp. 178–79, 193.

140. For the relation between Descartes's provisional morality and Spinoza see Strauss, "How to Study Spinoza's *TPT*," pp. 182–83.

141. René Descartes, *Discourse on Method*, in his *Philosophical Works*, trans. Elizabeth S. Haldane and G. R. T. Jones (Cambridge: Cambridge University Press, 1977), vol. 1, p. 95.

142. Descartes, *Discourse on Method*, p. 95.

143. *TEI*, p. 12; *G*, 2: 9 (23–27): "Ad captum vulgi loqui, et illa omnia operari, quae nihil impedimenti adferunt, quo minus nostrum scopum attingamus. Nam non parum emolumenti ab eo possumus acquiere, modo ipsius saptui, quantum fieri potest, concedamus; adde, quod tali modo amicas praebebunt aures ad veritatem audiendam."

144. See Powell, *Spinoza and Religion*, p. 65.

Chapter 3. The Critique of Scripture

1. Leo Strauss, "How to Study Spinoza's 'Theologico-Political Treatise,'" *Persecution and the Art of Writing* (Chicago: Free Press, 1952), p. 163; Berl Lang, "The Politics of Interpretation: Spinoza's Modernist Turn," *Review of Metaphysics* 43 (1989): 333–34; see also Friedrich Nietzsche, *Beyond Good and Evil*, trans. Walter Kaufmann (New York: Random House, 1966), par. 52, p. 66: "To have glued this New Testament, a kind of rococo of taste in every respect, to the Old Testament, to make *one* book, as the 'Bible,' as 'the book par excellence' — that is perhaps the greatest audacity and 'sin against the spirit' that literary Europe has on its conscience."

2. *TTP*, 150 [48] (30)–151(1); *Elwes*, chap. 10, p. 156.

3. Hermann Cohen, "Spinoza über Staat und Religion, Judentum and Christentum," in *Jüdische Schriften*, ed. B. Strauss (Berlin: Schwetschke, 1924), vol. 3, pp. 317–21, 337–38; Emil Fackenheim, *To Mend the World: Foundations of Future Jewish Thought* (New York: Schocken, 1982), p. 44; Emmanuel Levinas, "The Spinoza Case," in his *Difficult Freedom: Essays on Judaism*, trans. Séan Hand (London: Athlone, 1990), pp. 106–10.

4. Hans Frei, *The Eclipse of Biblical Narrative* (New Haven: Yale University Press, 1974), pp. 17–50, esp. pp. 42–46; Frank Manuel, *The Broken Staff: Judaism Through Christian Eyes* (Cambridge: Harvard University Press, 1992), pp. 108–61.

5. Joel C. Weinsheimer, *Eighteenth-Century Hermeneutics: Philosophy of Interpretation in England from Locke to Burke* (New Haven: Yale University Press, 1993), p. 57; Gerald Bruns, *Hermeneutics Ancient and Modern* (New Haven: Yale University Press, 1992), pp. 148–49.

6. Cf. Abraham Abulafia, the founder of *Hokmath ha-Tseruf,* or the "science of the combination of letters," described in Gershom Scholem, *Major Trends in Jewish Mysticism* (New York: Schocken, 1961), pp. 132–33, 134: "Basing himself upon the abstract and non-corporeal nature of script, [Abulafia] develops a theory of the mystical contemplation of letters and their configurations, as the constituents of God's name. For this is the real and . . . peculiarly Jewish object of mystical contemplation: The Name of God, which is something absolute, because it reflects the hidden meaning and totality of existence; the Name through which everything else acquires its meaning and which yet to the human mind has no concrete, particular meaning of its own. . . . This science of the combination of letters and the practice of controlled meditation is, according to Abulafia, nothing less than the 'mystical logic' which corresponds to the inner harmony of thought in its movement towards God."

7. *TTP,* 135 [33–34] (26–35): "But most people do not grant that any defect has cropped up even in the other parts of Scripture. Instead they maintain that by a certain special providence God has kept the whole Bible uncorrupted. Moreover, they say that the variant readings are signs of the most profound mysteries, and they allege the same about the asterisks which occur 28 times in the middle of a paragraph. Indeed, they claim that great secrets are contained in the very accent marks of the letters. Whether they have said these things out of foolishness and credulous devotion, or out of arrogance and malice, so that they alone would be believed to possess God's secrets, I do not know. I do know this: that in their writings I have read nothing which had the air of a secret, but only childish thoughts. I have also read, and for that matter, known personally, certain Kabbalistic triflers, whose insanity always taxed my capacity for amazement"; *Elwes,* chap. 9, p. 140.

8. Thomas Hobbes, *Leviathan,* ed. Michael Oakeshott (Oxford: Blackwell, 1955), chap. 33, pp. 247–48.

9. Hobbes, *Leviathan,* chap. 33, p. 248: "We read in the last chapter of *Deuteronomy,* verse 6, concerning the sepulchre of Moses, *that no man knoweth of his sepulchre to this day,* that is, to the day wherein those words were written. It is therefore manifest, that those words were written after his interment. For it were a strange interpretation to say Moses spake of his own sepulchre, though by prophecy, that it was not found to that day, wherein he was yet living."

10. On the spread of La Peyrère's ideas and their possible influence on Spinoza see Richard Popkin, "Spinoza and La Peyrère," in *Spinoza: New Perspectives,* ed. J. I. Biro and Robert W. Shahan (Norman: University of Oklahoma Press, 1978), pp. 177–95; Popkin, *Isaac La Peyrère (1596–1676): His Life, Work, and Influence* (Leiden, Neth.: E. J. Brill, 1987); Yirmiyahu Yovel, *Spinoza and Other Heretics,* vol. 1: *The Marrano of Reason* (Princeton: Princeton University Press, 1989), pp. 80–84; Yosef Kaplan, *From*

Christianity to Judaism: The Story of Isaac Orobio de Castro, trans. Raphael Loewe (Oxford: Oxford University Press, 1989), pp. 132–33.

11. Isaac La Peyrère, *Men Before Adam* (London, 1656), p. 208.

12. For the contents of Spinoza's library see Jacob Freudenthal, *Spinoza: Leben und Lehre* (Heidelberg: Carl Winter, 1927), vol 1, pp. 200–11.

13. Kaplan, *From Christianity to Judaism,* p. 133.

14. *TTP,* 118 [4] (20–21); *Elwes,* chap. 8, p. 121.

15. Isaac Husik, "Maimonides and Spinoza on the Interpretation of the Bible," in *Philosophical Essays: Ancient, Medieval, and Modern,* ed. L. Strauss and Milton Nahm (Oxford: Blackwell, 1952), pp. 148–51; Amos Funkenstein, *Theology and the Scientific Imagination: From the Middle Ages to the Seventeenth Century* (Princeton: Princeton University Press, 1986), pp. 219–20

16. The tendency to repudiate Spinoza's contributions to the historical debate about the Bible is typical of those who see him principally as a philosophical ethicist. Stuart Hampshire, in *Spinoza* (New York: Penguin, 1979), p. 194, comments that "the comparative lack of the idea of history, in the modern sense, in Spinoza's political thought is not accidental, a mere personal defect, but is the essential reflexion of his philosophy." See also R. G. Collingwood, *The Idea of History* (Oxford: Clarendon, 1956), p. 63; Collingwood says that despite "the brilliant work which made Spinoza the founder of Biblical criticism," it was "the sharply anti-historical bent" of his thought that led to its "general downfall." See also Ernst Cassirer, *The Philosophy of the Enlightenment,* trans. Fritz A. Koelln and James P. Pettegrove (Princeton: Princeton University Press, 1951), p. 185; Cassirer recognizes Spinoza's contributions to the historical debates of his time but decides that his hermeneutics are at best "an indirect conclusion from the logical premises of [his] system," which evinced "no interest in historical method as such."

17. *Ethics,* II, P 40, S 2, pp. 477–78; G, 2: 122 (3–11).

18. For works that show a greater appreciation of Spinoza's historical sense see Sylvain Zac, *Spinoza et l'interprétation de l'écriture* (Paris: Presses Universitaires de France, 1965), pp. 29–41; James C. Morrison, "Spinoza and History," in *The Philosophy of Baruch Spinoza,* ed. Richard Kennington (Washington, D.C.: Catholic University of America Press, 1980), pp. 173–95; Norman O. Brown, "Philosophy and Prophecy: Spinoza's Hermeneutics," *Political Theory* 14 (1986): 195–213; André Tosel, "Y-a-t-il une philosophie du progrès historique chez Spinoza?" in *Spinoza: Issues and Directions. The Proceedings of the Chicago Spinoza Conference,* ed. Edwin Curley and Pierre-François Moreau (Leiden, Neth.: E. J. Brill, 1990), pp. 306–26; Pierre Machery, "Spinoza: La fin de l'histoire et la ruse de la raison," in *Spinoza: Issues and Directions,* pp. 327–46.

19. Karl Marx, "A Contribution to the Critique of Hegel's Philosophy of Right," in his *Critique of Hegel's Philosophy of Right,* trans. and ed. Joseph O'Malley (Cambridge: Cambridge University Press, 1970), p. 131.

20. *TTP,* 98 [6–8] (16–28); *Elwes,* chap. 7, p. 99.

21. For some contemporary statements of this fundamentally antinaturalistic standpoint see Charles Taylor, "Self-Interpreting Animals," in *Human Agency and Language: Philosophical Papers,* vol. 1 (Cambridge: Cambridge University Press, 1985), pp. 45–76; Hans-Georg Gadamer, "The Problem of Historical Consciousness," in *Interpretive Social*

Science: A Reader, ed. Paul Rabinow and William Sullivan (Berkeley: University of California Press, 1979), pp. 103–60.

22. For some interesting similarities between Galileo and Spinoza see George Gross, "Reading the Bible with Spinoza" (unpublished MS).

23. *TTP,* 35 [26] (33)–36(2); *Elwes,* chap. 2, p. 33.

24. *TTP,* 36 [27] (8–9); *Elwes,* chap. 2, p. 33. Spinoza conjectures that the actual cause of the lengthened day may have been refracted light from the snow in the air, although the biblical text does not indicate that it was snowing at the time.

25. Jerry Bentley, *Humanists and Holy Writ: New Testament Scholarship in the Renaissance* (Princeton: Princeton University Press, 1983).

26. Cassirer, *Philosophy of the Enlightenment,* p. 185.

27. One of the few exceptions is Zac, *Spinoza et l'interprétation de l'écriture,* pp. 29–33.

28. Aristotle, *Poetics,* in *Introduction to Aristotle,* ed. Richard McKeon (Chicago: University of Chicago Press, 1973), 1451b: "The distinction between historian and poet is not in the one writing prose and the other verse . . . it consists really in this, that the one describes the thing that has been, and the other a kind of thing that might be. Hence poetry is more philosophic and of graver import than history, since its statements are of the nature rather of universals, whereas those of history are singulars."

29. Francis Bacon, *On the Dignity and Advancement of Learning,* in his *Works,* ed. James Spedding (New York: Garrett Press, 1870), vol. 4, p. 292.

30. Bacon, *Advancement of Learning,* p. 293.

31. *Cor,* #2, p. 76; *G,* 4: 8 (19–20)

32. *Cor,* #2, p. 76; *G,* 4: 8 (30). Wolff translates this phrase as "only makes assertions," which misses entirely the historical dimension of the term "narrates."

33. René Descartes, *Discourse on Method,* in his *Philosophical Works,* vol. 1, trans. Elizabeth Haldane and G. R. T. Ross (Cambridge: Cambridge University Press, 1977), p. 84.

34. Descartes, *Discourse on Method,* p. 84.

35. Descartes, *Discourse on Method,* p. 84.

36. Collingwood, *Idea of History,* p. 61.

37. *TTP,* 99 [12] (24–25); *Elwes,* chap. 7, p. 100.

38. *TTP,* 98 [9–10] (30)–99(8); *Elwes,* chap. 7, p. 100.

39. *TTP,* 99 [15] (34)–100(7); *Elwes,* chap. 7, p. 101.

40. *TTP,* 100 [16] (8–12); *Elwes,* chap. 7, p. 101.

41. *TTP,* 101 [23] (26–34); *Elwes,* chap. 7, p. 103.

42. *TTP,* 109 [59] (30–32) *Elwes,* chap. 7, p. 111.

43. *TTP,* 110 [61] (9–18); *Elwes,* chap. 7, pp. 111–12.

44. *TTP,* 111 [66] (3–15); *Elwes,* chap. 7, p. 112.

45. *TTP,* 253 (18–25); *Elwes,* p. 270 n. 7.

46. Weinsheimer, *Eighteenth-Century Hermeneutics,* p. 58.

47. *TTP,* 111 [67] (15–23); *Elwes,* chap. 7, p. 113.

48. *TTP,* 100 [16–17] (16–22); *Elwes,* chap. 7, p. 101.

49. *TTP,* 35 [26] (33)–36(7), 60 [11–12] (3–11), 167 [4–5] (22–30), 168 [6] (10–14), 174 [5, 7] (1–8, 13–17), 187 [38] (14–20), 237 [54] (20–24); *Elwes,* chap. 2, p. 33; chap. 4, pp. 57–58; chap. 13, pp. 175–76; chap. 14, p. 183; chap. 15, 197; chap. 19, p. 255.

50. For a useful discussion of this aspect of Spinoza's argument see Richard H. Popkin, "Spinoza's Skepticism and Anti-Skepticism," in *Spinoza: A Tercentenary Perspective*, ed. Barry S. Kogan (New York: Hebrew Union College, 1979), pp. 5–35; Jacqueline Lagrée, "Irrationality With or Without Reason: An Analysis of Chapter XV of the 'Tractatus Theologico-politicus,'" in *The Books of Nature and Scripture: Recent Essays on Natural Philosophy, Theology, and Biblical Criticism in the Netherlands of Spinoza's Time and the British Isles of Newton's Time*, ed. James E. Force and Richard H. Popkin (Dordrecht, Neth.: Kluwer, 1994), pp. 25–38.

51. *TTP*, 180 [2] (21–22): "Sed tam hos quam illos *toto coelo errare* ex jam dictis constat" (emphasis added); *Elwes*, chap. 15, p. 190.

52. *TTP*, 180 [1] (19); *Elwes*, chap. 15, p. 190.

53. *TTP*, 180 [3] (30); *Elwes*, chap. 15, p. 190.

54. For Alpakhar's role in the thirteenth-century debate over Maimonides see Bernard Septimus, *Hispano-Jewish Culture in Transition* (Cambridge: Harvard University Press, 1982), pp. 61–74; Daniel Jeremy Silver, *Maimonidean Criticism and the Maimonidean Controversy, 1180–1240* (Leiden, Neth.: E. J. Brill, 1965), pp. 176–82; Colette Sirat, *A History of Jewish Philosophy in the Middle Ages* (Cambridge: Cambridge University Press, 1985), pp. 222–26.

55. *TTP*, 119 [3] (15–18); *Elwes*, chap. 8, p. 121.

56. *TTP*, 120 [15] (32) 121(2); *Elwes*, chap. 8, p. 123. Husik, in "Spinoza and Maimonides on the Interpretation of the Bible," p. 150, notes that the *Gallic War* is also written in the third person, but no one has ever doubted Caesar's authorship of the text.

57. *TTP*, 121 [17] (21–27); *Elwes*, chap. 8, p. 124.

58. *TTP*, 119 [9] (18–23); *Elwes*, chap. 8, pp. 121–22.

59. *TTP*, 120 [10] (1–6); *Elwes*, chap. 8, p. 122.

60. *TTP*, 120 [11] (6–15); *Elwes*, chap. 8, p. 122.

61. *TTP*, 184 [19] (1–4); *Elwes*, chap. 15, p. 194.

62. *TTP*, 100 [18] (23–24); *Elwes*, chap. 7, p. 102.

63. *TTP*, 183 [16] (14–18); *Elwes*, chap. 15, p. 193.

64. Husik, "Maimonides and Spinoza on the Interpretation of the Bible," pp. 145–46.

65. *TTP*, 182 [10–11] (9–23); *Elwes*, chap. 15, p. 192.

66. For Orobio's relation to Spinoza see Kaplan, *From Christianity to Judaism*, pp. 150–51, 263–70; Yovel, *Spinoza and Other Heretics*, vol. 1, pp. 51–54, 58–68; Arthur Hertzberg, *The French Enlightenment and the Jews: The Origins of Modern Anti-Semitism* (New York: Columbia University Press, 1968), pp. 43–45.

67. The classic study of the revival of skepticism in early modern Europe is Richard H. Popkin, *The History of Skepticism from Erasmus to Spinoza* (Berkeley: University of California Press, 1964). Since Popkin's work there has been a flood of scholarly monographs on the subject; some of the better works are Henry G. Van Leeuwen, *The Problem of Certainty in English Thought, 1630–1690* (The Hague: Martinus Nijhoff, 1963); Don Cameron Allen, *Doubt's Boundless Sea: Skepticism and Faith in the Renaissance* (Baltimore: Johns Hopkins University Press, 1964); Charles Schmitt, *Cicero Scepticus: A Study of the Influence of the Academica in the Renaissance* (The Hague: Martinus Nijhoff, 1972); Myles Burnyeat, ed., *The Skeptical Tradition* (Berkeley: University of California Press, 1983).

68. For Luther's contributions see Frei, *Eclipse of Biblical Narrative,* pp. 18–25; Bruns, *Hermeneutics Ancient and Modern,* pp. 143–47.

69. Immanuel Kant, *Critique of Pure Reason,* trans. Norman Kemp Smith (New York: Saint Martin's, 1965), p. 29.

70. Luther said: "Scripture is through itself most certain, most easily accessible, comprehensible, interpreting itself, proving, judging all the words of all men" (cited in Frei, *Eclipse of Biblical Narrative,* p. 19).

71. Bruns, *Hermeneutics Ancient and Modern,* pp. 146–47.

72. Martin Luther, "Commentary on Galatians," in *Martin Luther: Selections from His Writings,* ed. John Dillenberger (New York: Doubleday, 1961), p. 129.

73. Martin Luther, "An Appeal to the Ruling Class of German Nationality as to the Amelioration of the State of Christendom," in *Martin Luther: Selections,* pp. 470–71.

74. Gilles Deleuze, *Spinoza: Practical Philosophy,* trans. Robert Hurley (San Francisco: City Lights Books, 1988), p. 31.

75. *Cor,* #21, p. 172; *G,* 4: 26 (14–17).

76. *Cor,* #21, p. 172; *G,* 4: 26 (23–25).

77. *Cor,* #21, p. 173; *G,* 4: 27 (1–6).

78. *Cor,* #21, p. 179; *G,* 4: 32 (14–16); emphasis added.

79. *Cor,* #21, p. 179; *G,* 4: 32 (19–24)..

80. *TTP,* 180 [3] (26–29); 167 [5] (4–5); *Elwes,* chap. 15, p. 190; chap. 13, p. 176.

81. *TTP,* 180 [4] (33)–181(1); *Elwes,* chap. 15, p. 190.

82. See, for example, Erwin I. Rosenthal, "Medieval Jewish Exegesis: Its Character and Significance," *Journal of Jewish Studies* 9 (1964): 265–81; and Rosenthal, "The Study of the Bible in Medieval Judaism," in *The Cambridge History of the Bible,* vol. 2, ed. G. W. H. Lampe (Cambridge: Cambridge University Press, 1969), pp. 252–79. For the messianic attempts to reconcile Scripture with truth see Marc Saperstein, *Decoding the Rabbis* (Cambridge: Harvard University Press, 1982), pp. 1–20.

83. Leo Strauss, *Spinoza's Critique of Religion,* trans. E. M. Sinclair (New York: Schocken, 1965), p. 148.

84. *TTP,* 114 [77] (10–14); *Elwes,* chap. 7, p. 115.

85. *TTP,* 104 [35] (24–25); *Elwes,* chap. 7, p. 106.

86. The issue of the esoteric dimension of Maimonides has become increasingly debated ever since Leo Strauss's classic essay "The Literary Character of the 'Guide for the Perplexed'" in *Persecution and the Art of Writing,* pp. 38–94. Works that have extended this analysis are Shlomo Pines, "Spinoza's 'Tractatus Theologico-Politicus,' Maimonides, and Kant," *Scripta Hierosolymitana* 20 (1968): 3–54; Aviezer Ravitzky, "Samuel Ibn Tibbon and the Esoteric Character of the 'Guide of the Perplexed,'" *AJS Review* 6 (1981): 87–123. For a lucid treatment of the problem as applied to medieval religious texts in general see Miriam Galston, *Politics and Excellence: The Political Philosophy of Alfarabi* (Princeton: Princeton University Press, 1990), pp. 22–54.

87. Maimonides, *The Guide of the Perplexed,* trans. Shlomo Pines, intro. Leo Strauss (Chicago: University of Chicago Press, 1962), intro., pp. 5–6.

88. Maimonides, *Guide of the Perplexed,* intro., p. 6.

89. Maimonides, *Guide of the Perplexed,* intro., p. 6.

90. Maimonides, *Guide of the Perplexed,* intro., pp. 6–7.

91. Maimonides, *Guide of the Perplexed*, intro., p. 15.
92. Maimonides, *Guide of the Perplexed*, intro., p. 15.
93. Maimonides, *Guide of the Perplexed*, intro., p. 7.
94. Maimonides, *Guide of the Perplexed*, intro., p. 11.
95. Maimonides, *Guide of the Perplexed*, intro., p. 15.
96. For a helpful gloss on Maimonides' use of this parable see Galston, *Politics and Excellence*, pp. 52–53.
97. *TTP*, 113 [75] (8–9); *Elwes*, chap. 7, p. 115.
98. *TTP*, 113 [75] (11–13): "For if it should be found contrary to reason according to its literal meaning, he would still think the passage was to be interpreted differently, however clear the literal meaning seemed to be"; *Elwes*, chap. 7, p. 115.
99. *TTP*, 105 [40, 42] (27–29), 106 (2–5); *Elwes*, chap. 7, p. 107.
100. *TTP*, 100 [17] (16–19); *Elwes*, chap. 7, p. 101.
101. Maimonides, *Guide of the Perplexed*, book II, chap. 25, pp. 327–28.
102. Maimonides, *Guide of the Perplexed*, book II, chap. 25, p. 328.
103. Maimonides, *Guide of the Perplexed*, book I, chap. 71; book II, chap. 16.
104. For a useful overview of the entire issue of eternity versus creation in time see Warren Zev Harvey, " A Third Approach to Maimonides' Cosmogony-Prophetology Puzzle," in *Maimonides: A Collection of Critical Essays,* ed. Joseph A. Buijs (Notre Dame, Ind.: University of Notre Dame Press, 1988), pp. 71–88.
105. "As concerns this issue of eternity, if Aristotle had given a clear demonstration of it by his laws of logic, he could have offered a figurative interpretation of the creation story" (cited in Ze'ev Levy, *Baruch or Benedict: On Some Jewish Aspects of Spinoza's Philosophy* [New York: Peter Lang, 1989], p. 52).
106. *TTP*, 114 [77] (6–10); *Elwes*, chap. 7, p. 115.
107. *TTP*, 114 [78–79] (17–31); *Elwes,* chap. 7, p. 116.
108. Pines, "Spinoza, Maimonides, and Kant," pp. 12–13.
109. *TTP*, 168 [5] (2–4); *Elwes*, chap. 13, p. 176.
110. *TTP*, 167 [5] (32)–168(2); *Elwes*, chap. 13, p. 176.
111. Maimonides, *Guide of the Perplexed,* book I, chap. 2, pp. 23–26. For a fascinating summary of the debate see Shlomo Pines, "Truth and Falsehood Versus Good and Evil: A Study in Jewish and General Philosophy in Connection with 'The Guide of the Perplexed' I, 2," in *Studies in Maimonides,* ed. Isadore Twersky (Cambridge: Harvard University Press, 1990), pp. 95–157.
112. *TTP*, 114 [80–81] (31)–115(5); *Elwes*, chap. 7, p. 116.
113. *TTP*, 115 [82] (8–11); *Elwes*, chap. 7, pp. 116–17.
114. *TTP*, 112 [69–70] (1–2); *Elwes*, chap. 7, p. 113.
115. *TTP*, 117 [94] (17–18); *Elwes*, chap. 7, p. 119.
116. *TTP*, 117 [94] (20–21); *Elwes*, chap. 7, p. 119.
117. *TTP*, 98 [8] (29–30); *Elwes*, chap. 7, p. 100.
118. *TTP*, 100 [19] (33)–101(1); *Elwes*, chap. 7, p. 102.
119. *TTP*, 102 [27] (21–29); *Elwes*, chap. 7, p. 104.
120. *TTP*, 135 [34] (35)–136(2); *Elwes*, chap. 9, p. 140.
121. *TTP*, 112 [73] (27–30); *Elwes*, chap. 7, p. 114.
122. *TTP*, 103 [29] (5–14); *Elwes*, chap. 7, p. 104.

123. *TTP*, 103 [30–31] (14–24); *Elwes*, chap. 7, pp. 104–05.

124. *TTP*, 103 [32] (24–35); *Elwes*, chap. 7, p. 105. The passage to which Spinoza alludes reads: "The Lord is good to those who wait for him, to the soul that seeks him. It is good that one should wait quietly for the salvation of the Lord. It is good for a man that he bear the yoke in his youth. Let him sit alone in silence when he has laid it on him; let him put his mouth in the dust — let him give his cheek to the smiter, and be filled with insults."

125. *TTP*, 104 [35] (20–21); *Elwes*, chap. 7, p. 106.

126. *TTP*, 102 [27] (29–32); *Elwes*, chap. 7, p. 104.

127. *TTP*, 102 [28] (32–35); *Elwes*, chap. 7, p. 104.

128. *TTP*, 98 [7] (22–25); *Elwes*, chap. 7, p. 99.

129. *TTP*, 111 [68] (27 — 29); *Elwes*, chap. 7, p. 113.

130. *TTP*, 116 [90] (29–32); *Elwes*, chap. 7, p. 118.

131. *TTP*, 165 [37] (34)–166(2); *Elwes*, chap. 12, p. 173.

132. *TTP*, 168 [8] (15–20); *Elwes*, chap. 13, p. 176.

133. *TTP*, 165 [34–35] (11–18); *Elwes*, chap. 12, p. 172.

134. *TTP*, 117 [91] (3–5); *Elwes*, chap. 7, p. 119.

135. *TTP*, 10 [24] (16–18); *Elwes*, pref., p. 9.

136. *TTP*, 167 [2] (10–12); *Elwes*, chap. 13, p. 175; emphasis added.

137. *TTP*, 186 [35] (30–32); *Elwes*, chap. 15, p. 197; emphasis added.

138. *TTP*, 184 [21] (22–23): "Nempe, uti diximus, ratio regnum veritatis, et sapientiae, Theologia autem pietatis, et obedientiae"; *Elwes*, chap. 15, p. 194.

139. *TTP*, 185 [27] (26–31) *Elwes*, chap. 15, p. 195.

140. *TTP*, 185 [28–29] (33)–186(1); *Elwes*, chap. 15, p. 196.

141. *TTP*, 188 [44] (19–26); *Elwes*, chap. 15, pp. 198–99.

Chapter 4. From Sacred to Secular History

1. G. W. F. Hegel, *Lectures on the History of Philosophy*, trans. E. S. Haldane and F. H. Simson (London: Routledge and Kegan Paul, 1955), vol. 3, p. 283.

2. Hegel, *History of Philosophy*, vol. 3, p. 257.

3. Hegel, *History of Philosophy*, vol. 3, pp. 257–58; translation modified.

4. Hegel, *History of Philosophy*, vol. 3., p. 258.

5. Hegel, *History of Philosophy*, vol. 3, p. 281.

6. Hegel, *History of Philosophy*, vol. 3, pp. 287–88.

7. Hegel, *History of Philosophy*, vol. 3, p. 252.

8. Hegel, *History of Philosophy*, vol. 3, p. 258.

9. Hegel, *History of Philosophy*, vol. 3, p. 288.

10. For a comprehensive contrast of, or "confrontation" between, Hegel and Spinoza see Pierre Machery, *Hegel ou Spinoza* (Paris: Decouverte, 1990). Machery acknowledges the writings of Louis Althusser as directly formative; see especially Louis Althusser, *Eléments d'autocritique* (Paris: Hachette, 1974). For a useful summary of some of the issues involved see Christopher Norris, *Spinoza and the Origins of Modern Critical Theory* (London: Blackwell, 1991), pp. 21–53.

11. Amos Funkenstein, *Theology and the Scientific Imagination: From the Middle*

Ages to the Seventeenth Century (Princeton: Princeton University Press, 1986), p. 206: "The many versions of reason in history from Vico to Marx are only speculative by-products of a profound revolution in historical thought in the sixteenth and seventeenth centuries, namely the discovery of history as *contextual reasoning*."

12. Funkenstein, *Theology and the Scientific Imagination,* pp. 213–15.

13. See, in particular, Hermann Lübbe, *Säkularisierung-Geschichte eines Ideenpolitischen Begriffs* (Freiburg, Ger.: Alber, 1965); Hans Blumenberg, *The Legitimacy of the Modern World,* trans. Robert Wallace (Cambridge: MIT Press, 1983); Peter Berger, *The Sacred Canopy: Elements of a Sociological Theory of Religion* (New York: Doubleday, 1967); José Casanova, *Public Religions in the Modern World* (Chicago: University of Chicago Press, 1994).

14. The best-known statement of this thesis remains Max Weber, *The Protestant Ethic and the Spirit of Capitalism,* trans. Talcott Parsons (New York: Scribner's, 1958).

15. Karl Löwith, *Meaning in History* (Chicago: University of Chicago Press, 1949), p. 38: "This philosophy of the proletariat as the chosen people is expounded in a document, the *Communist Manifesto,* which is scientifically relevant in its particular contents, eschatological in its framework, and prophetic in its attitude." See also Robert C. Tucker, *Philosophy and Myth in Karl Marx* (Cambridge: Cambridge University Press, 1961).

16. Carl Schmitt, *Political Theology: Four Chapters on the Concept of Sovereignty,* trans. George Schwab (Cambridge: MIT Press, 1988), p. 36. See also Löwith, *Meaning in History,* p. 201: "The modern world is as Christian as it is un-Christian because it is the outcome of an age-long process of secularization." For an extensive critique of the secularization thesis as a misguided anachronism see Blumenberg, *Legitimacy of the Modern World,* pp. 3–87.

17. Funkenstein, *Theology and the Scientific Imagination,* pp. 5–6.

18. Berger, *Sacred Canopy,* p. 111.

19. Berger, *Sacred Canopy,* pp. 111–12.

20. Löwith, *Meaning in History,* p. 209.

21. G. W. F. Hegel, *Philosophy of Right,* trans. T. M. Knox (Oxford: Clarendon, 1967), p. 12.

22. Immanuel Kant, "What Is Enlightenment?" in his *Political Writings,* ed. Hans Reiss, trans. H. B. Nisbet (Cambridge: Cambridge University Press, 1970), p. 54.

23. See Ernst Cassirer, *The Philosophy of the Enlightenment,* trans. Fritz C. A. Koelln and James P. Pettegrove (Princeton: Princeton University Press, 1951), pp. 275–78; Peter Gay, *The Enlightenment: An Interpretation,* vol. 1: *The Rise of Modern Paganism* (New York: Random House, 1968), pp. 127–32; Reinhart Koselleck, *Critique and Crisis: Enlightenment and the Pathogenesis of Modern Society* (Cambridge: MIT Press, 1988), pp. 98–123.

24. André Tosel, "Y-a-t-il une philosophie du progrès historique chez Spinoza?" in *Spinoza: Issues and Directions. The Proceedings of the Chicago Spinoza Conference,* ed. Edwin Curley and Pierre-François Moreau (Leiden, Neth.: E. J. Brill, 1990), p. 306.

25. Tosel, "Y-a-t-il une philosophie?" p. 307; Sylvain Zac, "Durée et Histoire," in *Philosophie, Theologie, Politique, dans l'oeuvre de Spinoza* (Paris: J. Vrin, 1979), p. 184; my translation.

26. Norris, *Spinoza and the Origins of Critical Theory,* p. 182.

27. *Ethics,* II, P 7, p. 459; G, 2: 89 (20–21). See Machery, *Hegel ou Spinoza,* pp. 129–33.

28. *TTP,* 15 [1] (5–6); *Elwes,* chap. 1, p. 13.

29. *TTP,* 15 [2] (17–19); *Elwes,* chap. 1, p. 15.

30. *TTP,* 15 [3] (31)–16(2): "at respectu certitudinis, quam naturalis cognitio involvit, et fontis, e quo derivatur (nempe Deo) nullo modo cognitioni propheticae cedit"; *Elwes,* chap. 1, p. 14.

31. *TTP,* 16 [4] (6–7); *Elwes,* chap. 1, p. 14.

32. *TTP,* 251 (20–25); *Elwes,* chap. 1, p. 269 n. 2.

33. *TTP,* 30 [5] (32–34); *Elwes,* chap. 2, p. 28.

34. *TTP,* 30 [6] (34–35): "This prophetic certainty was not mathematical, but moral"; *Elwes,* chap. 2, p. 28.

35. *TTP,* 16 [5] (13–15); *Elwes,* chap. 1, p. 14.

36. *TTP,* 32 [15] (32)–33(7); *Elwes,* chap. 2, p. 30.

37. *TTP,* 252 (7–8); *Elwes,* chap. 1, p. 269 n. 3.

38. *TTP,* 50 [31] (32–34). Spinoza mentions that both "sacred and profane" history bear out the fact that all nations possessed prophets; see *Elwes,* chap. 3, p. 49.

39. *TTP,* 53 [39] (1–5); *Elwes,* chap. 3, pp. 51–52.

40. *TTP,* 21 [25] (29–30); *Elwes,* chap. 1, p. 19.

41. *TTP,* 23 [30–31] (26)–24(8); *Elwes,* chap. 1, p. 21.

42. *TTP,* 19 [19] (26–33); *Elwes,* chap. 1, p. 17.

43. Maimonides, *Mishneh Torah,* ed. Moses Hyanson (New York: Bloch, 1937), book I, chap. 7, p. 42a.

44. Maimonides, *Mishneh Torah,* book I, chap. 7, p. 42a.

45. Maimonides' prophetology is the explicit theme of his *Guide of the Perplexed,* trans. Shlomo Pines, intro. Leo Strauss (Chicago: University of Chicago Press, 1962), book II, chaps. 32–48, pp. 360–412. For an excellent "guide" to Maimonides' account see Leo Strauss, *Philosophy and Law: Essays Toward the Understanding of Maimonides and His Predecessors,* trans. Fred Baumann (Philadelphia: Jewish Publication Society, 1987), pp. 81–110; see also Amos Funkenstein, "Maimonides: Political Theory and Realistic Messianism," in *Miscellanea Mediaevalia,* ed. Albert Zimmerman (Berlin: Walter de Gruyter, 1977), pp. 81–103.

46. Maimonides, *Guide of the Perplexed,* book II, chap. 32, p. 361.

47. Maimonides, *Guide of the Perplexed,* book II, chap. 32, p. 361.

48. Maimonides, *Guide of the Perplexed,* book II, chap. 40, p. 382.

49. Maimonides, *Guide of the Perplexed,* book II, chap. 32, p. 362.

50. Maimonides, *Guide of the Perplexed,* book II, chap. 36, p. 369.

51. Maimonides, *Guide of the Perplexed,* book II, chap. 36, p. 369.

52. Maimonides here follows the talmudic expression "The Torah speaks in the language of man" (*dibra tora kileshon bne' adam*); see T. B. Yevamot, 71a.

53. *TTP,* 21 [25] (25–26); 29 [1] (16–18); *Elwes,* chap. 1, p. 19; chap. 2, p. 27.

54. *TTP,* 32 [13–14] (17–32); *Elwes,* chap. 2, p. 30.

55. *TTP,* 35 [24] (14–17); *Elwes,* chap. 2, p. 33.

56. *TTP,* 35 [24] (21–23); *Elwes,* chap. 2, p. 33.

57. *TTP,* 37 [31] (13); *Elwes,* chap. 2, p. 35.

58. *TTP,* 37 [31] (15–18); *Elwes,* chap. 2, p. 35.

59. See H. H. Gerth and C. W. Mills, *From Max Weber: Essays in Sociology* (New York: Oxford University Press, 1976), pp. 294–98. The connection to Weber has been suggested in Robert McShea, *The Political Philosophy of Spinoza* (New York: Columbia University Press, 1968), p. 96; see also Shlomo Pines, "Spinoza's 'Tractatus Theologico-Politicus,' Maimonides, and Kant," *Scripta Hierosolymitana* 20 (1968): 23.

60. Maimonides, *Guide of the Perplexed,* book II, chap. 39, p. 379.

61. Maimonides, *Guide of the Perplexed,* book II, chap. 40, p. 381.

62. Maimonides, *Guide of the Perplexed,* book II, chap. 40, pp. 383–84.

63. Maimonides, *Guide of the Perplexed,* book II, chap. 40, p. 384.

64. Maimonides, *Guide of the Perplexed,* book III, chap. 27, p. 510.

65. Maimonides, *Guide of the Perplexed,* book III, chap. 27, p. 511.

66. Maimonides, *Guide of the Perplexed,* book III, chap. 27, p. 511.

67. Maimonides, *Guide of the Perplexed,* book III, chap. 27, p. 511.

68. Maimonides, *Guide of the Perplexed,* book III, chap. 27, p. 511.

69. Maimonides, *Guide of the Perplexed,* book III, chap. 28, p. 512.

70. Maimonides, *Guide of the Perplexed,* book III, chap. 28, p. 514.

71. Maimonides, *Guide of the Perplexed,* book III, chap. 28, p. 513.

72. Maimonides, *Guide of the Perplexed,* book III, chap. 28, p. 512.

73. Maimonides, *Guide of the Perplexed,* book III, chap. 28, p. 513.

74. *TTP,* 17 |10| (16): "It was by a true voice that God revealed to Moses the law" (*Voce enim vera revelavit Deus Mosi Leges*); *Elwes,* chap. 1, pp. 15, 18. See also *TTP,* 21 [23] (8–12), where Spinoza affirms that Moses heard a voice "surpassing human wisdom" (*supra humanam*).

75. Machiavelli, *The Prince,* trans. Harvey C. Mansfield, Jr. (Chicago: University of Chicago Press, 1985), chap. 6, p. 23: "It was necessary then for Moses to find the people of Israel in Egypt, enslaved and oppressed by the Egyptians, so that they would be disposed to follow him in order to get out of their servitude." See also Machiavelli, *The Discourses,* trans. Leslie J. Walker (London: Routledge and Kegan Paul, 1950), book I, chaps. 1, 9; book II, chap. 8; book III, chap. 30, p. 547: "He who reads the Bible with discernment [*sensatamente*] will see that, in order that Moses might set about making laws and institutions, he had to kill a very great number of men who, out of envy and nothing else, were opposed to his plans."

76. *TTP,* 40 [46–47] (35)–41(7); *Elwes,* chap. 2, pp. 38–39.

77. *TTP,* 9 [22] (34)–10(4); *Elwes,* pref., p. 8.

78. *TTP,* 49 [26] (31–34); *Elwes,* chap. 3, p. 48.

79. *TTP,* 48 [18] (4–6): "But neither were they chosen because of their virtue and true life. For in this respect also they were equal to the other nations and only a very few were chosen"; *Elwes,* chap. 3, p. 47.

80. Cf. Friedrich Nietzsche, *Beyond Good and Evil,* trans. Walter Kaufman (New York: Vintage, 1966), par. 251, pp. 187–88: "The Jews, however, are beyond any doubt the strongest, toughest, and purest race now living in Europe; they know how to prevail even under the worst conditions (even better than under favorable conditions), by means of virtues that today one would like to mark as vices — thanks above all to a resolute faith that need not be ashamed before 'modern ideas.' "

81. *TTP,* 48 [19] (10–11); *Elwes,* chap. 3, p. 47.

82. *TTP*, 48 [20] (18–21); *Elwes*, chap. 3, p. 47.

83. *TTP*, 47 [16] (26–31); *Elwes*, chap. 3, p. 46.

84. *TTP*, 50 [30] (24–29); *Elwes*, chap. 3, p. 49.

85. *TTP*, 44 [3] (33), 45 [6] (19); *Elwes*, chap. 3, pp. 43, 44.

86. *TTP*, 41 [47] (11–13); *Elwes*, chap. 3, p. 39.

87. *TTP*, 65 [37] (28–33); *Elwes*, chap. 4, p. 65.

88. See Gershom Scholem, *Sabbatai Zvi: The Mystical Messiah*, trans. R. J. Z. Werblowsky (Princeton: Princeton University Press, 1973). On Spinoza and the Sabbatian controversy see Yirmiyahu Yovel, *Spinoza and Other Heretics*, vol. 1: *The Marrano of Reason* (Princeton: Princeton University Press, 1989), pp. 53–54, 191.

89. *Cor*, #33, p. 217; *G*, 4: 178 (24–33).

90. *TTP*, 57 [56] (6–13); *Elwes*, chap. 3, p. 56.

91. *TTP*, 56 [53] (20–26); *Elwes*, chap. 3, p. 55.

92. On the politics of Jewish messianism see Michael Walzer, *Exodus and Revolution* (New York: Basic Books, 1985), pp. 117–25, 135–41, 144–47.

93. *TTP*, 57 [55] (1–6): "Signum circumcisionis etiam hac in re tantum posse existimo, ut mihi persuadeam, hoc unum hanc Nationem in aeternum conservaturum, imo nisi fundamenta suae religionis eorum animos effoeminarent, absolute crederem, eos aliquando, data occasione, ut sunt res humanae mutabiles, suum imperium iterum erecturos, Deumque eos de novo electurum"; *Elwes*, chap. 3, p. 56.

94. Machiavelli, *Discourses*, book II, chap. 2, pp. 361–66.

95. Machiavelli, *Discourses*, book II, chap. 2, p. 364.

96. Jean-Jacques Rousseau, *On the Social Contract*, trans. and ed. Roger D. Masters and Judith R. Masters (New York: Saint Martin's, 1978), book IV, chap. 8, pp. 124–32.

97. See Rousseau's letter to Usteri, in *Political Writings of Jean Jacques Rousseau*, ed. C. E. Vaughn (New York: Burt Franklin, 1971), vol. 2, p. 166: "The patriotic spirit is an exclusive one, which makes us regard all men other than our fellow citizens as strangers and almost as enemies. Such was the spirit of Sparta and Rome. The spirit of Christianity, by contrast, makes us regard all men as brothers, as children of God. Christian charity does not allow us to make odious distinctions between compatriots and strangers. . . . It is therefore true that Christianity by its very saintliness is contrary to the particularist social spirit."

98. Rousseau, *Social Contract*, book IV, chap. 8, p. 129.

99. Rousseau, *Social Contract*, book IV, chap. 8, p. 130.

100. We do know that the *Treatise* was held in high regard by the founders of political Zionism, to wit, the remark of David Ben-Gurion: "Under the conditions of the time and in the place the ban was perhaps justified . . . but as the condemnation of Socrates by an Athenian court did not turn that great Greek philosopher into a non-Greek, so the rabbinical ban in Amsterdam in the seventeenth century cannot deprive the Jewish people of its greatest and most original thinker" (cited in Joseph Dunner, *Baruch Spinoza and Western Democracy* [New York: Philosophical Library, 1955], p. vii).

101. *TTP*, 150 [48] (30)–151(1); *Elwes*, chap. 10, p. 156.

102. Pines, "Spinoza, Maimonides, and Kant," p. 22.

103. We know from their correspondence that Leibniz took an active interest in the author of the *Treatise* but that Spinoza held Leibniz at arm's length. In a letter to Spinoza

from G. H. Schuller, the latter reports that a mutual friend, one Tschirnhaus, had met in Paris a man of "uncommon learning," well versed in the sciences and "free from the vulgar prejudices of theology." This man named Leibniz was also said to think "very highly" of the *Theologico-Political Treatise* and had apparently expressed a desire to see some of Spinoza's unpublished work (*Cor,* #70, pp. 338–39). Spinoza replied to Schuller, "I think I know the Leibniz of whom he writes"; so far as Spinoza knew he seemed a man of "liberal mind" (*homo liberalis ingenii*) but thought that it would be "imprudent to entrust my writing to him so soon" (*Cor,* #72, p. 341). For an interesting account of the Spinoza-Leibniz relationship see Edwin Curley, "Homo Audax: Leibniz, Oldenburg, and the *TTP,*" *Studia Leibnitiana* (Supplement), vol. 27 (1990): 277–312.

104. *TTP,* 69 [4] (24–26): "Isaiah teaches nothing more clearly than that the divine law, taken absolutely, means that universal law which consists in the true manner of living, but not in ceremonies"; *Elwes,* chap. 5, p. 69. Spinoza cites Isaiah 1:16–17, "cease to do evil, learn to do good; seek justice, correct oppression," as evidence for this.

105. *TTP,* 56 [53] (19–26); *Elwes,* chap. 3, p. 56.

106. *TTP,* 54 [45] (26–27); *Elwes,* chap. 3, p. 53.

107. *TTP,* 180 [3] (30); *Elwes,* chap. 15, p. 190.

108. *TTP,* 41 [48] (17–27); *Elwes,* chap. 2, p. 39.

109. *TTP,* 21 [24] (13–15); *Elwes,* chap. 1, p. 19.

110. *Cor,* #74, p. 344; *G,* 4: 309 (10–13).

111. *Cor,* #74, p. 344; *G,* 4: 309 (13–15).

112. Pines, "Spinoza, Maimonides, and Kant," pp. 23, 45.

113. *PT,* chap. 1, pars. 1–2, pp. 261; *G,* 3: 273 (9)–274(9).

114. *TTP,* 104 [33] (2–3); *Elwes,* chap. 7, p. 105.

115. *TTP,* 103 [32] (27–30); *Elwes,* chap. 7, p. 105.

116. *TTP,* 163 [24] (8–12); *Elwes,* chap. 12, p. 170.

117. *TTP,* 70 [7] (21–25); *Elwes,* chap. 5, p. 70.

118. *TTP,* 70 [8–9] (26–32). As evidence Spinoza cites the famous claim in Matthew 5:28: "everyone who looks at a woman lustfully has already committed adultery with her in his heart"; *Elwes,* chap. 5, p. 70.

119. *TTP,* 48 [21] (19–20); *Elwes,* chap. 3, p. 47.

120. *TTP,* 57 [57] (13–20); *Elwes,* chap. 3, p. 56.

121. *TTP,* 70 [6] (13–16); *Elwes,* chap. 5, p. 70.

122. *TTP,* 71 [9] (5–7); 72 [14] (19–21); *Elwes,* chap. 5, pp. 71, 72.

123. *TTP,* 53 [40] (9–13); *Elwes,* chap. 3, p. 52.

124. *TTP,* 180 [4] (33)–181(1); *Elwes,* chap. 15, p. 190.

125. *TTP,* 21 [24] (19–22); *Elwes,* chap. 1, p. 19.

126. *TTP,* 64 [32] (31–33); *Elwes,* chap. 4, p. 64.

127. *TTP,* 64 [30–31] (10–12, 17–19); *Elwes,* chap. 4, p. 64.

128. *TTP,* 64 [31] (27–31); *Elwes,* chap. 4, p. 64.

129. Sylvain Zac, *Spinoza et l'interprétation de l'Ecriture* (Paris: Presses Universitaires de France, 1965), pp. 190–99.

130. *TTP,* 69 [1] (12–13), 70 [6] (10); *Elwes,* chap. 5, pp. 69, 70.

131. *TTP,* 76 [31] (1–4); *Elwes,* chap. 5, p. 76.

132. *TTP,* 76 [32–33] (8–17); *Elwes,* chap. 5, p. 76.

133. Michael Keren, "Moses as a Visionary Realist," *International Political Science Review* 9 (1988): 71–84. This essay draws on Walzer, *Exodus and Revolution*; Aaron Wildavsky, *The Nursing Father: Moses as a Political Leader* (Tuscaloosa: University of Alabama Press, 1984).

134. *TTP,* 74 [26–28] (34)–75(10); *Elwes,* chap. 5, pp. 74–75.

135. *TTP,* 152 [4] (7–11); *Elwes,* chap. 11, p. 158.

136. *TTP,* 153 [8] (19–22); *Elwes,* chap. 11, pp. 159. As evidence Spinoza cites Romans 15:15.

137. *TTP,* 153 [7] (8–17); *Elwes,* chap. 11, p. 159.138. *TTP,* 153 [7] (4–8); *Elwes,* chap. 11, p. 159.

139. *TTP,* 158 [2–3] (28)–159(2); *Elwes,* chap. 12, p. 165.

140. *TTP,* 221 [2] (22–24); *Elwes,* chap. 18, p. 237.

141. *TTP,* 54 [45] (21–26), where Spinoza concludes with the statement "So Paul teaches exactly what we require" (*Paulus itaque id, quod volumus, adamussim docet*); *Elwes,* chap. 3, p. 53.

142. *TTP,* 154 [10] (6–11); *Elwes,* chap. 11, p. 160.

143. *TTP,* 158 [24] (9–11); *Elwes,* chap. 11, p. 164.

144. *TTP,* 158 [24] (13–15); *Elwes,* chap. 11, p. 164.

145. Immanuel Kant, *Religion Within the Limits of Reason Alone,* trans. T. M. Greene and H. H. Hudson (New York: Harper and Row, 1960), pp. 116–20; G. W. F. Hegel, "The Spirit of Christianity and Its Fate," in his *Early Theological Writings,* trans. T. M. Knox, intro. Richard Kroner (Philadelphia: University of Pennsylvania Press, 1971), pp. 182–205; Karl Marx, "On the Jewish Question," in *The Marx-Engels Reader,* ed. Robert C. Tucker (New York: Norton, 1978), pp. 47–52.

146. Emmanuel Levinas is one of the few who have grasped the historically dialectical character of Spinoza's analysis; see "The Spinoza Case," in his *Difficult Freedom: Essays on Judaism,* trans. Sean Hand (London: Athlone, 1990), p. 108.

147. André Tosel, *Spinoza ou le crépuscule de la servitude* (Paris: Aubier, 1984), p. 264.

148. Levinas, "Spinoza Case," p. 108: "Within the history of ideas, [Spinoza] subordinated the truth of Judaism to the revelation of the New Testament. The latter is of course surpassed by the intellectual love of God, but Western being involves this Christian experience, even if it is only a stage."

149. *TTP,* 156 [18] (35)–157(6); *Elwes,* chap. 11, pp. 162–63.

150. *TTP,* 157 [21] (23–31); *Elwes,* chap. 11, p. 163.

151. *TTP,* 157 [22] (31)–158(2); *Elwes,* chap. 11, p. 163.

152. *TTP,* 237 [54] (20–24); *Elwes,* chap. 19, p. 255.

153. *TTP,* 237 [52, 55] (8–28); *Elwes,* chap. 19, pp. 254–55.

154. *TTP,* 223 [13] (23–27); *Elwes,* chap. 18, p. 239.

155. *TTP,* 224 [14] (1–2); *Elwes,* chap. 18, p. 240.

156. *TTP,* 174 [6] (8–9): "intentum Scripturae esse tantum obedientiam docere"; *Elwes,* chap. 14, p. 183.

157. Thomas Hobbes, *Leviathan,* ed. Michael Oakeshott (Oxford: Blackwell, 1955), chap. 43, pp. 394–95.

158. *TTP,* 174 [7] (13–17); *Elwes,* chap. 14, p. 183.

159. Hillel Fradkin, "The 'Separation' of Religion and Politics: Paradoxes of Spinoza," *Review of Politics* 50 (1988): 620–21: "In fine 'theological' fashion, confounding theology and philosophy, Spinoza has in this work presented the greatest simplification of biblical theology since Hillel the Elder was compelled to summarize the Bible while standing on one leg."

160. *TTP*, 177 [25–28] (21)2–178(10); *Elwes,* chap. 14, pp. 186–87.

161. Maimonides, *Guide of the Perplexed,* book III, chaps. 27–28, pp. 510–14; Leo Strauss, *Spinoza's Critique of Religion,* trans. E. M. Sinclair (New York: Schocken, 1965), pp. 245–50; Pines, "Spinoza, Maimonides, and Kant," pp. 30–36; Arthur Hyman, "Spinoza's Dogmas of Universal Faith in the Light of the Jewish Background," in *Biblical and Other Studies,* ed. Alexander Altmann (Cambridge: Harvard University Press, 1963), pp. 183–95; Harry A. Wolfson, *The Philosophy of Spinoza* (Cambridge: Harvard University Press, 1934), vol. 2, pp. 325–30.

162. Hyman, "Spinoza's Dogmas of Universal Faith," p. 185.

163. *TTP*, 178 [28] (9–10); *Elwes,* chap. 14, p. 187.

164. *TTP*, 176 [20] (18–19); *Elwes,* chap. 14, p. 185.

165. *TTP*, 179 [33] (4–5); *Elwes,* chap. 14, p. 188.

166. *TTP*, 179 [33] (7–9); *Elwes,* chap. 14, p. 188.

167. *TTP*, 177 [22] (4–6): "ad fidem catholicam, sive universalem nulla dogmata pertinere, de quibus inter honestos potest dari controversia"; *Elwes,* chap. 14, p 186.

168. *TTP*, 180 [40] (6–7); *Elwes,* chap. 14, p. 189.

169. *TTP*, 179 [39] (35)–180(2); *Elwes,* chap. 14, p. 189; emphasis added.

170. *TTP*, 176 [19] (13–15); *Elwes,* chap. 14, p. 185.

171. *TTP*, 175 [15] (19–20); *Elwes,* chap. 14, p. 184.

172. *TTP*, 175 [17] (34)–176(1); *Elwes,* chap. 14, p. 185.

173. Rousseau, *Social Contract,* book IV, chap. 8, p. 127.

174. For Rousseau's relation to Spinoza see Pines, "Spinoza, Maimonides, and Kant," pp. 46–47; Paul Vernière, *Spinoza et la pensée française avant la révolution* (Paris: Presses Universitaires de France, 1954), vol. 2, pp. 475–94.

175. Rousseau, *Social Contract,* book IV, chap. 8, p. 130.

176. Rousseau, *Social Contract,* book IV, chap. 8, p. 131.

177. Rousseau, *Social Contract,* book IV, chap. 8, p. 131. See Ronald Beiner, "Machiavelli, Hobbes, and Rousseau on Civil Religion," *Review of Politics* 55 (1993): 620–21: "What [Rousseau] offers in the last five paragraphs [of the *Social Contract*] is a highly attenuated, 'phantom' religion, an Enlightenment-style 'religion of tolerance,' one might say, in which liberal or negative tenets prevail over tenets that might positively build republican citizenship."

178. Rousseau, *Social Contract,* book IV, chap. 8, p. 130.

179. *TTP*, 178 [32] (30–34); *Elwes,* chap. 14, p. 188.

Chapter 5. A Democratic Turn

1. Alexandre Matheron, *Le Christ et le salut des ignorants chez Spinoza* (Paris: Aubier, 1971), pp. 14, 22–23.

2. *TTP*, 189 [1] (4–8): "Huc usque Philosophiam a Theologia separare curavimus et

libertatem philosophandi ostendere, quam haec unicuique concedit. Quare tempus est, ut inquiramus quo usque haec libertas sentiendi, et quae unusquisque sentit, dicendi in optima Respublica se extendat"; *Elwes,* chap. 16, p. 200.

3. *PT,* chap. 5, pars. 4, 6, p. 311: "A commonwealth [*Civitatis*] whose subjects are restrained from revolting by fear must be said to be free from war rather than to enjoy peace. For peace is not the mere absence of war, but a virtue based on strength of mind [*ex animi fortitudine*]. . . . Besides, a commonwealth whose peace depends on the apathy of its subjects, who are led like sheep so that they learn nothing but servility, may more properly be called a desert than a commonwealth. . . . A free people [*libera multitudo*] is led more by hope than by fear, a conquered people more by fear than by hope; for the former seeks to improve its life, the latter seeks only to avoid death"; *G,* 3: 296 (3–6, 8–10, 18–21); cf. Tacitus, *Agricola,* sec. 30: "Alone among men [the Romans] covet with eagerness poverty and riches. To robbery, slaughter, plunder, they give the lying name of empire; they make a solitude and call it peace [*ubi solitudinem faciunt, pacem appelant*]" (*The Complete Works of Tacitus,* ed. Moses Hadas [New York: Modern Library, 1942], p. 695).

4. Thomas Hobbes, *De corpore,* in his *English Works,* ed. William Molesworth (London: Bohn, 1839), vol. 1, p. ix.

5. See, for example, Robert McShea, *The Political Philosophy of Spinoza* (New York: Columbia University Press, 1968), pp. 137–38, where McShea says that the philosophy of Hobbes and Spinoza is "more than similar, it is identical," but adds somewhat anachronistically that Spinoza's philosophy is "identical not so much with what Hobbes actually said as with what he should have said had he been consistent." Leo Strauss, in *Spinoza's Critique of Religion,* trans. E. M. Sinclair (New York: Schocken, 1965), p. 229, goes to the opposite extreme, suggesting that "Spinoza's political theory, and in particular his theory of natural right . . . is *toto coelo* different from the theory of Hobbes, with whom his name is often coupled." Noel Malcolm, in "Hobbes and Spinoza," in *The Cambridge History of Political Thought, 1450–1700,* ed. J. H. Burns (Cambridge: Cambridge University Press, 1991), pp. 555–56, tries to split the difference between Hobbes and Spinoza by suggesting that Spinoza arrived at a "liberal, pluralistic theory of the state" out of Hobbes's "reductive style of power analysis" while at the same time maintaining that Spinoza's metaphysics was "radically different" from Hobbes's as was his theory of reason and human liberty. For a couple of excellent recent treatments see Alexandre Matheron, "Le 'droit du plus fort': Hobbes contre Spinoza," *Revue philosophique de la France et de l'étranger* 110 (1985): 149–76; Douglas den Uyl and Stuart D. Warner, "Liberalism and Hobbes and Spinoza," *Studia Spinozana* 3 (1987): 261–317.

6. Thomas Hobbes, *Leviathan,* ed. Michael Oakeshott (Oxford: Blackwell, 1955), chap. 13, p. 80: "Nature hath made men so equal, in the faculties of the body, and mind; as that though there be found one man sometimes manifestly stronger in body, or of quicker mind than another; yet when all is reckoned together, the difference between man, and man, is not so considerable, as that one man can thereupon claim to himself any benefit, to which another may not pretend, as well as he."

7. Hobbes, *Leviathan,* chap. 13, p. 80.

8. Thomas Hobbes, *Man and Citizen: Thomas Hobbes' De homine and De cive,* ed. Bernard Gert (New York: Doubleday, 1972), p. 99.

9. Hobbes, *Leviathan,* chap. 14, p. 103; see also Thomas Hobbes, *The Elements of Law, Natural and Politic,* ed. Ferdinand Tönnies (London: Frank Cass, 1969), book I, chap. 4, sec. 6.

10. Hobbes, *Leviathan,* chap. 13, p. 81; see also Hobbes, *De cive,* chap. 1, pars. 3–6, pp. 113–16.

11. *TTP,* 189 [2–3] (12–21); *Elwes,* chap. 16, p. 200.

12. *PT,* chap. 2, par. 3, p. 267: "The power of things in nature to exist and act is really the power of God. . . . For since God has the right to do everything, and God's right is simply God's power conceived as completely free, it follows that each thing in nature has as much right from nature as it has power to exist and act; since the power by which it exists and acts is nothing but the completely free power of God"; *G,* 3: 276 (27)–277(2).

13. *PT,* chap. 2, par. 2, p. 267; *G,* 3: 276 (23).

14. *Ethics,* IV, pref., p. 544: "That eternal and infinite being we call God, or Nature, acts from the same necessity from which he exists"; *G,* 2: 206 (23–25). See also *Ethics,* IV, P 4, pp. 548–49: "The power by which singular things (and consequently, any man) preserve their being is the power itself of God or Nature, not insofar as it is infinite, but insofar as it can be explained through the man's actual essence"; *G,* 2: 213 (1–5).

15. *PT,* chap. 2, par. 4, pp. 267–69; *G,* 3: 277 (3–5).

16. *PT,* chap. 2, par. 5, p. 269; *G,* 3: 277 (19–21, 24–25).

17. *TTP,* 189 [4] (25–30); *Elwes,* chap. 16, p. 200.

18. Hobbes, *Leviathan,* intro., p. 6.

19. *G,* 2: 146 (7–8); *E,* III, P 6, p. 498: "Each thing, as far as it can by its own power, strives to persevere in its being."

20. *TTP,* 189 [5–6] (30)–190(10); *Elwes,* chap. 16, p. 201.

21. Aristotle, *Nicomachean Ethics,* I. 1095a 10; II. 1103b 31–33; III. 1114b 29, 1119a 20; V. 1138a 10; VI. 1138b 25, 1144b 26–28, 1147b 3.

22. Aristotle, *Politics,* I, 1253a 7–38. For a useful discussion of this issue see Stephen Salkever, *Finding the Mean: Theory and Practice in Aristotelian Political Philosophy* (Princeton: Princeton University Press, 1990), pp. 74–79; see also David Keyt, "Three Basic Theorems in Aristotle's 'Politics,'" in *A Companion to Aristotle's Politics,* ed. David Keyt and Fred D. Miller, Jr. (Oxford: Blackwell, 1991), pp. 118–41.

23. Thomas Aquinas, *Treatise on Law* (Chicago: Regnery Gateway, 1988), question 94, art. 4, pp. 66–67: "the natural law, as to general principles, is the same for all, both as to rectitude and as to knowledge . . . and yet in some few cases it may fail, both as to rectitude, by reason of certain obstacles . . . and as to knowledge, since in some the reason is perverted by passion, or evil habit, or an evil disposition of nature; thus formerly theft, although it is expressly contrary to the natural law, was not considered wrong among the Germans, as Julius Caesar relates" (*De bello gall.* vi).

24. Hobbes, *Leviathan,* chap. 13, p. 84; chap. 15, pp. 104–05.

25. The following revealing story is related by Colerus in his "Life of B. De Spinosa," in Frederick Pollock, *Spinoza: His Life and Philosophy* (London: Duckworth, 1899), p. 395: "He also took pleasure in smoking a pipe of tobacco; or, when he had a mind to divert himself somewhat longer, he look'd for some spiders, and made them fight together, or he threw some flies into the cobweb, and was so well pleased with that battle, that he would sometimes break into laughter. He observed also, with a microscope, the

different parts of the smallest insects, from whence he drew such consequences as seemed to him to agree best with his discoveries."

26. *TTP,* 190 [9–11] (30)–191(10); *Elwes,* chap. 16, p. 202.

27. *PT,* chap. 3, par. 6, p. 289: "The whole teaching of reason is that men should seek peace. But peace cannot be achieved unless the general laws of the state are kept inviolate; and so the more a man is guided by reason . . . the more free he is, the more steadfastly will he observe the laws of the state and carry out his sovereign's commands"; *G,* 3: 286 (20–25).

28. *TTP,* 263 (20–26); *Elwes,* chap. 16, p. 276n.

29. Hobbes, *Leviathan,* chap. 14, pp. 84–85.

30. Hobbes, *De cive,* chap. 5, par. 5, p. 168.

31. Hobbes, *De cive,* chap. 5, par. 5, pp. 168–69.

32. Hobbes, *Elements,* book I, chap. 15, p. 1.

33. Hobbes, *Leviathan,* chap. 5, p. 25.

34. *Ethics,* IV, P 28, p. 559: "Knowledge of God is the Mind's greatest good; its greatest virtue is to know God"; *G,* 2: 228 (7–8).

35. *TTP,* 73 [20–22] (27)–74(3); *Elwes,* chap. 5, pp. 73–74.

36. *TTP,* 74 [22] (3–5); *Elwes,* chap. 5, p. 74.

37. *Ethics,* IV, P 37, pp. 566–67; *G,* 2: 237 (20–26).

38. *Ethics,* IV, P 35, p. 563: "Only insofar as men live according to reason must they always agree in nature"; *G,* 2: 232 (30–31). See also *The Federalist Papers,* ed. Jacob E. Cooke (Middletown, Conn.: Wesleyan University Press, 1961), No. 51, p. 349: "But what is government itself but the greatest of all reflections on human nature? If men were angels, no government would be necessary."

39. *G,* 2: 238 (23–27); *Ethics,* IV, P 37, pp. 567–68: "So in the state of nature no sin can be conceived. But in the civil state, of course, it is decided by common agreement what is good or what is evil. And everyone is bound to submit to the state. Sin, therefore, is nothing but disobedience, which for that reason can be punished only by the law of the state."

40. *Ethics,* IV, P 37, pp. 567–68; *G,* 2: 238 (18–19), 238 (35)–239(2).

41. See *The Federalist Papers,* No. 10, p. 60: "It is vain to say, that enlightened statesmen will be able to adjust these clashing interests, and render them all subservient to the public good. Enlightened statesmen will not always be at the helm."

42. For the use of this strategy see Albert O. Hirshman, *The Passions and the Interests* (Princeton: Princeton University Press, 1977), pp. 20–31.

43. *Ethics,* IV, P 7, p. 550: "An affect cannot be restrained or taken away except by an affect opposite to, and stronger than, the affect to be restrained"; *G,* 2: 214 (22–23).

44. *TTP,* 191 [15] (34)–192(2); *Elwes,* chap. 16, p. 203.

45. *PT,* chap. 2, par. 18, p. 279: "There is no sin in the state of nature; or rather, that if anyone sins, it is against himself, and not others. . . . [The law of nature] forbids absolutely nothing that is within human power"; *G,* 3: 282 (14–19).

46. *PT,* chap. 4, par. 6, pp. 305–07; *G,* 3: 294 (13–18).

47. Howard Warrender, *The Political Philosophy of Hobbes: His Theory of Obligation* (Oxford: Clarendon, 1957), pp. 99–100, 272–77.

48. Hobbes, *Leviathan,* chap. 15, p. 103.

49. *TTP,* 192 [20] (25–26); *Elwes,* chap. 16, p. 204.

50. *TTP*, 192 [21–23] (30)2–193(9); *Elwes*, chap. 16, p. 204.

51. Lewis S. Feuer, *Spinoza and the Rise of Liberalism* (New Brunswick, N.J.: Transaction, 1987), p. 101; Stanley Rosen, "Benedict Spinoza," in *History of Political Philosophy*, ed. Leo Strauss and Joseph Cropsey (Chicago: Rand McNally, 1972), pp. 431, 433, 441–42.

52. Plato, *Republic*, I. 338c; *Gorgias*, 483-c; Thucydides, *Peloponnesian War*, I. 76; V. 105: "Of the gods we believe, and of men we know, that by a necessary law of their nature they rule wherever they can."

53. *TTP*, 193 [25–26] (19–27); *Elwes*, chap. 16, p. 205.

54. Hobbes, *Leviathan*, chap. 16, pp. 105–06.

55. Hobbes, *Leviathan*, chap. 28, p. 209. Hobbes refers here to Job 41:25: "Upon earth there is not his like, who is made without fear."

56. Hobbes, *Leviathan*, chap. 22, p. 146.

57. Hobbes, *Leviathan*, chap. 17, p. 112; chap. 19, p. 121; *De cive*, pref., p. 104; chap. 10, par. 3, pp. 223–24.

58. Hobbes, *Leviathan*, chap. 18, pp. 116–17; chap. 30, pp. 224–25.

59. Hobbes, *De cive*, chap. 10, par. 7, p. 227.

60. Hobbes, *De cive*, chap. 10, par. 7, p. 227.

61. *Cor*, #50, p. 269.

62. Hobbes, *Leviathan*, chap. 21, pp. 163–66; *De cive*, chap. 2, pars. 14, 18, 19, pp. 128, 130–31.

63. Jean-Jacques Rousseau, *On the Social Contract*, trans. and ed. Roger D. Masters and Judith R. Masters (New York: Saint Martin's, 1978), book I, chap. 6.

64. *PT*, chap. 2, par. 16, p. 297; *G*, 3: 281 (32–33).

65. See *The Federalist Papers*, No. 9, p. 50: "It is impossible to read the history of the petty republics of Greece and Italy, without feeling sensations of horror and disgust at the distractions with which they were continually agitated, and at the rapid succession of revolutions, by which they were kept in a state of perpetual vibration, between the extremes of tyranny and anarchy." See also No. 10, p. 61: "Hence it is, that such Democracies have ever been spectacles of turbulence and contention; have ever been found incompatible with personal security, or the rights of property; and have in general been as short in their lives, as they have been violent in their deaths." On the tendency toward mob psychology see No. 55, p. 374: "Had every Athenian citizen been a Socrates; every Athenian assembly would still have been a mob."

66. *TTP*, 194 [28–29] (5–16); *Elwes*, chap. 16, pp. 205–06.

67. *TTP*, 195 [35] (17–21); *Elwes*, chap. 16, p. 207.

68. *TTP*, 194 [30] (16–23); *Elwes*, chap. 16, p. 206.

69. *TTP*, 195 [38] (26–34); *Elwes*, chap. 16, p. 207.

70. For the use of this term see Isaiah Berlin, "Two Concepts of Liberty," in his *Four Essays on Liberty* (Oxford: Oxford University Press, 1975), pp. 118–72; for a critique of the positive-negative liberty distinction see J. R. MacCallum, Jr., "Negative and Positive Freedom," in *Philosophy, Politics and Society*, 4th series, ed. P. Laslett, W. G. Runciman, and Q. Skinner (Oxford: Blackwell, 1972), pp. 174–93; see also Charles Taylor, "What's Wrong with Negative Liberty," in *Philosophy and the Human Sciences: Philosophical Papers 2* (Cambridge: Cambridge University Press, 1985), pp. 211–29.

71. Hobbes, *Leviathan*, chap. 21, p. 166.

72. Hobbes, *Leviathan,* chap. 21, p. 137.

73. Hobbes, *Leviathan,* chap. 6, p. 39; chap. 11, p. 63.

74. *Ethics,* IV, P 66 S, p. 584; G, 2: 260 (26–29).

75. Rousseau, *Social Contract,* book I, chap. 8, p. 56; *Ethics,* IV, P 68 D, p. 584; G, 2: 261 (15–16).

76. *Ethics,* IV, P 37, pp. 564–65; G, 2: 235 (12–14).

77. *TTP,* 193 [27] (34)–194(5); *Elwes,* chap. 16, p. 205.

78. Rousseau, *Social Contract,* book I, chap. 7.

79. *TTP,* 194 [32–34] (25)–195(5); *Elwes,* chap. 16, p. 206.

80. *Ethics,* III, P 7, p. 499: "The striving by which each thing strives to persevere in its being is nothing but the actual essence of the thing"; G, 2: 146 (20–21).

81. Berlin classifies Spinoza along with Hegel and Marx as a partisan of positive liberty and therefore as among the enemies of true freedom; see Berlin, "Two Concepts of Liberty," pp. 142, 146, 147. For an attempt to rescue Spinoza from this association see David West, "Spinoza on Positive Freedom," *Political Studies* 39 (1993): 284–96. In a rejoinder to this essay Berlin suggests that it is not Spinoza but merely a "distortion" of Spinoza's views that can be "easily twisted" in the direction of paternalism and social control. To this, one can only ask whose views are so impervious to misuse that they could not somehow be employed in the service of some corrupt cause? Employing a strategy of guilt by association, Berlin notes that Bismarck "greatly admired" Spinoza and borrowed his tactics in carrying out his *Kulturkampf* against the clerics of Germany; see Berlin, "A Reply to David West," *Political Studies* 39 (1993): 297. Berlin fails to note that Spinoza was also greatly admired by many more people, including Ben Gurion and the founders of the state of Israel. For a solid effort to rescue Spinoza from the charge of political illiberalism see Gerald M. Mera, "Liberal Politics and Moral Excellence in Spinoza's Political Philosophy," *Journal of the History of Philosophy* 22 (1982): 129–50.

82. Hobbes, *Leviathan* chap. 11, p. 63: "For there is no such *finis ultimus,* utmost aim, nor *summum bonum,* greatest good, as is spoken of in the books of the old moral philosophers.... Felicity is a continual progress of the desire, from one object to another; the attaining of the former, being still but the way to the latter." For a contemporary restatement of Hobbes's view see Judith N. Shklar, "The Liberalism of Fear," in *Liberalism and the Moral Life,* ed. Nancy L. Rosenblum (Cambridge: Harvard University Press, 1989), pp. 21–38.

83. *TTP,* 195 [36] (16); *Elwes,* chap. 16, p. 207.

84. *TTP,* 195 [34] (2–5); *Elwes,* chap. 16, p. 206.

85. *Ethics,* IV, P 18, p. 556: "From this it follows that men who are governed by reason ... want nothing for themselves that they do not desire for other men. Hence, they are just, honest, and honorable"; G, 2: 223 (15–18).

86. *Ethics,* IV, pref., p. 545; G, 2: 208 (15–17).

87. *Ethics,* IV, P 68, p. 584; G, 2: 261 (15).

88. *TTP,* 46 [12] (28–31); *Elwes,* chap. 3, p. 45.

89. *Ethics,* IV, P 67, 72, pp. 584, 586; G, 2: 261 (1–2), 264 (10).

90. *Ethics,* IV, P 28, p. 559; G, 2: 228 (7–8).

91. *TTP,* 73 [18–19] (13–24); *Elwes,* chap. 5, p. 73.

92. *Ethics,* IV, P 18, S, pp. 555–56; G, 2: 222 (27–28).

93. *Ethics*, IV, P18, S, p. 556; *G*, 2: 223 (5–14).

94. *TTP*, 57 [1] (23–31); *Elwes*, chap. 4, p. 57.

95. *TTP*, 57 [2] (31)–58 (6); *Elwes*, chap. 4, p. 57.

96. *TTP*, 58 [5] (28–29); *Elwes*, chap. 4, p. 58.

97. *TTP*, 46 [8] (4–6): "whether we say that all things happen according to the laws of nature, or whether we say that they are ordered according to the decree and guidance of God, we say the same thing"; *Elwes*, chap. 3, p. 45.

98. *TTP*, 45 [7] (34)–46(1): "By God's guidance I understand the fixed and immutable order of nature, *or* the connection of natural things [*rerum naturalium concatenationem*]"; *Elwes*, chap. 3, p. 44.

99. *TTP*, 58 [5] (33–35); *Elwes*, chap. 4, p. 58.

100. *TTP*, 59 [9] (25–26); *Elwes*, chap. 4, p. 59.

101. *TTP*, 61 [18] (21–22); *Elwes*, chap. 4, p. 61.

102. *TTP*, 60 [11] (9–11); *Elwes*, chap. 4, p. 59.

103. *Ethics*, V, P 33, p. 611; *G*, 2: 300 (29–30).

104. *TTP*, 60 [15] (34)–61(5); *Elwes*, chap. 4, p. 60.

105. *Ethics*, V, P 42, p. 616: "Blessedness is not the reward of virtue, but virtue itself"; *G*, 2: 307 (27–29).

106. Contemporary philosophers have had little patience with Spinoza's idea that philosophy issues into a kind of love. For one of the more bad-tempered responses see Jonathan Bennett, *A Study of Spinoza's Ethics* (Cambridge: Cambridge University Press, 1984). Bennett says that "the time has come to admit that this part of the *Ethics* has nothing to teach us and is pretty certainly worthless" (p. 372). Shortly thereafter he remarks that this material from the *Ethics* is "rubbish which causes others to write rubbish" (p. 374). And finally he pronounces that "those of us who love and admire Spinoza's philosophical work should in sad silence avert our eyes from the second half of Part 5" (p. 375). Would that the author had followed his own advice and passed over this part in "silence." The relation between philosophy and erotics is utterly incomprehensible from Bennett's point of view; it is, however, as old as philosophy itself. The classic work is Plato's *Symposium*.

107. For the sources of this doctrine see Harry Wolfson, *The Philosophy of Spinoza* (Cambridge: Harvard University Press, 1934), vol. 2, pp. 302–11; Shlomo Pines, "Spinoza's 'Tractatus Theologico-Politicus,' Maimonides, and Kant," *Scripta Hierosolymitana* 20 (1968): 25–27; Warren Zev Harvey, "A Portrait of Spinoza as a Maimonidean," *Journal of the History of Philosophy* 19 (1981): 167. Leon Roth, in *Spinoza* (London: Ernest Benn, 1929), p. 223, attributes intellectual love to the influence of Leon Abrabanel's *Dialogues on Love*, which Spinoza possessed in Spanish translation.

108. Maimonides, *The Guide of the Perplexed*, trans. Shlomo Pines, intro. Leo Strauss (Chicago: University of Chicago Press, 1963), book III, chap. 54, pp. 632–38.

109. For the view that the best life consists in the perfection of the theoretical intellect see Shlomo Pines, "Introductory Essay," in *Guide of the Perplexed*, pp. cxxii–cxxiii; Ralph Lerner, "Maimonides' Governance of the Solitary," in *Perspectives on Maimonides: Philosophical and Historical Studies*, ed. Joel L. Kraemer (Oxford: Oxford University Press, 1991), pp. 33–46. For the view that perfection consists in the life of moral or political virtue see Steven Schwarzschild, "Moral Radicalism and 'Middlingness' in the

Ethics of Maimonides," *Medieval Culture* 11 (1977): 65–94; Lawrence V. Berman, "The Political Interpretation of the Maxim: The Purpose of Philosophy in the Imitation of God," *Studia Islamica* 15 (1961): 53–61. For an attempt to reconcile these two positions see David Hartman, *Maimonides: Torah and Philosophic Quest* (New York: Jewish Publication Society, 1976), pp. 15–27, 204–05.

110. Maimonides, *Guide of the Perplexed,* book I, chap. 54, p. 128.

111. Maimonides, *Guide of the Perplexed,* book III, chap. 54, p. 636. The biblical text reads: "Let not the wise man glory in his wisdom, let not the mighty man glory in his might, let not the rich man glory in his riches, but let him who glories glory in this, that he understands and knows me that I am the Lord."

112. Maimonides, *Guide of the Perplexed,* book II, chap. 36, p. 372: "If the perfect man who lives in solitude thinks of [the multitude] at all, he does so only with a view to saving himself from the harm that may be caused by those who are harmful . . . or to obtaining an advantage that may be obtained from them if he is forced to it by some of his needs."

113. Maimonides, *Guide of the Perplexed,* book III, chap. 54, p. 635. Maimonides cites only part of the verse. In the Oxford Bible it reads: "Let them be for yourself alone, and not for strangers with you."

114. Maimonides, *Guide of the Perplexed,* intro., p. 6.

115. Maimonides, *Guide of the Perplexed,* book III, chap. 51, p. 624: "Now this is to my mind a proof that [the prophets] performed these actions with their limbs only, while their intellects were constantly in His presence, may He be exalted."

116. *Ethics,* II, P 40, S 2, p. 478; G, 2: 122 (15–30).

117. The conception of Spinoza as a "God-intoxicated man" (*Gott-trunkener Mensch*) was popularized by Novalis during the 1780s. For Spinoza's role in the *Pantheismusstreit* see F. H. Jacobi, "Über die Lehre des Spinoza," in *The Spinoza Conversations Between Lessing and Jacobi,* ed. Gerard Vallée; trans. G. Vallée, J. B. Lawson, and C. G. Chapple (Lanham, Md.: University Press of America, 1988), pp. 79–125; see also Frederick Beiser, *The Fate of Reason: German Philosophy from Kant to Fichte* (Cambridge: Harvard University Press, 1987).

118. *Ethics,* II, P 40, S 2, p. 478; G, 2: 122 (17–19).

119. See Gilles Deleuze, *Spinoza: Practical Philosophy,* trans. Robert Hurley (San Francisco: City Lights Books, 1988), pp. 28–29: "The *Ethics* is necessarily an ethics of joy: only joy is worthwhile, joy remains, bringing us near to action, and to the bliss of action. . . . Ethical *joy* is the correlate of speculative affirmation."

120. *Ethics,* V, P 32, p. 611; G, 2: 300 (21–27).

121. Feuer, in *Spinoza and the Rise of Liberalism,* pp. 217, 219, speaks of the intellectual love of God as displaying a significant degree of "gallows humor" and a "strain of intellectual masochism." This entirely misses the degree to which the Spinozist *amor Dei intellectualis* is inseparable from self-love. For an appreciation of Spinoza's philosophical therapeutics see José Benardete, "Therapeutics and Hermeneutics," in *Spinoza: Issues and Directions. The Proceedings of the Chicago Spinoza Conference,* ed. Edwin Curley and Pierre-François Moreau (Leiden, Neth.: E. J. Brill, 1990), pp. 209–20.

122. *TTP,* 58 [6] (35)2–59(2); *Elwes,* chap. 4, p. 58.

123. *Ethics,* V, P 42, S, pp. 616–17; G, 2: 308 (15–24).

124. See Harvey, "Portrait of Spinoza as a Maimonidean," pp. 168–69.

125. *Ethics*, V, P 42, S, p. 617; *G*, 2: 308 (26–27): "Sed omnia praeclara tam difficilia, quam rara sunt."

Chapter 6. From Jerusalem to Amsterdam

1. *TTP*, 201 [1] (9–14); *Elwes*, chap. 17, p. 214.

2. In the seventeenth chapter Tacitus is mentioned by name no fewer than five times; see Chaim Wirszubski, "Spinoza's Debt to Tacitus," *Scripta Hierosolymitana* 2 (1955): 176–86; see also Arnaldo Momigliano, "Tacitus and the Tacitist Tradition," in *The Classical Foundations of Modern Historiography* (Berkeley: University of California Press, 1990), pp. 109–31.

3. *TTP*, 203 [16] (30–33); *Elwes*, chap. 17, p. 217. See also Jean-Jacques Rousseau, *On the Social Contract*, trans. and ed. Roger D. Masters and Julia R. Masters (New York: Saint Martin's, 1978), book I, chap. 6, p. 53.

4. Robert McShea, *The Political Philosophy of Spinoza* (New York: Columbia University Press, 1968), pp. 102–03; see also Hans W. Blom, "Virtue and Republicanism: Spinoza's Political Philosophy in the Context of the Dutch Republic," in *Republiken und Republikanismus im Europa der Frühen Neuzeit*, ed. Helmut G. Koenigsberger (Munich: R. Oldenbourg, 1988), pp. 195–212, esp. 206–09; G. Groenhuis, "Calvinism and National Consciousness: The Dutch Republic as the New Israel," in *Britain and the Netherlands*, vol. 7 of *Church and State Since the Reformation*, ed. A. C. Duke and C. A. Tasme (The Hague: Martinus Nijhoff, 1981), pp. 118–33; Michael A. Rosenthal, "Why Spinoza Chose the Hebrews: The Exemplary Function of Prophecy in 'The Theologico-Political Treatise'" (unpublished MS).

5. For some useful comparisons of Machiavelli and Spinoza see Eco O. G. Haitsma Mulier, *The Myth of Venice and Dutch Republican Thought in the Seventeenth Century* (Assen, Neth.: Van Gorcum, 1980), pp. 170–74, 181–92; see also his "Controversial Republican: Dutch Views of Machiavelli in the Seventeenth and Eighteenth Centuries," in *Machiavelli and Republicanism*, ed. Gisela Bock, Quentin Skinner, and Maurizio Viroli (Cambridge: Cambridge University Press, 1990), pp. 254–57; Martin van Gelderen, *The Political Thought of the Dutch Revolt, 1555–1590* (Cambridge: Cambridge University Press, 1992), pp. 276–87.

6. See Joel Schwartz, "Liberalism and the Jewish Connection: A Study of Spinoza and the Young Marx," *Political Theory* 13 (1985): 58–89.

7. *TTP*, 246 [41–42] (11–25): "When the Politicians and the Estates of the provinces began to concern themselves with the religious controversy between the Remonstrants and the Counterremonstrants, it finally degenerated into a schism, and it was then manifest in many examples that laws passed to settle religious controversies aggravate people more than they correct them. . . . These examples establish more clearly than the noon light that the real schismatics are those who condemn the writings of others and seditiously incite the unruly mob [*vulgum petulantem*] against the writers, not the writers themselves, who for the most part write only for the learned [*doctis*] and call only reason to their aid, and again, that the real troublemakers are those who want, in a free state, to take away freedom of judgment, in spite of the fact that it cannot be suppressed"; *Elwes*, chap. 20, p. 264.

8. The term "theocracy" was first coined by the Hellenized Jew Josephus to describe

the political system of Israel. Josephus used this term to show that the law or Torah stems from God rather than from the will of the political sovereign and that this law is eternal and unchangeable; see Josephus, *Anti-Apion,* trans. H. St. J. Thackeray, Loeb Classical Library, vol. 1 (London:,William Heineman, 1926), book II, chap. 164, p. 359: "For us, with our conviction that the original institution of the Law was in accordance with the will of God, it would be rank impiety not to observe it. What could one alter in it? What more beautiful one could be discovered? What improvement imported from elsewhere? Would you change the entire character of the constitution? Could there be a finer or more equitable polity than one which sets God at the head of the universe, which assigns the administration of its highest affairs to the whole body of priests, and entrusts to the supreme high-priest the direction of the other priests? . . . But this charge further embraced a strict superintendence of the Law and of the pursuits of everyday life: for the appointed duties of the priests included general supervision, the trial of litigation, and punishment of condemned persons."

9. *TTP,* 206 [31–32] (9–19); *Elwes,* chap. 17, p. 219.

10. Feuer, *Spinoza and the Rise of Liberalism,* p. 121; Sylvain Zac, *Spinoza et l'interprétation de l'Ecriture* (Paris: Presses Universitaires de France, 1965), p. 210.

11. *TTP,* 74 [26–29] (34)–75 (25); *Elwes,* chap. 5, pp. 74–75.

12. *TTP,* 205 [26–28] (15–33); *Elwes,* chap. 17, pp. 218–19.

13. *TTP,* 206 [32] (19–22); *Elwes,* chap. 17, p. 220.

14. *TTP,* 206 [33] (23–29); *Elwes,* chap. 17, p. 220.

15. *TTP,* 212 [66] (31–35); *Elwes,* chap. 17, p. 227.

16. *TTP,* 209 [48] (4–8); *Elwes,* chap. 17, p. 223.

17. *TTP,* 213 [67] (2–4); *Elwes,* chap. 17, p. 227.

18. *TTP,* 216 [86] (7–10); *Elwes,* chap. 17, p. 230.

19. *TTP,* 215 [82] (16–22); *Elwes,* chap. 17, pp. 229–30.

20. *TTP,* 218 [96–97] (1–5); *Elwes,* chap. 17, pp. 232–33.

21. Michael Walzer, *Exodus and Revolution* (New York: Basic Books, 1984), pp. 55–66.

22. *TTP,* 217 [96] (31–35); *Elwes,* chap. 17, p. 232. See Ezekiel 20: 25–26: "Moreover I gave them statutes that were not good and ordinances by which they could not have life; and I defiled them through their very gifts in making them offer by fire all their first-born, that I might horrify them; I did it that they might know that I am the Lord."

23. *TTP,* 219 [102] (1–5); *Elwes,* chap. 17, p. 234.

24. *TTP,* 218 [97] (7–8); *Elwes,* chap. 17, p. 233. The phrase from Tacitus comes from the *History,* I, 3: "Non esse curae Deis securitatem nostram, esse ultionem [The Gods take no thought for our happiness, but only for our punishment]" (*The Complete Works of Tacitus,* ed. Moses Hadas [New York: Modern Library, 1942], p. 421; see also Wirszubski, "Spinoza's Debt to Tacitus," p. 181.

25. *TTP,* 218 [97] (6–12); *Elwes,* chap. 17, p. 233.

26. *TTP,* 217 [93–94] (19–26): "Nature, of course, creates individuals, not nations, individuals which are distinguished into nations only by differences of language, laws, and accepted customs [*linguae, legum et morum*]. . . . So if it must be granted that the Hebrews were more stiff-necked than other mortals, that must be ascribed to a vice either of the laws or of the accepted customs"; *Elwes,* chap. 17, p. 232.

27. Zac, *Spinoza et l'interprétation de l'Ecriture*, p. 212.

28. TTP, 218 [98–99] (12–21); *Elwes*, chap. 17, p. 233.

29. TTP, 218 [99] (21); *Elwes*, chap. 17, p. 233.

30. TTP, 219 [104] (15–16). *Elwes*, chap. 17, p. 234. See Feuer, *Spinoza and the Rise of Liberalism*, pp. 132–33; Walzer, *Exodus and Revolution*, pp. 111–12.

31. TTP, 219 [104] (20–21): "Quare tunc temporis seditio magis desierat, quam concordia coeperat"; *Elwes*, chap. 17, p. 234.

32. TTP, 219 [107] (33–35); *Elwes*, chap. 17, p. 235.

33. TTP, 220 [111] (28–30); *Elwes*, chap. 17, p. 236.

34. TTP, 221 [3] (29–31); *Elwes*, chap. 18, p. 237.

35. TTP, 222 [3–5] (1–13); *Elwes*, chap. 18, pp. 237–38.

36. TTP, 221 [2] (22–24); *Elwes*, chap. 18, p. 237.

37. TTP, 221 [2] (24–29); *Elwes*, chap. 18, p. 237.

38. TTP, 228 [1] (19–22); *Elwes*, chap. 19, p. 245.

39. TTP, 229 [3] (6–8); *Elwes*, chap. 19, p. 245.

40. TTP, 228 [2] (33)–229(3); *Elwes*, chap. 19, p. 245.

41. TTP, 229 [6] (19–22); *Elwes*, chap. 19, p. 246.

42. TTP, 232 [22] (9–10): "Certum est, quod pietas erga patriam summa sit, quam aliquis praestare potest"; *Elwes*, chap. 19, p. 249.

43. TTP, 232 [23] (19–22); *Elwes*, chap. 19, p. 249. See Machiavelli, *The Discourses*, trans. Leslie Walker (London: Routledge and Kegan Paul, 1950), book III, chap. 22, pp. 528–32; book III, chap. 34, 556–59.

44. TTP, 232 [25] (28–31); *Elwes*, chap. 19, p. 250.

45. TTP, 117 [91] (1–5); *Elwes*, chap. 7, pp. 118–19; emphasis added.

46. TTP, 117 [92] (8–10); *Elwes*, chap. 7, p. 119.

47. See José Faur, *In the Shadow of History: Jews and 'Conversos' at the Dawn of Modernity* (Albany: State University of New York Press, 1992), pp. 172–75.

48. For one possible source of Spinoza's views on sovereignty see *Pirke Avot*, trans. Leonard Kravitz and Kerry M. Olitzky (New York: UAHC, 1993), III, 2: "Rabbi Chaninah, the Assistant of the High Priests, said: 'Pray for the welfare of the government, for were it not for the fear of it, people would swallow each other alive.'"

49. Spinoza's view seems akin to Madison's in the *Federalist* No. 10, where Madison defines "faction" as "a number of citizens, whether amounting to a majority or minority of the whole, who are united and actuated by some common impulse of passion, or of interest, adverse to the rights of other citizens, or to the permanent and aggregate interests of the community" (*The Federalist Papers*, ed. Jacob E. Cooke [Middletown, Conn.: Wesleyan University Press, 1961], p. 57).

50. A similar paradox concerning the relation of individualism to absolutism has been noted in the writings of Hobbes; see Michael Oakeshott, "Introduction," in Hobbes, *Leviathan*, pp. lv–lviii; reprinted in *Rationalism in Politics and Other Essays* (Indianapolis: Liberty Press, 1991).

51. Feuer, *Spinoza and the Rise of Liberalism*, p. 119.

52. TTP, 236 [46–47] (9–19); *Elwes*, chap. 19, pp. 253–54.

53. TTP, 235 [41] (12–16); *Elwes*, chap. 19, p. 252.

54. TTP, 223 [13] (23–26); *Elwes*, chap. 18, p. 239.

55. *TTP*, 235 [43–44] (25–34); *Elwes*, chap. 19. p. 253.

56. *TTP*, 235 [41] (16–17); *Elwes*, chap. 19, p. 252.

57. *TTP*, 236 [50–51] (34)–237(8); *Elwes*, chap. 19, p. 254.

58. *TTP*, 237 [55] (28–30); *Elwes*, chap. 19, p. 255.

59. *TTP*, 228 [1] (19–20); *Elwes*, chap. 19, p. 245; emphasis added.

60. *TTP*, 239 (1–2): "Ostenditur, in Libera Republica unicuique et sentire, quae velit, et quae sentiat, dicere licere"; *Elwes*, chap. 20, 257. See also Tacitus, *The History*, in *Complete Works*, book I, chap. 1, pp. 419–20: "I have reserved as an employment for my old age . . . a subject at once more fruitful and less anxious [than] in the reign of the divine Nerva and the empire of Trajan, enjoying the rare happiness of times when we may think what we please, and express what we think." See also Wirszubski, "Spinoza's Debt to Tacitus," p. 184.

61. *TTP*, 239 [2] (9–10); *Elwes*, chap. 20, p. 257.

62. *TTP*, 239 [3] (12–16); *Elwes*, chap. 20, p. 257.

63. *TTP*, 239 [3] (17–18); *Elwes*, chap. 20, p. 257.

64. *TTP*, 202 [9] (26–28); *Elwes*, chap. 17, p. 216; emphasis added.

65. *TTP*, 202 [9] (29–35); *Elwes*, chap. 17, p. 216.

66. *TTP*, 11 [28] (1–8); *Elwes*, pref., p. 10.

67. *TTP*, 239 [4] (24–25); *Elwes*, chap. 20, p. 257.

68. *TTP*, 240 [6] (5–10); *Elwes*, chap. 20, p. 258.

69. *TTP*, 240 [9] (21–25); *Elwes*, chap. 20, p. 258.

70. *TTP*, 244 [29] (3–5); *Elwes*, chap. 20, p. 262.

71. *TTP*, 244 [30] (9–13); *Elwes*, chap. 20, p. 262.

72. For Spinoza's views on revolution see Feuer, *Spinoza and the Rise of Liberalism*, pp. 91–95; McShea, *Political Philosophy of Spinoza*, pp. 94, 193–96; Mulier, *Myth of Venice*, pp. 180–81.

73. At the same time that he expresses great caution about the legitimacy of revolution, Spinoza identifies himself with the Neapolitan insurgent Massanello; see Johannes Colerus, "The Life of B. De Spinosa," in Frederick Pollock, *Spinoza: His Life and Philosophy* (London: Duckworth, 1899), p. 392: "After [Spinoza] had perfected himself in that art, he applied himself to drawing, which he learned of himself, and he could draw a head very well with ink, or with a coal. I have in my hands a whole book of such draughts, amongst which there are some heads of several considerable persons, who were known to him, or who had occasion to visit him. Among those draughts I find in the fourth sheet a fisherman having only his shirt on, with a net on his right shoulder, whose attitude is very much like that of Massanello, the famous head of the rebels of Naples. . . . Which gives me occasion to add, that Mr. Vander Spyck, at whose house Spinoza lodged when he died, has assured me that the draught of that fisherman did perfectly resemble Spinoza and that he had certainly drawn it himself."

74. Machiavelli, *Discourses*, book III, chap. 1, pp. 459–63.

75. *TTP*, 227 [33–34] (8–21); *Elwes*, chap. 18, p. 243.

76. *TTP*, 227 [36] (33)–228(7); *Elwes*, chap. 18, p. 244.

77. *TTP*, 228 [37] (10–13); *Elwes*, chap. 18, p. 244.

78. *TTP*, 241 [12] (7–8): "Finis ergo Reipublicae revera libertas est"; *Elwes*, chap. 20, p. 259.

79. *TTP*, 241 [12] (3–6); *Elwes*, chap. 20, p. 259.

80. See Isaac Bashevis Singer, "The Spinoza of Market Street," in *An Isaac Bashevis Singer Reader* (New York: Farrar, Strauss and Giroux, 1971), pp. 71–92.

81. *Ethics*, IV, P 67, p. 84: "A free man thinks of nothing less than of death, and his wisdom is a meditation on life, not on death"; *G*, 2: 261 (1–2).

82. See Immanuel Kant, "What Is Enlightenment?" in his *Political Writings*, ed. Hans Reiss, trans. H. B. Nisbet (Cambridge: Cambridge University Press, 1970), p. 54.

83. *Ethics*, III, P 58, p. 529; *G*, 2: 187 (25–26)

84. *Ethics*, III, P 59, p. 529; *G*, 2: 188 (9–10).

85. *Ethics*, III, P 59, S. pp. 529–30; *G*, 2: 188 (21–33).

86. Among the few interpreters who have seen the importance of *fortitudo* see Robert Duff, *Spinoza's Political and Ethical Philosophy* (Glasgow: James Maclehose, 1903), pp. 115–16; Stuart Hampshire, *Spinoza*, (Harmondsworth, Eng.: Penguin, 1951), p. 167.

87. Aristotle, *Nicomachean Ethics*, IV. 4. 1124a 1.

88. René Descartes, *The Passions of the Soul*, in *The Philosophical Works of Descartes*, trans. Elizabeth Haldane and G. R. T. Ross, vol. 1 (Cambridge: Cambridge University Press, 1977), art. 150, pp. 400–01.

89. Descartes, *Passions of the Soul*, art. 152, p. 401.

90. Descartes, *Passions of the Soul*, art. 152, p. 401.

91. Descartes, *Passions of the Soul*, art. 153, p. 401.

92. Descartes, *Passions of the Soul*, art. 153, pp. 401–02.

93. Descartes, *Discourse on Method*, in *Philosophical Works of Descartes*, vol. 1, p. 120.

94. Descartes, *Discourse on Method*, pp. 119–20.

95. *TTP*, 243 [24–26] (16–24); *Elwes*, chap. 20, p. 261.

96. One of the few early thinkers to note the importance of commerce for Spinoza was Vico, who disapproved, noting that "Spinoza speaks of the commonwealth as if it were a society of hucksters"; see Giambattista Vico, *The New Science*, trans. T. H. Bergin and M. H. Fisch (Ithaca: Cornell University Press, 1970), par. 335, p. 54. For an appreciation of the role of commerce see Douglas J. Den Uyl and Stuart Warner, "Liberalism and Hobbes and Spinoza," *Studia Spinozana* 3 (1987): 286–90.

97. Both McShea, in *Political Philosophy of Spinoza*, pp. 108–9, and Feuer, in *Spinoza and the Rise of Liberalism*, p. 120, seem to believe that Spinoza favored a separation-of-powers doctrine with a considerable degree of pluralism. This seems false to me. Spinoza favored giving a wide latitude to individuals regarding freedom of speech and toleration, but not necessarily to groups.

98. *PT*, chap. 7, par. 8, pp. 341–43; *G*, 3: 311 (10–22).

99. Albert O. Hirshman, *The Passions and the Interests: Political Arguments for Capitalism Before Its Triumph* (Princeton: Princeton University Press, 1977), pp. 56–63.

100. See especially J. G. A. Pocock, *Virtue, Commerce, and History* (Cambridge: Cambridge University Press, 1985); and Pocock, "Cambridge Paradigms and Scotch Philosophers: A Study of the Relations of the Civic Humanist and Civil Jurisprudential Interpretation of Eighteenth-Century Social Thought," in *Wealth and Virtue: The Shaping of Political Economy in the Scottish Enlightenment*, ed. Istvan Hont and Michael Ignatieff (Cambridge: Cambridge University Press, 1983), pp. 235–52. For Pocock's

attempt to fit Spinoza into these debates see his "Spinoza and Harrington: An Exercise in Comparison," *Bijdragen en Mededelingen betreffende de Geschiedenis der Nederlanden* 102 (1987): 435–49.

101. Van Gelderen, *Dutch Revolt*, pp. 281–82.

102. For the dangers of regarding texts as illustrative of some preexisting paradigm, *mentalité*, ideology, or tradition of discourse see Ralph Lerner, *The Thinking Revolutionary: Principle and Practice in the New Republic* (Ithaca: Cornell University Press, 1987), pp. 1–38

103. *PT,* chap. 10, par. 5, pp. 433–35: "Many have tried to prevent these ills by passing sumptuary laws; but without success . . . since 'we always strive for what is forbidden, and desire what is denied.' Besides, men of leisure never lack the wit to get round laws which are framed to deal with things which cannot be forbidden absolutely, like feasting, gambling, personal adornment, and so forth, which are bad only in excess, and must be judged as excessive or otherwise in relation to the wealth of each individual, so that no general law can determine what is excessive and what is not"; *G, 3:* 355 (24–33). The inner quotation is from Ovid, *Amores,* III, 4, 17.

104. *PT,* chap. 10, par. 6, p. 435: "Thus every attempt must be made to ensure that the rich, if they cannot be thrifty, are at any rate greedy for gain. For if this passion for gain, which is universal and constant, is reinforced by the desire for glory, most men will certainly make every effort to increase their wealth by honorable means so as to obtain office and avoid great disgrace"; *G, 3:* 356 (5–8).

105. Not everyone agreed with this proposition. The most notable holdout was Rousseau, whose *First Discourse* was devoted to uncoupling enlightenment and moral progress; see also his preface to *Narcisse,* in his *Oeuvres complètes,* ed. Bernard Gagnebin and Marcel Raymond (Paris: Gallimard, 1964), vol. 2, p. 964n: "everything which facilitates communications between diverse nations brings to the others not their virtues but their crimes and alters everywhere the customs [*moeurs*] which are part of their climate and the constitution of their government." In the American context Thomas Jefferson also rejected the model of the commercial republic; see his letter to Thomas Leiper, January 21, 1809: "I have lately inculcated the encouragement of manufactures to the extent of our own consumption at least . . . this absurd hue and cry has contributed much to federalize New England; [the Federalists'] doctrine goes to the sacrificing of agriculture and manufacturing to commerce; to the calling of all our people from the interior to the sea shore to turn merchants, and to convert this great agricultural country into a city of Amsterdam" (*The Works of Thomas Jefferson,* ed. Paul L. Ford [New York: Putnam, 1955], vol. 11, pp. 90–91). For Jefferson's agrarian antimodernism see J. G. A. Pocock, *The Machiavellian Moment: Florentine Political Thought and the Atlantic Republican Tradition* (Princeton: Princeton University Press, 1975), pp. 532–33, 535–36, 540–43.

106. *TTP,* 245 [40] (35)–246(11); *Elwes,* chap. 20, p. 264.

107. For the theory of commercial republicanism see Lerner, *Thinking Revolutionary,* pp. 195–221; for an exhaustive account see Paul Rahe, *Republics Ancient and Modern* (Chapel Hill: University of North Carolina Press, 1992), part II.

108. Montesquieu, *L'esprit des lois,* book XX, chaps. 1–2, 5, 7; see Pierre Manent, *La cité de l'homme* (Paris: Fayard, 1994), pp. 53–72.

109. Alexis de Tocqueville, *Democracy in America,* trans. George Lawrence, ed. J. P. Mayer (New York: Anchor, 1969), vol. 2, part III, chap. 19, pp. 627–32, in the section entitled "Why There Are So Many Men of Ambition in the United States but So Few of Lofty Ambitions."

110. *Ethics,* IV, P 45 S, p. 572: "It is the part of a wise man, I say, to refresh and restore himself in moderation with pleasant food and drink, with scents, with the beauty of green plants, with decoration, music, sports, the theater, and other things of this kind, which anyone can use without injury to another. For the human Body is composed of a great many parts of different natures, which constantly require new and varied nourishment, so that the whole Body may be equally capable of all the things which can follow from its nature, and hence, so that the Mind also may be equally capable of understanding many things"; *G,* 2: 244 (28)–245(2).

Chapter 7. The Legacy of the Treatise

1. For Spinoza's influence on the French Enlightenment, see Ira O. Wade, *The Intellectual Origins of the French Enlightenment* (Princeton: Princeton University Press, 1971), pp. 27, 37–40; Paul Vernière, *Spinoza et la pensée française avant la révolution,* (Paris: Presses Universitaires de France, 1954), vol. 1, pp. 206–19; vol. 2, pp. 334–85; Arthur Hertzberg, *The French Enlightenment and the Jews: The Origins of Modern Anti-Semitism* (New York: Columbia University Press, 1990), pp. 29–30, 37–38, 39–40. On his place in the English debates see Leslie Stephen, *The History of English Thought in the Eighteenth Century,* (New York: Peter Smith, 1949), vol. 1, p. 33; Rosalie L. Colie, "Spinoza and the Early English Deists," *Journal of the History of Ideas* 20 (1959): 23–46; see also Jacob Freudenthal, *Spinoza: Leben und Lehre* (Heidelberg: Carl Winter, 1927), vol. 2, pp. 219–25.

2. The most notorious case was Voltaire; see Hertzberg, *French Enlightenment and the Jews,* pp. 280–86; Peter Gay, *Voltaire's Politics: The Poet as Realist* (New York: Random House, 1959), pp. 351–54; Gay, *The Party of Humanity: Essays in the French Enlightenment* (New York: Knopf, 1964), pp. 97–108.

3. David Sorkin, *The Transformation of German Jewry, 1780–1840* (New York: Oxford University Press, 1987), pp. 13–40; Jacob Katz, "The Term 'Jewish Emancipation,' Its Origin and Historical Impact," in *Studies in Nineteenth Century Jewish Intellectual History,* ed. A. Altmann (Cambridge: Harvard University Press, 1964), pp. 1–25; George Mosse, "Jewish Emancipation: Between 'Bildung' and Respectability," in *The Jewish Response to German Culture: From the Enlightenment to the Second World War,* ed. Jehuda Reinharz and Walter Schatzberg (Hanover, N.H.: University Press of New England, 1985), pp. 1–16.

4. Michael Meyer, *The Origins of the Modern Jew: Jewish Identity and European Culture in Germany, 1749–1824* (Detroit, Mich.: Wayne State University Press, 1967), pp. 85–114; Jacob Katz, *Out of the Ghetto: The Social Background of Jewish Emancipation, 1770–1870* (Cambridge: Harvard University Press, 1973), pp. 104–23.

5. Paul Mendes-Flohr, "Fin de siècle Orientalism, the 'Ostjuden,' and the Aesthetics of Jewish Self-Affirmation," in his *Divided Passions: Jewish Intellectuals and the Experi-*

ence of Modernity (Detroit, Mich.: Wayne State University Press, 1991), pp. 77–132. The classic study of this type of phenomenon is Edward Said, *Orientalism* (New York: Pantheon, 1978).

6. Zygmunt Bauman, "Exit Visas and Entry Tickets: Paradoxes of Jewish Assimilation," *Telos* 77 (1988): 56.

7. I hope to complete a companion volume to this book that covers Spinoza's legacy in the nineteenth and twentieth centuries.

8. For the view that the German-Jewish dialogue has never been anything more than a monologue carried on by German Jews see Gershom Scholem, "Against the Myth of the German-Jewish Dialogue," in *Jews and Judaism in Crisis,* ed. Werner Dannhauser (New York: Schocken, 1976), pp. 61–70. For some external evidence corroborating Scholem's opinion see Friedrich Nietzsche, *Beyond Good and Evil,* trans. Walter Kaufmann (New York: Random House, 1966), sec. 251, p. 187: "I have not met a German yet who was well disposed toward the Jews." Even as loyal a believer in the compatibility of Germanness and Jewishness as Franz Rosenzweig was compelled to wonder about it in a letter of 1923: "The liberal German-Jewish standpoint on which nearly all of German Jewry had a place for close to a hundred years has become so isolated today that only one human being, namely me, can still live on it: Poor Hermann Cohen!" (Rosenzweig, *Briefe,* ed. Edith Rosenzweig [Berlin: Schocken, 1935], p. 483). Rosenzweig's worst fears were realized a generation after his death when Germany's leading philosopher wrote in praise of "the inner truth and greatness" of National Socialism; see Martin Heidegger, *An Introduction to Metaphysics,* trans. Ralph Mannheim (New Haven: Yale University Press, 1959), p. 199. A powerful overview of these issues is given by Leo Strauss in his autobiographical "Preface," in Strauss, *Spinoza's Critique of Religion,* trans. E. M. Sinclair (New York: Schocken, 1965), pp. 1–31.

9. The immediate context of Lessing's Spinozism was his comment on Goethe's poem "Prometheus" in which he professed his belief in the *Hen kai pan* (One and All). When pressed as to what this meant, Lessing admitted his inability to believe any longer in the principle that God had created the world, and declared his belief in the infinite Substance of Spinoza. "There is no other philosophy but the philosophy of Spinoza" (Lessing, *Über die Lehre des Spinoza,* in *The Spinoza Conversations Between Lessing and Jacobi,* ed. Gerard Vallée; trans. G. Vallée, J. B. Lawrence, and C. G. Chapple [Lanham, Md.: University Press of America, 1988], p. 86). For a helpful discussion of the issues involved see Alexander Altmann, "Lessing und Jacobi: Das Gespräch über den Spinozismus," *Lessing Yearbook* 3 (1971): 25–70; reprinted in Alexander Altmann, *Die Trostvolle Aufklärung: Studien zur Metaphysik und politischen Theorie Moses Mendelssohns* (Stuttgart–Bad Cannstatt: F. Frommann, 1982), pp. 50–83.

10. Pierre Birnbaum and Ira Katznelson, eds., *Paths of Emancipation: Jews, States, and Citizenship* (Princeton: Princeton University Press, 1995), pp. 3–36.

11. For a full account of this story see Alexander Altmann, *Moses Mendelssohn: A Biographical Study* (Tuscaloosa: University of Alabama Press, 1973), pp. 593–653.

12. Moses Mendelssohn, *Jerusalem; or, On Religious Power and Judaism,* trans. Allan Arkush, intro. Alexander Altmann (Hanover, N.H.: University Press of New England, 1983), p. 36.

13. Altmann, *Moses Mendelssohn,* pp. 33–36, 50–53; Freudenthal, *Spinoza: Leben*

und Lehre, vol. 2, pp. 229–30; Julius Guttmann, "Mendelssohn's 'Jerusalem' and Spinoza's 'Theologico-Political Treatise,'" in *Studies in Jewish Thought,* ed. Alfred Jospe (Detroit, Mich.: Wayne State University Press, 1981), pp. 361–86.

14. Mendelssohn, *Jerusalem,* p. 33.

15. Altmann, *Moses Mendelssohn,* pp. 569–70.

16. For Mendelssohn's association with these groups see Altmann, *Moses Mendelssohn,* pp. 653–54; Norbert Hinske, ed. *Was ist Aufklärung? Beiträge aus der Berlinischen Monatsschrift* (Darmstadt, Ger.: Wissenschaftliche Buchgesellschaft, 1977), pp. xx–xxxi; James Schmidt, "The Question of Enlightenment: Kant, Mendelssohn, and the 'Mittwochsgesellschaft,'" *Journal of the History of Ideas* 50 (1989): 269–91.

17. Guttmann, "Mendelssohn and Spinoza," p. 383.

18. The intellectual background to the publication of *Jerusalem* has been usefully glossed in Altmann, *Moses Mendelssohn,* pp. 449–71.

19. Meyer, *Origin of the Modern Jew,* pp. 29–56.

20. John Locke, *A Letter on Toleration,* trans. J. W. Gough, ed. Raymond Klibansky (Oxford: Clarendon, 1968), p. 69.

21. Locke, *Letter on Toleration,* p. 65: "The toleration of those who hold different opinions on matters of religion is so agreeable to the Gospel and to reason, that it seems monstrous for men to be blind in so clear a light."

22. Locke, *Letter on Toleration,* p. 67.

23. Mendelssohn, *Jerusalem,* p. 39.

24. Mendelssohn, *Jerusalem,* p. 41: "Blessed be the state which succeeds in governing the nation by education itself."

25. Mendelssohn, *Jerusalem,* p. 45. Mendelssohn here directs his arguments to "the friends of the natural law."

26. Thomas Hobbes, *Leviathan,* ed. Michael Oakeshott (Oxford: Blackwell, 1955), chap. 15, p. 103.

27. Mendelssohn, *Jerusalem,* p. 56.

28. Mendelssohn, *Jerusalem,* p. 70.

29. Mendelssohn, *Jerusalem,* p. 52.

30. Mendelssohn, *Jerusalem,* p. 52.

31. Mendelssohn, *Jerusalem,* pp. 57–58.

32. Mendelssohn, *Jerusalem,* p. 70.

33. Mendelssohn, *Jerusalem,* p. 73.

34. For Locke's defense of the right of excommunication see his *Letter on Toleration,* p. 77.

35. Mendelssohn, *Jerusalem,* p. 74.

36. Mendelssohn, *Jerusalem,* p. 61.

37. Mendelssohn, *Jerusalem,* p. 63.

38. Mendelssohn, *Jerusalem,* pp. 62–63.

39. Mendelssohn, *Jerusalem,* p. 84.

40. Mendelssohn, *Jerusalem,* p. 85.

41. Mendelssohn, *Jerusalem,* pp. 89–90.

42. *TTP,* 48 [21] (19–20); *Elwes,* chap. 3, p. 47.

43. *TTP,* 47 [16] (26–31); *Elwes,* chap. 3, p. 46.

44. Mendelssohn, *Jerusalem,* pp. 91–92.

45. Mendelssohn, *Jerusalem*, p. 91.

46. Mendelssohn, *Jerusalem*, p. 93.

47. Mendelssohn, *Jerusalem*, p. 94.

48. Mendelssohn, *Jerusalem*, p. 94.

49. Mendelssohn, *Jerusalem*, p. 99.

50. Mendelssohn, *Jerusalem*, p. 98.

51. Mendelssohn, *Jerusalem*, pp. 118–19.

52. Mendelssohn, *Jerusalem*, p. 127.

53. Mendelssohn, *Jerusalem*, p. 133.

54. Mendelssohn, *Jerusalem*, p. 133.

55. Mendelssohn, *Jerusalem*, p. 135.

56. Mendelssohn, *Jerusalem*, p. 138.

57. Alexander Altmann, "Das Menschenbild und die Bildung des Menschen nach Moses Mendelssohn," in his *Die Trostvolle Aufklärung*, p. 19.

58. Mendelssohn, *Jerusalem*, p. 138; translation slightly modified.

59. Mendelssohn, *Jerusalem*, p. 139: "Reward and punish no doctrine, tempt and bribe no one to adopt any religious opinion! Let everyone be permitted to speak as he thinks, to invoke God after his own manner or that of his fathers, and to seek eternal salvation where he thinks he may find it, as long as he does not disturb public felicity and acts honestly toward the civil laws, toward you and his fellow citizens."

60. See Guttmann, "Mendelssohn and Spinoza," p. 382.

61. *TTP,* 229 [3] (6–8); *Elwes,* chap. 19, p. 245.

62. Alexander Altmann, "The Philosophical Roots of Moses Mendelssohn's Plea for Emancipation," in his *Die Trostvolle Aufklärung*, pp. 226–27.

63. Mendelssohn, *Jerusalem*, p. 139.

64. Thomas Jefferson, *Notes on the State of Virginia*, in *The Portable Thomas Jefferson*, ed. Merrill Peterson (Harmondsworth, Eng.: Penguin, 1977), p. 212: "Difference of opinion is advantageous in religion. The several sects perform the office of a Censor morum over each other. Is uniformity attainable? Millions of innocent men, women, and children, since the introduction of Christianity, have been burnt, tortured, fined, imprisoned; yet we have not advanced one inch towards uniformity. What has been the effect of coercion? To make one half the world fools, and the other half hypocrites."

65. George Washington, "Letter to the Hebrew Congregation of Newport," in *The Writings of George Washington,* ed. John C. Fitzpatrick (Washington, D.C.: Government Printing Office, 1939), vol. 31, p. 93.

66. Washington, "Letter to the Hebrew Congregation of Newport," p. 93.

67. Hermann Cohen, "Deutschtum und Judentum," in *Jüdische Schriften,* ed. Bruno Strauss (Berlin: Schwetschke, 1924), vol. 2, pp. 237–318. For a defense of Cohen's views see Steven S. Schwarzschild, " 'Germanism and Judaism' — Hermann Cohen's Normative Paradigm of German-Jewish Symbiosis," in *Jews and Germans from 1860 to 1933: The Problematic Symbiosis,* ed. David Bronsen (Heidelberg: Carl Winter, 1979), pp. 129–72.

68. The term is taken from Altmann, *Die Trostvolle Aufklärung*.

69. Reinhart Koselleck, "Aufklärung und die Grenzen ihrer Toleranz," in *Glaube und Toleranz: Das theologische Erbe der Aufklärung,* ed. Turtz Rendtorff (Gutersloh, Ger.: G. Mohn, 1982), pp. 269–71.

70. Gotthold Ephraim Lessing, *The Education of the Human Race*, in *Lessing's Theological Writings*, trans. Henry Chadwick (Stanford: Stanford University Press, 1992), sec. 4, p. 83.

71. Lessing, *Education*, sec. 76, p. 95: "The word *mystery* signified, in the first age of Christianity, something quite different from what it means now: and the development of revealed truths into truths of reason is absolutely necessary, if the human race is to be assisted by them. When they were revealed they were certainly not truths of reason, but they were revealed in order to become such."

72. Lessing, *Education*, sec. 91, p. 97.

73. Lessing, *Education*, sec. 8, p. 83; translation slightly modified.

74. Lessing, *Education*, sec. 23, p. 86; translation slightly modified.

75. Lessing, *Education*, secs. 16, 27, pp. 84, 87.

76. Lessing, *Education*, secs. 41–42, p. 90.

77. Lessing, *Education*, sec. 51, p. 91.

78. Lessing, *Education*, secs. 53, 64, pp. 91, 93.

79. Lessing, *Education*, secs. 86–89, pp. 96–97.

80. Lessing, *Education*, sec. 72, p. 94.

81. Lessing, *Education*, secs. 99–100, p. 98: "The recollection of my former condition would permit me to make only a bad use of the present. . . . And what then have I to lose? Is not the whole of eternity mine?"

82. So crucial is the theme of friendship to the play that Hannah Arendt has described *Nathan* as "the classical drama of friendship"; see Arendt, "Foreword," in *Nathan the Wise, Minna Von Barnhelm, and Other Plays and Writings*, ed. Peter Demetz (New York: Continuum, 1991), p. xv.

83. Lessing, *Nathan the Wise*, act II, scene 5, p. 214.

84. Lessing, *Nathan the Wise*, act II, scene 5, p. 213.

85. Lessing, *Nathan the Wise*, act IV, scene 7, p. 257.

86. Franz Rosenzweig, "Lessings Nathan," in Lessing, *Gesammelte Schriften*, ed. Reinhold Mayer and Annemarie Mayer (Dordrecht, Neth.: Martinus Nijhoff, 1984), vol. 3, p. 450.

87. Lessing, *Nathan the Wise*, act III, scene 7, pp. 234–35; see Chaninah Maschler, "On the Wisdom of Nathan," *Interpretation* 15 (1987): 362: "In Germany, Lessing seems to have been the first man of letters to appreciate and teach the power for the good of a mercantile mentality."

88. Hermann Cohen, *Religion of Reason Out of the Sources of Judaism*, trans. Simon Kaplan (New York: Ungar, 1972), p. 331: "Kant obtained from Spinoza his knowledge and judgment of Judaism"; Guttmann, "Mendelssohn and Spinoza," p. 362: "Yet nowhere can a clearer agreement with Spinoza be found than in Kant's view of Judaism, which strikes the reader as if it were a brief summary of Spinoza's theory"; Alfred D. Low, *Jews in the Eyes of the Germans: From the Enlightenment to Imperial Germany* (Philadelphia: Institute for the Study of Human Issues, 1979), p. 94: "Kant borrowed his conception of Judaism almost word by word from Spinoza." Cf. Nathan Rotenstreich, *The Recurring Pattern: Studies in Anti-Judaism in Modern Thought* (London: Weidenfeld and Nicolson, 1963), p. 25: "Kant's view is even more radical than those expressed in

Spinoza's *Tractatus Theologico-Politicus* and Mendelssohn's *Jerusalem,* though some-what influenced by them."

89. Immanuel Kant, *Religion Within the Limits of Reason Alone,* trans. T. M. Greene and H. H. Hudson (New York: Harper and Row, 1960), pp. 115–20.

90. Kant, *Religion,* p. 95.

91. Kant, *Religion,* p. 92: "Yet man is not entitled on this account to be idle in this business and to let Providence rule. . . . Rather man must proceed *as though* everything depended upon him" (emphasis added).

92. Kant, *Religion,* p. 116.

93. Kant, *Religion,* p. 116.

94. Kant, *Religion,* p. 116.

95. Kant, *Religion,* p. 156.

96. Kant, *Religion,* p. 118.

97. Kant, *Religion,* p. 120.

98. Kant, *Religion,* p. 155.

99. Kant, *Religion,* pp. 146, 147.

100. For some interesting parallels between Maimonides and Kant see Shlomo Pines, "Spinoza's 'Tractatus Theologico-Politicus,' Maimonides, and Kant," *Scripta Hierosolymitana* 20 (1968): 47–54.

101. Kant, *Religion,* p. 102.

102. Kant, *Religion,* p. 39.

103. Kant, *Religion,* p. 39.

104. Kant, *Religion,* p. 103.

105. Kant, *Religion,* p. 101.

106. Kant, *Religion,* p. 101.

107. Kant, *Religion,* p. 101.

108. In this context it is useful to recall that Kant's disciple Fichte was the author of a work entitled *Versuch einer Kritik aller Offenbarung* (1792).

109. Letter to Moses Mendelssohn, August 16, 1783, in *Kant: Philosophical Correspondence, 1759–99,* trans. Arnulf Zweig (Chicago: University of Chicago Press, 1967), p. 107.

110. Kant, *Philosophical Correspondence,* pp. 107–08.

111. Kant, *Religion,* p. 154.

112. Mendelssohn, *Jerusalem,* p. 87.

113. Kant, *Religion,* p. 154.

114. Immanuel Kant, *The Conflict of the Faculties,* trans. Mary J. Gregor (New York: Arabis, 1979), pp. 91–93.

115. Kant, *Conflict,* p. 93.

116. Kant, *Conflict,* p. 93.

117. Immanuel Kant, *Anthropology from a Pragmatic Point of View,* trans. Mary J. Gregor (The Hague: Martinus Nijhoff, 1974), p. 77n; translation modified.

118. Kant, *Anthropology,* p. 77n; translation modified.

119. Kant, *Conflict,* p. 95.

120. Kant, *Conflict,* p. 95.

121. Kant, *Religion,* p. 119; see also his *Critique of Practical Reason,* trans. Lewis

White Beck (Indianapolis: Bobbs-Merrill, 1956), p. 166: "Two things fill the mind with ever new and increasing admiration and awe, the oftener and more steadily we reflect on them: the starry heavens above me and the moral law within me."

122. Emil Fackenheim, *Encounters Between Judaism and Modern Philosophy* (New York: Schocken, 1973), p. 86.

123. For some of the more negative assessments see Lawrence Stepelevitch, "Hegel and Judaism," *Judaism* 2 (1975): 215–24. Rotenstreich, in *Recurring Pattern*, p. 49, notes that Hegel's critique of Judaism "certainly bears the character of an outbreak of emotional rejection rather than of conceptual analysis." Paul Lawrence Rose, in *Revolutionary Antisemitism in Germany: From Kant to Wagner* (Princeton: Princeton University Press, 1990), p. 109, claims that "it was Hegel's historical philosophy that provided revolutionary antisemitism with one of its theoretical pillars," although he has to admit later that Hegel "stopped well short of subscribing to the new ideology of Jew-hatred" and "made a more serious and sympathetic effort to understand Jews and Judaism than had Kant" (p. 116). For a more positive assessment of Hegel's role see Shlomo Avineri, "A Note on Hegel's Views on Jewish Emancipation," *Jewish Social Studies* 2 (1963): 145–51. For much of this section and the next I have drawn heavily on my article "Hegel and the Jewish Question: In Between Tradition and Modernity," *History of Political Thought* 12 (1991): 87–106.

124. G. W. F. Hegel, *Early Theological Writings*, trans. T. M. Knox, intro. by Richard Kroner (Philadelphia: University of Pennsylvania Press, 1971), p. 167: "The conception of the 'positivity' of a religion has originated and become important only in recent times . . . a positive religion is a contranatural or supernatural one, containing concepts and information transcending understanding and reason and requiring feelings and actions which would not come naturally to men: the feelings are forcibly and mechanically stimulated, the actions are done to order or from obedience without any spontaneous interest."

125. Hegel, *Early Theological Writings*, pp. 177–78.

126. Hegel, *Early Theological Writings*, pp. 68–69.

127. Hegel, *Early Theological Writings*, p. 69.

128. Hegel, *Early Theological Writings*, pp. 69–70.

129. The manuscript with commentary is printed in Franz Rosenzweig, *Kleinere Schriften* (Berlin: Schocken, 1937), pp. 230–77. Rosenzweig attributes the authorship of the piece to Hegel's friend Schelling. For a history of the disputed authorship see *Mythologie der Vernunft: Hegels "altesten Systemprogramm des deutschen Idealismus"*, ed. C. Jamme and H. Schneider (Frankfurt: Suhrkamp, 1984), pp. 63–69.

130. The early writings were so named by their first editor, Hermann Nohl, himself a student of Wilhelm Dilthey, in whose book *Der Jugendgeschichte Hegels* Hegel is interpreted as a religious thinker. For a revolt against this interpretation see Georg Lukacs, *The Young Hegel: Studies in Dialectics and Economics*, trans. Rodney Livingstone (Cambridge, Mass.: MIT Press, 1975), pp. 1–16.

131. Hegel, *Early Theological Writings*, p. 159. Hegel adds in a footnote: "A nation to which this [political independence] is a matter of indifference will soon cease to be a nation."

132. Hegel, *Early Theological Writings*, p. 159.

133. Richard Kroner, "Introduction," in Hegel, *Early Theological Writings*, p. 9.

134. Hegel, *Early Theological Writings*, p. 201.

135. Hegel, *Early Theological Writings*, p. 182.

136. Hegel, *Early Theological Writings*, p. 185.

137. Hegel, *Early Theological Writings*, p. 186.

138. Hegel, *Early Theological Writings*, p. 187.

139. Hegel, *Early Theological Writings*, p. 192,

140. Hegel, *Early Theological Writings*, p. 198.

141. Hegel, *Early Theological Writings*, p. 191.

142. Hegel, *Early Theological Writings*, p. 192.

143. Hegel, *Early Theological Writings*, p. 195.

144. Hegel, *Early Theological Writings*, pp. 210–11.

145. Hegel, *Early Theological Writings*, p. 209.

146. Hegel, *Early Theological Writings*, p. 212.

147. Hegel, *Early Theological Writings*, pp. 204–05.

148. See Hans Liebeschütz, *Das Judentum im deutschen Geschichtsbild von Hegel bis Max Weber* (Tübingen: Mohr, 1967), pp. 24–42.

149. G. W. F. Hegel, *Philosophy of History*, trans. J. Sibree (New York: Dover, 1956), p. 18.

150. Hegel, *Philosophy of History*, p. 195.

151. Hegel, *Philosophy of History*, pp. 195–96.

152. Hegel, *Philosophy of History*, p. 321.

153. Hegel, *Philosophy of History*, p. 321.

154. Hegel, *Philosophy of History*, p. 321.

155. Hegel, *Philosophy of History*, p. 321.

156. Hegel, *Philosophy of History*, p. 322.

157. Hegel, *Philosophy of History*, p. 323.

158. G. W. F. Hegel, *Lectures on the Philosophy of Religion*, trans. E. B. Speirs and J. B. Sanderson (London: Routledge and Kegan Paul, 1962), vol. 2, pp. 170–219. Hegel's use of the concept of the sublime is largely borrowed from Kant's aesthetics; see Immanuel Kant, *Critique of Judgment*, trans. James C. Meredith (Oxford: Clarendon, 1973), p. 97: "that is sublime in comparison with which all else is small." See also Rotenstreich, *Recurring Pattern*, p. 67.

159. Hegel, *Philosophy of Religion*, vol. 2, pp. 170–71.

160. Hegel, *Philosophy of Religion*, vol. 2, p. 174.

161. Hegel, *Philosophy of Religion*, vol. 2, p. 174.

162. G. W. F. Hegel, *Encyclopedia of the Philosophical Sciences (1830)*, trans. William Wallace (Oxford: Clarendon, 1957), par. 112, p. 164.

163. Hegel, *Philosophy of Religion*, vol. 2, p. 193.

164. Hegel, *Philosophy of Religion*, vol. 2, p. 194.

165. Hegel, *Philosophy of Religion*, vol. 2, p. 211.

166. Hegel, *Philosophy of Religion*, vol. 2, p. 211.

167. Fackenheim, *Encounters*, pp. 82–83.

168. G. W. F. Hegel, *Philosophy of Right*, trans. T. M. Knox (Oxford: Clarendon, 1967), par. 257, p. 155.

169. G. W. F. Hegel, *Philosophy of Mind*, trans. William Wallace and A. V. Miller (Oxford: Clarendon, 1978), par. 482, p. 240.

170. Hegel, *Philosophy of History*, pp. 342, 344, 412.

171. Hegel, *Philosophy of History*, p. 416.

172. Hegel, *Philosophy of History*, p. 416.

173. Hegel, *Philosophy of History*, p. 417.

174. Hegel, *Philosophy of History*, p. 420; translation slightly modified.

175. Hegel, *Philosophy of History*, pp. 422–24.

176. Hegel, *Philosophy of Right*, par. 279A, p. 288.

177. Hegel, *Philosophy of Right*, par. 187, p. 124.

178. Hegel, *Philosophy of Mind*, par. 522, p. 284.

179. Hegel, *Philosophy of Mind*, par. 522, pp. 286, 291.

180. Hegel, *Philosophy of Right*, par. 209R, p. 134.

181. Hegel, *Philosophy of Right*, par. 270, p. 169.

182. Hegel, *Philosophy of Right*, par. 270, p. 169.

Chapter 8. The Jewish Question Reconsidered

1. *TTP*, 7 [10] (6–12); *Elwes*, pref., p. 5.

2. Alexis de Tocqueville, *Democracy in America*, trans. George Lawrence, ed. J. P. Mayer (New York: Doubleday, 1969), pp. 290–91: "Moreover, all the sects in the United States belong to the great unity of Christendom, and Christian morality is everywhere the same." For some useful attempts to update and adapt Tocqueville's insights see George A. Kelly, "Faith, Freedom and Disenchantment: Politics and the American Religious Consciousness," *Daedalus* (Winter 1982): pp. 127–48; William Galston, "Liberalism and Public Morality," in *Liberals on Liberalism*, ed. Alfonso J. Damico (Totowa, N.J.: Rowman and Littlefield, 1986), pp. 129–47.

3. *TTP*, 11 [28] (1–8); *Elwes*, pref., p. 10.

4. Leo Strauss, *Spinoza's Critique of Religion*, trans. E. M. Sinclair (New York: Schocken, 1965), p. 6.

5. *TTP*, 57 [55] (1–6); *Elwes*, chap. 3, p. 56.

6. For a vivid discussion see David Bromwich, *Politics by Other Means: Higher Education and Group Thinking* (New Haven: Yale University Press, 1992).

Subject Index

Aaron, 149
Abraham: Hegel's view of, 188
absolutism, 197–98
Abulafia, Abraham, 224 n. 6
Advancement of Learning (Bacon), 61–62
Alfarabi, 39
Alpakhar, Jehuda, 66, 68, 69, 76
Altmann, Alexander, 177
amor Dei intellectualis, 141, 144
animositas, 161
Anthropology from a Pragmatic Point of View (Kant), 185
apostles: contrasted with prophets, 105–12
Aquinas, Thomas. *See* Thomas Aquinas
Areopagitica (Milton), 3
Aristotle, 61, 76, 125, 226 n. 28
Arnold, Matthew, 12
assimilation, 14–15, 168, 200–203
atheism: and Cartesian theology, 47–49
Aubrey, John, 33

autonomy: Enlightenment concept of, 167

Bacon, Francis, 61–62
Balibar, Etienne, 51
Balling, Pieter, 48
Bauman, Zygmunt, 168
Bayle, Pierre, 3, 39; Spinoza's *Treatise* as viewed by, 11
Bendavid, Lazarus, 185
Bennett, Jonathan, 243 n. 106
Berlin, Isaiah, 242 n. 81
Bible: Deuteronomy, 57–58, 67, 68, 97, 99, 149, 151; Exodus, 68, 99, 148, 149; Ezekiel, 72, 92, 149; Genesis, 67, 72, 76, 86, 191; James, 110; Jeremiah, 67, 142; Job, 193; 1 John, 116; Joshua, 60, 92; Lamentations, 80; Mark, 99; Matthew, 80; Numbers, 92, 151; Proverbs, 73; Psalms, 92, 183; Romans, 81, 109, 110; 1 Samuel, 67, 92; 2 Samuel, 67; 1 Timothy, 110. *See also* Scripture

Index of Passages Cited from
Spinoza's Tractatus Theologico-Politicus

The abbreviated titles are given in full on page 207. The numbers are all page numbers.